GOVERNING MEGACITIES IN EMERGING COUNTRIES

First published in French in 2011 by Presses de la Fondation Nationale des Sciences Politiques under the title *Métropoles XXL en pays émergents*, edited by Dominique Lorrain.

Governing Megacities in Emerging Countries

Edited by

DOMINIQUE LORRAIN
CNRS, France

Routledge
Taylor & Francis Group

LONDON AND NEW YORK

First published 2014 by Ashgate Publishing

Published 2016 by Routledge
2 Park Square, Milton Park, Abingdon, Oxon OX14 4RN
711 Third Avenue, New York, NY 10017, USA

Routledge is an imprint of the Taylor & Francis Group, an informa business

British Library Cataloguing in Publication Data
A catalogue record for this book is available from the British Library

The Library of Congress has cataloged the printed edition as follows:
Governing megacities in emerging countries / edited by Dominique Lorrain.
    pages cm
 Includes bibliographical references and index.
 ISBN 978-1-4724-2585-0 (hardback) – ISBN 978-1-4724-2588-1 (pbk.) –
1. Metropolitan government–Developing countries. 2. Metropolitan government–
Developing countries–Case studies. I. Lorrain, Dominique, author, editor of compilation.
 JS241.G66 2014
 320.8'5091724–dc23

                                                                    2013049437

ISBN 9781472425850 (hbk)
ISBN 9781472425881 (pbk)

Contents

List of Figures, Tables and Boxes

List of Figures

List of Tables

List of Boxes

Notes on Contributors

Alain Dubresson is Professor of Geography at the University of Paris Ouest Nanterre La Défense. His work focuses on local economic development in Sub-Saharan Africa, particularly on the relationships between economic trends and urban patterns in Southern Africa.

Sylvy Jaglin is Professor of Geography and Urban Planning at the University Paris-Est Marne-la-Vallée (France) and a researcher at Latts (Laboratoire Techniques, Territoires et Sociétés). She holds a PhD in urban planning (1991). Her research addresses the social and spatial issues associated with the regulation of, and reforms in, urban utility industries in developing countries. Her recent work has been on urban water management in Sub-Saharan Africa (*Services d'eau en Afrique subsaharienne: la fragmentation urbaine en question*, CNRS Éditions, 2005) and on metropolitan governance in Cape Town (Dubresson A. and Jaglin S. eds, *Le Cap après l'apartheid: gouvernance métropolitaine et changement urbain*, Éditions Karthala/IRD, 2008). Her current research focuses on urban energy issues in Sub-Saharan Africa.

Dominique Lorrain is Director of Research at CNRS, (Latts, Ecole des Ponts ParisTech). He graduated from Sciences Po, has a Masters in Economics (Paris 1), a Masters in Urban Planning (Sciences Po), and a PhD in Urban Sociology (EHESS). He has worked on urban affairs since 1972. His work bears on the transformations of urban public action and more specifically on infrastructure policies. Some recent publications include: Gestion de l'eau: conflits ou coopération? *Entreprises et Histoire*, 50, April 2008. Trous noirs du pouvoir *Sociologie du travail*, 49(1), 2007, (with Pierre Lascoumes). Urban Capitalisms: European Models in Competition. *International Journal of Urban and Regional Research*, 29(2), 2005: 231–67. He teaches at Ecole des Ponts, Paris and its joint MBA with Tongji University (Shanghai). He is a member of the editorial board of three Journals as well as the scientific committee of the Institute for Delegated Management since its creation in 1997. From 2000 to 2005, Dominique Lorrain was an independent expert for the Public Private Infrastructure Advisory Facility (PPIAF-World Bank). Since 2007 he has been a member of the Suez Environment Foresight Advisory Council (FAC). He is the head of 'Chaire Ville' Ecole des Ponts ParisTech.

Géraldine Pflieger is Senior Lecturer in urban and environmental policies at the Institute for Environmental Sciences and at the Department of Political Science of the University of Geneva, since February 2010. She has been Visiting Scholar at the University of California, Berkeley, in 2002, Senior Researcher at the Swiss Federal Institute of Technology of Lausanne from 2003 to 2008, and Assistant Professor in public policy and regulation at the University of Lausanne, from 2008 to 2009. She holds a PhD in Urban Planning from the Ecole Nationale des Ponts et Chaussées (Paris, 2003). As an urban and political scientist, she has undertaken research into the links between the management of network infrastructures, natural resources and the analysis of urban policies in various contexts (Chile, California, France and Switzerland). Since 2003, Géraldine Pflieger has developed her expertise on water, energy and urban utilities policies in Switzerland. Her current research projects cross the analysis of the regulation of network and natural resources and the transformation of metropolitan governance.

Marie–Hélène Zérah is a PhD holder in Urban Studies from the Paris Institute of Urban Studies. She is currently a Senior Researcher with the Institute of Research for Development (Paris) and is deputed to the Centre de Sciences Humaines of New Delhi. She previously worked with the Water and Sanitation Program of the World Bank and with Ondeo (Suez Group). She was also involved in projects and consultancy for a number of organisations, including the European Union. She has worked extensively in the area of water supply and sanitation in Indian cities as well as other urban services. Recently, her research interests concern the shifts in urban governance in India. She has published a book on the question of water access in Delhi and recently co-edited a book on the Right to the City in India.

Acknowledgments

This book is part of Chaire Ville's research program (http://www.enpc.fr/chaire-ville). It started as a small working group for the five authors to present their research on the cities they had been working on for several years. Other colleagues joined the 'club' and contributed to enrich the final result – Charlotte Halpern and Patrick Le Galès (CEE, SciencesPo), Frédéric Gilli (Chaire Ville) – and the editing work by SciencesPo Les Presses also improved the manuscript. Behind the scene are the infinite contacts and personal exchanges that each author has established in 'his' metropolis. Without this support, the interviews and open discussions, this book would have been impossible. Once published in French it received valuable comments from several colleagues: Christophe Defeuilley (EDF R&D), Juliette Galonnier (SciencesPo), Jean Philippe Leresche (Lausanne University), Pauline Prat (SciencesPo) and Eric Verdeil (CNRS, EVS, University of Lyon). It has also been discussed at several seminars: SciencesPo's 'Cities are back in Towns'; Latts Ecole des Ponts; Fondation Braillard in Geneva; Agence Française de Développement's research seminar; and World Water Summit 2012 an event organised by Suez Environment and CGLU.

In terms of institutional support we acknowledge funding from our present partners in Chaire Ville – Agence Française de Développement, GDF SUEZ, Suez Environnement – and past partners, Caisse des Dépôts et Consignations, DATAR, Suez Environnement. Not only did they bring financial support, but also their interest in the substance of the research.

Karen George translated the introduction and the chapters on Shanghai, Cape Town and Santiago de Chile. Sharmila Sarkar and Vandana Kawlra were responsible for the translation of the chapter on Mumbai and the conclusion was translated by Amy Jacobs. Before delivery to the publisher, Jonathan Rutherford (Latt, Ecole des Ponts) performed a final English language quality check.

Chapter 1

Introduction:
The Institutions of the Urban Fabric

Dominique Lorrain

This book focuses on the government of megacities and large cities in emerging countries.[1] In 2008, the population of cities equalled the rural population for the first time in history (United Nations, 2008). This fact has been widely commented upon, but one partially hidden aspect merits particular attention, because it presents a major challenge: the formation of large cities with populations of more than 10 million. These megacities present challenges not only in terms of their numbers and the speed at which they are changing, but also because they need to develop the appropriate institutions. Like their pace of development, the fact that most of them are in emerging countries raises the stakes to a level never encountered before. How will the actors manage to develop appropriate institutions in these densely populated, built-up spaces that are constantly, rapidly changing? Will they be stable enough – and fair enough – to allow the organisation of mutually beneficial exchanges? The capacity to govern is meaningless unless it solves essential problems; will those who govern these large cities be able to bring progress for all, reduce poverty and protect the environment?

For better or worse, megacities – by virtue of their resources, their size and their impact – are at the leading edge of change in many countries. Reading the social science literature seems to tell us that this is for the worse. A very broad current in urban sociology has associated economic globalisation with the creation of a wider spectrum of jobs and with a challenge to traditional social ties, leading to more segregated societies (Castells 1989; Fainstein, Gordon and Harloe, 1992; Graham and Marvin 2001; Harvey, 1973; Marcuse and van Kampen, 2000). Many urban scientists and urban geographers continue to condemn gigantism. Lewis Mumford made the medieval town his ideal-type (Mumford, 1964); according to Paul Bairoch, half a million represents the upper population limit and, in the interests of preserving well-being, the size of a town should be no more than about 300,000 people (Bairoch, 1985). Given their size, these emerging megacities deviate totally from these ideals. So how can their existence and their continued development be explained? Are there internal regulation mechanisms in urban

---

1   Our subject, the government of large and very large cities, covers megacities above 10 million people (according to United Nations definitions) and large cities above 4 million: a total of 100 urban areas.

societies that these authors did not understand? Or are we seeing the prophecy of urban disaster described by Mike Davies and taken up by the cinema in *Blade Runner* come true? (Davis, 1997 and 1998; Soja, 2000).

The hypothesis that we develop here does not tackle these questions head-on; instead, we argue that the situation is not a scenario for disaster since large cities are being organised and *de facto* governed through their networked services. If these technical systems are to be built and managed, institutional issues must be tackled, consciously or otherwise, from the angles of their legal status, mode of organisation and mode of financing. Let us look at a megacity with its international airport, several railway stations, a public transport system (with metro lines, sometimes tramways and always buses), a system for producing and distributing electricity, another for drinking water and one for rainwater drainage; we can also add communications systems ranging from cell phones to high-speed cable networks. And so that this quick tour will be complete, we should also mention the major amenities that mark each era of the city's history. The pedestrian city was structured around symbolic buildings (citadel, palace, places of worship); the transition to megalopolis was expressed through the construction of the first urban highways and the development of department stores, big hotels, railway stations and high-rise buildings; the current stage of the very large cities – which I have also called the gig@city – has seen the advent of mega shopping centres and integrated leisure/conference centres. Large cities must provide this technical infrastructure, both in order to be machines of production and in order to be functionally habitable.

Here we argue that these artefacts (major amenities and all the networks that are in fact often considered 'natural') should be viewed as representing a gateway to the issue of governing large cities. First, they form the city's 'bone structure', since they manifestly help to organise its spaces in such a way as to prevent it turning into an indistinguishable urban stew. They act as hooks or pegs that provide structure, while also allowing activities to go on. Second, these technical systems correspond to operations that are out of the ordinary, in terms of the amounts of money invested, their technical challenges or their architecture – and because they have irreversible consequences for the structure of cities. In order to create them, urban governments must solve numerous institutional problems. They must define who is responsible for them, who is going to operate them using what methods, and how to guarantee financing. This list of choices can be refined, but the main point remains: in order to solve these major functional problems, city officials must make choices that impact on the question of urban government. We all have a tendency to think spontaneously about these issues of government in terms of elected assemblies and democracy. This book maintains – although with an open mind – that policy issues can be tackled by asking how one designs a service for everyone, who is to coordinate it, who is to manage it and how would it be paid for. These practical questions come under the heading of everyday politics, although the decisions that have to be made are out of the ordinary. In our spontaneous representations, they occupy a less elevated position on the league table of public activities than do 'grand politics'. However, choices made at these levels have consequences for the everyday lives of millions of city dwellers.

In terms of the theoretical landscape, we are approaching the urban question and the government of cities via an institutional history of technical systems that employs a few key words: problems, actors, institutions (North, 1990; Hughes, 1983). We think that actors react above all to problems; among these problems, the provision of essential services and major infrastructure occupies a significant place. This 'way in' through problems and through the material city also enables us to confirm the hyperconstructed nature of the environment in which the actors are evolving, and this in turn is a way of recalling the often-forgotten material nature of phenomena. There is a city, produced over the long term and through a largely irreversible process. The way in which it is organised has a direct bearing on the actor, through various parameters: how smoothly it runs, ease of access to it, whether it adheres to principles of equality or not. The organisation of this material city comes about through political choices that are expressed in institutions. These choices may be made with varying degrees of transparency and with varying levels of awareness of the political consequences; but it remains the case that, when they are made for all major amenities and utilities and then pieced together, these choices shape a public space and, in their own way, play a part in the government of cities.

In other words, in order to develop physical infrastructure it is necessary to define institutional infrastructure. The approach that we are proposing starts from problems, affirms the material dimension of the city and takes the view that the latter forces the actors to develop appropriate institutions, dedicated to solving practical problems, and that these – over time – allow them to evolve and – over the long-term – lead to the creation of 'models of urban services' with division of tasks between the public sector and the market and with formal institutions (the rules of the game), second-level institutions (tools and instruments) and informal institutions (culture and collective mentalities).

The Newness of Megacities.

The formation of megacities with populations of between 15 and 20 million represents a historic transformation. This is manifested first and foremost through numbers. The biggest cities in antiquity, in Mesopotamia and in China, had populations of around 500,000 (Bairoch, 1985: 292; Mumford, 1964; Nicolet, 2000). Byzantium, Rome and Teotihuacan, each with a million inhabitants, were exceptional (Soja, 2000: 68). According to Jacques Le Goff, in the thirteenth century, when European cities were becoming stronger, only Florence and Venice had populations of over 100,000 – except for Paris, which, with double that number, topped the mediaeval hierarchy (2003: 139). It was not until several centuries had passed, bringing the Industrial Revolution and later the spread of the automobile, that these levels were surpassed. After the Second World War, only New York and

Tokyo recorded populations of 10 million (Beaujeu-Garnier et al., 1966). These kinds of figures were exceeded dramatically in just a few decades at the end of the twentieth century. There are now 19 megacities with populations over 10 million, and seven of these have populations of 15 million or more: Tokyo with 35.7; Mexico City, 19.0; New York-Newark, 19.0; São Paulo, 19.0; Mumbai, 18.8; Delhi, 15.9; Shanghai, 15.0 (UN-HABITAT, 2008: data for 2007). By 2050, world population could reach about 8½ billion, and two thirds of these people would be living in cities. Forecasters expect a rise in the urban population of around 2.5 billion over 40 years – which means accommodating the equivalent of a new population of France every year.

These megacities are developing primarily in emerging countries. The latest United Nations statistics on this are absolutely clear (see Box 1.1). Fifteen megacities with populations of over 10 million are currently recorded in these countries; and the phenomenon is going to become stronger, by 2025, 22 out of a total of 26 megacities in emerging countries will have crossed this threshold. The new members of the club will be: Kinshasa, Lagos,[2] Djakarta, Guangzhou, Lahore, Shenzhen and Chennai. These megacities are changing at a much faster rate than anything that the industrial countries have experienced. Mumbai is on course for a population increase of 7.6 million over the 18 years from 2007 to 2025, Karachi 7 million, Delhi 6.6 million and Shanghai 4.4 million, while their counterparts in the industrial countries are progressing modestly, with less than a million for Tokyo, 1.2 million for Los Angeles-Long Beach and 1.6 million for New York -Newark. What is more, even in their accelerated growth phase, these Western cities never experienced such increases; New York took 50 years (1880–1930) to increase its population by 5 million and Chicago, 30 years (1870–1900) to go from a population of 300,000 to 1.7 million.

Box 1.1   Fifteen megacities with populations of over 10 million in emerging countries.

Mexico City 19.0	São Paulo 19.0	Mumbai 18.8	Delhi 15.9
Shanghai 15.0	Kolkata 14.8	Buenos Aires 12.8	Dhaka 13.5
Karachi 12.2	Rio de Janeiro 11.9	Cairo 11.3	Beijing 11.1
Manila 11.1	Moscow 10.5	Istanbul 10.1	

Source UN-HABITAT, 2008

To this numerical challenge, we have to add the challenge of institutions. This is obvious, since if these countries had stable, incentivising institutions, certain technologies, a well-trained labour force and capital, they would already be fully

2   The fact that these two megacities are located in 'poor' countries will present them with even greater challenges.

developed. Therefore, for each one to remain a viable whole – or, at the very least, viable enough to continue to attract people and money – the leaders of these megacities are going to have to fast-track two kinds of response: acting quickly to meet the challenge of urbanisation and developing appropriate institutional frameworks that will enable them to achieve a lasting policy regime. Collision between speed of change and inadequacy of institutions may lead to disaster. Some cities may function in a primitive accumulation regime in which one group of actors appropriates the city's rent-seeking opportunities for itself, controls its sources of profit and maintains a segregated form of social organisation. In order to avoid this worst-case sequence of events, the leaders of these large cities are going to have to design institutions that define the rules of the game: property rights, general planning regulations, fiscal rules, mechanisms for financing fixed assets. Institutions cannot take everything upon themselves, of course, but they are a precondition for any collective action (North, 1990). It is also through institutions that strategic leaders can act in order to guide social change; these rules allow individual energies to operate cumulatively.

These megacities form *worlds in themselves*. Perhaps this is putting it a bit strongly, since – like all the actors – they still have linkages to the state and are embedded in inherited institutions and social relations (Dupuy and Halpern, 2009); nevertheless, their size and the diversity of their activities give them a capacity to bring together things that were separate. We have not really got the measure of them yet, since our imaginations are still bound up with a hierarchy that runs from the small town to the capital city. This is a reading in terms of continuities; there is no difference between the nature of a medium-sized town and that of a large city – there has simply been an increase in numbers. With megacities, this historical interlocking no longer holds good: there has been a structural change. In order to clarify these ideas, let us first consider Paris, which has a population of two million in the 'city proper', lying within its inner ring road. Including both the inner and the outer suburbs, its metropolitan population rises to 10 million. At first glance, the Municipality of Shanghai has double this number of inhabitants; starting from Pudong in the east and running across to the western administrative boundaries, its built-up space stretches for almost 90 kilometres. However, large agricultural spaces are not to be found beyond that (as they are in the Ile de France region): the urban region continues towards Nanjing; the urbanised expanse stretches for almost 200 km and there are about 70 million urban dwellers. Even though the numbers are different, the phenomenon remains the same when we look at Mumbai and its linear suburbs, at Mexico City – which extends far beyond the Federal District alone – and at the urban regions of São Paulo and of Guangzhou[3].

---

3   The authorities in Guangzhou, Hong Kong and Macau are working on highway and rail infrastructure schemes that would link these three focal points in a vast urban triangle and, thereby, the cities in between (Shenzhen, Zhuhai, Foshan) to form an urban complex with a population of about 27 million.

Megacities and large cities have specific properties that relate just as much to their economic base and the intensity with which they function as to the invention of new lifestyles. From an economic point of view, some of these properties are conflicting ones. On the one hand, they concentrate into one space functions that in the past were divided between several towns or cities which gives them a certain autonomy. In contrast, when they trade in goods or services, they function more through linkages with other hyperurban spaces than with their own 'hinterland'; in a global economy, they function as hubs and their technical networks allow them to organise exchanges.

In many respects, these large cities are the leading edge of a society. They are more subject than other cities to the forces of globalisation and they raise the stakes, increasing the pace of the changes (Marcuse and van Kempen, 2000). By comparison with the calm, settled life of so many well-ordered, sophisticated, medium-sized cities in old Europe, these megacities are melting pots for opposing forces. They bring intensity to everything. They attract migrants who are ready to put up with a great deal in order to advance in life. In these cities, fortunes are made in industrial production, in trading on the markets or in the production cycle of the built environment. They concentrate loci of economic and political power. They act as gigantic accelerators of social forces. They are places of innovation where new urban technologies are implemented and where soaring buildings mark the spirit of the times. The scenario is almost the same everywhere, with buildings that testify to their investors' ambitions: high-rise office buildings rising ever higher, giant multi-functional shopping centres, luxury hotels and business centres; and to these must be added public buildings (a city hall) and public amenities (a museum, a stadium).

All these factors combine to make megacities places where lifestyle change is accelerated. The city has always represented freedom. In the Middle Ages, it enabled people to break the bonds of feudalism – indeed, we talk about 'free cities' (Le Goff, 2003: 137). By comparison with rural societies, they offered freedom: going to the city meant that people could shrug off the influence of previous generations and try out a new way of life (Handling, 1979). In every country, the large city has always been the port of entry for rural migrants in search of a better, modern way of life. *'Stadt Luft macht frei'*. It is the same story whether we are talking about the migrants who have settled in Paris since the eighteenth century (Le Bras, 1986) or the English and Irish peasants pushed out by enclosures, who flocked to the ports and migrated to the colonies (Rediker and Linebaugh, 2001). Nowadays, it is the peasants of Cappadocia who converge on Istanbul and those from the plains of Uttar Pradesh and Bihar who descend on Mumbai. Shanghai draws in a flow of peasants from the central provinces of Hubei and Henan, or from distant Sichuan; they come to sell their labour to construction companies. They earn a bit of money – certainly more than they would if they stayed in their villages – and they discover a new world. As they sit smoking during their breaks, they observe the stream of passers-by and express their astonishment at this fresh new world. This too is what the large city represents.

In the *longue durée* of migrations to cities, the present moment represents a discontinuity. As Michel Serres evokes,

> in the early 20th century, 60% to 65% of people in the West were peasants; in the year 2000, there are just 1.8% left. This abrupt fall ... marks the end of a period that started ... . with the Neolithic. ... Therefore it is a significant upheaval, the consequences of which are only now beginning to be felt. The rural animal is not the same as the urban animal – not the same 'being in the world'.[4]

Already in the early twentieth century, Georg Simmel (1900, 1903) and Werner Sombart (1902) in Germany, and subsequently the Chicago School, were investigating the impacts of the large city on lifestyles (Bruhns, 2001: 68; Joseph, 1990; Gottdiener and Budd, 2009: 1–10). Perhaps we are now seeing the emergence of *Homo urbanus*. The formation of megacities is transforming an age-old cycle from several points of view, and the strength of the impact is greater because the transition from a traditional rural society to the very large city is taking place within a compressed timeframe. The first point is that the recognition of the individual has transformed various kinds of collective solidarity; this phenomenon relates not only to the West and is not explained simply by the immediate political circumstances of the late twentieth century and the extension of market principles. Next, sociability which for a long time was organised on a face-to-face basis (proximity) has been enriched by connectivity. Gigantism, increased travel and the advent of new communications techniques are transforming relations to the other and introducing the principle that in order to communicate, you have to be connected to a network; technology is supplementing the old face-to-face ways. Finally, ties to the natural world are loosening. Someone who lived in a small or medium-sized city was able to maintain a close bond with nature. But in megacities, which have to be seen as gigantic constructs, the natural elements are disappearing or have in fact been created by human beings. This helps to make technical networks a strategic element in preserving various kinds of balance, as is highlighted by disaster situations (Harris and Keil, 2008; Zimmerman, 2001) or challenges to law and order (Gandy, 2005 and 2006; Graham, 2010).

A New Kind of Object, to be Viewed with an Open Mind ...

All this invites us to move away from our usual frames of interpretation and to approach megacities as new objects waiting to be discovered. In many respects, the large cities in emerging countries represent a new object that shakes up some of our knowledge about the city. The history of urban ideas and of the policies pursued in industrial countries – as it is described by Peter Hall (2002), for example – illustrates this property perfectly. In the nineteenth century, there was

---

4   Michel Serres, interview, *Le Monde* 22 December 2009, p. 5.

general thinking on the urban, inspired by Greco-Roman antiquity, but institutions largely remained to be built. Nor was there a real 'city industry', with developers and major network operators. When the urbanization phenomenon began, the world was feeling its way forwards, experimenting. Politicians were reacting to problems or to crises, while entrepreneurs were trying to construct a market. In the industrial countries, urban public policy formed part of a long sequence: construction in stages led to the contemporary landscape. Emerging countries do not have to make the whole of this journey. They can take the world as it already is, with megacities, technologies and feedback from other countries' experiments; firms are ready to engage with them and international development institutions to advise them. The city is no longer an unknown territory that can be only reached by following a given sequence. They can tackle it head-on by setting out all the options on the same level. The result is an eclecticism of choices and architectures.

The problems to be settled are not those of industrial countries, which have a long history and a legacy of fixed assets and institutions to rely on and where growth follows a gentle curve. In this 'first world', fashionable writers can concern themselves with the role of a creative class, since everything else is already available there; the result is that cities are advised to get involved in 'branding' (Florida, 2002). In the second, emerging world, accumulation remains primitive, as it was at the beginning of Western capitalism (Goody, 1996: 55–6). There are pressing problems, and although some social groups are getting richer by leaps and bounds, the hopes of many remain focused on simply acquiring the essentials: access to decent housing and to an unrestricted supply of electricity, gas and water at reasonable prices. What is just ordinary for the first world represents hope for many people in the second. The forces involved are not of the same intensity. So we should not be surprised to observe that the solutions found in these countries take liberties with our model.

Our view of forms of government is based on the idea of *political democracy*, with an elected assembly that runs a local administration in charge of city affairs. This representation first became weaker as more or less independent public or private institutions contributing to urban public policy increasingly came onto the scene. The terms used to describe these at first were 'quangos' (in the UK) or '*secteur paramunicipal*' (the French 'paramunicipal sector'), before the academic community settled on the general expression 'governance'.[5] Through their size, megacities challenge these models of government or governance, which are inspired to a greater or lesser degree by Greek democracy: assemblies made up of small numbers of people who debate in a public space, a model that has led to our delegate assemblies. But do these really work in identical fashion? It is far from the case that the majority of emerging megacities have accountable, elected governments. However, since not all of them have sunk into chaos, it must be the

---

5   For France, Le Galès (1995), Jouve and Lefèvre (2002), Lorrain (1989); in the United States, Stone (1989 and 1993); in the UK, Dunleavy (1980), and see Sellers' overview (2002).

case that these metropolitan areas are *de facto* governed. What kind of government mechanisms do not arise from a perfectly democratic regime, but are nevertheless still accepted by the population? And on the other hand, are large cities that have prioritised reform of their political institutions actually any better governed?

Our *view of the shape of the city* corresponds to a historic centre surrounded by its suburbs, and it is this whole that is governed. The spatial development of megacities is often uneven, combining a primary centre, newly structured spaces ('edge cities') (Garreau, 1991) and fringe areas with few or no amenities. In terms of both surface area and speed of change, the megacity is constantly pushing beyond its administrative territory. The dominant model is polycentric in form, and no longer hierarchical; the old division between city and countryside, on which the geography of the West was based, is being blurred by a new kind of interdependence. Three questions arise in emerging countries much more strongly than in industrial countries. First, what balance will emerge between the administered territories and their urban fringes? Are the latter just spaces waiting to be integrated or do they represent 'other' towns and cities that are going to be permanently self-regulated (Agier, 2002)? In that case, what are the forces at work? Are voluntary-sector NGOs going to take over failing institutions, or will it be major private-sector operators who function as quasi-organisations, or will bits of the city fall into the clutches of gangs and cartels? Second, steering these vast constructs always involves multiple administrative territories, and these may include the state level, the provincial level and the regional level. In these large cities, complexity is part and parcel of public policy; the political sciences talk about 'multilevel governance' (Sellers, 2002). Can these multilevel urban institutions be effective? Third, size favours spatial specialisation; planning also strengthens this tendency, in the name of efficiency. All this carries a risk of segregation. This has been urban sociology's most dominant theme[6]. But are these megacities moving solely towards communities behind barricades? Even if there are separation factors at work, can we also identify opposing agglomerative forces which are substantively laying the foundations for belonging to the whole of the large city?

Differences are also to be found in choices made in relation to *utilities*. The option used in industrial countries since the late nineteenth century has been that of the single technical network, managed by an integrated monopoly company and operating a single tariff (Stoffaës, 1995; Curien, 2000; Coutard and Rutherford, 2009). This solution enabled the urbanised space to be provided with amenities, while reducing unit costs by sharing the fixed costs across the largest number of people. In megacities, this approach is far from universal. These cities develop very quickly; land occupation may precede the provision of technical networks. Alongside the city that is equipped with systems and amenities, we also have to consider the urban fringes, where institutional and infrastructure density is looser. This shows us another dimension of the very large city, with entire sections that are situated outside official channels and where residents cobble together their

---

6   See references at the beginning of this text.

own solutions as best they can (Kennedy and Ramachandraiah, 2006; Jaglin and Bousquet, 2008; Blanc and Botton, 2010).

So emerging megacities bring their own unusual responses to urban challenges, and this is true for several underlying factors: political regime, spatial organisation and utilities model. They invite a specific study approach – an approach that thinks of them as worlds in themselves, to be investigated in several dimensions.

The Urban Dimension of Economic Accumulation

The very large city can also highlight properties that are less often taken into account in studies of economic accumulation phenomena, and this relates not only to emerging countries. It makes the place of cities in the production of value more perceptible. If we start from the Marxist distinction between production and reproduction (Boccara, 1974; Castells, 1972; Castells and Godard, 1974; Palloix, 1978) or from the two circuits of capital (Lefebvre, 1970: 206 and 212; Harvey, 1978), the factory represents the locus of production of surplus value, while consumption and reproduction of the labour force corresponds to the built environment; the whole political problem is knowing how to switch the surplus from the first circuit to the second. This view has been totally changed by the globalisation of production systems, their reorganisation according to a principle of flexible specialisation (Piore and Sabel, 1984; Storper, 1997) and the new importance of technical networks. The city now plays a direct part in the production of value. With the emergence of a 'city industry', it can be thought of as an economy in itself (Brenner and Theodore, 2002; Brenner, 2004; Lorrain, 2002 and 2008a).

For a long time, the primary explanation was through the production economy and, first and foremost, economists stressed markets in their orthodox definition (atomised, competitive). It took many years for the local dimension of trade and of production systems to be taken into account. Urban geographers and industrial economists helped to demonstrate the importance of spatialised production relations.[7] In both these schools, there was to be an insistence on cooperation, on embeddedness in social relations[8] and on the importance of class relations. So we were moving away both from the microeconomics that takes the factory as the starting-point and from the macroeconomics of supply-demand adjustment models. However, in this view, what happens in the production process remains primary to understanding the economic order.[9] As Manuel Castells sums it up, the innovations that are going on there are transforming the space of flows and they

---

7   See in particular Bagnasco, Maurice, Piore and Sabel, Scott, Storper, Trigilia, Veltz. One writer, Aydalot, coined and developed the concept of 'innovative milieu'.

8   See also, for a less spatialised approach, Polanyi (1944).

9   See the vast literature on the topic of the new international division of labour (NIDL), published since the mid-1980s by the *International Journal of Urban and Regional Research*.

bring us an understanding of the space of places (Castells in Pflieger 2006, p. 165). Fundamentally, this reading sets up a non-equivalence in which the production part (production relations, factory, technology) carries greater weight than the reproduction, collective consumption and city side.

Megacities enable us to reconsider this reading, because they highlight the specifically urban properties of production. They give visibility to the respective significance of the production economy and of the services that make it possible. Megacities are subject to three sets of linkages in relation to the functioning of the economy and to the production of value:

- With the globalisation of trade, the functions necessary for exchange take on greater importance. Large technical networks contribute directly to the movement of goods along increasingly extended value chains. In a globalised economy, the large city functions as a 'switching system'. In order to guarantee that it can function as a hub in this way, it must develop fixed assets.
- These assets can have two faces: they are directly linked to production, but are also fixed assets that serve the domestic economy (utilities, buildings, major amenities). They represent markets for private-sector firms and their performance impacts on other firms since they have an influence on the cost of goods and services as well as on the free flow of trade. In many industrial countries the economy of the urban fabric represents on average between 7 and 10 per cent of the active population. Since the 1980s, with liberalisation policies, these activities have been increasingly financed and managed by large private-sector firms (Lorrain, 2002).
- The service economy (finance, leisure/conferences, education) is largely tied up with the large city and with the functional resources that it can bring. Their concentration within one dense space generates economies of agglomeration. They are at the heart of the development of cities and of innovation functions. In the future, with increasing attention paid to sustainable development (environmental protection and conservation of finite resources), there will certainly be a growing role for technical networks since they deal with the environment.

In explaining these properties, a graphic form of expression converges with the historical explanation. In its descriptive form, a flow is represented by an arc that joins two points; a network (a major technical system) corresponds to the arc, while a single place (a gas terminal, for example) or an urban space can correspond to a point (Dupuy, 1991; Offner and Pumain, 1996). Because of their cost, large technical systems are limited in number and concentrated in a few places: network nodes. Nodes that draw together several technical networks become hubs. These hubs, or large cities, agglomerate large populations and develop other networks in order to provide them with services: utilities networks. The economy therefore becomes more infrastructure-based. The space of technical networks directs the movement of flows and so represents an explanatory factor in the value chains of goods and services. This is the outcome of a long process that was ignored for a long time.

In a study of the economic development of the United States over the period 1790–1860, Douglass North maintained that development starts through the success of an export sector. In order to run smoothly, this requires 'transport, warehousing, port facilities and other types of social overhead investment' infrastructures (North, 1966: 5), which go on to create externalities favourable to the development of other activities. So a development cycle gets underway. This export sector goes on to generate a surplus; if this is distributed unequally and leaves the territory in order to be reinvested elsewhere, its impacts are weak. Conversely, when it is distributed equitably, household consumption creates a demand on the domestic market, from which industry and services benefit; the economic base becomes bigger and more diverse. The nature of the institutions also plays a part. The export base and the productivity changes are 'a nearly automatic response' because they are an intrinsic part of 'an acquisitive society under competitive market conditions … . The structure of a competitive market provided important rewards for successful innovation in a society whose value system prized such activity' (op. cit.: 8). Finally, there is a very important general factor relating to the dimensions of markets. Greater size leads them towards specialisation and division of labour, both of which increase efficiency; the economic actors move from an integrated form of organisation to a disintegrated form.

At the start of the Industrial Revolution, most of the building-blocks that would later become the basis of the big hubs were already in place together in rural America. As a general rule, the principle of efficiency and its corollaries of specialisation and trade, which North discusses, require the infrastructures (port, road – and later – highway, railway, airport, telephone and internet) that all form the basis of the large modern city (World Bank Report 1994: 3). In turn, the formation of a domestic economy leads to demand for other urban networks and for the construction of a built environment.

Early twenty-first-century large cities now represent a sizeable accumulation of investments in fixed assets. No society could possibly abandon these places and rebuild them elsewhere – the cost would be prohibitive. The cities built by the Romans in order to conquer Germany, like Genghis Khan's capital cities and his nomadic towns (Inoue, 1990), disappeared because they were not very dense in accumulated capital; their network level was low. The transition from pedestrian city (*polis*) to megalopolis and then to very big, very network-dense metropolis (*gig@city*) has set the large city once and for all on a path along which there is no going back (Tarr and Konvitz, 1981; Lorrain, 2001 and 2008a). So megacities and large cities are here to stay, established in their territories, and they are certainly going to continue to grow. Equipped with infrastructure, human resources and institutions, as 'hyperdense bodies' they capture both capital and people. They act as giant magnets.

This property raises several questions. Firstly, are they politically acceptable for those who live in them? Doesn't their gigantic size damage the fragile bond between governors and governed? Secondly, is it always to society's best advantage that they are so attractive? The megacity captures many activities because it has the capital and the political backing – but is this optimal? Wouldn't these activities be better located elsewhere – in other regions or in smaller cities? Thirdly, are they sustainable? This question can be stated in a number of ways, taking land consumption (areas covered), energy consumption or volumes of pollutants discharged (greenhouse gases, untreated wastewater, waste) as its starting-point.

This material reading of the large city establishes that in some cases actors invest in activities to develop the built environment; and here we find growth coalitions (Logan and Molotch, 1987). Some are driven by public-sector actors who are both strategists and developers, as in Singapore (Haila, 2002), Hong Kong (Castells, 1985) and a large number of Chinese cities (Logan 2002). In other cities where the local authorities are less involved, the driving force is provided by large private-sector actors, as in Latin America or India. In addition to these sophisticated coalitions, we also find primitive accumulation regimes; the city represents a means of laundering and protecting surpluses that arise from war, expropriation or various kinds of illegal or semi-lawful trafficking. This reminds us that regulated growth regimes have sometimes found their origins in a wild untrammelled, primitive form of accumulation.

In essence, our argument involves bringing together results from several separate bodies of research. We have the literature of the 'new economic geography' which puts forward the idea of globalisation of exchanges and at the same time their embeddedness in spatialised factors; we intend to draw on their conclusions while also taking into account the infrastructures that enable these global movements and these local services. This approach is backed up by literature from the Science, Technology and Society current which specifically tackles technical networks through their morphological, social and economic properties[10] (Dupuy and Offner, 2005; Coutard et al., 2004; Summerton, 1994). Finally, our argument is completed by consideration of the vast corpus of economics literature on infrastructure liberalisation policies. This establishes that types of financing and management previously guaranteed by the public authorities (and thought of under the headings of public services or utilities) are now provided by private-sector firms. Therefore, the large city viewed as a locus of fixed-assets accumulation no longer represents just a place determined by direct production as it was considered by theory. It must also be viewed as another place of accumulation, producing the value that forms an integral part of economic performance – the city as a meta-means of production. The urban fabric has necessarily led to the formation of a 'city industry'.

---

10   See the journal *Flux* or the *Journal of Urban Technologies* for this line of research.

A Way in Through Institutions

Clearly, the large city in emerging countries questions several elements of our established knowledge: accumulation regime and speed of development, forms of government, social relations, the relationship between city and countryside. It is an enormous and enormously rich object in many different regards. We have chosen to enter this city by starting from the issue of institutions of government and steering. There are several reasons for this. Like the neo-institutional economists, we think that the issue of institutions is primary in the *organisation* of a society; they are the rules of the game that allow the actors to cooperate (North, 1990; Vietor, 2007). Moreover, these institutions represent a raw material on which proactive actors can act; they are not imposed by the laws of nature but are the product of human action. Finally, when we consider this question about institutions in relation to urban affairs, we get an interesting result – one that underlines the importance of second-level institutions, alongside the classic distinction between formal and informal institutions (Lorrain, 2008b). Formal institutions lay down property rights, define general rules and provide incentives to the actors, but they do not explain everything. In order to act, the actor draws on a stock of informal institutions (culture, values, behavioural norms) and also relies on the more casual, familiar institutions that we call 'second-level institutions' (instruments). The idea is that between the two general categories of formal and informal, each policy sphere has produced instruments that guide the actor in the detail (Bezes et al., 2005; Lascoumes and Le Galès, 2004). To put this another way, there is a 'lower order of institutions' (Cattaneo cited by Ingold 2008: 31) that lies between legally defined property rights and loose custom.

The study of cities and in particular of large cities in emerging countries enables us to highlight this genealogy in the development of institutions. First come problems that cannot be avoided. Spatial development presupposes investment in major infrastructure and city dwellers need basic services; rainwater drainage and transport issues must be solved, otherwise disasters can ensue. These ever-present problems can be tackled first of all from a technical angle but it is not long before institutional choices must be made. Therefore, faced with problems, actors take decisions based on technical constraints and then supplement them with institutional choices. These are not major choices, like those that are made within the articles of a constitution; they are second-level choices. However, in this way, institutions for steering technical systems are invented and they have some of the attributes of political institutions. So there are several ways of building institutions. The political route and the formal institutions have been the most studied. In large cities, it is worth focusing attention on the more low-profile route of second-level institutions with their starting-point in urban networks. It is by starting from this institutional approach and reconsidering it through the prism of technical issues and second-level institutions that we intend to tackle the issue of governing megacities.

Generally speaking, the approach that we are proposing in this book consists of tackling the urban question through its 'hard' or permanent nature, through its material basis, since we believe that, in the end, choices made at this level help to structure the everyday existence of millions of urban dwellers. This material city can be thought of both as the framework that structures the space of movements and possible movements and as the medium for building numerous institutions. The fact that these choices may be forgotten, become naturalised and disappear over the long term cannot be seen as proof of their secondary nature. By inserting technology and the network into our reading of the city – in brief, by 'ballasting' our approach to the urban question – we also want to shift several of our habitual keys to interpretation.

By comparison with the debate on *the postmodern city* embodied by Los Angeles (Soja, 2000; Gottdiener and Budd, 2005: 121), our reading of urban history through material changes – the city of nomads, the polis, the megalopolis, the gig@city – suggests that there is no end of history, no impassable horizon of which we are to be the guardians. There are simply cities that are changed by human will, according to the available techniques and the customs of the day. This will continue and the emerging cities will probably surprise us.

As far as the urban economy is concerned, before advancing the idea that *the global city* is a site of innovation (Sassen, 1991), it is not irrelevant to point out that the actors will be all the more innovative if they are working in well-equipped, well-governed cities. This means re-establishing the importance of 'back-office jobs' and support functions; of course they are less glamorous, but they represent the first stage on the road to progress that affects everyone.[11] It is a way of reminding ourselves that the 'genius' of the creatives, of the financial aces and the high-flying designers, could not be expressed without the work of other, smaller hands (to use Pierre Sansot's turn of phrase, *les gens de 'peu'*). They drive the metro trains, guard and maintain the power stations, collect the waste, manage the drinking-water production plants and work in the hospitals. Large cities form a whole, whose different parts remain indissociable. If we focus too much on global cities, making London, New York and Tokyo our models, we shall end up producing a deformed picture of the world.[12]

The question of *institutions* is central to the development of emerging countries, which suffer a combination of pressure from problems and incomplete development of their legal and regulatory frameworks. Our argument is that these arrangements do not arise *ex nihilo*, even if some heads of international development organisations take the view that they can be exported (Bafoil, 2006; Boyer, 2001; Fukuyama, 2006). Our hypothesis is that the actors build the institutions above all in order to provide solutions to practical problems. They experiment with trial-and-error processes; they seek compromises between the rational solution and

---

11   See, for example, Michael Harloe's observations on London and the differences between the Boroughs and the City (2003).

12   See Hammett's 1994 critique, in Gottdiener and Budd (2005: 41).

existing interests. Therefore, in order to retrace their path, we too should start from the problems. This reading diverges from the dominant bodies of literature on more than one account. First, it reintroduces technical phenomena, often forgotten by the social sciences. Cities offer us a powerful invitation to integrate this component, since issues linked to the built environment occupy a central place in any city. Second, this reading introduces necessity into action, in a context where many people see only a proactive, strategic actor. Our approach is to move away not just from the standard economics fiction of the mathematical exchange of pure, perfect markets, but also from the strategic-actor reading and even from the city-as-collective-actor reading shared by organisational sociologists and political scientists (Friedberg, 1993; Le Galès, 2002: 37 and 323 et seq.). In both cases, the actor seems to move in a flat world where the constraints on him are so weak that he can map out his path with ease. Yet, when it comes to the built environment or to institutions and when the existing laws, norms and rules that organise any action are taken into account, cities are above all inherited constructs. In this reading, action becomes less flamboyant (Lorrain, 2004): the actor must conduct himself more modestly – and if he has a strategy, he must come to terms with this legacy city and integrate the variable of the *longue durée*.

Four Research Sites, One Method

In order to deal with these questions, my first preference was for a small number of extended essays, rather than quantitative surveys; we already have UN-HABITAT research and World Bank databases to provide us with a quantitative framework. It was also essential to stick to a limited number of case studies, since these very large cities are obviously complex objects; we needed to be able to describe and to demonstrate. Therefore I contacted several colleagues who work on cities in emerging countries. We shared several of the hypotheses put forward – sufficiently, at least, to adjust to one other quickly and with ease.

Approaching our topic through individual chapters does carry the risk of idiosyncrasy; nothing lends itself to a cumulative approach, and it is not possible to produce results of general significance. The solution that we have adopted is an intermediate one, somewhere between complete freedom for each writer on her or his own terrain and a highly structured framework for analysis. My preference was to offer a series of questions and a flexible analytical framework. This choice reflected a desire not to box things in and so risk finding that we had set up *a priori* conceptions; instead, I wanted to let each place speak for itself. Each of these cities exists on a site that positions it in its neighbouring territory and in major global flows; each city has its own – sometimes tragic – history, economic base and social groups. All this gives the city an identity, sets an agenda and allows us to draw out a common theme that acts as a starting-point for linkages between a large number of issues. The account given in these four chapters is an illustration of this property of the city. Any attempt at literal comparison would flatten out this reality. The use of a few comparative indicators is only meaningful once the overall organisation of each city, on which its singularity is based, is understood.

So we worked in a threefold register: i) sharing common questions and hypotheses that have their origins in a fairly long research practice, ii) tackling each city in detail and organising each chapter in a particular layout, iii) finally, a comparison.

With a population of around 23 million, **Shanghai,** China's economic capital, is emblematic of the emerging megacities. What holds the attention first and foremost are issues relating to the speed of change and the leaders' capacity to elaborate a new institutional architecture; enacting policy through infrastructure plays a primary foreground role in this city. When President Deng Xiaoping embarked on the economic modernisation of China in 1978, the urbanised part of Shanghai was no bigger than 300 km², the city was dominated by industry and had lost its international role, Pudong New Area did not exist and the other districts (some 5,500 km²) were still rural. As in the rest of China, urban government was a matter for direct administration. There was a pyramid system of interlocking commissions and bureaux – all part of the public sector. Their resources came from taxes and public subsidies, tariffs played little part in financing public services and overall coordination depended on central planning.

From the mid-1980s, with the support of central government, the Municipality of Shanghai instigated a modernisation plan. This of course related to economic infrastructures (industrial zones, a financial city development, technology zones) but it was also backed up by a very ambitious programme of investment in urban infrastructure – a programme for spatial change. According to Dominique Lorrain's description, modernisation of primary infrastructures – the metro, sanitation, electricity – was to play a very significant role in this process of change. Faced with major challenges in terms of finding technical solutions, financing and project control, local officials decided to undertake experiments that would lead them towards a different management model. The old bureaux were converted, in small stages, into shareholder companies; some of the instruments of a market economy were introduced. Partnerships were formed with the World Bank, its consultants and foreign firms. These exchanges, modest to begin with, acted as an incubator. Shanghai's elites are learning; they test the options and try out partnerships; they travel all over the world and compare different institutional choices ranging from deregulated markets to more contract-based formulas. And in the end they have forged their own doctrine. In the period roughly from 1999 to 2003, the solutions found in these first experiments were generally extended to most infrastructures – highways, bridges and tunnels, the port, the drinking-water system, waste treatment and the organisation of a chemical industrial park. The result was that, in 15 years or thereabouts, this city was able to move from a direct administration regime that was fairly broadly autarkic to a socialist market economy – an economy that opened up to the world. This translated into a separation between directive functions and management functions, into the adoption of shareholder company status for the bureaux and into a proliferation of partnerships with foreign firms. At the end of this process, municipal government has emerged with a very different face.

Lorrain argues that this institutional history represents the invisible, essential side of economic success. Shanghai has been materially transformed because its elites have built a new institutional framework and new institutions that have borrowed from both Chinese tradition and Western market economics. It is thanks to these quiet reforms that the city has been able to carry through its enormous material transformation successfully. A large number of technical networks that structure the space are less than 20 years old. The city has provided amenities, its offer to residents has seen marked progress and Shanghai has broadly escaped the ills suffered by a good number of emerging cities. This success is explained partly by its strategic position near the mouth of the Yangzi and partly by the support of central government, but also by engagement on the part of its elites. This is a metropolis governed by a 'public-sector growth coalition', where political leaders and administration officials draw in and work alongside major private-sector companies. This limited decision-making group has accumulated a large part of the city's political and economic resources and this enables it to lead major projects while avoiding the usual obstacles (detailed public enquiries, opposition through the courts, criticisms in the press, etc.) and the costs of coordinating these. This case study is certainly intended to feed into debates on social change and, conversely, on path dependency theory. Shanghai's elites have been able to get off their existing track and drive a new way forward. But this accumulation regime has its own weaknesses. How long can the megacity go on developing once the environmental impacts and the growing inequalities of income and wealth are taken into account? In the present schema, 'the city is paying for the city': it is the increase in land values that allows state-owned development companies to fund the new infrastructures that, in their turn, feed growth. What are the forces that are going to moderate this coalition's ambitions and enable it to make the transition into a more sustainable regime?

Mumbai is a megacity with a population of 12 million (above 20 million in the whole urban region) – and one which combines extremes. As Marie-Hélène Zérah emphasises from the outset, it is India's economic capital, cosmopolitan and opulent, yet at the same time it is a poor city with a large informal economy. It appears to be a modern city, open to the world, attracting migrants from Maharashtra and other parts of India; its elites dream of making it a world city, but it is also a city organised on the basis of caste, unequal and underequipped. It functions on a twofold economic base, of which one element is part of the globalised economy and the other governed by the informal economy – and the first needs the second in order to succeed. These two elements also make Mumbai a melting-pot, bringing together heterogeneous social micro groups; at the local level, it is a ferment of cultures. Everything is jostling together and this creates a stir – occasionally even a riot. Mumbai is energetic and violent. Now it is suffering from the defects of its infrastructure and is seeing competition from Chennai, Bangalore and Hyderabad to the south and Delhi to the north. The situation is problematic, and not just for the poor: there are difficult transport conditions, water and power cuts, an endemic shortage of social housing. One international consultancy has advocated that the city should undertake a massive programme of investment in infrastructure. This policy is seen as a lever for economic growth and as a way of improving living conditions. The ambition is to haul the city up into the ranks of global megacities by reproducing the elements that have created Shanghai's success; but there is a risk that this strategy will come up against several stumbling-blocks: i) an unstable political system, ii) a growth coalition without any utilities and large construction firms, iii) major social inequalities expressed in the form of endemic poverty.

This megacity is difficult to govern and Zérah's description of the institutions gives us the first reason why. Responsibilities are divided between a powerful State institution (Maharashtra), with authority over a lot of strategic issues, and the Municipal Corporation of Greater Mumbai (led by a Municipal Commissioner[13] and a Municipal Council) which appoints the Mayor. In this architecture, the Mayor has very few resources when it comes to political legitimacy, budgets, technical expertise or knowledge. Where there are opposed interests between institutions at different levels, he is not in a position to impose his own choices. To this factor must be added the dynamic of the political arenas, with the extreme fragmentation of a caste society and of migrant groups, strengthened by the British legacy of political democracy – the same situation as is found in Cape Town. The mixture of a political system that guarantees individual rights and a socially fragmented society leads to an unstable system, both in the interplay of political parties and in the conduct of public policy. Unregulated confrontations between interests lead to extreme volatility in public policy; and this reflects Lester Thurow's analysis of the difficulties faced by pluralist societies in coordinating their interest groups, with the risk of 'the zero-sum society' (1981). In Mumbai, this situation is not balanced out by a growth coalition largely driven by professional practitioners in the urban development field who would act as strategy leaders. This metropolis does not fit in with the '3S' schema – Shanghai/Singapore/Santiago – where urban actors declare themselves publicly as the leaders of major projects. We may seek them in the infrastructure groups or among developers, but in Mumbai such actors still remain silent. In fact, it is the large industrialists and their institutions who carry projects forward. So Zérah gives us an account of the tribulations of investing in electricity or drinking water and of disputes around bridges and urban highways. The issue of a viaduct bridge led to a confrontation between two figures in the industrial establishment, the Ambani brothers, which received a great deal of media attention – however, the surprising thing was not the family dispute but the fact that one of them controls the country's leading petrochemical group and the other is at the top of the telecomms industry (Reliance). Their activities in spheres where other countries would see major construction groups becoming involved simply serve to tell us that Mumbai – and probably India as a whole – lacks a 'city industry' capable of meeting its urban challenges.

---

13   The equivalent of a city manager in a North American city.

Cape Town can be described as a second-level world city. With a population of 3.7 million for the Metropolitan area (and 4.1 for the urban region) it is South Africa's third metropolis and has its own special characteristics. It is situated a long way from the megacity of Johannesburg-Pretoria, which concentrates both political power and economic power; it is not governed by the ANC (Nelson Mandela's party). Its position at the southern tip of the African continent gives it the potential status of global trade hub, but here it finds itself in competition with Durban and Port Elisabeth. As Alain Dubresson and Sylvy Jaglin show, it is not a poor city by comparison with other African cities; but it is a city where there are poor people whom the City of Cape Town wants to reduce in number and provide services for. The 'indigent policy', which gives access to several utilities free of charge, comes into play at an income threshold of 3,000 rand (300€), a high level in comparison to a good number of neighbouring countries. There are two important dates in the city's contemporary history. 1994 saw the end of apartheid. Although this represented a major break with the past, the long history of that system has left a deeply traumatic legacy; infinite divisions criss-cross society and put social groups into many different micro classifications. 2000 was the year of a very important reform of metropolitan government with the merger of 61 local authorities (racially segregated and until then overseen by the Regional Services Council, a management body) to form a Unicity.

Measured by the standard of many African cities, Cape Town is characterised by the quality of its institutions. Networked public services work properly (relying on the legacy of pre-apartheid state-owned enterprises). The government has allocated massive public investments in Cape Flats, subsidies are directed to the poor, and to a certain extent the government ensures public-sector steering of private-sector investments. Despite these efforts, and as Dubresson and Jaglin show, this policy has not managed to stem the rise in poverty or the worsening inequalities that can be measured by different indicators: the city's Gini coefficient is 0.67;[14] in 2005, 38 per cent of households were living below the poverty line; there has been an increase in the indebtedness of the poorest households; and black Capetonians are underskilled (affirmative action measures in their favour see some businesses with vacant posts). There are problems in the housing market, with a risk of segregation and of return to apartheid. The influx of retired people, often British, pushes prices up and accentuates divisions between residential areas. Employment is becoming another source of problems. In Cape Flats, not only drugs but also taxis are controlled by gangs.

The situation in this large city can be summed up by saying that at the outset it had a segregated social system coupled with efficient utilities delivering universal services. Extensive political and institutional reform has not yet managed to reduce segregation, but neither is it improving the quality of services. Political

---

14   For the record, in 2005 the Gini coefficient was 0.25 for Denmark and Japan, 0.33 in France, 0.36 in the United Kingdom and 0.41 in the United States. UNDP, Human Development Report (2006).

segregation has been abolished but individual rights are being asserted within a society that is atomised by extreme socio-economic diversity, which in turn is exacerbated by microdifferentiated identities. In this kind of context, public-sector decision-making can be very complex. Spatial segregation is maintained and poverty increases it further. Since the introduction of pro-market reforms, technical networks that used to be unified (despite apartheid) are now more fragmented. For some activists, 'the only revolution is the "tender revolution"'. Public expenditure is now only committed following compulsory competitive tendering procedures; these give more businesses increased chances and, in particular, allow black businesses to gain access to these markets. Looking at the whole picture, some researchers talk about a 'tragedy' of governance.

Santiago de Chile, with a population above 6 million, belongs to the family of 'large' cities – a far larger family than that of the megacities. Firstly, Santiago's geographical position in South America sets it apart from the world's major flows; it has grown up in a valley separated from the Pacific Ocean by the cordillera (the Andean Belt). In addition, its economy dominates the country; the GDP of the metropolis represents about 40 per cent of Chile's GDP, with the result that there is often confusion between national and local interests. Finally, it has had a tragic political history with the Allende Government's democratic experiment brought to a halt in 1973 by General Pinochet's coup d'état and military dictatorship. This political split was to be expressed in the economy: Chile was the first testing-ground for economic liberalization policies influenced by the Chicago economists.

This large city, as presented by Géraldine Pflieger, is original because of a combination of factors. It is a highly governed metropolis, but one without a true government; by comparison with other large cities in this part of the world, it guarantees all its residents a satisfactory level of service and yet is also characterised by strong spatial segregation. The path taken by its institutions, as put forward by Pflieger, clearly highlights the links between the major issues of four historical periods and the political responses.

Decision-makers first of all tackled housing reform. This has been a major problem since the 1960s, with insufficient production of social housing and concentration of social housing in certain working-class municipalities. The dictatorship relied on these characteristics in order to develop formulas for granting public subsidies. These led to a form of financial and management zoning; working-class municipalities continued to get social housing, while up-market districts saw development initiated by private property developers out towards the Andes cordillera. The second stage of public policies was marked, as in other countries at the time, by the modernisation of networked services (electricity, drinking water, bus transport). The government introduced liberalisation of these sectors by various methods: privatisation through the sale of shares or, for bus transport, 'competition in the market'. At a third stage, in the mid-1990s, a policy known as 'conditional urban development' was undertaken. So that development could be pursued despite slow progress in providing infrastructure, all infrastructure costs were incorporated in the sale price of building land; economists thought it was possible to calculate and integrate externalities. This approach was not to be successful, but metropolitanisation continued in the shape of highways extensions and major urban projects driven by the private sector. The resulting spatial fragmentation and the environmental impacts called for new responses, in particular investments in urban transport. In this fourth phase, difficulty in implementing these highlighted the limitations of sector-based steering and of decentralisation to individual municipalities.

Although the dominant problems in each period have changed, responses to them have always revolved around variant forms that in fact mark out a very particular model of government, where three forces play a role: the state, network services companies and developers. Firstly, a large part of metropolitan government depends on the central state, which itself has delegated some of the tasks to networked services companies or to a private-sector growth coalition. There is no true metropolitan government; the Regional Governor in charge of these affairs has to compromise with the municipalities which themselves are dependent on the central state; their fiscal receipts come from redistributed national taxes. Secondly, this large city is characterised by efficiently functioning technical networks. There is a long tradition in this sphere, first of all with efficient national state-owned enterprises which were subsequently privatised. As in Cape Town under the apartheid regime, networked services were provided to everyone; segregation was going on elsewhere. Pflieger also points out that the organisation of these networks was not disrupted by political changes, as if the elites were taking the view that there was a layer of urban government based solely on the city's technical and economic properties. Thirdly, urban development is largely driven by a growth coalition dominated by developers and large landowners. They have a great deal of influence on public policies and command sufficient financial resources to be capable of driving long-term strategies and far-reaching policies: creating land reserves, urbanising entire districts and developing a new quasi city.

These four large and very large cities offer different features in their histories, in their general contexts and their institutional frameworks. Their histories open a debate about the way that change is managed. The approach adopted in Cape Town as in Mumbai contrasts fairly strongly with the one taken in Shanghai: steering takes place through policy rather than technical reforms, with comprehensive proactive engagement rather than a gradual approach. It is probably too soon to come to a firm verdict, but both these cases raise several questions. What is the right balance between political reform and practical approaches? And in what order should they be undertaken? Is there a limit to what institutions can bring to the results of policy put into action? These large cities show us that everything is not dependent on 'good' governance; there are factors exogenous to the actors that carry them forward or rein them in; their position in the major flows of globalisation are not the same and nor are their respective capacities to capture wealth. These cities have each inherited a history, with different elites and different social groups; these can drive ambitions forward or exacerbate conflicts of interest. These factors also have a strong influence on the outcomes of urban public policy.

Table 1.1   Four large cities: a few facts and figures

	Mumbai	Shanghai	Santiago de Chile	Cape Town
Site	port	port, plain	valley surrounded by mountains	port mountains to the north
Global flows	hub for India	hub for China	in south of continent	in south of continent
History	1990 liberalisation	1992 socialist market economy	coup d'état 1973 testing ground for economic liberalisation	end of apartheid 1994 ref. local institutions 2000
Economy	economic capital	economic capital	political/ economic capital	
GNP, % of national			60%	
Municipal authority	city/metropolis gap	strong	weak	strong
Population				
City	12.0			
Metropolis	18.4	23.0	6.3	3.7
Urban region	20+	70+	–	4.1
Population, % of national	–	–	40%	–
Area of city	435 km²	100 km²	–	–
Area of metropolis	–	6,340 km²	650 km²	2,500 km²
Density of city	27,000 people/ km²	35,000 people/ km²	9,231 people/ km²	–
Density of metropolis	–	3,230 people/ km²	394 people/km²	1,440 people/ km²

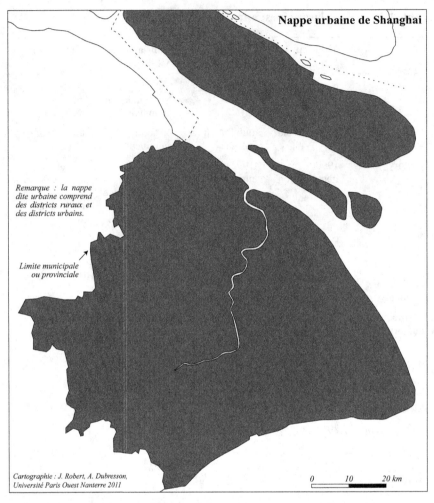

Nappe urbaine de Shanghai

Remarque : la nappe dite urbaine comprend des districts ruraux et des districts urbains.

Limite municipale ou provinciale

Cartographie : J. Robert, A. Dubresson, Université Paris Ouest Nanterre 2011

0   10   20 km

Figure 1.1   Map of Shanghai

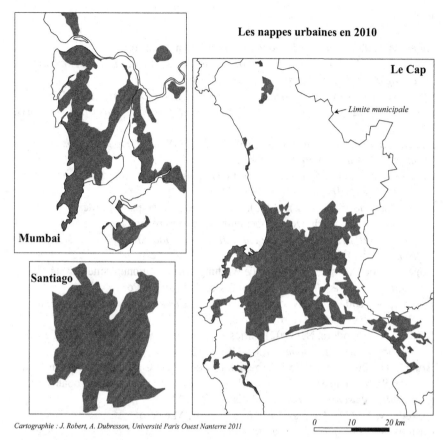

Les nappes urbaines en 2010

Le Cap

Mumbai

Santiago

Limite municipale

Cartographie : J. Robert, A. Dubresson, Université Paris Ouest Nanterre 2011

0   10   20 km

Figure 1.2   Maps of Cape Town, Mumbai and Santiago

References.

Agier, M. (2002). *Aux bords du monde*. Paris: Flammarion.

Bafoil, F. (2006). *Europe centrale et orientale, mondialization, européanization et changement social*. Paris: Presses de Sciences Po.

Bagnasco, A. (1988). *La costruzione sociale del mercato*. Bologna: Il Mulino.

Bairoch, P. (1985). *De Jéricho à Mexico, Villes et économie dans l'histoire*, Paris: Gallimard, 705.

Beaujeu-Garnier, J., Gamblin, A., Delobez, A. (1966). *Images économiques du monde* (11e année). Paris: SEDES.

Bezes, P., Lallement, M., Lorrain, D. (2005). Les nouveaux formats de l'institution. *Sociologie du Travail*, 47(3): 293–300.

Blanc, A., Botton, S. (dir.) (2011). Services d'eau et pays en développement. Agence Française de Développement, collection recherche.

Boccara, P. (1974). *Etudes sur le capitalisme monopoliste d'Etat, sa crise et son issue*. Paris: Editions sociales.

Boyer, R. (2001). L'après consensus de Washington: institutionnalisme et systémique? *L'Année de la régulation*, 5. Paris: Presses de Sciences Po, 13–56.

Brenner, N. (2004). *New State Spaces. Urban Governance and the Rescaling of Statehood*. Oxford: Oxford University Press.

Brenner, N., Theodore, N. (2002). Cities and the Geographies of 'Actually Existing Neoliberalism'. *Antipode*, 34(3): 349–79.

Bruhns, H. (2001). La ville bourgeoise et l'émergence du capitalisme moderne, Max Weber: Die Stadt (1913/1914–1921). In B. Lepetit and C. Topalov (dir.), *La ville des sciences sociales*, Paris: Bélin, 2001, 47–78.

Castells, M. (1972). *La question urbaine*. Paris: Maspero.

Castells, M. (1985). *High Technology, Space, and Society*. Beverly Hills: Sage.

Castells, M. (1989). *The Informational City: Information Technology, Economic Restructuring and the Urban-Regional Process*. Oxford; Cambridge, MA: Blackwell.

Castells, M. (1997), *The Rise of the Network Society*. Oxford: Blackwell Publishers.

Castells, M., Godard, F. (1974). *Monopolville. L'entreprise, l'Etat, l'urbain*. Paris La Haye: Mouton.

Coutard, O., Hanley, R., Zimmerman, R. (eds) (2004). *Social Sustainability of Technical Networks*. New York: Routledge.

Coutard, O., Rutherford, J. (2009). Les réseaux transformés par leurs marges: développement et ambivalence des techniques 'décentralisées'. *Flux*, 76/77(avril-septembre): 6–13.

Curien, N. (2000). Economie des réseaux, La Découverte, coll. Repères, Paris.

Davis, M. (1997). *City of Quartz, Los Angeles, capitale du futur*. Paris: La Découverte.

Davis, M. (1998). *Ecology of Fear. Los Angeles and the Imagination of Disaster*. Metropolitan Books.

Dunleavy, P. 1980. *Urban Political Analysis*. London: MacMillan.

Dupuy, C., Halpern, C. (2009). Les politiques publiques face à leurs protestataires. *Revue française de science politique*, 59(4): 701–22.

Dupuy, G. (1991). *L'urbanisme des réseaux, théories et méthodes*, Paris: Armand Colin, 198.

Dupuy, G., Offner, J.M. (2005). Réseau: bilans et perspectives. *Flux*, 62: 38–46.

Fainstein, S., Gordon, I., Harloe, M. (eds) (1992). *Divided Cities: New York and London in the Contemporary World*. Oxford: Blackwell.

Florida, R. 2002. *The Rise of the Creative Class: and How it's Transforming Work, Leisure, Community and Everyday Life*. New York: Basic Books.

Friedberg, E. (1993). *Le Pouvoir et la Règle*. Paris: Seuil.

Friedmann, J. (1986). The world city hypothesis, *Development and Change*, 17(1): 69–84.

Fukuyama, F. (2006). *D'où viennent les néo-conservateurs?* Paris: Grasset.

Gandy, M. (2005). Cyborg Urbanization: Complexity and Monstrosity in the Contemporary City. *International Journal of Urban and Regional Research*, 29(1): 26–49.

Gandy, M. (2006). Planning, Anti-Planning and the Infrastructure Crisis Facing Metropolitan Lagos. *Urban Studies*, 43(2): 371–96.

Garreau, J. (1991). *Edge City, Life on the New Frontier*. Anchor Books, New York: Doubleday.

Goody, J. (1996). *The East in the West*. Cambridge: Cambridge University Press.

Gottdiener, M. and Budd, L. (2005). *Key Concepts in Urban Studies*. London: Sage.

Graham, S. (2010). *Cities Under Siege: The New Military Urbanism*. London, New York: Verso.

Graham, S. and Marvin, S. (2001) *Splintering Networks: Networked Infrastructures, Technological Mobilities and the Urban Condition*. London: Routledge.

Haila, A. (2002). State-Present Capitalism: Property and Development Companies in Singapore. *Entreprises et Histoire*, 30(septembre): 63–72.

Hall, P. (2002). *Cities of Tomorrow* (3rd edition). Malden, MA: Blackwell.

Handlin, O. (1979). *The Uprooted: the Epic Story of the Great Migrations that Made the American People*. Boston: Little, Brown and Company, 1st edition 1951.

Harris, A., Keil, R. (eds) (2008). *Network Disease: Emerging Infections in the Global City*. Oxford: Wiley Blackwell.

Harloe, M. 2003. Le nouveau gouvernement métropolitain de Londres: vers la terre promise? *Revue d'administration publique*, 107: 319–31.

Harvey, D. (1973). *Social Justice and the City*. Oxford: Basil Blackwell.

Harvey, D. (1978). The Urban Process Under Capitalism: A Framework for Analysis. *International Journal of Urban and Regional Research*, 2: 101–31.

Hughes, T. (1983). *Networks of Power: Electrification in Western Society 1880–1930*. Baltimore: John Hopkins University.

Ingold, A. (2008). Les sociétés d'irrigation: bien commun et action collective. *Entreprises et Histoire*, 50: 19–35.

Inoue, Y. (1960). *Le loup bleu (le roman de Gengis-Khan)*. Traduction française 1990, Paris: Editions Philippe Picquier.

Jaglin, S. and Bousquet, A. (2007). Conflits d'influence et modèles concurrents: l'essor de la privatization comunautaire dans les services d'eau d'Afrique subsaharienne, working paper, Latts-Ecole des Ponts

Joseph, I. (1990). *L'école de Chicago: naissance de l'écologie urbaine*. Paris: Aubier.

Jouve, B. and Lefèvre, C. (dir.) (2002). *Des métropoles ingouvernables*. Paris: Elsevier.

Kennedy, L. and Ramachandraiah, C. (2006). Logiques spatiales d'une stratégie régionale 'high tech'. L'exemple de HITEC City à Hyderabad (Inde), *Flux*: 63–4, 54–70.

Lascoumes, P. and Le Galès, P. (dir.) (2004). *Gouverner par les instruments*, Paris: Presses de Sciences Po.

Le Bras, H. (1986). *Les trois France*. Paris: Editions Odile Jacob.

Lefebvre, H. (1970). *La révolution urbaine*, Paris: Gallimard idées*nrf*, 1970.

Le Galès, P. (1995). Du gouvernement des villes à la gouvernance urbaine. *Revue Française de Science Politique*, 45: 57–95.

Le Galès, P. (2002). *European Cities: Social Conflicts and Governance*. Oxford: Oxford University Press.

Le Goff, J. (2003). *L'Europe est-elle née au moyen âge?* Paris: Seuil.

Logan, J. and Molotch, H.L. (1987). *Urban Fortunes, the Political Economy of Places*. Berkeley: University of California Press.

Logan, J. (ed.) (2002). *The New Chinese City*. Oxford: Blackwell.

Lorrain, D. (1989). La montée en puissance des villes, *Economie et Humanisme*, 305: 6–20.

Lorrain, D. (2001). Gig@city: the Rise of Technological Networks in Daily Life, *Journal of Urban Technology*, 8(3): 1–20.

Lorrain, D. (2002). Capitalismes urbains : la montée des firmes d'infrastructures. *Entreprises et Histoire,* 30: 5–31.

Lorrain, D. (2004). Les pilotes invisibles de l'action publique, le désarroi du politique? In P. Lascoumes and P. Le Galès (dir.), *Gouverner par les instruments*, Paris: Presses de Sciences Po, 163–97.

Lorrain, D. (2008a). La Gig@city, nouveau lieu de la production de capital. *Annales des Mines, Réalités Industrielles*, spécial sur l'économie urbaine, février: 63–9.

Lorrain, D. (2008b). Les institutions de second rang. *Entreprises et Histoire*, 50(avril): 6–13.

Marcuse, P. and van Kempen, R. (eds) (2000). *Globalizing Cities, (A New Spatial Order?)*, Oxford: Blackwell.

Maurice, M., Sellier, F., Silvestre, J.J. (1979). La production de la hiérarchie dans l'entreprise : recherche d'un effet sociétal. Comparaison France-Allemagne, *Revue française de sociologie*, 20(20-2): 331–65.

Mollenkopf, J. and Castells, M. (eds) (1991). *Dual City*. New York: Russell Sage Foundation.

Mumford, L. (1964). *La Cité à Travers l'Histoire*. Paris: Seuil.

Nicolet, C. (dir.) (2000). *Mégalopopoles méditerranéennes, Maisonneuve et Larose*, Paris: Ecole Française de Rome, 117.

North, D.C. (1966). *The Economic Growth of the United-States 1790–1860*. New York: The Norton Library.

North, D.C. (1990). *Institutions, Institutional Change, and Economic Performance*. Cambridge: Cambridge University Press.

Offner, J.M. and Pumain, D. (dir.) (1996). *Réseaux et territoires, significations croisées*, La Tour d'Aigues: Editions de l'Aube.

Palloix, C. (1978). *Travail et production*. Paris: Maspero.

Pflieger, G. (2006). *De la ville aux réseaux, dialogues avec Manuel Castells*. Lausanne: Presses Polytechniques et Universitaires Romanes.

Piore, M. and Sabel, C. (1984). *The Second Industrial Divide: Possibility for Prosperity*. New York: Basic Books.

Polanyi, K. (1983). *La Grande Transformation. Aux origine politiques et économiques de notre temps*. Paris: Gallimard.

Rediker, M. and Linebaugh, P. (2008). *L'hydre aux mille têtes, l'histoire cachée de l'atlantique révolutionnaire*. Paris: Editions d'Amsterdam.

Sassen, S. (1991). *The Global City*. Princeton, NJ: Princeton University Press.

Sellers, J. (2002). *Governing from Below. Urban Regions and the Global Economy*. Cambridge: Cambridge University Press.

Scott, A.J. (1998). *Regions and the World Economy*, Oxford: Oxford University Press.

Scott, A.J. (ed.) (2001). *Global City-Regions (Trends, Theory, Policy)*, Oxford: Oxford University Press.

Scott, A.J. and Storper, M. (eds) (1988). *Production, Work, Territory*. Boston: Unwin Hyman.

Scott, A.J. and Soja, E.W. (eds) (1996). *The City, Los Angeles and Urban Theory at the End of the Twentieth Century*. Berkeley: University of California Press.

Simmel, G. (1987). *Philosophie de l'argent* (1900). Paris: PUF.

Simmel, G. (1903). Die Grosstädte und das Geistesleben. Conférence à la Gehe Fondation. In Wolff K.H. (trans.) 1950, The Sociology of Georg Simmel. New York: Free Press.

Soja, E.W. (ed.) (2000). *Postmetropolis, Critical Studies of Cities and Regions*. Oxford: Blackwell.

Sombart, W. (1902). *Der moderne Kapitalismus*. Leipzig.

Stoffaës, C. (ed.) (1995). *Services publics question d'avenir*. Paris: Editions Odile Jacob.

Stone, C. (1989). *Regime Politics*. Lawrence: University of Kansas Press.

Stone, C. (1993). Urban Regimes and the Capacity to Govern. *Journal of Urban Affairs*, 15(1): 1–28.

Storper, M. (1997). *The Regional World: Territorial Development in a Global Economy*. New York: The Guilford Press.

Summerton, J. (ed.) (1994). *Changing Large Technical Systems*. Westview: Boulder (Co).

Tarr, J., Konvitz, J. (1981). Patterns in the Development of the Urban Infrastructure. In *American Urbanism*, Gillette H. et Miller Z. (eds). New York: Greenwood Press, 196–225.

Thurow, L. (1980). *The Zero Sum Society: Distribution and the Possibilities for Economic Change*. New York: Basic Books.

Trigilia, C. (1998). *Economic Sociology, State, Market, and Society in Modern Capitalism*. Oxford: Blackwell.

UN-Habitat (2008). State of the World's Cities 2008/2009. *Harmonious Cities*. New York: United Nations.

Veltz, P. (2000). *Le nouveau monde industriel*. Paris: Gallimard.

Vietor, R. (2007). *How Countries Compete (Strategy, Structure and Government in the Global Economy)*. Boston: Harvard Business School Press.

World Development Report 1994. Washington D.C., World Bank.

Zimmerman, R. (2001). Social Implications of Infrastructure Network Interaction, *Journal of Urban Technology*, 8(3): 97–119.

Chapter 2

Governing Shanghai: Modernising a Local State

Dominique Lorrain

Today's Shanghai is a captivating megacity with a population above 23 million;[1] it attracts investments, tourists and migrants from all over the country. The intense, electric atmosphere of this city of extremes reflects much of the vitality and many of the tensions of contemporary China. In the early 1990s, central government made the city the symbol of its policy of opening up 'a socialist market economy'. As a gateway for foreign capital, a counterweight to the dynamism of Hong Kong after its 'handover' in July 1997 and an illustration of change throughout the whole of China (Pairault, 2008: 10; Sanjuan, 2006: 236), Shanghai became a priority for development policy. The city's ambitions have been served by politics and geography. As regards the first, Shanghai has enjoyed unfailing government support. Two of its former mayors have occupied top positions in Beijing: Jiang Zemin, who succeeded Deng Xiaoping first as Secretary of the Chinese Communist Party in 1993 and then as President of the People's Republic, had been Mayor of Shanghai from 1985 to 1989. Zhu Rongji, Jiang's future Prime Minister, followed him as Mayor.[2]

Geography has also played a key role: the megacity occupies a strategic position on the mouth of the Yangzi (Chang Jiang), the 'blue river' that flows from Wuhan in central China and, further to the west, Sichuan's great metropolis, Chongqing. The completion of the Three Gorges Dam relieved this major communication route of the terrible floods that were once typical (Bernis, 1930; Bonavia, 2002; Lynn, 1997), allowing the river to become a strategic transport route, like the

---

1   23 million people is the population of 2013 including the 'floating' population. In November 2006 the number was 17.8 million, including 4.38 million migrants and foreigners resident in the city for over six months. The natural population increase for 2005 was 123,900 births and 107,000 deaths. The city is growing by an average of 270,000 people a year, largely due to migration (Shanghai Statistics Bureau; Shanghai Daily, 18–19 November, 2006). The age pyramid is distorted by the low proportion of young people (10 per cent) and the large number of people aged over 60 (21 per cent); if we include the 'floating' population, the active population (18–60 years) rises to three quarters. This very distinctive structure partly explains Shanghai's economic performance: it is a 'production machine'.

2   See the entries about these significant political figures by Tran (p.140), Cabestan (p.65) and Gipouloux (p.276) respectively, in Sanjuan, 2006.

Rhine in Europe (Sanjuan, 2001). Shanghai dominates an urban region of 80 million inhabitants, of whom 66 million live in towns or cities. This greater urban region is bordered by the Yangzi to the north and stretches to Nanjing in the west and Hangzhou and Ningbo in the south (Chreod, 2003); it is a rectangle measuring roughly 300 by 200 kilometres.

'Shanghai' was long viewed as being solely the historic urban area of Puxi, with its nine urban districts (Yusuf and Wu, 2002: 1218–19). However, this is a restricted reading as the Municipality of Shanghai in fact administers an area of 6,340 km², two and a half times the size of Luxembourg.[3] Puxi, with its nine districts, covers 300 km², while the real urban core, roughly bounded by the Inner Ring Road, measures 100 km², equivalent to the City of Paris (see Box 2.1). References to 'Shanghai's municipal government' mainly mean this area. The gap between this immediate perception and the reality of the megacity relates to the nine so-called 'rural' districts and to Pudong, the new district on the other side of the River Huangpu. But, from an administrative point of view, the city also includes these formerly rural districts, which have undergone rapid urbanisation – and will to a large extent determine its future development.

Another salient feature of Shanghai's development is that it is recent – very recent, in fact. Policy decisions were taken in the mid-1980s and construction of the major infrastructures and development zones that have shaped today's megacity began between 1992 and 1995. It could be said that in just 15 years the Chinese authorities managed to haul Shanghai up from a run-of-the-mill Chinese city to a global metropolis, which, by increasing its network density, is in the process of joining the closed club of gig@cities (Lorrain, 2008a). The city developed its infrastructure, including the metro, urban highways, bridges and tunnels, the international airport, a deep-water port, heavy industrial zones for automobile, steel and petrochemical production and a complete, newbuild financial centre. Its surface area expanded to cover a large part of its administrative territory. These are the visible signs of change. However, there is also an invisible, institutional dimension, which this chapter will try to reveal. The argument here is based on the simple proposition that policy is inseparable from the institutions and tools that the actors make in order to act. If we are interested in the political economy of development, it makes sense to examine the institutions that actors create. This field has been expanded by American institutional economists (North, 1990; Vietor, 2007), while others, including myself, have attempted to add more detail through studies of the role of second-level institutions in policy (Lascoumes and Le Galès, 2004; Lorrain, 2004; Bezes, Lallement and Lorrain, 2005; Lorrain, 2008b).

This enormous question can itself be divided into two parts. First, on what foundations are institutions and instruments built? In introducing his political economy of institutions, North rightly states that institutions represent the

---

3   As an additional comparison, the Île de France region of Paris is 10,900 km². Pre-unification Berlin covered 481 km². The total area of the city-state of Singapore, including islands, is 647.5 km².

framework: 'Institutions are the rule of the game in a society ... In consequence they structure incentives in human exchange, whether political, social, or economic' (North, 1990: 3). However, they do not arise out of nowhere. The proposition put forward here is that the process of institution building is largely based on the nature of the problems to be solved: it is from these anchor points that actors move forward. If we want to understand how they transform institutions and come to accept a departure from their routines, we must proceed from the challenges they face. This does not just mean looking at the results of policy, i.e. what can be observed *ex post*; we should also examine the substance of policy. Networked infrastructures are a key issue in urban planning: not only can they act as bottlenecks for development but they also present technological, financial and other challenges. Therefore the modernisation of these sectors stimulates the creation of new institutional frameworks that form part of city government reform. I also think that such processes should be read more as being driven by necessity than as proactive, rational plans. This approach to examining institutions makes particular sense in the context of emerging economies, as the issue of institutions lies at the crux of their development or stagnation. Such countries are insufficiently developed, and they struggle to emerge from this state not only because they lack various factors of production (such as capital markets, a skilled workforce, high-quality infrastructure and entrepreneurial ability) but also – and equally – because they do not have good-quality institutions. While this precondition remains unmet, all the aid given by development banks can have only a limited effect. This is a chicken-and-egg problem: where should modernisation begin?

The second question relates to the nature of institutional change. This debate pits proponents of incrementalism against supporters of institutional shock therapy (Stiglitz, 2002; Thelen, 2003; Bafoil, 2006). The latter, largely represented by the IMF and the World Bank, believe that a package of institutional measures, along the lines of the reforms imposed on Japan and Germany after the Second World War, should be introduced *en bloc* in order to establish a coherent system that features – among other things – electoral reform, decentralisation, privatisation of enterprises, a market economy, an independent central bank and laws on the protection of foreign investment. The idea is that this new foundation will unleash the actors' energies and that, with the help of foreign investment, a virtuous circle of development will be set in motion.

In relation to these institutional debates, Shanghai's transformation – ahead of the rest of China – offers a wonderful opportunity for field observation and represents an original model of change management.[4] At the outset, all the actors

---

4 This chapter is based on a good deal of research. In 1996, I worked with other researchers to produce a study for the Ministry of Industry on environmental markets in the Shanghai region. In 2004, SOGREAH entrusted me with the task of producing the institutional report for a study conducted in Shanghai for the Ministry of Finance and the World Bank. Since 2000, I have been teaching a course – Infrastructure and Sustainable Development – in the joint ENPC (Paris)-Tongji University MBA programme (known as

in this story worked in the public sector, with its strict hierarchy of commissions, bureaux and offices. They were restricted by the Communist Party, economic planning and the public finance system. The economy was largely unmonetised and public utility tariffs were extremely low. Resources were allocated according to the state budget. To meet the challenge of development, the Municipality converted administrative bodies into state-owned companies. It changed its accounting tools and opened up to the market and to international partners. Major institutional transformation was achieved in around 15 years (1988–2003). This change partly explains Shanghai's capacity for development, but it was not accomplished all in one piece. The process was gradual and based primarily on the reform of networked industries.

In examining the issues, this chapter will start by looking at physical changes to the megacity. It will then go on to describe the original institutional system, in order to show how profoundly it has changed while trying to solve practical problems. Experimental reforms were initially made to several networked industries (the metro, sanitation and electricity distribution), and these then served as points of reference. 'Good' solutions were subsequently replicated in other sectors, and by the mid-2000s this had led to a new configuration. Looking at the internal workings of institutions reveals that the process of change can be effective only if it goes beyond mere reform of formal institutions; the instruments used by the actors in their everyday actions must also be revised. Finally, the chapter will discuss issues that are still on the agenda: growing inequalities, massive environmental degradation and greater difficulty in coordination.

'SIMBA'). Several of my students have held managerial positions in municipally-owned companies, and a number of dissertations have focused on urban issues. In 2006, 2008 and 2009, my colleagues from the University helped me to conduct a new series of interviews. All this research, spread over several years, allowed me to access a number of sources in the Municipal Government (i.e. officials in commissions, bureaux, rural districts, SOEs and several joint ventures). This information was supplemented by the *Statistical Yearbook* and the websites of numerous bodies. I was able to access the accounting records of several companies in the environmental management sector. Finally, with my students, I attempted to tackle the difficult task of gathering information on 'real' household incomes and public service pricing. I would like to thank Alain Guéguen and Gary Moys from SOGREAH, my colleagues at Tongji Dr Yang Mengying and Prof. Chen Song (School of Economics & Management and SIMBA), my MBA students and everyone who agreed to meet me. Without their help, these investigations into the machinery of the Municipality would not have been possible.

Box 2.1   Demography and densities

Population   (in thousands)

1957, census data   6,900
2000, census data   16,408(a)
2020, World Bank estimate   23,830

Sources: for 1957, Beaujeu-Garnier et al., 1966. For 2000 and 2020, SHUEP, Inception Report, SOGREAH, March 2004.

Population and spatial density, 2000

	Pop. (thousands)	Area, km²	Density: people/km²
Puxi (9 urban districts)	6,930	289.44	23,943
Pudong New Area	2,402	522.75	4,596
3 rural districts (MJB)(b)	3,198	1,245.75	2,567
6 rural districts (c)	3,877	4,282.57	905
Total	**16,407**	**6,340.50**	

Source: SHUEP, Inception Report, SOGREAH, March 2004.

Comparisons of areas and densities:

	Pop. (thousands)	Area km²	Density: people/km²
Shanghai, 'inner ring' <9 districts	3,500	100	35,000
Shanghai, 'outer ring' >9 districts	9,000	600	15,000
City of Paris	2,300	100	23,000
Remainder of metropolitan Paris	8,200	10,900	752
Singapore, urban area	4,000	140	28,571
Singapore, total area (d)	4,100	647	6,337

Compiled by the author

(a) Including 3.8 million migrants resident in the city for over six months. Statistics from different sources may vary depending on the extent to which they take migrants into account.

(b) Minhang, Jiading, Baoshan

(c) Jinshan, Songjiang, Qingpu, Nanhui, Fengxian, Chongming

(d) The total area of the city-state of Singapore includes islands

Physical Changes: Economic Base and Major Infrastructure

Shanghai is the only metropolis in the world to combine industries that are usually spread between several cities. An American analogy would be a mixture of Detroit for automobiles, Pittsburgh for steel, Houston for petrochemicals and New York for its port, finance and commerce. A French comparison would be a combination of Paris, Le Havre and Dunkirk. So Shanghai is a complete urban space which unites opposites. There is a central zone with shops, services and small-scale industry. On the other side of the Huangpu, the financial district of Lujiazui aspires to become Asia's leading stock market.[5] This economic base also includes long-standing industrial areas and high-tech development parks in new towns, in particular Pudong. Heavy industry is located further from the centre at the city limits. To the north is the largest steel producer in the world that is located in one place (Baoshan), to the south-west is one of the world's ten leading petrochemical production sites (the Shanghai Chemical Industrial Park) and, bordering neighbouring towns to the west, there is a string of areas given over to the automotive industry. Shanghai also has a port, which nowadays rivals Hong Kong and Singapore for container transport, and an international airport, which is becoming a hub for that part of the world. Finally, in its rural districts, the megacity also includes areas dedicated to market gardening;[6] its water is supplied from the west by a lake that is linked to the enormous Lake Tai, the freshwater reservoir for the entire region. Lastly, the island of Chongming in the middle of the river is a haven of peace in this densely populated space: at a little over a thousand square kilometres, it has a population of just 650,000. It has so far been spared from development, as it can only be reached by boat.[7]

In 1986, Shanghai had a population of 9.5 million, including 3 million migrants, mostly living west of the Huangpu River (Dale and Edwards, 1980).[8] The district of Pudong, on the east bank, had been little developed; there was no bridge, and

---

5   Perhaps this gamble is about to pay off. Unflagging economic growth has led to an exponential increase in stock market flotations and in volume of transactions. In November 2006, the daily volume of transactions was $5 billion. On 30 March 2007, it was $16.4 billion and on 9 May 2007, $48.6 billion. This record figure places the Shanghai Stock Exchange ahead of London ($29.4 billion) and Tokyo ($26.9 billion) (*Financial Times*, 10 May 2007). The global financial crisis of Autumn 2008 only strengthened Shanghai's ambitions. In 2009, an index that ranked megacities according to their importance as financial centres and ports placed Shanghai third in the world, after New York and not far behind London (*Shanghai Daily*, September 9, 2009: B3).

6   *Statistical Yearbook 2003*, pp 236–7. See the tables entitled 'Output of Major Farms'.

7   This situation will soon come to an end, as the Municipality has built a bridge-tunnel that links Chongming to the coast and Shanghai to the Province of Jiangsu. It remains unclear whether this will limit Chongming's development and help to conserve its environment (as has been promised) or if the area will fall victim to the pressure for real estate.

8   See their lively illustrated portrait of the city in 1980.

a ferry was the only means of crossing. The road network had remained largely unchanged since 1949, and most enterprises were located within the city limits. In the 1970s, the city still specialised in textiles. Journeys from home to work were short and could be done on foot or by bicycle.[9] Public transport consisted of 100 bus routes within the Inner Ring Road, (Zhongshan Road). Private cars enjoyed mythic status; they were unaffordable and registration plates were not granted to privately-owned vehicles.

However, once the city had been recognised as a national priority in 1992, an accelerated development process began. Local GDP rose from \$9.2 billion in 1990 to \$49.2 billion in 1998 (Shi, Hutchinson and Xu, 2004). Shanghai became a centre for the steel, automotive, telecoms, IT and petrochemical industries while also establishing itself as a major centre for the service industries. The city expanded beyond its historical boundaries, and residential areas, shopping centres and amenities sprang up in its new districts. To get to this point, as the statistics show, infrastructure had to be constructed at breakneck speed. According to the *Statistical Yearbook*, 6 billion yuan were invested in urban infrastructure[10] between 1950 and 1978, 25 billion yuan between 1979 and 1990 and 895 billion yuan between 1991 and 2007 (see Appendix B). It is worth examining the key developments in this transformation, because it was from these that Shanghai's leaders began to learn a new mode of government.

The greatest feat of urban development was without doubt the construction of *Pudong*, which presented both a technical and a political challenge. The technical challenge arose from the fact that the district was not very built up, except in a few residential areas close to the port and the Huangpu. The remaining 500 km² was farmland. A new town had to be built from scratch. The political challenge lay in the lack of support from international development institutions (the World Bank in particular) for the construction of a financial centre at the heart of Pudong. A rather heated confrontation ensued: the Chinese authorities refused to back down in any way and made the project a symbol of their economic policy independence, in the face of the Washington consensus. For this reason, Pudong New Area was largely financed by Chinese capital. It was shaped around several major facilities, of which the Lujiazui Finance Centre deserves first mention. Construction work began around 1991–1992, and today the Television Tower (1994) and the Jinmao Tower (1999) looking out over the Bund, are a sign of the project's success. At a height of 421 metres, the Jinmao Tower was the tallest structure in China until it was surpassed by the Shanghai World Financial Center (492 metres) in 2008. The district is also organised around large-scale housing developments, three major industrial zones (see Box 2.2) and several huge shopping centres.

---

9 Even bicycles were expensive, costing on average two months' salary.

10 The statistics distinguish between investment in 'fixed assets' and urban infrastructure, which covers electricity, transport, the postal service and telecoms, utilities and public works (see Appendix D).

Box 2.2   Pudong's zones

- Waigaoqiao Free Trade Zone. The first phase (1990) was China's first free trade zone, and it covers 4 km² out of a planned total area of 10 km².
- Jinqiao Export Processing Zone. This zone in central Pudong initially covered 4 km² but there are plans to extend it to 19 km². It also includes technology-based industries such as automotive equipment and chemical processing.
- Zhangjiang Hi-Tech Park. This zone was established in 1992 with a total surface area of 17 km². The first phase was completed in 2006 and covers 2.5 km².

The *international airport* is located 35 km from the centre, on the eastern edge of the city near the sea. Construction began in 1996, and the first phase became operational in October 1999. A third of the finance for this phase was provided by the Municipal Government, with the remaining capital supplied through loans from the State Development Bank and the Japanese government. The second phase started in 2003. At that time, the airport was handling 20 million passengers a year, but its capacity needed to be increased to 60 million for World Expo 2010.[11] To enhance Pudong as a showpiece district, the authorities decided on a public transport experiment in the form of a train line that uses magnetic levitation – the *Maglev*. It was brought into service in early 2003, connecting the airport with an industrial park. It was only a few kilometres long, but it was the only line in the world to make commercial use of this technology, and so it showcased both the city and its developers, Siemens and ThyssenKrupp. In 2007, the same technology was selected to connect Shanghai to the major historic city of Hangzhou, making the journey possible in around half an hour instead of two hours and strengthening the development of the greater urban region.[12]

The *port* was developed in three stages, which illustrate Shanghai's rise as a global city. The first port was located on the banks of the Huangpu, a stone's throw from the Bund. It dated from the 1920s and dealt mainly with traffic from the urban region. Its first container-handling gantry crane was not installed until 1985.[13] Then, with the development of Pudong and the traffic generated by the free trade zones, the port migrated to Waigaoqiao on the right bank of the Yangzi; the

---

11   For comparison, Atlanta was the busiest airport in the world in 2009, with 88 million passengers, followed by London Heathrow, Beijing International and Chicago O'Hare with around 65 million. Charles de Gaulle handled around 57 million passengers a year.

12   This project and its proposed route through the urban space were widely criticized by residents of Shanghai's southern districts when it was unveiled in 2007, with articles, blogs and a demonstration. There are concerns that the new line will be unsightly, cause health hazards and noise and reduce property values.

13   In a move that symbolised the cycle of urban change, the site of the first port was rehabilitated and used to host part of World Expo 2010.

focus of its operations shifted from the city to the sea. Several terminals were constructed and managed by joint ventures between the port authority and private-sector companies. Between 1991 and 2001, the port saw growth of around 30 per cent a year. Construction of a third port in Yangshan began in the 2000s, marking a new era in trade flows. This deep-water port is situated 30 kilometres out from the coast in Hangzhou Bay, on several islands linked to the mainland by a 31-kilometre viaduct. This location means it is capable of handling super cargo vessels with their deep draughts. The first phase was completed in record time: it was finished at the end of 2005 at a cost of $1.24 billion (*Moniteur du commerce international* No. 7, 2004; *Financial Times*, 20 December 2005). This facility aims to make the megacity China's leading exchange node and the busiest container seaport in the world, ahead of Singapore and Hong Kong (see Box 2.3). This was achieved in 2010, with 29.05 million containers handled. So, in just 20 years and starting from scratch, the Shanghai authorities have made their port the busiest in the world. The state-owned company that manages the port aspires to become a global operator.

Box 2.3   Container traffic at the Port of Shanghai

1985	1990	1995	1998	2000	2001	2002	2003	2004	2005	2006	2010
0.20	0.46	1.53	3.07	5.61	6.34	8.61	11.28	14.55	18.08	22.60	29.05
World ranking			10	5		3	3	3	3	3	1

Million TEUs (Twenty-foot Equivalent Unit) and world ranking of the Port of Shanghai

Urban transport is among the major facilities that have supported and allowed such stupendous growth. In 1985, the decision was taken to build a *metro*. The first section of Line 1 was brought into service in May 1993, and the line was completed two years later. Other lines followed, and by 2006 the network comprised five lines with a total length of 123 kilometres. Convinced of the importance of transport, the Municipality undertook a vast programme to put in place a metropolitan network. By the end of 2007, after three new lines were made operational, the network consisted of eight lines; including the Maglev line and extensions the network was then 273 km long with 174 stations. Investment continued apace, and by the time of World Expo 2010 the network comprised 10 metro lines and, including the Maglev, was 400 kilometres long with 280 stations and a large number of interchanges. Several lines serve the so-called 'rural' districts.[14]

A great deal has also been accomplished since the early 1990s in terms of *bridges, tunnels* and *urban highways*. Puxi and Pudong needed to be linked together. Moreover, several years of intensive economic development had led to significantly

---

14 500 km and 12 lines are planned for the longer term.

increased vehicle numbers and worsening traffic conditions. Average speed had fallen to around 13 kilometres an hour and even dropped to five kilometres an hour during peak times. The Municipal Government therefore planned a network of elevated urban highways, accompanied by bridges and tunnels linking the banks of the Huangpu. This had a significant impact on the city. Three tunnels were built between 1985 and 2004, and four bridges between 1988 and 1995 (see Box 2.4). Construction of the first Inner Ring Road began in 1993. It was supplemented by the North-South Elevated Highway and then the Yan'an Elevated Highway, which runs east-west. The central section of this highway consists of six elevated lanes; in addition, there are four lanes on each side at ground level. So these highways cut a huge swathe through the city; buildings were destroyed and roundabouts completely altered. For example, Wu Fulong notes that the 8.5 km link between Chengdu Road and the Inner Ring Road displaced 180,000 households and thousands of small work units (Wu, 2000; Baye, 2001).

Box 2.4   Bridges and tunnels

Bridge	opened	work started	duration	length	cost	finance
Nanpu	November 1991	12/1988	3 years	7.99 km	0.82 GY	state
Yangpu	October 1993	05/1991	2.5	7.66	1.32	Chengtou
Xupu	June 1997	04/1994	3	6.02	2.26	Chengtou; BOT
Fengpu	October 1995	1994	1.5	2.32	0.30	BOT
Lupu	2003	10/2001	< 2	8.79	(2.21)	

Sources: Data compiled by the author
Cost shown in billions of yuan (GY)
Three <u>tunnels</u> were built between 1985 and 2004:
Yan'An Road Tunnel (December 1984–1987); Fuxing Road Tunnel (January 1994–November 1996); and Dalian Road Tunnel (2004)

Growth in *private car ownership*, encouraged by this new infrastructure and by public policy decisions, has also contributed to a profound change in the urban space. In the 1980s, Volkswagen was the first foreign company to establish a joint venture with a municipally-owned company: the aim was to manufacture Passats in Shanghai and modernise the taxi fleet; the German company subsequently introduced the newer models of this car. In the mid-1990s, Chinese manufacturers established other partnerships, in particular with General Motors. The rate of private car ownership saw continued growth. Initially, the opening of the first urban highways improved the traffic flow and the Municipality regulated the number of cars coming onto the roads by auctioning registration plates. Prices were very high, with the coveted plate costing 40,000 yuan (€4,400),[15] so cars remained a rare and expensive good. Then from 1997 onwards, the Municipality encouraged car ownership and increased the number of plates available in order to bring down prices. The desired effect was achieved: prices dropped and the number of private cars increased (Box 2.5). But the other side of the coin was that average traffic speeds fell again: in 2003, they were no more than 8–10 kilometres an hour. At the November 2006 auctions, the average price of a registration plate rose to 38,460 yuan; 6,500 registration plates were offered for sale and there were 11,860 bidders, indicating the size of pent-up demand (*Shanghai Daily*, 20 November 2006). Shanghai is the only Chinese city to have such expensive registration plates. Between 2000 and 2009, this system brought in around 15 billion yuan (€1.6 billion) (see Box 2.5).

However, the effectiveness of this system in regulating traffic flows is limited. First, much of the traffic consists of vehicles whose numbers cannot be reduced, such as 180,000 commercial vehicles (which register a rapid increase with economic growth), 18,000 buses and 48,700 taxis (*Statistical Yearbook*, 2003). Second, thousands of vehicles enter Shanghai from other towns every day. Third, some creative Shanghai residents get round the rules by registering as residents in another town, which allows them to obtain the sought-after plates. Finally, the enormous number of two-wheeled vehicles needs to be taken into account; in 2003, there were 985,000 of these registered under the heading of 'motorcycles' alone, (a rise of 33 per cent since 2002).[16] According to the Statistics Bureau, at the end of 2005 there were 2.2 million vehicles in the city (up 8.7 per cent in one year) and over 410,000 private cars (up 29.1 per cent in a year). It is worth noting that planners in the mid-1980s estimated there would be 2 million vehicles by 2020. In fact, this figure was exceeded more than 15 years early – an indication of the pressure on road use and the density of traffic flows. Despite the fact that a policy involving prohibitive registration-plate prices is hardly an incentive, 230,000 new cars appeared on the streets of Shanghai within a 6-year period (see Box 2.5).

Box 2.5   New cars on the road and prices of registration plates

	2000	2001	2002	2003	2004	2005(1 Oct)	total
New cars coming onto the road	14,000	15,900	31,850	53,064	58,500	55,678	228,992
Price of registration plates, yuan	14,416	14,444	31,721	34,354	31,940	33,972	
Income (million yuan)	202	203	1,010	1.823	1,868	1,891	7,024 MY

Source: Statistics Bureau, Transport Department, according to Shanghai International MBA (SIMBA) dissertation PT5a, May 2006

---

15 We have adopted an exchange rate of 1 euro = 9 yuan.
16 *Shanghai Statistical Yearbook*, Chapter 13.9

The city has also changed physically as a result of *property development*: housing programmes, urban renovation and commercial urban planning schemes. The traditional (dense, low-rise) *lilong* and the uniform five-storey blocks built after 1949 are giving way to 15- or even 30-storey towers. The transformation is substantial and palpable. Even experts in urban issues are amazed at how radically a district can change in just a few months (Logan, 2002). This massive transformation started around 1992, when the Municipality implemented national reform of property ownership,[17] establishing a type of private ownership that contrasted with the previous total state control of the sector and making it possible to sell housing (Pairault, 2008:28; Guiheux, 2006: 130). 'Housing went from being a good managed by the state to a consumer product governed by the market' (Zhuo, 2006: 144). Chinese leaders were inspired by the sale of social housing in the UK, the first of Margaret Thatcher's privatisations. Tenants could buy their home at an extremely low price, calculated by one academic expert to be around 10 per cent of the replacement cost.[18] This was also a way for the Municipality to reduce the burden on its finances: in the early 1980s, building and maintenance costs were running at around 35 billion yuan, against annual rental income of about 1 billion yuan.[19] This reform would have a major impact. In ten years, Shanghai went from a system of total state ownership to very strong private ownership of housing. Wu Fulong explains that, in 1996, market-based production accounted for two thirds of new housing with 80 per cent of purchasers being private individuals (Wu, 2002, p. 156). A new circular flow of income for production of the built environment came into being. There were opportunities for private individuals to invest their savings and for developers to launch programmes in the new districts of Pudong and Minhang, in addition to all the districts of Puxi. In just a few years, a whole sector of the economy linked to housing sprang up – estate agencies, banks, developers, construction companies, tradesmen carrying out improvements, distributors of household goods.

At the same time, dozens of department stores were established in Shanghai, contributing to the restructuring of the urban space. The Hong Kong group New World opened a store in 1996, and Sincere in 1997. Hotel groups moved in. Developers of all types flourished, including large state-owned construction companies (such as the Shanghai Construction Group and the Shanghai Urban Construction Group[20]), subsidiaries of development companies and new entrants

---

17 Transactions recorded by the *Statistical Yearbook* clearly show the macroeconomic impact of this reform.

18 In 1993, the same academic bought his own 75 m² flat for 10,000 yuan, i.e. 133 y/m²; by Autumn 2002, it was worth around 300,000 yuan, i.e. 4,000 y/m² (*Financial Times*, 13 November 2002: 13).

19 Source: a Goldman Sachs analyst based in Hong Kong. Richard McGregor, Shanghai's property boom, *Financial Times*, 13 November 2002: 13.

20 As recently as 1996, the SUCG had been simply a design institute (Baye, Lorrain & Guillemot, 1996, p. 45).

to the market. Developers from Hong Kong also arrived on the scene, and foreign firms such as Macquarie, GE Real Estate and Temasek have followed more recently. Alongside standard schemes consisting of several towers within an enclosed space, some developers have built more distinctive neighbourhoods. One that has an obvious target market is named 'Richville'. In another part of the city, developers are offering a replica of England – 'Thames Town' – with English-style houses, a church and a pub. In a district to the north, near the Volkswagen factories and the new science and technology university, a 'mini town' has been built: the German agency responsible has employed a more European, Bauhaus-inspired style of planning.

Not all investors met with success. In 1995 and 1996 came speculation, a price bubble, an overly rapid increase in supply and the risk of an over-production crisis. The Asian economic crisis that began in 1997 led to a business slowdown. Some companies went bankrupt and some construction programmes were halted. According to the Municipality's data, 21 department stores recorded losses in the first four months of 1998 (*Financial Times*, 12 July 1999). Office developments stood partly empty and housing prices dropped. Office rents in 'prime locations' could rise and fall dramatically. They peaked at $90 a square metre in 1995, dropped to $10/m² in March 2000, and then rose by $15-$20/m² in July. These variations are also to a great extent explained by the development of Pudong, as large amounts of office space came onto the market with the completion of each tower. When construction of the district began in the early 1990s, the total supply of office space was 300,000 square metres; ten years later, it had increased to 5.5 million m².

In order to offset the effects of the 1997/1998 recession, central government relaxed the regulations and allowed foreign investment in this sector. The cycle reversed from 2000 onwards, and construction began at a frenetic pace once more. Prices rose sharply. In 2004, the average cost of housing was 6,000 yuan/m², making a flat of about 100 m² the equivalent of 40 years' average salary for a Shanghai resident (average earnings, 2003: 14,860 yuan). In Spring 2006, there was a pause in new construction programmes. Newbuild properties were being offered for sale at an average of 6,000–10,000 yuan/m², varying according to whether they were located in Pudong or in the central districts. In September 2008, prices in the Puxi districts stood at between 15,000 and 25,000 yuan/m² depending on the quality of the product and its exact location.[21]

Over a period of five years, the Land Administration put an area equivalent to a third of the size of Manhattan up for sale. According to the *Shanghai Economic Yearbook*, quoted by Zhang, 'Between 1988 and 1998, 4337 land parcels were transacted, involving a total area of 14 436 hectares', although there was a severe lack of transparency in the management of these land-use rights (Zhang, 2003: 1556). Thousands of ordinary residents were forced to leave their homes; the procedure for setting compensation left them little room to negotiate. In contrast, some economic actors benefited from preferential treatment. Fortunes

---

21 Field study in February and September 2008, checked with agencies and databases.

were made rapidly at the intersection of political power, banking and construction. In 2003, the Forbes list placed four Shanghai developers among China's 11 richest people (*Financial Times*, 4 June 2003). But in the same year, a scandal made a developer and his company, the Nongkai Development Group, infamous – and others were to follow. These discreditable affairs call into question the procedures and networks of influence that connect the worlds of business and politics, with critics nicknaming those involved 'the Shanghai Gang'.

Shanghai's development may not have taken place in one smooth stroke, but the city's economic vitality has overcome all obstacles. Forecasts could doubtless have been more exact, and at times there was a glut of supply, but in the end it met a demand so great that the city both densified – developing upon itself – and expanded into new spaces.

Reforming through Networks

In the late 1980s, the city began growing and transforming its economic base. It needed to gear up and develop its infrastructure. The visible signs of this process were elevated highways and buildings going up; but institutions inherited from the Communist period were also undergoing invisible radical change.

In the Beginning was Direct Administration ...

When the reforms began and Shanghai's major transformation got underway, municipal administration was mainly focused on the urban area served by basic technical networks – electricity distribution, drinking water, urban transport and waste collection. This area covered only a part of Puxi's nine urban districts, equivalent to the area of the City of Paris and its inner suburbs.[22] Under the system in force in China at that time (Lorrain 1998), the municipality had extremely wide-ranging powers that included not only the production and management of the built environment (housing, public amenities and infrastructure) but also numerous other activities that, in a market economy, are managed by separate organisations: economic development and industry regulation, international relations, transport, fishing, agriculture, forestry, education and research, health. Other functions were carried out by state-owned enterprises (SOEs) under the authority of the municipal government. In this completely state-run economy, SOEs acted as 'total organisations', managing the production of goods or services and providing numerous facilities for their employees, such as housing, health care and some amenities (Eyraud, 2003; Pairault, 2008: 20).

This wide range of tasks explains the protean structure of the Shanghai Municipality. A study carried out in 1993 counted no fewer than nine large commissions and 51 bureaux (Mott MacDonald, 1993). However, even this

---

22   See Box 2.1 above.

organisation chart is a simplification. It does not take account of the upstream influence of the Communist Party and various political commissions and the downstream extension of the bureaux through state-owned water, cleansing, construction, electricity and urban transport companies. Nor does it mention the significant intermediate role played by district-level in some areas of activity. As regards cleaning, for example, the standard chain of commission/bureau/company was supported in each district by an office responsible for street sweeping and transporting waste to local transfer stations. The Chinese referred to this as a system with three levels of administration: municipalities, districts and streets.Nor does this organisation chart include the financial institutions that were attached, directly or not, to the city government: its construction bank, the local branch of the Bank of China, the development companies. In 1981, the Municipality created its first investment company, the Shanghai Industrial Investment (Holdings) Company (SIIC), and floated it on the Hong Kong Stock Exchange. Then the Jiushi Corporation was founded in 1986. These trust companies or, as the Chinese call them, 'window companies' act as intermediaries: 'The banks deal with deposits and loans. Financial actors who are not authorized to receive deposits are intermediaries or trusts'.[23] A trust company can borrow, as well as issue bonds and shares through public offerings. Under Chinese law, local governments cannot undertake such operations and therefore many have set up trust companies – Shanghai being one of the first. The SIIC was charged with raising funds to finance major infrastructure projects.[24] In the 1980s, Jiushi financed hotels, two bridges, the first metro line and the main sewers constructed as part of the pollution management programme.[25]

The whole of this massive structure was based on a hierarchy of deputy mayors, commissions, bureaux and companies. A commission set out the main priorities and policies and carried out studies. 'It doesn't get involved in the details'. The bureaux had executive powers and acted either as operators or through state-owned companies. However, in practice the commission/bureau hierarchy was not absolute: some bureaux, such as the finance bureau or the police bureau, were at the same level on the organisation chart as commissions.[26] All were public legal entities. The Municipality was the sole owner of assets such as land, infrastructure and equipment. The economy was not really monetised. Rents and utility tariffs were low. For example, in 1995, drinking water cost a very cheap 0.48 yuan per cubic metre and there was no charge for wastewater. So, at the beginning of the 1990s, a 'municipality' wielded a combination of political,

---

23 Interview with the CEO of a development company, November 2006.

24 In 2006, SIIC declared group assets totalling €5 billion, of which €2 billion were held by the SIIC company itself. It has three main areas of activity: property and infrastructure, trading, manufacturing medical equipment (web site and interview, November 2006).

25 Web site accessed September 2008.

26 Shanghai is not alone in this: we had previously seen it in our research in Chengdu and in Chongqing (Lorrain, 2000).

regulatory and management powers. Coordination of the whole structure was achieved through the concentration of power in the hands of several influential members of the Communist Party and the most important commissions (the economic planning commission, the finance commission and the construction commission). Monitoring was carried out through central planning and state subsidy mechanisms. The actors had little autonomy outside this framework. In other words, the hierarchical organisational architecture, the legal status of each subdivision, property law, state budgetary mechanisms and credit control kept the whole system firmly in hand.This form of organisation had been established in 1949, and it operated throughout a period of relative demographic and economic stability and of tight control by Beijing, which redistributed resources. It was still in place when the first transport infrastructure was built. It could even be said that this state-run, centrally planned system allowed progress to be achieved within a short space of time. The concentration of decision-making and financial power and, above all, the absence of property rights allowed the Municipality to move fast. It had a complete system at its disposal, with public-sector engineering companies (including the Shanghai Municipal Engineering Design Institute), investment companies to finance the fixed assets (SIIC and Jiushi) and state-owned construction companies (SCG and SUGC).

However, when China started opening up in the 1990s and Shanghai's radical transformation began, the weaknesses of this organisational form became obvious. First, the structure was complex and several administrative levels were involved in decision-making, since the hierarchical principle was combined with that of isomorphism; this is rooted in the ancient principle of *tiao* (Zhong, 2003: 72) or duplication of administrative structures, from the ministries down through all the other levels – provinces, municipalities, rural districts, villages. This meant that the functional structure at the top of the system was replicated at all its lower levels. Let us take as an example the water sector and two elements that were very important at that time: economic planning and price regulation. A planning bureau and a pricing bureau were at the top of the Municipality's organisational structure, with the same rank as commissions. Two bureaux with the same remit also formed part of the structure of the construction commission, which was responsible for all urban affairs. Planning and pricing bureaux were found again at the next level, within the utilities bureau – and then again in the water company that was responsible to the utilities bureau. Therefore any important decisions that involved pricing or economic planning in some way or another (i.e. practically everything) would set this whole chain of actors in motion. The same style of organisation was to be found in other sectors, with the result that decision-making was slow. This functional division also meant that few actors had an overview. And isomorphism did not stop there, as the equivalent tiers at provincial or central levels of administration could also intervene. Second, the operators of the large technical systems – who were the true actors, putting policy into practice – were confined to the end of the administrative chain of deputy mayor/commission/bureau/company or office and hence had little influence. At the extreme end of the spectrum, the head of the pricing bureau had as much authority in a coordination meeting as the directors of the water company or the electricity bureau, despite the fact that they were managing organisations with several million customers and several thousand employees.Third, despite the Municipality's wide-ranging powers, public-sector accounting did not separate the various sub-units. China's standard accounting system had been designed for exchanges of materials within a centrally planned economy, and it lacked sophistication (Pairault, 2008). The lowest-ranking actor would record salaries, consumables and maintenance equipment as expenses. Other items of expenditure came under general accounting, but tended to be incorrectly allocated. Assets were not depreciated, and the idea of reserves (to prepare for future expenses that were certain to be incurred) seems to have been foreign to this system.[27] The Municipality frequently dipped into receipts from tariff charges to carry out other policies. This must be understood in the context of the time – when the government was seen as the 'owner'. If 'everything belonged to everyone', why introduce an element of ownership, even public ownership? So the operators of technical networks did not have the legal autonomy that would have allowed them to implement the policies needed, nor the accounting tools to enable them to measure events, nor any financial resources. In this system, in the end, 'everyone helped themselves from the same pot' (Eyraud, 2003) and resources were shared out according to the political and administrative balance – or rather, balance of power.

The rest of the territory of the metropolis – the nine *xian* – remained rural. There were no interconnecting large networks – no highways, no sewerage system and no gas supplied directly to homes. Water was distributed through separate technical systems, bus routes were few, electricity consumption was low, and the waste collection service took the most primitive form (organic waste was spread over gardens, some rubbish was recycled, and the rest was simply put in a hole known as 'the dump'.) This period was characterised by a marked separation between town and country not only in operations and lifestyles but also in modes of government. Each rural district had an administration based in its central town, which formed an additional tier of government over smaller towns and villages.However, several coordination mechanisms ensured a certain degree of cohesion between city and rural district administrations. First, the isomorphism mentioned above meant that each segment of an organisation had a functional equivalent on the level above. Civil servants in a district bureau were therefore not left to their own devices; they had easy access to their more competent, better-informed counterparts in the Municipality. Second, we must not forget the Chinese Communist Party (CCP). It had representatives in every organisation, with salaries paid from the state budget; they were involved in all major decisions. Administration and politics

---

27 It is worth noting that local authorities in France took a while to introduce depreciation into the enterprises that they controlled. See the annual reports of the Cour des Comptes for 1969 and 1976 and Cour des Comptes (2003) *La gestion des services publics d'eau et d'assainissement*. Paris, Les éditions des journaux officiels.

were not separate; they formed a single world combining meritocratic competence and membership of the Communist Party. Access to responsible positions was restricted to Party members, but the larger the organisation, the more room there was for people with professional skills. This was the case for Shanghai and its large-scale services but in rural districts, where there were fewer human resources, the political factor took on greater importance. This meant there was a certain amount of coordination between city and countryside administrations through the Communist Party's internal networks.

First Reforms: Starting from the Networks

In just 15 years, Shanghai Municipality undertook reforms that reconfigured the institutional architecture. It introduced market principles into a formerly state-run economy; the whole machine was restructured. However, this was not a single continuous movement. Reforms were initially introduced in a few sectors where there were priority projects. These sectors began to adopt a more autonomous mode of organisation. Over time, this change continued, deepened and spread to more areas, eventually giving rise to a new mode of government.

Twenty years after the first decisions it is possible to look back and discern Chinese incrementalism at work – a 'step by step' approach to change. Although this way of putting things is not inaccurate, it reflects a retrospective reading that introduces the idea of rationality where, in fact, there was a great deal of pragmatism. No one theorised this strategy at the beginning. There was no manual on change management or how to organise the transition from direct administration to a socialist market economy. In reality, these changes should be primarily read as driven by necessity. The old system no longer enabled solutions to the issues on the agenda, among which major infrastructure was of particular strategic importance. First, it constituted a very real bottleneck for development. Second, each separate infrastructure required the use of people skills, financial resources and technology, making it essential to open up to the outside world. A problem of this kind could not be resolved in the codified game of relations between Beijing and the Municipality.

In other words, the argument here hinges around the following points:

1. Beginning from a state-run economy, the Shanghai Government arrived at a new model of local government.
2. This process was not driven by rationality but by necessity. The actors took the problems to be solved as their starting-point.
3. At this time, the main problems were largely connected with the production of major infrastructures. Change was therefore introduced using a technical approach which was perceived to have no political or institutional dimension.
4. This approach lent itself equally easily to external cooperation with the World Bank, consultancies and foreign firms. These actors not only provided subsidised loans or technology, they also introduced their policy

regimes – their decision-making procedures, institutional architecture and accounting rules.

5. Time is another factor that needs to be considered. It took time for these outside contributions to be accepted and then assimilated by local actors. These changes were achieved within a span of 20 years, from 1985 to 2005. The first reforms were introduced into specific priority sectors. Over time, they were taken further in these sectors and then extended to others.

6. When we view these reforms – which were originally separate – with the benefit of hindsight, we can see that they shared common principles, so that in the end they were cumulative and led to a new geometry of municipal policy and activities.

To substantiate this interpretation, we must examine the order in which institutional reforms took place. The timeline mirrors the development of major infrastructures. The first change came when bureaux were converted into companies. This fundamental act prefigured changes in practices, as it introduced the principle of autonomous decision-making and financial accounting.

The Shanghai Metro Corporation (SMC) was set up in 1985 to build the city's metro. It is an SOE which has two state-owned development companies, SIIC and Jiushi, as shareholders. The first metro line was totally state-funded. The second was 31 per cent financed by commercial loans, with repayment guaranteed by the development companies. The World Bank supported this organisational autonomy: like any banker, it sought to control the risk of default. It wanted to be able to identify the operations that it was supporting by making them discrete accounting units, and so its loans were conditional on the existence of separate legal entities that were distinct from the Municipality as a whole. The reform experiment was pursued fairly radically in the sphere of urban transport. At the outset, the city had a single SOE operating 315 lines and 6,000 buses.[28] The quality of service left much to be desired. Probably influenced by the UK's 1986 bus deregulation experiment with competition 'in' the market, the Shanghai authorities opted for a new arrangement, to be introduced in two stages. In 1992, several state-owned limited companies were set up and granted a monopoly over routes: Bashi was allocated 13 routes, Great Wall two routes, Guan Zhong three and Hua Bus three. In 1996, bus services were completely opened up. Licenses were granted to 13 'self-financed companies'. They managed services route by route and subcontracted to bus operators. The bus (and its driver) became the basic unit for measuring results – and it was at this level that competition took place.

The influence of the World Bank is again evident in sanitation programmes. The Bank's concern for environmental protection and urban services provision meant it was consistently involved from the beginning; it went on to finance engineering studies, grant loans and help supervise works. In the mid-1980s, Shanghai did

---

28   Sources: SIMBA dissertation PT8, October 2008, and an interview with a professor from the Urban Planning Department of Tongji University.

not have a proper networked utility – certainly nothing that could be described as a service. People who visited the city at the time remember Suzhou Creek as completely polluted.[29] There were so many plastic bottles floating on its surface that one could have walked across on them, and some commentators wondered whether it was time to demolish a nearby bridge! In 1988, at the request of the Bank, two companies were set up within the framework of the First Shanghai Sewerage Project – a project company and a management company. The principle of autonomy was introduced, as was the principle of policy being steered by a legal entity constituted as a company (and no longer by a segment of the administration) – even though these companies' operations were to a large extent controlled by the sanitation bureau, known as the Municipal Engineering and Administrative Bureau (MEAB). The 1988 reform triggered others, proving that change was well underway. A clean-up programme for Suzhou Creek was launched. Main sewers were built to discharge wastewater at the mouth of the Yangzi. The next step was to connect the maximum number of buildings to the main network, which represented a big challenge. Major works could be carried out without much input from the sanitation service but, in contrast, it had to be involved in every aspect of the process of connecting properties to the sewerage network, such as constructing collector sewers in the streets and linking each building to them. In 1995 the service underwent radical reorganisation. The sanitation bureau (MEAB) retained its role as the organising and supervisory authority for the rural districts (on behalf of the Municipal Government), but its operational responsibilities were given to a state-owned company, the Shanghai Municipal Sewage Company (SMSC), which absorbed the two companies created in 1988.

In the electricity sector, the existing bureau was converted into a state-owned company, the Shanghai Municipal Electric Power Corporation, in 1991. It is worth noting that the first reform of this type dated from the creation of an autonomous company for the Shenzhen Special Economic Zone several years earlier. Although we can talk about incremental change in China, it should be pointed out that this is a spatialised process: several places and projects are used as experiments, and operations that work are then rolled out. So, with its electricity company, Shanghai was one of the first reformers. The company had a monopoly over a 531-km² area, covering the urban area of Puxi and the district of Baoshan (where the Baosteel steelworks was expanding). It served 2.7 million customers, sold them 17.2 billion kWh in 2001 and recorded revenue of 10.69 billion yuan (about €1.19 billion). Around the same time, Shenergy was added to the system. This state-owned company had been set up in 1987 and converted five years later into the Shenergy Power Company, part of the ShenNeng Group.[30] It invested in the energy sector,

---

29   Suzhou Creek is a small river that passes right through the centre of Shanghai (to the north of Nanjing and Beijing Roads) and flows into the Huangpu just downstream from the Bund.

30   The ShenNeng Group is a state-owned company with seven major subsidiaries. Its growth really began in the mid-1990s, as its revenue – in billions of yuan –

in areas such as electricity production and gas transmission. The scope of its activities was later expanded: in Spring 1997, it assisted the electricity company in a major project, supported by the World Bank, for the construction of two power stations using a type of project financing that was new to China – design-build-finance-operate-transfer.[31] After several years growth at 10 per cent or higher, electricity production capacity could no longer keep up with needs. The city was experiencing blackouts, and investment was urgently required.

At the same time, policy tools such as accounting methods, tariffs and financing instruments were also undergoing reform. In 1993, China's central government adopted a general accounting reform (Pairault, 2008: 27), which allowed business accounting to be introduced into utilities and networked-public services. Up to this point, bookkeepers at bureau level had recorded only direct operating costs (such as wages and related charges, supplies and minor works). They took less account of overheads (premises, electricity, payroll administration, transport, telephone bills and so on) and did not allow for any depreciation. It took a while for the accounting rules published by Beijing, with their accompanying regulations, to be implemented in practice. Little effect was noted in 1996, but by 2004 all the companies in our study were drawing up income statements and balance sheets; they had valued their assets and partially depreciated them.[32] In 1996, a charge for wastewater was introduced. This was highly novel, since sewage removal had traditionally been free and drinking water tariffs low. As was the case with the accounting reform, some time was needed for practices to change, but transformation was underway. In ten years, household tariffs increased from 0.48 yuan to 1.03 yuan/m³ for drinking water and from zero to 0.90 yuan/m³ for wastewater (see Box 2.6). State-owned companies totally changed the way in which they recorded transactions. They had developed within a logic of central planning, with exchanges of materials between sectors of the economy. Ten years after the adoption of the new accounting system, managers had taken on the logic of the firm: they saw it as normal to record expenditure so they could measure costs and set tariffs. This new way of thinking did not extend to the political dimension of tariff-setting but – in distinct contrast to the past – the actors now had precisely recorded figures that allowed them to substantiate their choices in this area.

---

shows: 1996 – 0.34, 2002 – 3.04, 2007 – 13.5. Source: SIMBA dissertation PT8, October 2008.

31   The Waiqaoqiao I and II Power Stations were built using the design- build-finance-operate-transfer model. The breakdown of the pool of investors was as follows (in millions of dollars): International Bank of Reconstruction & Development (400), Ministry of Environmental Protection (216.2), East China Electric Power Group (108.1), Shenergy (216.2), local banks (703.8), cofinancing (500); total $2,144.4 million (SIMBA dissertation PT8, October 2008).

32   I saw this for myself in Shanghai and other towns in the region during a field trip in 1996 (Baye, Guillemot, Lorrain, 1996). This mode of operation was still in use in Chongqing during my 1997 and 1998 studies (Lorrain 2000). My survey of Shanghai's water and sanitation companies in 2004 showed that these concepts had been completely assimilated.

Box 2.6   Changes in water and wastewater tariffs (yuan/m3)

	1995	1996	1997	1998	1999	2000	2001	2002	2003	2004	2005	2008
Water	0.48	0.48	0.68	0.88	0.88	0.88	1.03	1.03	1.03	1.03	1.03	1.03
wastewater		0.12	0.12	0.24(a)	0.45	0.70	0.70	0.70	0.70	0.70	0.90	0.90

Sources: Inception Report, SOGREAH, March 2004; Implementation Completion Report, APL1, World Bank, 30 June 2003; interviews conducted with Shanghai Municipal Sewage Company (SMSC) by the author, June 2004 and September 2008

(a) The tariff of 0.24 yuan/m3 applied to domestic users; for other customers, the tariff was 0.37 yuan/m3.

As we have already seen, in 1981 the Shanghai Government created the SIIC, a development company listed in Hong Kong, to get round the ban on Chinese municipalities borrowing from banks or issuing bonds. It was involved in financing most of the city's major infrastructures, industrial as well as urban. But after ten years of development at breakneck speed, the situation had become more complicated. 'The main task of raising funds (for infrastructure) was done by different actors: municipal government, local districts and SOEs. The situation was too complex'. The authorities decided to restructure in order to simplify responsibilities, and in 1992 a new development company, Chengtou, was set up to focus on urban infrastructure alone.

The 2000s: Widespread Application of Successful Experiments

At the beginning of the 2000s, the pace of reform intensified as the economy continued to grow at an unprecedented rate. After the Asian economic crisis, and contrary to alarmist predictions, annual growth remained extremely high. It was constantly above 10 per cent, with a high point of 13.5 per cent in 2004. The Municipality had to continue to invest in infrastructure and it needed to find new sources of finance. But, in stark contrast to the early 1990s, it was not starting from scratch. A new architecture had begun to appear, guided by several principles. First, regulatory and operational functions were separated. Bureaux (or other, newer authorities) continued to be responsible for the former, while companies took charge of the latter. Without expressly saying so, the municipal authorities adopted the principal-agent theory (Jensen and Meckling, 1976) and separated the functions of organising authority and operator, which until then had been combined. Second, a kind of private-sector accounting was introduced, enabling cost calculation and tariff reform. Third, financing vehicles were set up, allowing capital to be raised from financial markets and partnerships with foreign firms to be established more easily.

Overall, this new configuration was conceived and refined in the sanitation and electricity sectors and in transport (buses and, partly, the metro). Now there was nothing to stop it being rolled out to other areas and nothing to prevent market principles being introduced on a wider scale. State-owned companies could be floated on the stock exchange. They could sell capital stakes to preferred partners; they could assign particular activities or set up subsidiaries to deal with them. In short, once the basic architecture was in place, there were many roads to reform. In three years, between 2000 and 2003, partnerships were formed for the metro, drinking water, sanitation, waste, highways, the deep-water port and the huge petrochemical industrial park, all evidencing an acceleration of reform. They led to a new municipal government configuration, which should now be discussed in more detail, starting with transport infrastructure.

Transport Infrastructure

In order to continue the development of the metro while keeping down the cost to the public purse, the Municipality carried out a large-scale reorganisation in the early 2000s. Four specialised companies took the place of the Shanghai Metro Company that had been created in 1985: a vehicle for raising finance (the Shentong Group), a construction company, an operating company to manage Lines 1 to 4 (the Shanghai Shentong Metro Corporation) and a company based on a more horizontal partnership to run other lines (the Shanghai Modern Railway Transport Corporation[33]). The Shentong Group is a state-owned company set up in 2000 with public sector shareholders.[34] Its object is to raise finance for the metro. Its first project, the extension of Line 2, was achieved through a rather convoluted arrangement that demonstrates Chinese managers' capacity for institutional innovation. In 2001, with the Municipality's support, Shentong took control of a listed water company. This company sold its water operations for 218 million yuan and bought up Line 1's assets, which belonged to the Shentong Group. Once this transaction had been carried out, the water company was renamed Shanghai Shentong Metro Corporation Ltd (Shentong Metro for short). It is 58 per cent controlled by Shentong Group and quoted on the stock exchange, allowing finance to be raised from the equity markets. This deconsolidation of the metro company was justified by the need to share competencies and financing. The Shentong Group owns the tunnels, which it leases to its subsidiary Shentong Metro at prices calculated on the basis of their depreciation over the very long term. The latter

---

33   Source: SIMBA dissertation PT6b, January 2007. In April 2000, five Shanghai companies created the Shanghai Modern Railway Transportation Corporation with share capital of 100 million yuan. It was initially put in charge of Line 5, then Lines 6 and 11. In 2003, it was licensed to run Line 8. It also considered a partnership with the Hong Kong metro company for a future Line 9 to serve Chonqming, but that came to nothing.

34   The Jiushi Corporation (66.13 per cent) and the Shanghai Urban Construction Group (33.87 per cent).

owns the rolling stock and other equipment; it seeks additional finance through the stock market and subcontracts operations to another company, Shanghai Metro Operation Company. In 2005, Shentong Metro paid 26.35 million yuan in rent for the tunnels and other assets, equivalent to 0.5 per cent of total investment in Line 1 and corresponding to depreciation over a period of more than 200 years. In other words, Shentong Group is responsible for a good part of the fixed costs, whereas Shanghai Metro Operation Company operates the lines and its earnings derive from fares.

As regards roads, the Ninth Plan (1996–2000) set out a programme for the construction of roughly 440 kilometres of highways and improvements to an additional 170 kilometres, for a total investment of 40 billion yuan. The Tenth Plan (2001–2005) added another 510 kilometres. The Municipality intended to make extensive use of the private sector through 'build-operate-transfer' contracts.[35] However, we should not make too much of this private-sector aspect: in fact, it is often SOEs connected to the Municipal Government that get involved, and income is derived from rent paid by the public authorities[36] rather than from direct payments by users. All these BOT infrastructures employ shadow toll schemes, so that Chinese commentators have referred to them as 'BOST' contracts – build, operate, *subsidise* and transfer. Involvement of genuine private-sector companies has been less frequent – and more problematic. This programme started with a pilot project in October 1999. Chinese investors understood little of BOT arrangements and did not come forward. Instead, the contract was won by a UK engineering consultancy, the Maunsell Group, and the municipally-owned Shanghai Urban Construction Group.[37] In Spring 2000, the Municipality approved four BOT highways, which formed the third ring road,[38] and two other projects undertaken by the private sector with financial support from SOEs. By the end of 2006, a total of 17 billion yuan[39] had been invested and the four highways and their extensions

---

35   In this type of contract, the firm designs, finances and build, then operates and maintains the facility. If the contract is not renewed, the facility has to be transferred to the public authority in good condition. The first experiment of this type was the Jiangsu Expressway Company, set up in 1992. The idea was to create a company to manage and value existing assets and to raise capital through a stock market flotation, with the Province of Jiangsu remaining a shareholder. This technique subsequently became widespread (SIMBA dissertation PT6b, November 2006: 11).

36   Payments come from the various local authorities whose administrative territories are crossed by the highways.

37   SIMBA dissertation PT6, December 2006.

38   These projects consisted of 52 km westbound towards Qingpu District (the Huqingping Highway), split into two sections (urban and extra-urban), and 53km northbound to Jiading District (the Jia Liu Highway) and southbound to the district of Jishan (the Xin Feng Jin Highway) (SIMBA dissertation PT6a, December 2006).

39   The official total was 17 billion yuan – but 20 billion yuan if operations underway were included. (Interview with a private-sector manager who subsequently transferred to a state-owned development company, November 2006).

were operational. Overall, this policy allowed investment to be stepped up without putting a strain on municipal finances, and the network increased from 108 to 407 kilometres.[40] However, this general success was peppered with a number of issues that illustrate the difficulty of creating a private sector *ex nihilo*. The private-sector companies selected were newly formed, and several had originated in the property sector. They did not have enough capital to cover the investments required,[41] so they borrowed a great deal. One of them (Fuxi) involved a municipal pension fund in its financial arrangements, which led to a corruption scandal that touched Municipal Government officials at the highest level (*Financial Times*, 27 September 2006; *Le Monde*, 26 September 2006). Central government handling of this crisis allowed the situation to be brought under control and some rules of the game to be laid down for the possible use of pension funds. A Hong Kong developer, Shui On Land, who was using the same sort of arrangement, had to pay back 875 million yuan to the municipal pension fund (*Shanghai Daily*, 17 November 2006: B7).

In contrast, for the first BOT bridges and tunnels (see Box 2.4), the Municipality relied on large state-owned companies. Citic Pacific – a subsidiary of the state-owned conglomerate Citic Group, listed on the Hong Kong Stock Exchange – holds a 20-year franchise to operate three bridges and a 30-year contract for the Yan'An tunnel.[42] Two other tunnels, Fuxing and Dalian, are managed by a listed company, Shanghai Tunnel Company. The recent history of these operations is interesting, since it illustrates how public policy adapts to suit the context, how public authorities learn from experience and revise their judgements, and how negotiations are far easier when they involve only public-sector actors. At the outset, the BOT contract for the Yan'An tunnel guaranteed a fixed rate of return of 12 per cent. Then the Municipal Government changed its policy, adopting the view that the private sector must shoulder its share of the risk and that there was no place for guaranteed high rates of return: 'if there is no risk, then it is a loan'.[43] By 2003 or 2004, the government had renegotiated all contracts of this type (the same went for a drinking-water production contract signed with Thames Water and Bovis in 1996). In the case of the Yan'An Tunnel, the contract and the assets were bought up by Chengtou (at a 'discount rate for the assets'), but in return Chengtou involved Citic in the new tunnel management company. The payment made by the development company was not calculated on the basis of traffic flow or economic criteria (nor were the assets evaluated on these bases when Chengtou bought them): 'it is a contribution to the common wealth'.[44] This suggests that the

---

40   SIMBA dissertation PT6a, December 2006.

41   The legislation in force stipulates that operators, in addition to meeting construction costs, have to acquire land-use rights. Calculations are often based on a figure of 3,000 yuan per *mou* (unit of 666 m^2). Acquiring an area 100 m wide by 10 km long therefore costs around 4.5 million yuan (1,500 *mou* x 3,000 yuan).

42   SIMBA dissertation PT2, 2002, and interviews conducted in 2006.

43   Interview with a development company manager, November 2006.

44   Interview with a Chengtou manager, November 2006.

old principles of direct administration are still in force despite the transformation of the institutional architecture. This legacy means that the prevalent attitude is: 'It all belongs in one big pot, so it all more or less evens out in the end'.

In 2003, in order to ensure the success of the massive project of building a new deep-water port (Yangshan), the Municipality converted the port authority into a company, the Shanghai International Port Group (SIPG).[45] Shanghai Municipality held 70 per cent of the shares through various companies,[46] while China Merchants International, a company listed in Hong Kong, held 30 per cent. The SIPG was floated on the Shanghai Stock Exchange three years later. It controls 30 direct subsidiaries and its annual revenue is 9.55 billion yuan. It has also formed six partnerships to finance, build and operate the terminals, pulling in some of the biggest names in maritime transport and port services: the Danish shipping firm AP Moller-Maersk, the Hong Kong-based group Hutchison Ports, the Singapore Port Authority, the French group CMA-CGM and Cosco, a Chinese company. Also in 2006, the SIPG acquired a 40 per cent interest in a subsidiary of AP Moller in Zeebrugge (B), and its senior management made no secret of the fact that it would not stop there (*Financial Times*, 26 March 2007).

Environmental Infrastructure

The institutional and financial innovations that took place in transport also applied to the environmental services. The project portfolio of the infrastructure development company Chengtou has expanded[47] considerably since the company was created in 1992. In 2000, it set up three specialised subsidiaries: the Shanghai Water Assets Operation and Development Company (SWAOD) for the specific water cycle, Chengtou Environment for waste and Chengtou Traffic for transport, with the aim of allowing more precise operational steering and more flexibility in the pursuit of external finance.

---

45   SIMBA dissertation PT6a, December 2006, and an interview with the CEO of a maritime company, September 2008.

46   The shareholders linked to the Municipality were: i) the State-owned Assets Supervision and Administration Commission (SASAC) (50 per cent); ii) Shanghai Tongsheng Investment, a municipally-owned company set up in 2002 for the construction and operation of the new deep-water port (19 per cent); iii) Shanghai State-owned Assets Operation, a municipally-owned company formed in October 1999 to manage municipal assets (0.5 per cent); it conducts its operations through five subsidiaries (which include Shanghai Da Sheng Operation Co); iv) Shanghai DaSheng Holdings, a municipally-owned holding company created in November 2002 to manage and exploit public assets (0.5 per cent).

47   In 2004, the assets of the Chengtou group amounted to 128.3 billion yuan. Bridges and highways were worth 30 billion yuan, water 29 billion, property 15–20 billion and sanitation 1 billion. Source: web site (in Chinese); interviews with Chengtou management, Autumn 2004 and November 2006.

The drinking water sector had been administered by a single company since 1952, the Shanghai Municipal Water Corporation, and was in charge of the whole specific water cycle in the area covered by the networks. It was responsible to the Public Utilities Bureau (PUB), itself under the authority of the Construction Commission. (The 'rural' districts had their own separate technical systems.) It was a very large company: in 1990–1993, before the development of Pudong, it sold around 3.5 million cubic metres of water a day. In December 1999, it was broken up into five municipally-owned companies: one for pumping and transporting raw water (the Raw Water Company) and four others to manage distribution and the rest of the specific water cycle. They divided up the metropolitan space in a straightforward fashion: one company took charge of the north, one the south, another the new district of Minhang in the south-west and the last, Pudong. From an operational point of view, these companies were independent, but they applied the same tariff, set by the Municipal Government using the same procedure as previously. This reform was supplemented in 2000 by the creation of a new entity, the Shanghai Water Authority (SWA), which became the organising authority for the whole specific water cycle. It combined the functions that had previously come under two separate bureaux, the PUB for drinking water and the MEAB for wastewater. The influence of Western consultants through previous programmes and the need for a more efficient coordination mechanism led to this solution, putting an end to a century-long tradition that was not unique to China. In organisational terms, drinking water had been grouped with other services to which a tariff was applicable. In China, the utilities bureau controlled drinking water, gas distribution, urban transport and taxis. Germany provides an example of something similar: the *Stadtwerke* combine responsibilities for drinking water, electricity, gas distribution and urban transport. In contrast, drainage of wastewater (before the days of pollution management) was seen as an activity covered by tax in the same way as road maintenance,[48] waste or cemeteries; the Germans group these under the heading of *Entsorgung*. Therefore, this seemingly simple measure had a profound impact for Shanghai: it replaced division on administrative grounds with a more environmentally-sound approach and the idea of a complete cycle, representing a shift from administrative organisation to 'the circular economy'.

The reform continued in 2002 with the sale of half the capital of the Pudong Water Company. This transaction signalled a change in the Chinese authorities' analysis at the highest level. Up to this point, the law forbade foreign investors from contact with the end-customers of networked public services, a matter considered too politically sensitive to be delegated. For this reason, cooperation was restricted to engineering services or equipment procurement, or based on service contracts or a few BOT agreements for new production plants. In 2002, this principle was revised. The Chinese authorities realised that intervention was needed throughout the product cycle in order to improve the service, in keeping with the idea that a

---

48   The link with roads came about naturally, since they were used for the disposal of rainwater and effluent before the industrial era and the widespread use of mains drainage.

chain is only as strong as its weakest link. In the drinking-water sector, it is futile to spend vast amounts on state-of-the-art technology in production facilities, only for the water to be lost or deteriorate in badly maintained networks. Chengtou looked for a foreign partner to take a 50 per cent stake in the Pudong Water Company and operate it. An international call for tenders was organised, and Suez, Thames Water and Veolia Environnement bid against one other. Veolia emerged as the winner in May 2002.[49] Shortly afterwards, direct negotiations were opened for Thames Water to acquire a 50 per cent interest in the northern company (Shibei). These were suspended by the firm after 18 months because the brief was overly complex and too much of the data was insecure.

The Pudong deal is significant in more than one respect. For the French firm, Pudong was the ideal showcase in China, guaranteeing the opportunity to display its expertise. It also represented a big contract – lasting 50 years, covering 2.6 million residents (2004) and with a production capacity of 1.27 million cubic metres. For the Chinese authorities, this deal had a double advantage. An association with a foreign firm would allow them to acquire better network management techniques – the area which remained their weakest link. There was also a financial dimension. The sale of half the Pudong Water Company brought in a sizeable sum: Veoila had agreed to pay about 2 million yuan ($260 million).[50] This was allocated as a credit to Chengtou and allowed it to finance other infrastructures. Having previously issued bonds and floated companies on the stock exchange, the Shanghai authorities now realised that selling assets to foreign partners was another way of raising funds and financing infrastructure. Pudong would be just the tip of the iceberg.

In the sanitation sector, the company formed in 1995 (SMSC) continued its reforms, but along different lines than in the water sector. It retained its organisational unity and outsourced its activities. In 1999, it set up a construction subsidiary and an *ad hoc* company for the Suzhou Creek Rehabilitation Project, financed by the Asian Bank. In July 2001, it created three sewerage operating companies to lay and maintain networks and connections. In other words, over a period of six years the old administrative 'bureau' that had combined all the functions in the sector was converted into a company, and then subdivided its activities among several specialist entities, of which some could compete with private sector companies for network contracts.

------

49   At the same time, Suez signed a drinking-water production contract for 25 years in Qingdao and a contract in Shanghai to reconstruct two drinking water plants (*Financial Times*, 25 June 2002, p.22). In November 2002, Suez went on to sign a joint-venture contract with the Chongqing Municipality to operate in a new, rapidly growing district of the city. The two French firms have since signed several agreements of this kind.

50   Interviews conducted in Shanghai (June 2002 and June 2004) with two firms that participated in the tender. See also Liu Qiang, 'Summary of International Investment, Transfer of Shanghai Municipal Waterworks Pudong Co'. In SCTF, *Sustainable Urban Services*, Shanghai Seminar, April 2003, PECC, M. de l'Equipement, Paris, pp 149–55. See also *Financial Times*, 25 June 2002, p.22. According to the Chairman of Chengtou, Veolia put in 2.03 billion yuan (www.worldbank.org).

As part of the large pollution management programme that had started in 1988 with World Bank support, the Chinese authorities decided to build a huge treatment plant. Two phases were planned, with treatment capacities of 1,700,000 cubic metres a day and 600,000 m³/day respectively. The authorities selected a BOT scheme, this was the largest wastewater treatment plant ever constructed in China under a contract of this type (SUCG web site).[51] In May 2002, a consortium – the Youlian Development Company – won the tender, which had been open only to Chinese companies, at a price of 0.222 yuan per cubic metre of wastewater treated; the contract was for a period of 20 years. The price paid by the public authorities was supposed to cover the costs of construction and operation while generating a 6 per cent return.[52] Construction began in the autumn. Phase II was launched in early 2003, and a year later the same consortium was selected for a 25-year contract, following its offer of 0.299 y/m³. To begin with, the Municipality was delighted with its decision. Its sanitation company had estimated the break-even price at 0.38 y/m³, so if the first plant functioned at three quarters of its capacity, the annual saving would be around 73 million yuan.[53] In fact, the saving to the Municipality was a little less, as the private sector consortium's offer was only possible with public financing in the form of the provision of land, a World Bank loan and financing on preferential terms by a state-owned construction company, the Shanghai Construction Group (SCG),[54] which was a member of the consortium.[55] Four years later, officials were more sceptical.[56] The plant had never functioned as it should have done. Youlian, the project holder, withdrew; its shares and those of the construction company had to be bought up by the Shanghai Urban Construction Group (SUCG), another state-owned construction group specialising in infrastructure. Managers interviewed in November 2006 recognised two sources of difficulty: 'they didn't have the expertise, and the price was very low'. It was true that Youlian had no expertise in this area at the outset. It was a private-sector company with interests in property, supermarkets, golf courses and taxis (the last regulated by the Utilities Bureau). Its bid prices bore no relation to reality. This affair shows that reforms are sometimes introduced in a spirit of optimism with little thought

---

51   As the plant operator does not have any contact with customers, it is paid by the public authority on the basis of the volume of wastewater treated.

52   It was not entirely settled at the time what factors (such as the amount of investment or the amount of capital actually freed up) were to be taken into consideration when calculating the return. The rate of return is now calculated as a percentage of net assets, defined as the difference between assets after depreciation and liabilities.

53    $(0.38y - 0.222y) \times (1\ 700\ 000\ m3 \times 0.75) \times 365$ days = 73.5 million yuan.

54   The Shanghai Construction Group, a heavyweight in the construction industry, is a state-owned company created in 1994. With revenue of around 20 billion yuan in 2005, it is the third biggest company in China and the largest in Shanghai (SCG web site and shanghaiwater.gov.cn).

55   SIMBA dissertation PT4a, May 2005, and www.sucgcn.com.

56   Interview with participants in the operation, November 2006.

for the future, and that not all developments follow a rational course. When interviewed in 2004, the same respondents had not envisaged that there might be any problems.[57] After all, the price had been set following a call for tenders (and surely the market couldn't be wrong?). The project holder's lack of experience was considered of secondary importance, since technical skills could be acquired by employing specialists. These responses demonstrated profound optimism and a notion of change that made light of the need for organisations to accumulate competencies. Any problem could be solved with sufficient capital – and human resources could be bought in. Despite their background in a state-run system, these interviewees unwittingly employed the same reasoning as private equity funds in their indifference to the substance of the project.

Up to this time, the waste management sector had been left behind by the reform process; it represented a locus of just as little attention in China as elsewhere.[58] In Shanghai, as in other Chinese cities, it was the responsibility of a 'City Appearance and Environmental Sanitation Administration Bureau' under the authority of the Construction Commission (Lorrain, 1998). This Bureau was extended in each district by offices in charge of street cleaning and of collecting waste and taking it to transfer stations. In 2002, a reform was introduced that followed the principles already applied in other fields: a distinction was made between the functions of the organising authority and the operator (or the principal and the agent) and public/private partnerships were established to operate the services. The Bureau was reorganised into two departments. One had a regulatory function and granted household waste tipping permits. The other had operational competencies and managed two partnerships: an incinerator and a 'sanitary landfill'. In early 2003, the Bureau invited international tenders for the fourth phase of the sanitary landfill. The winner of this process was a consortium involving Onyx (Veolia), Citic Pacific and Chengtou Environment. The parties signed a 20-year concession agreement; 51 million euros were invested up front, partly financed by a World Bank loan. The landfill site was located 60 km from central Shanghai and had a surface area of 361 hectares.[59]

Industrial infrastructure was also affected by this opening up to the private sector. In the late 1990s, the municipal authorities decided to build a large petrochemical complex, the Shanghai Chemical Industrial Park, located in the district of Jinshan, 70 kilometres from the centre and facing the sea. The first phase covered an area of 10 square kilometres. It became operational in late 2004

---

57   Interviews conducted in September and December 2004.

58   In industrialised countries and emerging economies, investment tends to be allocated in the following order: telecommunications > electricity > public transport > drinking water > sanitation > waste.

59   It could receive around 6,300 tonnes/day and had a total capacity of 34 million tonnes. As a comparison, the landfill in northern Hong Kong that Sita has operated under a 20-year contract since 1995 has a total surface area of 95 hectares and a maximum height of 240 metres, with a total storage capacity of 34 million cubic metres.

when the central cracker, with an annual production capacity of 900,000 tonnes of ethylene, came online.[60] The park may ultimately cover 30 square kilometres. From the beginning, the authorities have paid particular attention to environmental protection: in contrast to normal practice, industry is not in charge of these issues. The park development company has engaged specialists in order to ensure a world-class service. Since 2002, it has formed partnerships with leading names in each sector: Vopak (Netherlands) to manage the terminal and storage tanks; SembCorp (Singapore) for energy and steam; Air Liquide (France) for industrial gases; and Suez and its partners for drinking water, sanitation and waste incineration. For each network, an ad hoc company has been formed between the state-owned company and the foreign partner. The price paid for half the capital (the highest stake permitted) depends on the total amount of assets provided by the Chinese side. This 'specialist' company is responsible for running the operation; directorships in the joint venture company are shared between the two parties in order to ensure balanced control.

Recombining Formal Institutions, Acting through Instruments

So within the space of a few years, many sectors were completely transformed. A more complex landscape emerged, with widespread recourse to the market and to partnerships with the private sector. In 2004, the Municipality introduced overall coherence into this system through a total overhaul that replaced its previous structure of nine commissions and 51 bureaux with a new format. First, the reformed system introduced the new category of 'government organs' or departments (www.shanghai.gov.cn) (Appendix A), consisting of nine commissions and 11 bureaux. Among the commissions responsible for urban issues, the Development and Reform Commission (previously the State Planning Commission) and the Municipal Commission of Construction and Administration are particularly important for our purposes. The 'bureaux' include the Auditing, Finance and Water Affairs Bureaux (with the Shanghai Water Authority). Then come 23 'organisations directly under' the authority of the Shanghai Government: the Environmental Protection Bureau, the Housing, Land and Resources Administration, the Urban Communications Administration Bureau (covering urban transport) and the Harbour Administration. A third category of 'organisations under' the Shanghai Municipality' covers seven bureaux. The Bureau of Public Works Administration is responsible for roads, bridges and tunnels and gas distribution. The street scene and urban environment are managed by the City Appearance and Environmental Sanitation Administration Bureau, which takes care of rubbish, street lighting and outdoor advertising. Formally, the whole structure was simplified because the

---

60 On-site interviews conducted in 2004 and 2006; data from the SCIP web site.

number of bureaux was reduced by 10 (to 41).[61] However, this simplification is deceptive when the enormous growth in the number of state-owned companies, with their subsidiaries and partnerships, is taken into account; some 20 important ones are identified in Appendix A.

Finally, this reform formalised a separate 'special' organisation – the Shanghai Municipal State-owned Assets Supervision and Administration (SASAC). It acts as the ultimate owner on behalf of the public authority. With ownership rules modified by stock market flotations, BOTs and joint ventures, the boundaries had become more complicated and needed to be clarified. The question was, who holds the rights in property? In a socialist market economy, they remain in the hands of the public authorities. As Thierry Pairault comments, state-owned companies are the private-law heirs of enterprises ' … owned by the people as a whole' (Pairault, 2008: 32). This principle has been clearly reaffirmed, even though a March 2004 amendment to the Constitution lays down 'inviolable' rights of private ownership (Guilheux, 2006: 76). From 2004, all the large municipally-owned enterprises transferred their assets to SASAC, and some operations were sold off to the private sector at the same time. The change lay in a shift in the lines of responsibility. Previously, an SOE's assets belonged to the commission to which it was attached – for example, the Construction Commission (in the case of urban infrastructure) or the Communications Office (in the case of the port) – in keeping with the prevailing principle of hierarchy. Now, powers are concentrated in SASAC. 'They represent the government; they establish regulations for managing an SOE's assets. They appoint the CEO; they supervise; they have a lot of power'.[62] The change has been a significant one.

The Shanghai Municipality has opened up to the market, converted its bureaux into companies and increased the number of partnerships with private-sector companies; to counterbalance this, it has established SASAC as a tool to ensure coherence and ultimate ownership. But it is worth asking if equilibrium has in fact been established, and whether it is the Government or the market that is driving the megacity.

Taking Back Control of Transport

In answering this, it is important to remember that the rules of the game (i.e. institutions) represent a variable that is far more adaptable in China than in Western countries. The weight of the single-party system, the concentration of power in the hands of an elite and the extreme weakness of the normal forces of opposition (the law, a political opposition, the press) mean that the authorities can

---

61   This process of reorganisation is still going on. According to the latest data (2011), there are now 16 'organisations directly under' the authority of the Shanghai Government, rather than 23, and the 7 'organisations under' have been reduced to 3. The scope of some major commissions and bureaux has been modified, as have their names.

62   Interviews conducted in November 2006 with municipal commission and SOE.

very quickly redefine the rules of the game to suit themselves. Urban transport is a good example of this kind of institutional bifurcation. We have seen earlier in this chapter that the sector underwent radical reorganisation. The metro company was floated on the stock market and broken up into several subsidiaries. Bus transport was deregulated in 1996 and several companies competed in operating the same line. For the sake of completeness, the following should also be mentioned: management of a fleet of about 50,000 taxis by several companies (some of the biggest of which also operated buses), the two long-distance bus stations, the two railway stations and the two airports. In short, the system was complex and was divided between various public and private sector actors, while the line of reform chosen had primarily made use of the market and of competition.

However, within an exceedingly short time, the authorities totally revised this schema in order to return to steering from the centre through state-owned companies. In 2007, the Ba-Shi group (buses and taxis) transferred its shares in the second metro operator (Shanghai Modern Railway Transport Corporation) to the Shentong Group, the state-owned holding company that oversees the metro (and is itself a subsidiary of Jiushi). In September 2008, three of the main bus companies[63] were taken over by Jiushi, the municipal investment company in this sector. The transaction was accomplished quickly and quietly, with the shareholders in the 'private-sector companies' receiving instructions to transfer their holdings. There are two lessons to be learnt from this. First, the fact that these companies operate in the new private sector must not blind us to the fact that the great majority are undertakings in which the Municipality has invested official capital, and therefore it wields considerable power to readjust the balance. The second lesson is that the Municipality, through Jiushi and its subsidiaries, now has a tight grip on the whole system (i.e. control of the metro and bus services, with influence over taxis) throughout the entire metropolitan space (Puxi, Pudong and the 'rural' districts). 'Government direct investment will dominate'.[64]

Two considerations lay at the origin of this sudden recentralisation. First, competition 'in' the market had not lived up to its promise. Many Shanghai residents, from officials to people in the street, were dissatisfied with the system. Fares were high and badly coordinated between lines that were managed by different operators. The level of service was poor and connections to the formerly rural districts were inadequate. Lastly, coordination between bus routes and the metro was problematic. Second, the argument for coordinated transport carried particular weight 18 months

---

63   These were the Ba-shi Group, created in 1992 (7,500 buses, 340 routes and revenue of 5.5 billion yuan), the Dazhong Transport Group, created in 1988 (6,000 buses, 311 routes and revenue of 5.2 billion yuan), and Qiangsheng, created during the First World War and floated on the stock market in 1992 under the name 'Pudong Qiangsheng Taxi Co'. – though in fact bus transport represented a quarter of its business (1,000 buses and 45 routes). Source: SIMBA dissertation PT8a, interview with an academic from the University of Tongji.

64   Interview with a specialist from the University of Tongji, September 2008.

before the opening of World Expo 2010. The city was expecting 70 million visitors between May and October, i.e. an average of 400,000 people a day and more at peak times. In order to make sure it could cope with these flows, the Municipality decided to focus its efforts on public transport. It needed not only to guarantee that visitors would be able to travel around easily but also to present Shanghai as a sustainable city – the theme of the exhibition. It therefore embarked on a highly ambitious investment programme for various means of transport, reinforced by intermodal coordination. As we have seen, the metro expanded from five to 10 lines within a few years, with the Municipality investing about 30 billion yuan each year. The capacity of the two airports was stepped up and, most importantly, they were linked in to the public transport network: the metro was extended and an intermodal station was built for Hongqiao Airport;[65] situated inside the airport, this facility connects the Beijing-Nanjing-Shanghai railway line, a long-distance bus station and the metro. The railway was upgraded to a high-speed line and it was planned to extend the experimental Maglev line to Hangzhou at the same time. Most districts in the metropolis are now served by the metro and by buses, and Shanghai has various fast train links to other towns in the urban region.

With this transport reform, the Municipality took back control and produced an integrated technical system. We might observe that this new institutional configuration is a rather good illustration of the cycle of public transport organisation described by José Gomez Ibanez and John Meyer (Gomez Ibanez and Meyer, 1993: 17). In this case, state-run organisation underwent a first phase of reforms in 1992, which was succeeded by opening up to the market in 1996 and then by a return to local-state control in 2008.

Macroeconomics of Investments in Fixed Assets

The balance between government and the market can also be examined by taking a seemingly technical detour to study the macroeconomics of investments in fixed assets, taking a look at the volume of fixed assets and the ways they are financed. These mechanisms require a great deal of decision-making power and the capacity to coordinate this massive set of institutions. According to data published by the Statistics Bureau for the period 1991–2007, Shanghai Municipality invested 3,526 billion yuan (€392 billion) in fixed assets (see Box 2.7 and Appendix D). These are vast sums. Sixty per cent of this investment went into fixed assets financed by SOEs and public-sector institutions in order to increase production or engineering efficiency. It therefore fell into the category of production-related investment. Thirty per cent of investment went into 'property development' – understood in a broad sense that encompassed every type of construction and of post-demolition

---

65 This involved an urban development operation in the west of the metropolitan area. A 26.26 km² plot was earmarked and a 36 billion yuan investment announced. An ad hoc company was set up with three shareholders: the Shanghai Airport Group (40 per cent), Shanghai Jiushi (30 per cent) and the Shanghai Land Centre (30 per cent).

reconstruction: housing, apartment blocks, factories, warehouses, restaurants, hotels, leisure facilities, offices, public amenities and so on. Finally, agricultural investments (whether production-related or not) accounted for 9 per cent of the total. This breakdown has its own coherence, but the figure can also be analysed using a different logic. The Statistics Bureau produces data on investments in housing and in infrastructure. By subtracting these figures from total investment in fixed assets, we can estimate investment in production-related fixed assets (see Box 2.7). Using this approach, the total of 3,526 billion yuan breaks down into a quarter for housing, a quarter for infrastructure (895 billion yuan) and half for production-related fixed assets.

Box 2.7   Investments in fixed assets (IFA) for Shanghai Municipality (1991–2007)

Investments in fixed assets (IFA) for Shanghai Municipality (1991–2007) in billions of yuan (GY)					
Total IFA	Production-related investment and replacement		Property development	Agricultural investment	Various
3,526 GY	2,082	60%	1,084 30%	316 9%	44%
Total IFA	Infrastructure		Housing	Production-related fixed assets	
3,526 GY	895	25.4%	874 24.8%	(1,757) 49.8%	

For definitions and methodology, see Appendix D

Source: Shanghai Statistical Yearbook

IFA and first breakdown: Table 6.1; Infrastructure: Tables 10.1 and 10.2; Housing: Table 18.2

Investments in infrastructure can be studied in more detail, since precise statistical data in this area are available (see Appendix B). Up to 1990, infrastructure accounted for around 15 per cent of total investment in fixed assets. For the next 17 years, it settled at around 25 per cent, with fluctuations depending on the economic situation. Such a steady outlay deserves attention, as it was made against a background of very strong growth. The gross figures are impressive. In 1991, a total of 6.1 billion yuan was invested in infrastructure. The 50 billion yuan mark was passed in 1997/1998. Investment continued apace, reaching 147 billion yuan in 2007 (€16.3 billion). As a comparison, the preliminary budget estimate for the Greater Paris transport plan is between €19 billion and €35 billion (according to the scenario) – but that is a multi-year programme (*Les Echos*, 6 August 2009, p. 4).

A breakdown of Shanghai's expenditure by sector is also instructive (see Box 2.8). The two largest items are transport and public works, accounting for 39 per cent and 29 per cent of the total respectively. These are followed by the electricity sector (14 per cent) and telecoms (12 per cent). Drinking water and wastewater treatment (3.2 per cent) and gas (1.9 per cent) come last by a sizeable margin. If we use comparison with expenditure for the gas sector to rank all the other sectors, we see that investment in transport was 20 times higher and in public works 15 times higher – a clear indication of hierarchies and priorities.

Box 2.8   Ranking of investment in infrastructure over the period 1991–2007

Ranking of investment in infrastructure over the period 1991–2007 shown in billions of yuan (GY)

Total investment in fixed assets (IFA)	3,526 GY		
including: Housing	874		
Infrastructure	895		
Infrastructure:	in GY	in %	multiple/gas
Transport (metro, buses, highways, airport and ports)	351.57	39.3	20.2
Public works (roads, lighting, bridges, tunnels and sewers)	263.62	29.4	15.1
Electricity	125.28	14.0	7.2
Post and telecoms	107.94	12.1	6.2
Water and wastewater	29.02	3.2	1.7
Gas	17.43	1.9	1

See Appendixes B and D for sources and methodology.

Financing Fixed Assets from Land- Sale Income.

Such vast investment in infrastructure between 1991 and 2007 (895 billion yuan, around €100 billion) inevitably raises the issue of the mode of financing. This topic has been widely debated by urban sociologists and economists.[66] The explanation often put forward is that, having at first financed their development through public-sector mechanisms (such as subsidies and state-owned bank loans), Chinese cities increasingly turned to the market – a move reflected in a rise in foreign direct investment (FDI) and bond issues (Zhang, 2003; Wu and Li, 2002). The market

66   See for example articles on urban development in China published in the journals *IJURR* and *Urban Studies*. For an overview, see Logan 2002.

compensated for the government's loss of power. These analyses suggest that power structures in China have been reshaped over time, with central government and Communist Party networks losing influence. Both our research and an in-depth examination of the detailed facts and figures contradict this explanation. Data published in the *Statistical Yearbook* since 1995 allow us to measure sources of financing for all fixed assets. Six sources are listed (Appendix C). We started with Zhang's analysis for the years 1995–1999 and extended it to cover the years 2000–2007. With the exception of a few details resulting from duplications, these sources enable us to understand how the Municipality financed its enormous investments in fixed assets (including infrastructure) and what the implications of this are in terms of the balance of power.

i) State subsidies (budgetary allocations) played a very minor role, accounting for less than 2 per cent of financing. This may seem somewhat paradoxical in the light of the argument that Shanghai has enjoyed constant central government support; but this support was presumably expressed through two other types of contributor – state-owned banks and SOEs.

ii) Chinese (state-owned) banks contributed just over a fifth, and their involvement even slightly increased during the 2000s.

iii) Bond issues, which supposedly compensated for decreased state funding, in fact made a negligible contribution – just over 2 per cent in the period 1995–1999 and a token amount (0.14 per cent) in the 2000s.

iv) Foreign direct investment, which accounted for 14.3 per cent in the first period, did not fulfil its promise, and subsequently fell to 6.5 per cent. Since the volume of FDI went from 16 billion yuan in 2000 to 26 billion yuan in 2007, this fall must be seen as relative – but it did not follow the general rate of increase. Trends in the type of investment are also instructive. Loans were predominant at the outset, providing more than half of investment. The balance shifted gradually towards direct investment: from 2005 onwards, it accounted for 77 per cent of the total. This shows that foreigners (who may come from Hong Kong, Taiwan, Singapore, etc.) are investing directly in the metropolis – a sign that they have a long-term policy and confidence in the Chinese economy. The fall in the proportion of foreign loans also reflects the increasing strength of the Chinese banking sector, which has resources available and is capable of taking matters into its own hands.

v) 'Other' financing represented almost 16 per cent in the first period and 24 per cent subsequently, making it the second largest source of finance, equal with bank loans. This somewhat vague classification covers 'collective

Foreign direct investment (FDI) as a proportion of total foreign investment						
2000	2002	2003	2004	2005	2006	2007
45%	55%	65%	75%	77%	77%	77%

funds from employees'[67] as well as contributions made by public bodies, chiefly SOEs, to the investments from which they would benefit. This is a type of prefinancing. For example, when the Shanghai Chemical Industrial Park (SCIP) undertook enormous site development works, it needed to find funding. It therefore involved the Sinopec Petrochemical Group (and other industrial concerns), which was interested in the project because it had formed a joint venture with British Petroleum to build and operate a huge ethylene cracker. In this mechanism, the petrochemical group acted as a client of the development company, in that it bought the developed site, and as a partner by 'contributing' to initial investments and becoming a shareholder. This type of mechanism is widely used to finance industrial investments. Its primary, practical effect is that of balancing the finance plan; but its institutional impact is just as great. This type of financing, with its two-way trade, forms social networks that bring together political and administrative elites and senior managers of major companies.

vi) The last source of finance is unknown in Europe: the 'self-raised funds' that represent around 45 per cent of resources – in other words, a large share. This proportion remained relatively stable over the 13 years we studied. The category covers: 1) profits from industrial enterprises, 2) capital raised on the financial markets (a modest proportion) and 3) income from sales of land and other assets. This last mechanism is essential. It shows that the Municipality's development companies – SIIC, Jiushi, Chengtou and Shentong – have made enough money as developers to finance half the megacity's fixed assets directly. They bought land, built infrastructure and other amenities and sold it on to property developers, shopping centre management companies, hotel groups, industrialists and so on. The added value that this created meant they could carry on and finance infrastructures that would not find a counterparty for a market transaction. The emergence of this important mechanism also explains the paradox of the water and sanitation company financing that we encountered in our 2004 research.[68] We were told officially that tariffs balanced out costs, but a close examination of the accounts of several companies revealed that they did not cover repayment of the debt incurred to finance major facilities, i.e. networks and plants. The tariff covered running costs, repairs and the depreciation of small equipment – and no more. Major infrastructure was still covered by Chengtou (which acted as development bank to this sector). The same was true in other sectors. In fact, it is land-sale income (and betterment) that provide the large development companies with a large share of their finance.

---

67   We observed this in the case of the Minhang Water Company, which has invested heavily in the 'new town' where it is located.

68   Survey carried out in June, September and December 2004: interviews; examination of the accounts of water and sanitation companies. See SHUEP 2005, section 7 'The microeconomics of companies', p.52 et seq.

A Growth Coalition

This examination of sources of financing reveals that Shanghai Municipality has financed its enormous fixed-assets accumulation by behaving largely like a private developer, with the advantage of not being constrained by private ownership. It is worth taking a moment to reflect on the sums involved. Over the period 2000–2007, the total invested in fixed assets rose to 2,429 billion yuan (€270 billion).[69] The 'self-raised funds' mechanism (i.e. land-sale income) contributed around 1,100 billion yuan (Appendix C). Behind these hard figures, we can sense the infinite number of transactions involved in exploiting the value of land and building development.

Despite their background in a state-run economy, the actors quickly understood land-sale income mechanisms. Since the economy was not really monetised at the outset, the development companies received land from the Municipality free of charge or at extremely low rates. They developed this land, installed amenities and sold it at the market price. As Shanghai was rising quickly through the hierarchy of cities, the gap between entry and exit prices was very large. This mechanism was used to develop the Pudong New Area (from scratch), as well as in the urban renovation of Puxi and in new districts. A different technique has been used to finance several other urban infrastructures, but the logic is identical. Whether it is a matter of constructing toll tunnels and bridges, setting up the Pudong Water Company or providing infrastructure for the chemical park, the development companies build the first infrastructures with their available funds. Then they transfer the assets to a company and a proportion of the shares in this is sold at market price to an investor, whether a foreign firm or a state-owned company such as Citic. Another possibility is that they may transfer the assets to another company in return for a fixed rent. The details of this proliferation of mechanisms vary – a testament to the financial ingenuity of the Chinese elites – but basically they allow income to be generated in a number of different ways. The first transaction monetises the land, which was undervalued in the state-run economy. Next the selling price of the land with amenities includes the general rise in the value of assets, itself a function of the metropolis's progress up the world hierarchy of cities. The partial sale of shares in a state-owned company is another mechanism that allows the costs incurred to be recouped and the value of intangible assets – which appreciates in proportion to the city's potential development – to be exploited.

To account for this mode of government, we need to take the term 'socialist market economy' at face value. The actors have retained socialism's weak property rights (this explains the speed at which projects are completed), fairly low prices and strong coordination through a nucleus of actors who are connected to political power. From the markets, they have imported legally independent companies that allow assets to be circulated and offer greater flexibility to arrange any kind of

---

69   For comparison, before the 2007–2008 financial crisis, the California Public Employees' Retirement System (CalPERS) pension fund was managing assets of $250 billion.

deal. However, the profusion of organisational forms borrowed from the capitalist economy and the very strong coordination through just a few decision-making nodes are unique to Shanghai and probably to China's development. These institutions of power include several deputy mayors, a number of commissions (including the Construction Commission and SASAC), the large development companies and industrial and construction companies (see Appendix A). Although Shanghai is a huge metropolitan area, important decisions are taken by a small number of bodies where meritocratic competence is combined with links to the CCP. This state-present growth coalition[70] mirrors characteristics already identified in Hong Kong and Singapore[71] – but Shanghai has introduced something extra. The scales of urban change in Shanghai are far greater, whether in terms of the area of land involved, the speed, or the gap between initial and current values. By moving out of a closed, non-monetised economy and becoming a world city in just 15 years, the Municipal Government met the challenge of development. It managed to produce infrastructure and buildings at a rate that kept pace with extremely rapid economic development. The city has acquired essential amenities; it does not suffer from the problems afflicting numerous megacities in emerging countries, such as unfit housing or lack of access to networks.[72] To achieve these goals, the Municipality behaved strategically. It also benefited from a situation that allowed it to derive the maximum possible amount of land-sale income: assets acquired at extremely low prices, and sales on a market that has risen close to the standard of major world cities.

Unresolved Issues

However, this growth coalition is facing several limitations that to some extent dictate the major issues on the political agenda. First, the mechanism of using land-sale income as a principal source of financing will not always provide the same return: i) there is not an infinite number of (Fortune 500) Western companies ready to buy fixed assets, and the city has already attracted many major firms; ii) in the future the differential between purchase and selling prices, which determines the income, will be lower. In this event, will tariff charging – the principal technique used in Western countries – be able to make up the difference? The answer is 'yes', if we take into consideration that, historically, tariffs have been set on the low side. However, if we examine the impact of tariff increases on all essential goods, it quickly becomes 'yes, but … '. The technical question of modes of financing rapidly leads to an examination

---

70   The term 'growth coalition' is a reference to the works of Logan and Molotch on 'growth machines' (1987).

71   For further reading on Singapore, see Anne Haila, 2002.

72   See the *Fourth* Session of the *World Urban Forum*, UN Habitat, Nanjing, November 2008.

of incomes and the realisation that the income gap has widened considerably. A second problem is therefore presented by inequalities in income and wealth. Before the 1990s, such inequalities were insignificant. Nowadays they mark a real dividing line in civil society and could jeopardise its unity. Although some of the population have comfortable incomes, a much larger section is financially more insecure. Third, the accumulation regime has taken its toll on the environment, which has been considerably degraded by land consumption and by water and air pollution. Development cannot continue in this direction. Fourth, the coordination of public policy at the level of the megacity presents an acute problem. The incorporation of formerly rural districts into the urbanised area and the replacement of the former 'bureaux' with autonomous companies, which themselves have generated partnerships and subsidiaries, have both resulted in greater institutional complexity. The old method of steering the economy according to a central plan is not enough to meet the challenge.

Tariffs: Policy Adjustment Variable or Recurring Resource?

Historically, tariffs have been extremely low, since they formed part of a particular social model. Water tariffs are a striking example of this: Shanghai's are nearly at the bottom of the Chinese ranking (31st out of the 36 largest Chinese cities[73]), even though it is the country's economic capital. The city authorities, as guardians of the principles of the socialist market economy, have been extremely careful not to increase the prices of public utilities by too much. This policy is resolutely justified by the fact that incomes are said to be low. The minimum income was 675 yuan a month in the mid 2000s and the average income 1,400 yuan, although it should be noted that little heed is taken of shadow incomes (which, in a megacity with 4.5 official migrants, must be far from negligible). To what extent are tariffs too low, if indeed this is the case? To consider this question, we collected information on incomes and the cost of water services in Shanghai and compared this with our own data on France. Our comparison showed that people with identical social status spent a far smaller proportion of their household income on water in Shanghai than in France (see Box 2.9). This went for every social group: a single-income blue-collar couple, an unskilled blue-collar couple with two incomes, a single person in a managerial job, and a couple consisting of a manager and a white-collar worker. Proportionate expenditure in Shanghai and in France was equal only among elderly people living alone – but this was equality by default, as their rate of expenditure is high.

---

73   www.researchinchina.com/report/ – China Water Affair Report (Investment and Development), 2005–2006.

Box 2.9   Comparison of proportion of household income spent on water (2006–07)

	Shanghai		France	
	Monthly income	Water bill	Monthly income	Water bill
Elderly single person (on minimum income)	400y	4.6%	700€	4.3%
Unskilled blue-collar couple, one income	1,100y	1.7%	1,100€	2.7%
Unskilled blue-collar couple, two incomes	2,200y	0.83%	2,100€	1.4%
Manager or technician, single	4,000y	0.46%	3,200€	0.94%
Manager and white-collar worker, couple	10,200y	0.18%	4,600€	0.65%

Data on monthly salaries was taken from the *Statistical Yearbook* and checked with my students in Shanghai; data for France was provided by INSEE and FP2E. For water consumption, we used the standard international rate of 120 m3/year per household, allowing a comparison to be made. We ignored any possible changes in consumption resulting from levels of income.

The average Shanghai household spent 18.4 yuan a month on water (120 m3 water x 1.03 yuan = 124 yuan/year) + (108 m3 wastewater x 0.90 yuan = 97 yuan/year). Annual total: 221 yuan

The total spent on water in France was €360 a year, i.e. €30 a month

By choosing to restrict the prices of public utilities in order to protect low-income individuals, the government creates several problems. First, and most obviously, under-pricing is tantamount to subsidising medium and high earners. They have to spend a lower proportion of their income (when placed in an identical position among a cohort of income recipients) than their counterparts in industrialised countries, even though Shanghai is accumulating fixed assets at full tilt and so consumers there should be contributing more. Second, companies lack a source of regular income that would allow them to pursue network modernisation policies – long-term policies that, although low-profile, are essential to get results. It is not enough to finance a few large amenities: networks and services need to be upgraded, and for that operating profits are necessary. Third, the impact of under-pricing does not stop there. Low tariff charges means that infrastructure is largely financed through the land-sale income mechanism. This encourages state actors to act as developers and to feed the land and property price boom. Price rises trigger further rises, in a dangerous spiral from which it is difficult to break free, as too many interests are involved: the horde of new owners, the whole production system for the built environment, the officials of the state. Everyone expects the boom to continue. The megacity is developing upon itself and districts are becoming denser. Public and private actors are investing in major fixed assets, which increase its attractiveness, but without considering whether they are optimally located at the national level.[74] Within the balance of power as it currently stands, there is virtually no force opposing this growth coalition.

However, raising tariffs poses other questions. If this were done within the existing single-price regime, it would create a distortion between companies that do not have the same costs or financing requirements. Those operating in the new districts – Minhang and Pudong – have the advantage of a new network that is expected to provide a good return, as the number of leaks is low; but if the population there continue to increase, they will have to step up their production capacities and develop their networks. Companies operating in the old part of the metropolis face a fall in population, but have a lot to do to modernise the old networks. It is not clear whether the existing management system is capable of taking all these differences on board. So if the Municipality were to make greater use of tariffs it would need to improve its knowledge tools and perhaps even accept different tariffs in different areas. Price revision would also mean the end of a political compromise between the Communist Party and the middle and working classes. Shanghai attracts workers; life in the city is tough, but in return migrants have access to all the goods of modernity at low prices. The unwritten deal is basically: 'Come to our city, work hard and get rich' – and this presupposes that compulsory charges will remain reasonable.

In other words, behind a seemingly technical discussion of mechanisms for financing infrastructure, the Shanghai Government is in fact having to make a choice of accumulation regime. After 20 years of rapid growth, it faces the problem of moving from a growth coalition to an equilibrium coalition. With the first, the city continually develops, new infrastructure is built and the land-sale income mechanism allows the city to meet the challenge. But this growth cannot be infinite. A slowdown always comes, and with it the obligation to maintain the existing asset base. This is the investment and operational cycle. Methods of financing cannot stay the same, and a recurring resource needs to be mobilised: tariffs. The Municipal Government is fully aware of the problem and of the political risks that threaten the social equilibrium. On the one hand, as the city has opened up economically, its policy options have become more limited, and price-setting in the public services allows it to retain an important lever of power. The economic crisis of 2007–2008 highlighted tariff control as an adjustment variable that can cushion households against fluctuations in their purchasing power: in Autumn 2008 the Municipal Government decided to freeze tariffs, following central government's instructions to fight inflation. On the other hand, tariff rises are essential as a way of accessing new resources and are sometimes necessary to prevent waste. In June 2009, the Municipality decided on a two-step

---

74   See Pairault (2008), op. cit.

increase in the water and sanitation tariff, which had remained unchanged for seven years. The price first went up from 1.84 yuan/m3 to 2.3 yuan/m^3, and then to 2.8 yuan/m^3 in November 2010.

Inequalities in Income and Wealth

Until the economy was opened up to the market, two mechanisms combined to make Shanghai socially homogenous with little spatial segregation. Under Communism, wages were tightly controlled and there was no private ownership of housing. This homogeneity was reinforced by the spatial effect of SOEs: these 'total organisations' provided their employees with housing and services, so that households were not geographically distributed by earnings but by employment. This situation changed rapidly, first and foremost with the advent of high incomes. Managers working for market-oriented companies can earn 40,000 yuan a month, which contrasts strongly with the 400 yuan received by the stereotypical 'granny' living alone in the poor *lilongs* of the central districts. Inequalities are even more pronounced, although invisible, when wealth is taken into account. With the liberalisation of the housing market, private ownership has come into existence, and people increasingly choose their place of residence based on property prices. Some people do not own property: they rent their homes, in settlements that are substandard or far from the centre, and they travel by bicycle or by bus. At the opposite end of the scale, senior managers, big retailers/wholesalers and top civil servants own a car and several properties. If the average cost of housing is 15,000 yuan/m^2,[75] then a property portfolio consisting of one main residence and two rental apartments (totalling 270/m^2) is worth about 4 million yuan. It is not uncommon to own assets worth between €300,000 and €500,000.

If the Shanghai Government opted for greater use of tariffs to raise finance, it would be confronted by this inequality, which has so far been obscured. It is worth asking what impact an across-the-board rise in the price of essential goods would have, and my Tongji University students and I spent several years collecting information on this question. Our idea was to measure the 'real' incomes of various social groups, establish how much they spent on six essential goods (housing, water, electricity, gas, transport and telephone), calculate the proportion of their household income they were forced to spend on these items and then explore the impact of various tariff rises. This information was supplemented by data from the Statistics Bureau on the distribution of the population between the various social groups. Even though our calculations (Appendix E) are based on expert assessments rather than statistical sources, they provide a good outline of the problem.

Our first finding was that the population can be divided into three main groupings. The highest income grouping represents just under a quarter of the population; it consists of top managers and their counterparts in the public sector

75   See discussion on property prices towards the end of Section 1.

(2 per cent), big retail/wholesale traders (5 per cent) and – the most numerous sub-group – senior managers and technicians (16 per cent). Their incomes vary between 10,000 and 40,000 yuan a month. Next comes a middle grouping, representing around 44 per cent of the population. It corresponds to the traditional working class (39 per cent of the total population) and consists of skilled/unskilled blue-collar workers and white-collar workers, plus retired people from these groups (5 per cent of the population). Monthly incomes vary on a scale from 2,000 to 4,000 yuan a month. At the bottom of the distribution, we identified several low-income groups that make up around a third of the population: the single elderly (15 per cent), unskilled single-income blue-collar couples (10 per cent) and small retail/wholesale traders (8 per cent). They receive between 350 and 3,000 yuan a month. Overall, the monthly disposable incomes of around half the population are restricted by the irreducible cost of essential goods (see Box 2.10). However, the restriction does not always follow the income curve – and that is the central difficulty of a tariff policy. Five types of household spend 29 per cent or more of their monthly income on these essential goods – and for unskilled workers, the figure soars to over 40 per cent.

Box 2.10   Proportion of monthly household income spent on essential goods, by socio-occupational class

Financially insecure (50% of the population)			
3 classes (35% of the population):			
Unskilled blue-collar couple, 1 income	43%	Unskilled blue-collar couple, 2 incomes	38%
Young single white-collar worker	39%		
2 classes (15% of the population):			
Single retired person	31%	Single elderly person	29%
Stable but vulnerable (27% of the population)			
Retired couple (5%)	25%	Blue-collar couple living with parents (14%)	19%
Small retail/wholesale trader (8%)	13%		
Well-off (23% of the population)			
Big retail/wholesale trader (5%)	12%		
Top manager, public or private sector (2%)	30%	Manager or technician (16%)	45%

Research by the author, Appendix E. The (%) figure shows the proportion of a group in the whole population

In addition to this pressure on disposable incomes, there are two factors that apply to certain households and further undermine their situation: housing and employment. A comparison between two unskilled blue-collar couples is revealing. The first couple live independently and spend 38 per cent of their income on essential goods. The second live with their parents and are better-off: essential goods absorb just 19 per cent of their income, although this situation will last only as long as the parents are alive. The same situation applies to single-income as against dual-income blue-collar households: essential goods consume 43 per cent of household income in the first case, but 38 per cent in the second. When we look at elderly people, we should not be under any illusions about the lower proportion of their income that goes on essential goods: it simply reflects the continuation of traditional lifestyles with substandard housing and limited consumption. As for people involved in wholesale or retail trade, they can attribute a large percentage of their housing and travel costs to their work. This analysis is confirmed when we look at people in the opposite situation. Although they can earn around 10,000 yuan a month, the proportion of income spent by managers and technicians on essential goods was the highest in our survey, at 45 per cent. This is explained by the fact that such households are buying a home and running a vehicle.

In other words, the Shanghai Government is going to have to deal with the issue of income and income redistribution. Undiscriminating tariff reform would put half the population – already forced to spend a large proportion of their income on essentials – under greater financial pressure. It could also affect a much bigger number – around a quarter of the population – if these households were to go through an adverse life event such as loss of one wage, loss of a spouse's pension or the end of an advantageous housing situation. The equation is therefore not as straightforward as it may seem on a first reading.

Environmental Degradation

Twenty years of economic development have profoundly changed Shanghai. It has developed, acquired amenities and become wealthy. However, this has all come at the price of serious environmental degradation – the 'dark side' of success. The megacity, like China as a whole, will have to find a new model of development that is more environmentally sound. The challenge is enormous. Travellers can see this for themselves as soon as they venture outside Puxi. Residents suffer from air pollution, traffic jams and the urbanisation of previously rural areas. Life is tough in Shanghai and you need a lot of energy to survive. The city is a production-and-consumption machine which is not really a place for the vulnerable, such as young children or the elderly. Geriatric studies have looked at this problem, sounding the alarm about links between deteriorating quality of life and the silent depression of older people (Chan et al., 2006). A study based on a systems approach using a set of indicators (consumption of resources, economic development and social welfare) to compare highly developed Shanghai to Chongming – which is still protected from polluting industries – has clearly established that degradation has taken place:

'the development process in Shanghai is one of weak sustainability with relatively rapid social and economic development at the cost of environment and resource degradation' (Shi et al., 2004: 335). Using somewhat similar indicators for the period 1978–1998, Yuan and James demonstrated that the majority of correlation coefficients between economic and environmental indicators were negative (Yuan and James, 2002). Two sectors – air pollution and water pollution – offer clear illustrations, allowing many aspects of the problem to be explored.

As far as levels of air pollution are concerned, on a first reading it appears that Shanghai is not among the worst cities in China. According to a World Bank study and 2004 data, Shanghai's concentration of 100 PM_{10}/m^3 (10-micron particles per cubic metre) means that it ranks somewhere in the middle: pollution is lower than in exceptionally polluted industrial cities (which have over 200 PM_{10}/m^3) and significantly lower than Beijing (150 PM_{10}/m^3) and other cities such as Chongqing, Xian and Wuhan. However, looked at globally, the situation is worse than in Hong Kong, Mexico, Rio de Janeiro, Bangkok and Cape Town, which have levels of around 50 PM_{10}/m^3 (*Financial Times*, 3 July 2007, p.2). Measurement of suspended particulates has shown that they decreased in the urban area between 1986 and 1998 (Li et al., 2004: 51). These results reflect the introduction of stricter technical standards for coal-burning power stations[76] and for industries. The location of the megacity near the Chinese coast is also beneficial, as the winds blow pollution away. However, the situation remains worrying. Everything depends on the focus of a given study. First, what is the territory under consideration? The improvement cited applies to Shanghai's urban area (Puxi, the older part of the city), from which a large number of polluting industries have been relocated. However, a study of the distribution of particulates in the megacity as a whole shows that they have increased in rural districts (Li et al., 2004). Second, using macro particles (>10 microns) to measure air quality underestimates other pollutants, such as ozone, sulphur dioxide, nitrogen oxide and derivatives of these, such as sulphates and nitrates (Kan et al., 2004: 101). Third, when micro particles measuring less than 2.5 microns, which are particularly dangerous to the respiratory system, are taken into account, the situation appears just as grave. These are produced by fuel combustion and by vehicles, and so their concentrations have increased due to the considerable rise in motorised transport (Ye et al., 1999). However, according to some studies, coal-fired power stations may be more to blame than vehicle fuels for increased levels of lead particles (Chen et al., 2005).

Water pollution is another difficulty, and is partly explained by geography. Shanghai has developed over a vast flood plain that slopes gently; this reduces the flow rate of water courses that could carry pollutants away. At the same time, sea water can enter the canals, and in periods of drought it travels right up the Yangzi. The urban region, bounded to the north by this great river, is crossed by the Huangpu River, other tributaries and numerous canals that form a huge network, 21,000 km in length (Yin et al., 2005). Originally, the city's water was

---

76   For information on the situation in the 1990s, see Tong and Xi (1997).

provided by the Huangpu, while villages and towns in rural districts used the canals. However, geography is not the whole story: there is also the economic factor. The city's rapid urbanisation and its development model have led to a decline in water quality; a study of the period 1947–1996 provides revealing data (Ren et al., 2003). At the beginning of the 2000s, water in some canals was so polluted that specialists deemed it unfit for consumption even after it had been treated (SHUEP, 2004: 4–8). As a result, many pumping stations were closed and the villages affected had to be connected to the technical network of the nearest town. The Municipality's primary response to these problems was to develop major facilities, such as drinking-water treatment plants and sewers, with World Bank support. Pumping stations were moved upstream. Municipal officials also took refuge behind statistics claiming that 98 per cent of industrial wastewater was being treated. These different policies represented only a partial response to a problem that is at once more specific and more general. It appears more specific when we look at the sources of pollution. A 2001 survey of 55,000 outfalls by the Environmental Protection Bureau showed that 33,000 of them discharged untreated pollutants directly into waterways (Yin et al., 2005: 199). To this should be added non-localised pollution (non-point source contamination). This covers discharges of domestic wastewater[77] (significant in villages), the first flush of rainwater runoff from streets and frequent flooding. Finally, poor management of solid waste adds to the problem. According to a study conducted in the late 1990s, around 2,000 small and three large landfill sites discharged highly polluting leachate into canals and groundwater (Zhao et al., 2000). However, the problem also appears more general if Shanghai is seen as part of the greater urban region. Pollution measured along the Huangpu River in Shanghai originates partly from upstream activities. The quality of water in the lake that supplies the city with some of its drinking water depends on Lake Tai, which itself is surrounded by the cities of Suzhou, Wuxi and several other districts.

All these analyses lead to the same conclusions. First, the environment has been degraded. Second, technical solutions are not enough – pollution can only be reduced if separate fields are coordinated. There is a link between public energy, transport policies and public health objectives. Land use is another key factor in explaining environmental degradation. The fight against water pollution must start at the source and involve every sector responsible for pollution – housing, industry, trade and agriculture. The challenge is to act at two levels simultaneously, implementing highly specific measures while ensuring overall coordination.

---

77   According to a 1995 study, a third of domestic wastewater was treated. The rest was used in agricultural sewage sludge spreading, collected by canals and discharged to the Yangzi River or the ocean, or discharged to local waterways (Yin *et al*, 2005, p. 214).

Coordination: A Complex Exercise

The conversion of 'bureaux' into companies, the proliferation of specialised subsidiaries and the use of partnerships with the private sector means that multiple actors are involved in municipal government, posing a further problem of coordination. 'The number [of organisations] has increased nowadays because more works and policies are being implemented. But the commissions have less power than before, as opening up to a market economy means they have to share it'.[78] The spatial extension of urbanisation to the nine formerly rural districts will compound this problem. The scale at which matters are being steered is changing. The western Qingpu District is 45 kilometres from the city centre, and Jinshan District 75 kilometres. The system of government that we have described was functional when it operated in Puxi and Pudong. Even though its complexity clearly increased, three forces have worked against fragmentation and maintained a certain degree of unity: administrative authority, the role of the Communist Party and financial oversight. It is by no means certain that this system can be easily applied to the new urban districts, as other factors are now in play. These districts used to be a long way from the 'big city' and were less wealthy. Now they have been absorbed by the city, and large technical networks link them to the centre and to the entire urban region. They are attempting to safeguard their autonomy for a variety of reasons. First, the appraisal system for local officials has, up to now, been based on performance (Edin, 2004),[79] so that they have had to take on the additional role of developer. Second, competition between districts is strengthened by local fiscal mechanisms. The district is the basic unit for tax collection.[80] When a company registers in a district, it also pays VAT, turnover tax and corporation tax there. The issue of location is therefore extremely important and districts compete to attract companies. Third, urban pressure is intense in areas where new districts are springing up. Their development brings the chance to earn a great deal of money and power.

The managers of a Shanghai development company told us that they have experienced great difficulty working in these districts, which are not rich enough to finance their own infrastructure but nevertheless do not want to give up land that would allow it to be financed through a development deal. 'Land belongs to the districts, we belong to the Shanghai Municipal Government and we have

---

78 Commission official, November 2006.

79 'Since the early 1980s, the cadre management system introduced both individual and collective performance contracts for leading and medium-level township cadres, which were not unlike those given to enterprise managers. Subsequently, they were integrated within the civil servants' evaluation system, which became a powerful tool of governance [...] Leading township cadres are evaluated by the county on the basis of their performance contracts, which include a hierarchy of soft, hard and priority targets'. (Edin, 2004, p. 14).

80 This applies to the nine urban districts that make up Puxi, as well as to Pudong and the nine 'rural' districts.

the resources of the SMG'.[81] So districts often keep land for their own benefit. Our study included one district in the west that needed to invest in environmental infrastructure, but refused to take part in a special World Bank programme, arguing that 'it is complex and there are a lot of procedures'.[82] In fact, this masked the district's desire to remain independent and to drive projects forward while retaining as much freedom as possible. This district is in the perfect location to attract private developers who will build hotels, leisure facilities and office developments. In another case, a site in Pudong had been earmarked by the Shanghai Government for an industrial equipment manufacturer. 'One company came and was shown the site, but it was contacted by other, cheaper parks and went elsewhere'.[83] This example fell within the remit of the Economic Commission: this body advocates concentration in industrial zones, but it cannot exert much influence on the districts, which are autonomous, or on businesses, for the sake of free trade. China has signed world trade (WTO) agreements, and direct intervention would look like interference in the private sector.

In short, coordination 'was easier in the past'. The institutional diversity that characterises the Municipal Government after 15 years of reforms poses new problems of coordination – between districts, municipal enterprises, joint ventures and the requirements of free-trade agreements. This is also a problem with respect to neighbouring provinces. Shanghai Municipality wants to build up its financial services and industrial base, but other cities (such as Nanjing and Tianjin) also want to attract financial services. 'The decision must be taken not only on the basis of market criteria, but also on political grounds'. Despite these real difficulties, the Construction Commission and the Development and Reform Commission are working together on an urban-rural planning system called '1, 9, 6, 6' meaning one city specialising in services (Shanghai), nine satellite cities with industry and services, 60 towns and 600 villages. (The Municipality currently has 1,800 villages, but they will be grouped together for the purposes of this scheme.)

Conclusion: Inventing a New Accumulation Regime

In 15 years, Shanghai has undergone radical change, in terms of both its physical transformation and its mode of government. Shanghai has risen to the rank of megacity while avoiding the pitfalls faced by many cities in emerging countries (like shanty towns or anarchic urbanisation).[84] The current schema is very different from the direct administration in place at the outset. In this process, infrastructure has been a vehicle for learning and reform. The chronology of events shows that

---

81   Interview conducted in November 2006.
82   Interview conducted in September 2004.
83   Interview with a municipal commission official, November 2006.
84   See the glowing praise in a speech delivered by the director of UN-Habitat in Nanjing, November 2008.

it was in the context of networked services that the authorities redesigned the institutional architecture and introduced cost measurement, the idea of return on investment and partnerships with the West, initially with the World Bank and subsequently with private sector firms. Time has been a key factor. It took between 15 and 20 years to transform institutions and certain practices; this was the time that elapsed between creation of the first metro company (1985) and flotation of the port company (2006). It is often considered that it takes a generation to transform a mode of government.[85] From this point of view, the Chinese have remained in control of the timescale and of their agenda, despite exhortations from the IMF and the World Bank to speed up reform of state-owned enterprises.[86] However, time has not run in a simple straight line. We should see it more as a sequential process with a learning phase (1988–1996) followed by an acceleration during which the same schema was rolled out to a large number of sectors. This second stage took place over a brief period, between 1999 and 2003. The first reforms (the metro, sanitation, the electricity sector) acted as incubators, and these new experiences circulated between the elites.

Here the organisation of power from a few concentrated networks allowed great efficiency. The cognitive sciences talk about 'distributed knowledge' (Borzeix and Cochoy, 2008), a notion that can be applied to the Shanghai elites. Once they had been convinced of the benefit of reforms, including the operational dimension, they moved easily to the second stage. The members of this club had already exchanged ideas and started to draw up a shared grammar of public policy. Among the internal mechanisms that have facilitated cooperation between sectoral elites, it is worth mentioning the role of the Communist Party and the existence of a solid meritocracy in the administration, fed by the city's major universities – Fudan, Jiaotong and Tongji. This is the major decision-making group. These elites constitute a network, travel in China and abroad and exchange experiences. The importance of this group of decision-makers must also be assessed on the basis of the very fact that a development strategy exists. How many emerging countries in the world have received sizeable aid from their former colonial rulers or from international development institutions and yet are still embroiled in infighting or state capture? Shanghai's strength lies in an elite that is proud of its history and ambitious both for itself and the city, seeming almost to have been inspired by Colbert or Frederick II of Prussia.

The success of Shanghai's transformation also relates to its capacity to act in several registers, combining the reform of formal institutions with action on second-level institutions. The authorities have converted their bureaux

---

85 I arrived at this result during my previous work on local government in France: the first modernisation programmes were introduced in 1972–1974, but decentralisation in the cities reach maturity only in the late 1990s. More recently, I came to the same conclusion in a study of the international policy of Lyonnaise des Eaux (Lorrain, D.(2007) The local-global firm: Lyonnaise des Eaux, 1980–2004, *Sociologie du travail*, 49S, e90–e109).

86 For a critical overview, see Stiglitz, 2002.

into companies, and the latter have set up subsidiaries that produce ever more innovative partnerships. However, the government also tackled accounting reform, tariff policy and financing methods at a very early stage. Each reform progressed at its own speed. It was only when they came up against new problems that actors saw the benefit of adopting certain rules (such as private-sector accounting and depreciation), which others would have tended to see initially as orders from the World Bank and free-market reformers. The situation meant that certain reforms made practical sense, and this helped them to be rolled out.

In its initial operations, the World Bank always asked for the actors to be made autonomous ('corporatisation'). This was a way for the Bank to exercise better control over the risk of default and to introduce a market economy without actually saying it was doing so. If numbers of companies created, stock market flotations and other partnerships are considered, then it succeeded beyond its expectations. However, it could also be said that the Chinese authorities were boxing clever with the Bank. They did what was asked of them, but took their time over it, in order to make sure they derived maximum benefit. The resulting web of institutions means that lines of responsibility have never been clearly defined. This appears to be all the more true when we take into account the flawed reform of property rights and the patchy introduction of accounting reform. At the outset, the Bank's staff, with their rational perspective, wanted to deconstruct a municipal machine that they saw as a 'black box' over which they had no control. They succeeded in doing so – but the result is scarcely more transparent. In each sphere, the structures interlock; yet the institutional system is constantly shifting, and so the local actors have found room for manoeuvre within these interlockings. But this desire for freedom is also a risk factor. The Shanghai authorities act like firms in a market economy, playing the role of 'super developer'. However, they lack the most important check and balance that acts on Western firms: information. These firms are answerable to their shareholders, banks and the public authorities. In Shanghai, the overall dynamic is largely orchestrated by a fairly limited group of actors who have accumulated political, industrial and financial power. By and large, they have escaped the forces that structure market economies, such as property rights, accounting rules and a critical press. This is the hidden side of Shanghai's growth coalition.

The Municipality has found a solution to the financing of urban development by making itself a developer: the city is paid for by the city. This is the model employed in Singapore and Hong Kong – the Asian version of the 'growth machine'. Thanks to their control of the whole chain of production of the built environment, the local authorities have managed to harness land-sale income to drive urban development. In this macroeconomic equilibrium, growth is a pull factor for more growth, though it has to be said that the city is also caught up in a headlong rush. Future infrastructure will continue to be financed for as long as growth holds out. Is it really sustainable? The Municipality is going to be faced with managing the end of an exceptional period and of the factors that have favoured it: Beijing's support in making Shanghai a 'world city', the abrupt transition from a demonetised economy to an international market, an influx of migrants who could be put to work immediately. The Municipality will have to confront growing inequalities, environmental degradation and the issue of an ageing population. One of the challenges of the coming years will be to steer the megacity to a soft landing and to develop a new, more harmonious accumulation regime.

References

Bafoil, F. (2006). Les apprentissages du changement dans l'entreprise polonaise. Entre continuité et rupture. *Sociologie du travail*, 48(2): 240–56.

Baye, E. (2001). *De la ville chinoise à la cité mondiale*. Cahiers TTS, Paris, Ministère de l'Equipement.

Baye, E., Lorrain, D., Guillemot, M. (1996). *Shanghaï; la protection de l'environnement et les éco-industries*. Ministère de l'Economie des Finances et de l'Industrie, coll. Etudes, 168.

Bernis, A. (1996). *Les Nuits du Yang-Tsé, chez les pirates du Grand Fleuve dans la Chine des années 1920*. (1st édition 1930), Paris.

Bezes, P., Lallement, M., Lorrain, D. (2005). Les nouveaux formats de l'institution. *Sociologie du Travail*, 47(3): 293–300.

Bonavia, J. (2002). *The Yangzi River and the Three Gorges*. Odyssey Publications, Hong Kong.

Borzeix, A., Cochoy, F. (2008). Travail et théories de l'activité: vers des workspace studies? *Sociologie du travail*, 50(3): 273–86.

Chan, S.W., Shoumei, J.I.A., Thompson, D.R., Yan, H.U., Chiu, H.F.K., Chien, W., Lam, L. (2006). A Cross-Sectorial Study on the Health Related Quality of Life of Depressed Chinese Older People in Shanghai. *International Journal of Geriatric Psychiatry*, 21(9): 883–9.

Chen, J., Tan, M., Li, Y., Zhang, Y., Lu, W., Tong, Y., Zhang, G., Li, Y. (2005). A Lead Isotope Record of Shanghai Atmospheric Lead Emissions in Total Suspended Particles During the Period of Phasing out of Leaded Gasoline. *Atmospheric Environment*, 39: 1245–53.

Chreod (2003). The Shanghai Metropolitan Region, Development Trends and Strategic Challenges. The World Bank (EASUR), Shanghai Development Planning Commission.

Dale, B., Edwards, M. (1980). Shanghai Portfolio; China's Born-again Giant. *National Geographic*, July: 2–43.

Edin, M. (2004). Local State Corporatism and Private Business. In Ho, Eyferth and Vermeer (eds), *Rural Development in Transitional China*. New York, London: Frank Cass.

Eyraud, C. (2003). Pour une approche sociologique de la comptabilité. Réflexions à partir de la réforme comptable chinoise. *Sociologie du travail*, 45(4): 491–508.

Gomez Ibanez, J.A., Meyer, J.R. (1993) *Going Private, the International Experience with Transport Privatization*. Washington, D.C.: The Brooking Institution.

Guiheux, G. (2006), Immobilier. In Sanjuan T. (dir.), *Dictionnaire de la Chine contemporaine*, Armand Colin, Paris, 130–31.

Haila, A. 2002. State-Present Capitalism: Property and Development Companies in Singapore. *Entreprises et Histoire*, 30: 63–72.

Jensen, M.C., Meckling, W.H. (1976), Theory of the Firm: Managerial Behavior, Agency Cost, and Ownership Structure, *Journal of Financial Economics*, 3(4): 305–60.

Kan, H., Chen, B., Chen, C., Fu, Q., Chen, M. (2004). An Evaluation of Public Health Impact of Ambient Air Pollution under Various Energy Scenarios in Shanghai, China. *Atmospheric Environment*, 38: 95–102.

Lascoumes, P., Le Galès, P. (dir.), 2004. *Gouverner par les instruments*, Paris, Presses de Sciences Po.

Li, J., Guttikunda, S.K., Carmichael, G.R., Streets, D.G., Chang, Y-S. Fung, V. (2004). Quantifying the Human Health Benefits of Curbing Air Pollution in Shanghai. *Journal of Environmental Management*, 70: 49–62.

Logan, J., Molotch, H.R. (1987). *Urban Fortunes, the Political Economy of Places*. Berkeley: University of California Press.

Logan, J. (ed.), (2002). *The New Chinese City*, Malden, MA: Blackwell.

Lorrain, D. (1998). Les réseaux techniques urbains à Chengdu, *Flux*, 33(juillet-septembre): 4–21.

Lorrain, D. (2000). La Banque mondiale, telle Janus, (expériences d'études en Chine). *Annales de la Recherche Urbaine*, 86(juin): 101–10.

Lorrain, D. (2004). Les pilotes invisibles de l'action publique, le désarroi du politique? In P. Lascoumes et P. Le Galès (dir.), *Gouverner par les instruments*, Presses de Sciences Po, Paris, 163–97.

Lorrain, D. (2008a), La Gig@city, nouveau lieu de la production de capital. *Annales des Mines, Réalités Industrielles*, spécial sur l'économie urbaine (février): 63–9.

Lorrain, D. (2008b), Les institutions de second rang. *Entreprises et Histoire*, 50(avril): 6–13.

Lynn, M. (1997). *Yangzi River: The Wildest, Wickedest River on Earth*. Oxford University Press.

Mott, MacDonald, North West Water International, KPMG, Mouchel Environmental (1993). Shanghai Environment Project, Water Sector Institutions Report. Shanghai.

North, D.C. (1990). *Institutions, Institutional Change, and Economic Performance*. Cambridge: Cambridge University Press.

Pairault, T. (2008). *Petite introduction à l'économie de la Chine. Editions des archives contemporaines*, Paris: Agence universitaire de la francophonie.

Ren, W., Zhong, Y., Meligrana, J., Anderson, B., Watt, W.E., Chen, J., Leung, H-K. (2003). Urbanization Land Use and Water Quality in Shanghai. *Environment International*, 29: 649–59.

Sanjuan, T. (dir.) 2006. *Dictionnaire de la Chine contemporaine*. Paris: Armand Colin.

Shanghai Statistical Yearbook, (2003 et suiv.). Beijing: China Statistics Press.

Shanghai Urban Environment Project (SHUEP), (2004). Design Review & Advisory Services, Inception Report. Shanghai Municipal Government, SOGREAH Consultants.

Shanghai Urban Environment Project (SHUEP), (2005). Institutional Strengthening and Training Report (IST). Shanghai Municipal Government, SOGREAH Consultants.

Shi, C., Hutchinson, S.M., Xu, S. (2004). Evaluation of Coastal Sustainability: An Integrated Approach Applied in Shanghai Municipality and Chong Ming Island. *Journal of Environmental Management*, 71: 335–44.

Stiglitz, J.E. (2002). Globalization and its Discontents. New York: WW Norton.

Thelen, K. (2003). *Comment les institutions* évoluent: *Perspectives de l'analyse comparative historique. L'Année de la régulation, no.7*, Paris: Presses de Sciences Po., p. 13–43.

Tong, J., Xi, S. (1997). Energy Consumption Structure and Atmosphere Environment in Shanghai, *Fuel and Energy Abstracts*, 38(6): 452.

HT 147.C6 Wu Duo, Li Taibin (2002). The Present Situation and Prospective Development of the Shanghai Urban Community. In J. Logan (ed.), *The New Chinese City*. Malden, MA: Blackwell, 22–36.

Wu, Fulong (2000). The Global and Local Dimensions of Place-making: Remaking Shanghai as a World City, *Urban Studies*, 37: 1359–77.

Wu, Fulong (2001). Housing Provision under Globalization: A Case Study of Shanghai. *Environment and Planning*, 33: 1741–64.

Wu, Fulong (2002). Real Estate Development and the Transformation of Urban Space in China's Transition Economy with Special Reference to Shanghai. In J. Logan (ed.), *The New Chinese City*. Malden, MA: Blackwell, 152–66.

Vietor, R. (2007). *How Countries Compete* (Strategy, Structure and Government in the Global Economy). Boston: Harvard Business School Press.

Ye, S-H., Zhou, W., Song, J., Peng, B-C., Yuan, D., Lu, Y-M., Qi, P-P. (1999). Toxicity and Health Effects of Vehicles Emissions in Shanghai. *Atmospheric Environment*, 34: 419–29.

Yin, Z-Y., Walcott, S., Kaplan, B., Cao, J., Lin, W., Chen, M., Liu, D., Ning, Y. (2005). An Analysis of the Relationship Between Spatial Patterns of Water Quality and Urban Development in Shanghai, China. *Computers, Environment and Urban Systems*, 29: 197–221.

Yuan, W., James, P. (2002). Evolution of the Shanghai City Region 1978–1998: An Analysis of Indicators. *Journal of Environment Management*, 64: 299–309.

Yusuf, S., Wu, Weiping (2002). Pathways to a World City: Shanghai Rising in an Era of Globalization. *Urban Studies*, 39(7): 1213–40.

Zhang, L-Y. (2003). Economic Development in Shanghai and the Role of the State. *Urban Studies*, 40(8): 1549–72 ; cité pp. 1556, 1557.

Zhao, Y., Liu, J., Huang, R., Gu, G. (2000). Long-term Monitoring and Prediction for Leachate Concentrations in Shanghai Refuse Landfill. *Water, Air and Soil Pollution*, 122: 281–97.

Zhong, Yang (2003). *Local Government and Politics in China*. New York: East Gate Books.
Zhuo, Jian (2006), Logement. In Sanjuan, T. (dir.) *Dictionnaire de la Chine contemporaine*, Paris: Armand Colin, 144–5.

List of Acronyms and Abbreviations

BOT: Build Operate Transfer
BOST: Build Operate Subsidize Transfer
DBFO: Design Build Finance Operate
FDI: Foreign Direct Investment
GDP: Gross Domestic Product
MEAB: Municipal Engineering and Administrative Bureau
CCP: Chinese Communist Party
PUB: Public Utilities Bureau
SASAC: State-own Assets Supervision and Administration Commission
SCG: Shanghai Construction Group
SHUEP: Shanghai Urban Environment Project
SIIC: Shanghai Industrial Investment Co.
SMSC: Shanghai Municipal Sewage Co.
SUCG: Shanghai Urban Construction Group
SWA: Shanghai Water Authority

Appendix A: The New Institutional Architecture (2004)

(www.shanghai.gov.cn and research by the author)

- 'Government organs':
  - 9 commissions, including Development and Reform Commission and Commission of Construction and Administration
  - 11 bureaux including Auditing, Finance and Water Affairs Bureaux (with Shanghai Water Authority)

- 23 'organisations directly under the authority of the Shanghai Government', including:
  - Environmental Protection Bureau
  - Housing Land, and Resources Administration
  - Urban Communications Administration Bureau (urban transport)
  - Harbour Administration

- 7 'organisations under the authority of the Shanghai Government':
  - Public Works Administration (roads, bridges and tunnels, gas distribution),
  - City Appearance and Environmental Sanitation Administration (rubbish, street lighting, outdoor advertising)

- 'Special' organisation: Shanghai Municipal State-owned Assets Supervision and Administration (SASAC)

State-owned Companies that Play a Role in Management of the City

- SIIC, development company floated on Hong Kong Stock Exchange in 1981. Industrial infrastructure and property.
- Jiushi, development company created in 1986, dominates transport sector
- Chengtou, development company founded in 1992 (water, sewage, transport), has several affiliates

- SMEDI, design institute for urban infrastructure
- Eastern China Electric Design Institute (specializing in energy)
- Shanghai Urban Construction Group (SUCG), created in 1996. Specialises in infrastructure construction. Has an engineering subsidiary. Shareholder in Shanghai Tunnel Co. (listed).
- Shanghai Construction Group (1994), major national building and public works company

- Shanghai International Port Group (2003) floated in 2006. Controlled by SASAC and Tongsheng Investment. Company created in 2002 for third

port. 6 joint ventures to manage terminals (HIT, PSA, Cosco, CMA-CGM), 30 direct subsidiaries.
- Shanghai Airport Authority. Joint venture with Hong Kong Airport Authority.

- Shanghai Municipal Electric Power Corp. (1991)
- Shenenergy (1987), converted into Shenenergy Power (1992), then ShenNeng Group (1996)

- Shanghai Chemical Industrial Park (2002). Joint ventures for infrastructure: fluid, gas (Air Liquide), port (Vopak), energy and steam (SembCorp), water/sanitation, waste (Suez Environnement).

- Shentong Group (2000), with quoted subsidiary Shanghai Shentong Metro Corp. Operating company (Shanghai Metro Operation Corp.)
- Shanghai Modern Railway Transportation Corp. (partnership between 5 state-owned companies)

- Shanghai Chengtou Holding (company listed in 2008) controls existing water companies: 4 water distribution companies and 1 raw water company (1999), Shanghai Municipal Sewage Co. (1995); operational subsidiaries (2001). Pudong Water Company: joint venture between Chengtou and Veolia (2002)
- BOT for wastewater treatment plants (2002 and 2004), taken over by Shanghai Urban Construction Group
- Waste landfill concession (2003): Veolia Propreté, Citic Pacific and Chengtou. Partnership between Shanghai Environment Group (an affiliate of Chengtou) and Waste Management (2010).

Appendix C: Sources of Investment in Fixed Assets (IFA)

Year	IFA in GY	Funding of fixed assets (a) BA(b)	Loans	Bond	FI	SRF	Others	
1995	160.18	*1.9*	*18.4*	*0.1*	*11.2*	*51.5*	*16.9*	
1996	195.20	*1.5*	*19.2*	*4.2*	*17.1*	*48.2*	*13.9*	
1997	197.76	*1.4*	*22.4*	*4.0*	*15.8*	*46.1*	*14.3*	
1998	196.48	*2.1*	*21.8*	*3.2*	*15.4*	*45.3*	*15.2*	
1999	185.67	*2.1*	*19.0*	*0.8*	*16.5*	*45.0*	*16.6*	
1995/99	935.29	*1.9%*	*20.5%*	*2.2%*	*14.3%*	*47.2%*	*15.8%*	*101.9%*
2000	182.06	4.83	37.92	0.48	16.18	90.55	32.10	
2001	219.91	5.78	48.22	0.18	20.26	101.32	44.14	
2002	242.01	2.93	56.36	1.00	21.51	104.20	56.00	
2003	284.44	3.55	67.43		21.05	120.34	72.06	
2004	361.08	3.85	90.74		23.40	148.40	94.69	
2005	424.76	4.64	95.53	0.20	23.56	197.67	103.16	
2006	495.20	7.43	116.22		27.12	226.50	117.93	
2007	551.17	9.80	129.69	1.88	26.24	236.49	147.64	
	2760.63 (c)	42.81	642.11	3.74	179.32	1,225.47	667.72	2761.17
		1.55%	*23.25%*	*0.14%*	*6.50%*	*44.38%*	*24.18%*	*100%*

Source: *Shanghai Municipal Statistical Yearbook*, our researches 2004, 2006, 2008.

(a) For the years 1995–99 breakdown (in percentage) from Zhang L.Y., *Urban Studies*, 2003, p. 1555.
For the years 2000-07 figures in yuan billions from the *Statistical Yearbook*, compiled by the author.
Years 2000, 2001: http://www.stats-sh.gov.cn/2002shtj/tjnj/2002/table/6_9d.htm.
Years 2002, 2003: http://www.stats-sh.gov.cn/2003shtj/tjnj/2004tjnj/C0609/60609d.htm.
Years 2004, 2005: http://www.stats-sh.gov.cn/2003shtj/tjnj/nj06.htm?d1=2006tjnj/C0707.htm.
Years 2006, 2007: http://www.stats-sh.gov.cn/2003shtj/tjnj/2008tjnj/C608.htm.

(b) BA = budgetary allocation; FI= foreign investment; SRF= self-raised funds;
Others = largely contributions from the collective funds of State Owned Enterprises.

(c) Because of different data sources, the total of fixed assets from appendix B (*Statistical Yearbook* table 6.1) does not equal the total calculated from the sources of funding.

Appendix B: Investment in Fixed Assets and Infrastructure (Billion of Yuan, GY)

Year	IFA*	INFRA**	INFRA/ IFA	Infrastructure						Pb. Works	Polution Management***
				Power	Transp.	Post&Tel.	Utilities	(incl. Water,	Gas)		liquid, solid air
1981	5.42	0.78	14.4%	0.35	0.24	0.004	0.06	–	–	0.09	
1985	11.86	2.35	19.8%	0.40	0.55	0.12	0.78	–	–	0.49	
1986	14.67	2.48	16.9%	0.57	0.77	0.18	0.45	0.27	0.18	0.50	
1991	25.83	6.14	23.8%	1.98	1.68	0.46	0.68	0.23	0.45	1.34	0.76
1992	35.74	8.43	23.6%	1.97	1.82	0.64	0.94	0.32	0.61	3.06	1.52
1993	65.39	16.79	25.7%	2.58	4.61	1.47	2.36	0.69	1.67	5.78	3.21
1994	112.33	23.82	21.2%	4.16	4.43	3.59	1.93	1.15	0.78	9.71	3.91
1995	160.18	27.38	17.1%	5.73	3.48	5.34	2.61	1.31	1.30	10.21	4.65
1996	195.20	37.88	19.4%	7.76	8.12	7.76	3.67	2.21	1.46	10.56	6.88
1997	197.76	41.29	20.9%	8.02	10.02	6.10	3.71	2.71	1.00	13.43	8.22
1998	196.48	53.14	27.0%	8.96	13.94	7.27	2.77	1.46	1.31	20.20	10.21
1999	185.67	50.14	27.0%	8.31	15.01	6.39	1.63	0.64	0.99	18.80	11.16
2000	186.97	44.99	24.1%	6.46	14.10	6.87	1.22	0.53	0.69	16.33	14.19
2001	199.47	51.08	23.2%	7.22	14.12	10.77	1.18	0.60	0.58	17.70	15.29
2002	218.71	58.35	25.6%	6.21	19.60	10.82	1.54	0.86	0.68	20.17	16.24
2003	245.52	60.46	26.2%	6.60	27.38	7.66	3.69	2.29	1.40	15.14	19.15

2004	308.47	67.26	21,8%	8.95	31.70	5.44	2.69	1.66	1.03	18.48	22.54
2005	354.25	88.57	25,0%	12.42	38.56	5.83	4.13	2.97	1.16	27.63	28.12
2006	392.51	112.55	28,7%	11.62	58.95	11.37	5.62	4.38	1.24	24.98	31.08
2007	445.86	146.63	32,9%	16.33	84.05	10.16	6.09	5.01	1.08	30.01	36.61
1991/07	**3,526.34**	**894.90**	25,4%	125.28	351.57	107.94	46.46	(29.0)	(17.43)	263.62	**233.77**

*Total IFA (investment in fixed assets), *Statistical Yearbook*, table 6.1, www.stats-sh.gov.cn
** *Shanghai Statistical Yearbook*, table 11.1, Investment in infrastructure,
*** *Shanghai Statistical Yearbook*, table 20.1, Investment in environment protection (the three wastes : liquid, solid, air)
Concerning the years 1981-1999 see Yusuf S. and Wu W., *Urban Studies*, vol. 39, 2002 p. 1123

Publisher's note: Appendix B has been introduced after C in order to maintain a comprehensive view of the table.

Appendix D: Methodological Note

Shanghai Municipality's Office of Statistics produces statistics that can be used to assess investment in urban infrastructure and other fixed assets, with certain precautions.[1]

Total Invested in Fixed Assets (Table 6.1 of the *Statistical Yearbook*)

This statistic, available over 30 years (1978–2007), corresponds to the 'total investment for fixed assets in the whole society'. It is a broad category that covers all types of investment and breaks them down into seven subcategories. In order to ensure homogeneity with other statistical tables (in particular 'the three pollutions'), we worked on the period 1991–2007. Over this period, the total invested in fixed assets was 3526.34 GY.

i. The category 'fundamental construction' refers to construction, expansion engineering and other related work entailing total investment of 500,000 yuan or more, done by enterprises, institutions and administrative units in order to expand production capacity or engineering efficiency. This corresponds to productive investment. It is the first category of investment, representing a total of 1647.64 GY. If we track the trends, we see that in 1991, it stood at around 11 GY, a level reached three years earlier; in 1994 it exceeded 50 GY. Then the total settled at around 75 GY for several years from 1997. After 2004, there was a considerable surge to 172 GY, then 277 GY in 2007; in part, this result is explained by the suspension of the next two categories.

ii. The category 'renewal and reconstruction' refers to the renewal and technical renovation of fixed assets, as well as related supporting projects and work (not including heavy repair and maintenance) for existing facilities done by enterprises and institutions, with a total investment of 500,000 yuan and more. This statistic was suspended in 2004. The total invested since 1991 is 434 GY.

iii. A category 'other investment', also suspended in 2004, represents a sum of 25.77 GY. It covers investment not included in categories i), ii) and iv).

iv. The category of investment in 'real estate development' refers to real estate development and operation activities, including residential buildings, factories, warehouses, restaurants, hotels, holiday resorts, office buildings and supporting facilities, which are built, or commissioned, or rebuilt after demolition, by real estate development companies, real estate construction and other legal entities involved in real estate development, as well as

---

1   My thanks to my colleague Yang Menying who liaised with the offices of statistics and explained the meanings of the headings of the general sections.

other organisations affiliated with other legal entities, engaged in real estate development or operation activities. Simple land transactions are not included. This statistical series begins in 1987 and the trend in the figures is a fairly clear reflection of the transformation of the real estate sector from the early 1990s, following reforms in real estate ownership. The threshold of one billion yuan (1 GY) was crossed in 1992, 50 GY in 1995/96 and 100 GY between 2003/04. The total investment in this category amounts to 1084.24 GY.

v. The category of investment in agriculture and collectives stands at 298.5 GY.
vi. The category of 'urban and private construction' amounts to 1.68 GY.
vii. The category of 'rural and private construction' amounts to 17.22 GY.

Investment in Infrastructures (Table 10.1; 11.1 of the *Statistical Yearbook*)

The previous statistic (Table 6.1) cannot be used to calculate infrastructure investment (electricity, transport, telecommunications, water, gas, public works and depollution), because it is divided between one or other of the three main categories: fundamental construction (or productive investment), real estate development and agricultural investment.

Infrastructure investment is obtained from tables 10.1 and 11.1. It is broken down between five major entries. An additional table (10.1 and 11.2) disaggregates certain categories and can be used to break down the 'utilities' category between water, gas and transport expenditure for reassignment to the transport category.

i. Power, total for the period 1991–20007, 125.28 GY.
ii. Transport. This very significant category (351.57 GY) includes investment in public transport and motorways (another part is in public works) and also in ports and airports. Until 2002, certain cost items such as the acquisition of buses were included in the 'utilities' category. This classification was administratively convenient, since the 'utilities' office covered the water, gas distribution, taxi and bus sectors. From 2003 onwards, all transport-related investment was reassigned to this category. This explains the sharp drop for 'utilities' and the rise for transport in the statistical series (tables 10.1 and 11.1 before adjustment) in 2002/2003.
iii. Post and telecommunications (107.94 GY).
iv. Utilities covers investment for drinking water and gas (total 46.46 GY). Water also includes investment in depollution, which corresponds to water treatment. Investment in water networks as such pipework is assigned to the 'public works' category. Until 2002, this category also included investment

in transport. We recalculated the two statistical series (utilities, transport) to obtain a homogeneous series.[2]

v. Municipal works, total of 263.62 GY (see Table 10.2 for a breakdown). This large category includes several subcategories: parks and gardens; city appearance, which covers street cleaning, public toilets. The main item (Municipal Engineering Management, 85 per cent of the total) corresponds to investment in the street network (new works, extension, maintenance); it also covers bridges, tunnels and elevated expressways; finally, it includes the big sewage networks.

Out of this discussion emerges the fact that statistical categories have themselves been modified by material changes to the city. Initially, they reflected administrative classifications. The 'offices' responsible for a sector also had the task of recording the figures, but this procedural convenience led to a number of mismatches in the description of real-world phenomena. We have shown that investment in transport was recorded in the 'transport' category (fortunately), but also in 'utilities'; the official adjustment was made in 2003. Similarly, the introduction of sewage treatment and then waste treatment became another assignment problem. The current statistical classifications led to the separation of these policies into two categories: anything relating to treatment is recorded in 'utilities', whereas engineering works fall into the category of 'public works'. To obtain an overall view, statisticians created a new table (Table 20.1, Environmental protection and the use of the three wastes: solid, liquid, air (SO_2, NO).

---

2   We took investment in wastewater treatment to be included in 'water', with the result that utilities − (water + gas) = transport. The statistical series from 2003 onwards, the date of the adjustment for transport, confirms this point: (water + gas) = utilities; there is no remainder that would correspond to a specific assignment of water treatment.

Appendix E: Household incomes and essential goods in Shanghai in 2006–2007

	Income (yuan/month)	Essential goods						TOTAL	% Income
		Hous.	water	elec	gas	transp	Telecom		
49% of total population									
Worker couple	3625	800	52	92	53	285	105	1387	38%
Worker couple at parents	3867	127	50	87	50	300	110	724	19%
Worker couple (1 income)	1700	500	39	43	24	83	40	729	43%
Office worker (young unmarried)	4000	1000	35	75	30	300	125	1565	39%
20% of total population									
Destitute old person, alone	350	16	17	25	20	5	17	100	28.6%
Retired unmarried person	800	50	30	40	50	50	25	245	30.6%
Retired couple (**5% of TP**)	2000	100	50	80	100	150	30	510	25.5%
13% of total population									
Small shopkeeper (**8% of TP**)	3000	50	36	50	42	100	100	378	12.6%
Wealthy shopkeeper (**5% of TP**)	9000	750	50	100	50	50	50	1050	11.7%
16% of total population									
Middle managers. Technicians	10,200	2930	71	201	192	850	377	4621	45.3%
Sen Man./civil servant (**2% TP**)	37,000	7250	140	470	202	2,500	375	10,937	29.6%

Method. Initially, I wanted my students on the joint Tongji/ENPC Paris MBA to think about price policies. The first idea was to get away from a sectoral approach to include all essential goods, because if a government applied an economic mechanism for one of them, it would have to extend them to all the other public services. The second idea is that a prices policy must be related to real incomes, which means trying to assess non-monetary benefits or undeclared income. This exercise was organised as a game. The group (around 45 students) was divided into different household categories, and an expert team checked the data from each 'household' (which gave rise to some heated discussions) while one group representing the municipality set a price rise policy. By playing this game over several years, I put together seven identical matrices, the sum of which produced the table shown below and is the basis for the analysis in section 5, pages 74–6.

Method for weighting households within the total population. The data provided by the statistics are incomplete. There is therefore a degree of construction on my part, arrived at as follows.

Table 3.9 of the *Statistical Yearbook* gives the age structure of the population in millions; I then added the floating population, allocating three quarters to the working population

Age		<17	18–59	60+
TP	14 Mh	1.5	9.5	3
Floating	4 Mh	1	3	0
Total	18 Mh	2.5	12.5	3

Assuming that the under 17s are part of their parents' households, elderly people represent between **17** and **20 per cent** of the population.

Table 3.11 based on a sample of 811,000 people of working age gives a breakdown. Managers and technicians represent **16 per cent**. Unskilled and office workers combined **49.5 per cent**. The figure for shopkeepers (**13 per cent**) is my estimate.

Chapter 3
'Transforming Mumbai' or the Challenges of Forging a Collective Actor

Marie-Hélène Zérah

Introduction

At the outset, three long-term constants that have characterised Mumbai over two centuries need to be underlined. To begin with, Mumbai is the fruit of man's action on his natural environment. This metropolis of 12.5 million inhabitants was originally no more than seven little islands inhabited by fishing communities. It was in the late eighteenth century, under British rule, that the city started flourishing. The building of the railroads and port gave a fillip to the growth of manufacturing industries (especially the textile industry) as well as trade (including the opium trade – illicit activities in the city being one constant) and encouraged the emergence of an innovative and diversified entrepreneurial class (Markovits, 1995), which turned Mumbai into India's economic capital in around a century. The proactive actions taken by the British authorities to transform (and control) the city also contributed to its rapid expansion. Throughout the nineteenth century, major public works projects were undertaken: construction of the port, major drainage and land reclamation projects aimed at merging the seven islands, the first water supply network, etc. Lastly, migrants from Maharashtra and other regions of India constituted the bulk of the labourers, turning Mumbai into both an industrious and 'cosmopolitan' city. An open city, a symbol of modernity and the melting pot of different peoples in the imagination of the elite, the city was also a place where survival strategies and confrontations between social classes, castes and religions punctuated everyday life (Hansen, 2001, Heuzé, 2007). Even today, these social and communal tensions stem from deep divides about the identity of Mumbai, which structure political life and debates to a large extent.

At a time when the Indian economy's liberalisation process was initiated, with a growth strategy based on urban centres, the 1993 Hindu-Muslim riots testified to the city's fragility – both social and economic – as it had started its transformation from an industrial society into a services-based society. It also suffered from infrastructural fragility due to chronic under-investment in major public utility networks. Transport congestion, insufficient water treatment and supply, stagnation in the power generation and distribution network and the saturation of garbage dumps affected the entire population, around half of which lived in slums

(54.5 per cent in 2001 and 41.3 in 2011 according to the census)[1]. These factors and a restrictive legislative environment weakened its competitiveness, while other cities, such as Bangalore or Hyderabad, were growing rapidly. The rhetoric (as also the reality) of the crisis was persistent, given the disastrous sanitary conditions in the nineteenth century (Klein, 1986) and helplessness in the face of post-Independence demographic growth and spatial expansion (Shaw, 1999b). To this was added the feeling of decline at the dawn of the century. In the eyes of several observers, the 2005 floods that took a toll of over 1000 lives proved that this was a metropolis that was badly governed by multiple institutions incapable of coordination and devoid of accountability toward their users. The city was ruled by a corrupt political class utterly indifferent to it and lacking a long-term vision for undertaking large-scale public action, such as those implemented by other cities in response to the following questions: what conditions were required to restore 'urban performance' while simultaneously providing support to the city's economic transition? How could the considerable problems of transportation, congestion, water supply, drainage and, more recently, the supply of electricity be resolved in an extremely volatile political and social context?

During this period of upheaval brought about by the 'crisis', deliberations were conducted on the role of the infrastructure and major urban projects as a means of reviving urban competitiveness and improving living conditions. Some quoted Singapore as a model and, more frequently, Shanghai, which though disputed by others, served as a yardstick for gauging the extent of transformation in the production and governance of urban utility networks, among other sectors (real estate and financial reforms for instance). The idea of a 'governability crisis' in an emerging metropolis like Mumbai, faced with managing a number of long-term tensions emblematic of the Indian economy's transformation, continued to be called into question: how much time did a perennially poor city need to meet its material requirements, the aspirations of the middle and well-to-do classes and the housing needs of the most deprived? How could the tensions between a tradition of direct state administration and the persistence of clientelism or crony capitalism be resolved? Lastly, how could this direct administration model be transformed into a more decentralised and less hierarchical model, given that political fragmentation and civil society protests were increasing the complexity of public arenas and public debates?

This chapter relies on surveys conducted between 2003 and 2008 on several aspects of the reform of urban services in Mumbai. The research is based on the analysis of a number of sectors (water, garbage, drainage) or urban projects so as to throw light on the following issues: i) what are the new instruments of public action (participation, delegation, public-private partnerships)? ii) To what extent do these action modalities correspond to changes in the sluggish institutional building process? If they do, then what are the new rules of the game? iii) Does the

---

1   One shall note that the decline in the slum population share observed by the Census is contested.

change in the governance of urban networks and services make the city more or less governable? This chapter also attempts to understand the unexpected effects of public policies by analysing how certain social groups have (or have not) seized hold of the means developed so as to enhance their power in a less hierarchical urban governance system. Finally, apart from questions concerning governability (is there a 'governability crisis'? what are the proper scales for governing the city?), the question that arises is that of the main orientations at the heart of the urban projects selected, in an emerging city that remains perpetually 'poor' over the long term.

A 'Poor Global City' with Complex and Competitive Metropolitan Governance

The Reality of a Global City

Between the seventeenth and nineteenth centuries, Mumbai was transformed into a modern city. A process of rapid expansion, accelerating in the late eighteenth century, started once the East India Company transferred its head office to the city (Pacione, 2006). In the nineteenth century, spectacular changes took place. The population quadrupled: from 229,000 inhabitants in 1830 to 644,000 inhabitants in 1872, and 928,000 in 1901. The economy developed swiftly, supported by major public works carried out by the British (Dossal, 1991).

The growth continued throughout the twentieth century, marked by three characteristics. Firstly, the population spread beyond the island city to the well-off, sea-facing western suburbs and the eastern suburbs along the railway tracks. In 1961, these suburbs were incorporated in the municipality that was to become the Municipal Corporation of Greater Mumbai (MCGM). The city (or Municipality) thus comprising the 'island city' (which includes the city centre) and 'suburbs' (see Figure 3.1) had around 12 million inhabitants in 2001 and 12.5 million inhabitants in 2011.[2] Mumbai is one of the most densely populated cities in the world, with more than 27,000 inhabitants per square kilometre over a surface area of 435 sq. km. Nonetheless, although the density remains very high, it must be noted that less than 25 per cent of Mumbaikars live in the island city, whose population has been stagnant since 1961 and has even declined between 2001 and 2011 (Figure 3.1). Secondly, the economic structure of the activities undertaken in the city has been evolving. The decline of the textile industry started straight

---

2   The terms MCGM or Municipal Corporation of Greater Mumbai will be used interchangeably for the city of Mumbai. The 'suburbs' therefore form part of the Mumbai municipality, but this term – corresponding to a spatial and living reality that differs from the 'centre' – will be retained. The term 'peripheries' will be employed for the metropolitan region's cities for easier reading and language. It must, however, be noted that the metropolitan region, as defined in the MMRDA's statutes, also includes 982 villages with different governance structures.

after World War II, while investments were made in sectors such as chemicals, petrochemicals and pharmaceuticals (Pacione, 2006). In 1962, the manufacturing industry accounted for 41 per cent of jobs and 50 per cent of the city's income (Harris, 1995). Ten years later, Mumbai was to host most of the corporate offices in the banking sector and held 70 per cent of bank deposits in India (Shaw, 1999a). Thirdly, urban development policies contributed to transforming the urban space, with the development of Navi Mumbai (New Bombay) across the Arabian Sea, the Bandra-Kurla institutional complex to ease traffic flow in the business centre built at the southern tip of the peninsula (Nariman Point) and, more recently, the development of an industrial zone in Andheri.

Today, Mumbai is a polynuclear metropolis. The city's weight in the metropolitan region is decreasing, although it still predominates: in 1961, the Mumbai municipality's population accounted for 90 per cent of the Mumbai region's total population, with the figure plunging to 67 per cent in 2001and below 60 per cent in 2011 (Figure 3.1).

In the 1980s, Thane and Kalyan (each with a population of more than 1 million inhabitants in 2001) witnessed a very strong growth, followed in the next decade by the corridor north of Mumbai (Vasai/ Virar) and Navi Mumbai. Economically, the 1980s were marked by a decline in industrial employment and shrinking economic activities (with a total growth in production of a mere 1.9 per cent per annum in the 1980s – Harris, 1995). In particular, the collapse of the textile industry also marked the end of a certain working-class culture (D'Monte, 2002). In this context, the peripheries benefited and small textile industries developed in the Thane-Bhiwandi areas. The changes in regional employment bear testimony to this fact. Between 1965 and 1981, employment in the districts adjacent to Mumbai (Thane and Raigad) rose swiftly. In 1986, 43 per cent of the jobs in the chemical sector were to be found in Thane and in this very city, jobs in the banking sector increased by 360 per cent between 1977 and 1987 (Harris, 1995). But this was coupled with the emergence of the informal sector – job distribution figures in the formal and the informal sectors reversed between 1961 and 1981 (65 per cent of jobs were in the formal sector between 1961, falling to 35 per cent in 1981)[3] (MMRDA, 2003). Since the early 1970s, the slow growth in formal sector employment (a mere 0.2 per cent between 1971 and 1993) can be explained by the very distinct decline in manufacturing sector jobs (47.3 per cent in 1983 and 25 per cent in 1993). Simultaneously, a rise in employment in the services sector could also be observed: 19.6 per cent in 1983 and 25 per cent in 1993; and for the financial sector, 7.6 per cent in 1983 and 11.5 per cent in 1993.

Overall, the metropolitan area corresponds to a definition of the 'city-region' given by Scott (2001, pp. 4–5) – i.e. a central metropolitan area with a hinterland of variable size, comprising less dense auxiliary developing territories, often characterised by high income inequalities and low salaries. Although not

---

3 More recent statistics should be available soon, with the publication of the latest employment surveys.

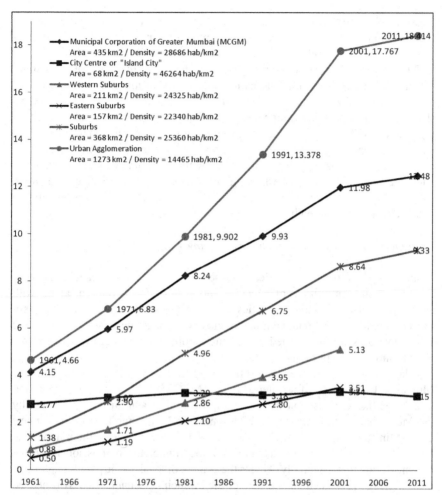

Source: Census of India (2003, 2011).

Note: The urban agglomeration's curve does not take into account the villages included in the metropolitan region.

Figure 3.1   Distribution of Mumbai's population (1961–2011) (in millions)

many figures are available on Mumbai, the rise in informal sector employment was concomitant with an increase in average per capita income, consequently suggesting rising inequalities. According to Sassen (2001), this combination of growth, increasing informal sector employment and the polarisation of inequalities constituted one of the driving forces for the consolidation of the 'global city'. Thus, although Mumbai is not a premier global city, it is rising in the hierarchy of cities. The classification established by the Globalisation and World Cities

Research Network[4] for the period 2004 to 2008, raises Mumbai from the fourth to the third rank among global cities, corresponding to cities that play an important role at the regional level. Although its GDP, estimated at around 20 billion Euros in 2003, remains modest in comparison with major international cities, it plays a strategic role in integrating its national economy in the global economy – it accounts for 4–5 per cent of India's GDP (Prud'homme, 2007). Hence, as we shall see later, supporting Mumbai's growth has implications beyond the local or regional context alone. All things being equal, it is part of a national strategy that explains the central government's mobilisation with regard to the city. The central government's actions are being implemented within the framework of a competitive and fragmented, strongly overlapping institutional and political environment, which has produced a hybrid infrastructure production and management model that needs to be presented here.

Institutional Complexity of Institutions Steering Technical Systems

Mumbai suffers from the typical problems of large cities, caught between fragmentation, a multitude of agencies and scales of intervention, along with ambivalent relations between politics and bureaucracy. It is therefore necessary to examine this institutional complexity closely, through the prism of how public utility networks are run, as the Mumbai metropolitan region's growth has led to a mushrooming of institutions.

The only administrative organisation that also has a policy jurisdiction is the Municipal Corporation of Greater Mumbai (MCGM). The municipal corporation is a Janus-like organisation as it is composed of an administration headed by the Municipal Commissioner – a high-ranking official appointed by the State's Chief Minister – and a Municipal Council that indirectly elects the mayor. The latter's powers are more limited than that of the Municipal Commissioner. It is the administration that essentially decides the content of local public policies, although the budget requires the final approval of the Municipal Council. This twin-headed system, inherited from the British, apparently from the 'Commissioner System' (Pinto, 2000), curbs the powers of the Municipal Council's elected members. The MCGM is a central player in Mumbai's governance structure. It is the largest urban local authority in India, both in terms of budget and responsibilities, and therefore investment capacities. It is in charge of public transport, health, education, water supply and treatment, as well as power supply in the island city.

At the metropolitan region's level, the other urban local self-governing bodies are less powerful. These fall under two categories: the 'Municipal Corporations' for the six largest cities and 13 'Municipal Councils' for the smaller ones. Among those under Municipal Corporations, Kalyan-Dombivili and Thane have crossed the million-inhabitant mark (1.19 and 1.26 million inhabitants respectively in 2001) and keep growing, albeit at a lower pace (1.24 and 1.8 million inhabitants

---

4   http://www.lboro.ac.uk/gawc/index.html

respectively in 2011). After Mumbai, Thane and Navi Mumbai (704,000 inhabitants in 2001 and 1.12 million inhabitants in 2011) are the ones with the most solid economic base as they host industries as well as services. The development of Navi Mumbai[5] actually started in the early 1970s. For this purpose, the public sector acquired land and then put it up for auction. Most of it is a planned city with considerable infrastructural investments, inhabited by the middle class[6]. Its development model is a complete contrast to the cities situated in northeast Mumbai, as these are dormitory cities that developed illegally and chaotically, without urban planning rules and land regulations being applied. Thus, the Vasai-Virar area is controlled by a few elected officials and landowners that control the real estate market[7], and a local party dominated by the biggest landowner in this periphery (Angueletou-Marteau, 2009).

Cities like Thane or Navi Mumbai enjoy considerable investment capacities and autonomy as they have a solid economic foundation (industries and services). Moreover, the State administration is more professional: each department is headed by a high-ranking official and includes qualified engineers. The situation is different in the 'Municipal Councils' in which the staff is largely composed of unqualified employees; these municipalities are essentially in charge of daily infrastructure maintenance and management. Investments are made and planned by the regional state ministries or para-public establishments, which often impose conditions on them. The regional State institutions thus wield considerable power.

The most important of these State institutions is the MMRDA (Mumbai Metropolitan Region Development Authority), founded in 1996 to define the development plan for the entire metropolitan region. It is an urban planning agency, reporting to the Government of Maharashtra. It acts both in the metropolitan region (financing water supply and drainage systems, along with infrastructure projects), but also, increasingly, in Mumbai. The scale of its activities has grown with its implementation of major governmental programmes, such as the Megacity Scheme for infrastructure construction. It is also the nodal agency for the majority of projects aimed at transforming the city, especially two major transport projects partially funded by the World Bank. Lastly, the MMRDA is a rich agency as it owns plots in the Bandra-Kurla complex which has become the city's second biggest

---

5   This new city was planned by CIDCO (City and Industrial Development Corporation of Maharashtra) to ease congestion in Mumbai.

6   Although some areas remain unplanned.

7   In the 1970s, a family that had grown rich through illegal activities purchased large tracts of agricultural land and turned it into urbanisable land (with the support of a certain number of elected representatives who had themselves purchased land at very low rates). While the MMRDA was to have been designated as the area's urban development agency, an agreement was signed three months before that could take place, approving the change in land use. It is estimated that between 1980 and 1990, land prices multiplied a hundred-fold and that 70 per cent of title deeds were held by one family and the network that it had built (Angueletou-Marteau, 2009).

business centre. By auctioning these plots to companies setting up their corporate offices, this public body operates as a real estate promoter and has therefore acquired working capital that enables it to finance numerous infrastructure projects. Hence, it is an extremely influential institution throughout the region. In Mumbai, it is in constant competition with the MCGM. The MMRDA, being under the direct control of the State's Chief Minister, is perceived as the government's instrument for controlling city affairs (Pinto and Pinto, 2005).

There are other direct operators that play a role in governing the city. First of all, the MSRDC (Maharashtra State Road Development Corporation) was established in 1996 to be able to borrow and then invest in the construction of highways in Maharashtra. In the course of time, its prerogatives extended to other areas and it started increasing its operations in the city of Mumbai. It built 50 flyovers and was the contracting authority for two major sea-bridge projects, the first for linking the eastern suburbs with the city centre and the second for opening a new road between Navi Mumbai (and Raigad district) and Mumbai (Table 3.2).

There are two public bodies for settlement and housing. The MHADA (Maharashtra Housing and Development Authority) is in charge of building public housing for Maharashtra as a whole, while the more recent SRA (Slum Rehabilitation Authority), established in 1995, looks after slum planning and rehabilitation. This organisation is, for instance, in charge of the ambitious programme of transforming Asia's largest slum, Dharavi[8], as well as new rehabilitation programmes implemented since the 1990s, based on market mechanisms. It is partly in charge of the rehabilitation of persons displaced by the city's infrastructure projects in cooperation with the MMRDA – involving around 136,000 families, almost 680,000 people (Modi, 2009).

Other decentralised Central government departments also operate here, such as the Maharashtra Pollution Control Board or other technical operators such as the Maharashtra Jeevan Pradhikaran[9] – which designs water supply networks for the metropolitan region's municipalities – as well as the various ministerial departments of the regional government. However, the very visible exception of the power sector in this institutional landscape must be noted, marked as it is by the strong presence of State institutions. Four operators are present in the distribution segment: a municipal board (BEST), which supplies power to Mumbai's city centre, two private companies (Reliance for the Mumbai suburbs and Tata – essentially for industrial consumers) and the Maharashtra State Electricity Distribution Company for the rest of the region. The region's main power generation players are the two private companies, Tata and Reliance, and a

---

8   The Dharavi project is the subject of much debate in Mumbai, as also internationally in development professional circles and the academic world. It will not be dealt with in this article. In a sense, Dharavi is a 'global slum', much like Rosario in Rio de Janeiro, which is the focus of much research, press articles and development activities.

9   Maharashtra Water Board.

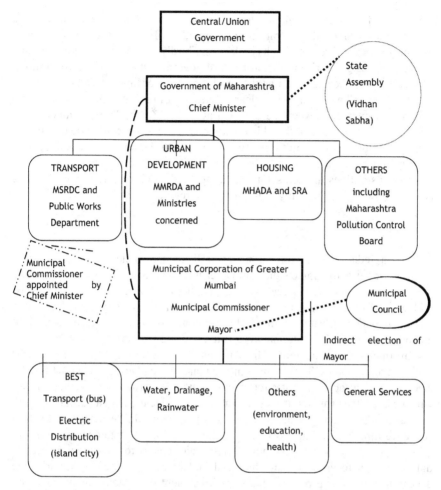

Source: Adapted from Urban Age (2007: 22)

Figure 3.2   Institutional steering structure for urban public utility networks

public sector undertaking (Mahagenco). This particular unusual configuration can be explained by the atypical history of the constitution of this sector (Zérah, 2008).

To summarise in brief the institutional landscape in the sphere of the production of major public utility networks in Mumbai, the following elements need to be borne in mind. Firstly, there is a plethora of public institutions acting at various scales and with different sources of legitimacy. The city of Mumbai and other local self-governing authorities have an elected Municipal Council, whereas the state government controls the direct operators. This situation generates strong tensions, particularly for Mumbai city, as there is no elected body (council or regional committee) for the metropolitan region. Secondly, the abundance of institutions forms part of a direct administrative model in India, which creates new institutions as time goes on to deal with fresh challenges. Thirdly, this fragmentation of public institutions has given rise to the problem of governability and of the constitution of a collective actor, more so as the resolution of coordination and cooperation problems as well as the lack of a clear delineation of responsibilities is subject to conflicts of interest between the different agencies (Zérah, 2009c). Nonetheless, this chapter would suggest that this institutional complexity cannot be interpreted merely as a problem of multi-level governance. On the contrary, it is necessary to fully understand the extent of the role of politics in metropolitan management as these institutions are tools for allocating funds and, therefore, for wielding political power in a politically highly-disputed region.

A Competitive Political Structure

India is a federal State with strong centralising tendencies. The Constitution defines three lists of subjects that fall under the ambit of the central government, the state government or shared by both. Each state has a legislative assembly, with a Chief Minister heading the state government. It was only in the late 1980s that the debate on greater autonomy for regional governments was revived. Two amendments to the Constitution were voted in 1992 for introducing a third level of governance for local rural (73rd Amendment) and urban (74th Amendment) self-governing bodies. These amendments made it mandatory to conduct regular elections and introduced quotas for women, scheduled castes and schedules tribes, which paved the way for the democratisation of local political officials. With regard to urban management, some responsibilities could be delegated to local self-governing bodies but it depends on the desire of the state concerned. More often than not, the states have not offered their support to these new municipal duties by transferring adequate financial and human resources. Similarly, the decentralisation law provides for the establishment of a Metropolitan Planning Committee (a kind of regional council), two-thirds of which was supposed to be constituted by elected members, and which was to look after urban development in metropolitan zones.

No big city, apart from Kolkata (Calcutta) had been endowed with such a Metropolitan Planning Committee, which highlights the reluctance of the states to delegate more power to locally elected officials and create a metropolitan political space. Thus, issues regarding land policy or transport policies remain the states' prerogative. The Indian federal structure is hierarchical and tensions between centralising and decentralising forces can also be seen in issues related to major public utility networks. Although Mumbai is more capable of seizing the opportunities offered in the 74th Amendment than other cities due to its size, its budget, the influence of some elected representatives, but also because of a longstanding tradition of local democracy, the power of locally elected officials remains marginal and is often exerted at an infra-local level.

The stakes involved in regional politics are thus central to understanding how the metropolitan region is steered. Regional legislative assembly elections are conducted every five years. Until the late 1980s, Maharashtra's political regime was marked by a single dominant party, along with a hegemonic Congress Party (Vora, 2009:226). This 'Congress system' (Kothari, 1964) – based on an ability to maintain a structure dominated by the Maratha caste while simultaneously ensuring a minimum level of representation of the state's social diversity – started to develop cracks in the late 1970s. In 1978, after the Emergency[10], the Congress lost the Legislative Assembly elections for the first time in Maharashtra. It resumed power in 1980 and retained it until 1995. But the process of the fragmentation and polarisation of political arenas was the order of the day, with the split in the Congress in 1999 on one hand, and the emergence of the regionalist, xenophobic party, the Shiv Sena, on the other, with the latter resorting to violence as a means of action and winning the 1995 elections along with the BJP (Bharatiya Janata Party) – the Hindu right-wing national party.

According to Vora (2009: 226), Maharashtra had entered a phase that resembled a bipartite system and an era of competition between 'the Congress and Hindutva' (the Congress being allied to the National Congress Party and the Shiv Sena being allied to the Bharatiya Janta Party or BJP). The recent elections depict an increasingly fragmented state with the emergence of small parties[11] unwilling to enter the pre-poll alliance game, preferring to play kingmakers after poll results are declared.

The municipal elections, too, are held every five years. They are less important and the voter turnout rate is much lower (below 50 per cent), but assuming power in major cities makes it possible to wield a certain counter-power and gain access to certain resources. The Thane and Mumbai municipalities are Shiv Sena bastions. In Mumbai, the coalition led by the Shiv Sena has also dominated the Municipal Council since 1992. Since the Municipal Commissioner is appointed by the State's Chief Minister and the MMRDA is controlled by the local government, held by a Congress-NCP majority (Table 3.1), the conflicts between the administration and local representatives, and the coordination problems between the municipality and para-public establishments should be viewed in the context of this political rivalry. Hence, Mumbai is an arena of political competition for the State. As will be seen hereafter, the 'Vision Mumbai' reform programme is one of its components.

Nonetheless, despite the surplus (or hyper-expansion) of politics, formulating urban policies does not dominate the political agenda. The functioning of the Indian

---

10   Between 1975 and 1977, the prime minister of India, Indira Gandhi, imposed a state of emergency where she could rule by decree and suspended elections and civil liberties. This period is seen as one of the darkest moments for Indian democracy since the independence.

11   The Maharashtra Navnirman Sena, in particular, which broke away from the Shiv Sena despite its strong ideological closeness, leading to the splitting of the 'Marathi' vote during the previous elections and paving the way for the re-election of a Congress-led coalition.

democracy is based on a regulatory mode that is at the same time competitive, accommodates diversity and is respectful of pluralism. One of its consequences is the sidelining of the public interest and the competition for access to the resources by various interest groups (based on community, caste, regional belonging, etc.). Political success largely depends on the ability to reconcile conflicting interests without ignoring pluralism and debate (Jaffrelot, 1998). In concrete terms, in Mumbai, the challenges related to the city's identity (a Maharashtrian city versus a cosmopolitan city) and the attitude towards migrants from the states of Uttar Pradesh and Bihar (some advocate a policy of 'regional preference' or respect for Marathi culture) occupy the centre stage in politics. Let us take an example that directly concerns the metropolitan region's future. Some economists and corporate decision-makers had postulated the idea of turning Mumbai into a State, so that the city could perform better (and no longer be used to finance the rest of Maharashtra). This argument is a non-starter – not on grounds of regional solidarity, but because the current boundaries of the state of Maharashtra were carved out of a fierce struggle during the re-delimitation of states, based on language, by a particularly powerful social movement in Mumbai.

Table 3.1   Parties dominating the Municipality and the State in 1997–2013

	Municipality	State Government
From 1990 to 1992	Shiv Sena	Congress Party
From 1993 to 1995	Congress Party	Congress Party
From 1995 to 1997	Congress Party	Shiv Sena – BJP Coalition
From 1997 to 1999	Shiv Sena – BJP	Shiv Sena – BJP Coalition
From 1999 to 2013	Shiv Sena – BJP	Congress – Nationalist Congress Party

Hence, the economic challenges involved in Mumbai's transformation remain technical issues that have been ignored in political debates; but that is due to change. Demographic changes are resulting in an increase in the weight of urban constituencies during regional elections. With the new delimitations for the 2009 elections, 60 of the 288 seats for Members of the Legislative Assembly (MLAs) now fall under the metropolitan region. In the more or less long term, this transformation of the body politic will certainly impact on the perception of Mumbai's role. Moreover, the Union government level cannot be ignored. In fact, in the central government's view, cities are the driving force for India's growth; it has therefore set up a new urban development programme called JNNURM (Jawaharlal Nehru National Urban Renewal Mission), which aims to fund major investments, especially in infrastructure. It will enable cities to avail of the most substantial funding since Independence for urban infrastructure, but it all goes hand in hand with incentives and conditions for reforms to be undertaken based on several guiding principles: introduction of the private sector, intensifying the decentralisation process and real estate market reforms. To a certain extent, this paradoxically appears to herald the return of the Central State in formulating urban policies. It marks a radical change in the perception of the role that India's major cities play in economic growth (Kennedy and Zérah, 2008). In keeping with this logic, Mumbai has been one of the chief recipients of JNNURM funds. The central government wishes to encourage the upgrading of the city and earnestly wants the World Bank's involvement to support reforms. In this fragmented and volatile political landscape, the aim would be to somehow create incentives for the physical transformation of India's economic capital. This ambitious policy, which provides considerable investments, on the flip side also delivers a relatively negative statement on the direct administration model that has prevailed for the provision of urban services and on which it will be necessary to dwell later.

A City in Perpetual 'Crisis'

An acknowledged infrastructure 'crisis'

The aim here is not to proceed to a detailed analysis of all the sectors, but to put the condition of infrastructure in Mumbai in perspective, along with a series of explanations that would help understand why so many urban problems remain to be solved which provides fodder for so much 'crisis' oriented rhetoric.

First of all, although Mumbai boasts of the highest per capita income among all Indian cities, 45 per cent of the metropolitan region's inhabitants live in slums (MMRDA and LEA, 2007), with the figure rising to 55–60 per cent for the Mumbai municipality[12]. There is a disastrous scarcity of housing. While on an average, 35 per cent of households live in one room in urban India, in Mumbai the figure is 64 per cent, the space per inhabitant being estimated at 2.9 square metres (Bertaud, 2004). This low figure should be seen in conjunction with the some of the steepest real estate prices in the world, be it the real estate buyer's market or rented property, or the commercial or residential segment.

Along with the housing issue, transport is the second major challenge for the metropolis. Public transport occupies a very important place, with a network of trains and public buses totalling 88 per cent of the 11–12 million daily rides.[13] Nonetheless, here too, Mumbai assumes the status of a world record-making city: the 'maximum city'.[14] Rush hours last four hours (morning and evening), double the 'international norms', and trains carry 2.7 times more passengers than their capacity. The situation is even more critical as predictions foresee an extremely sharp rise in trips (which have already grown from 7 million in 1975 to 15 million in 2001). Part of this growth is due to the increase in the number of

---

12   The latest number provided by the 2011 Census is 41.3%.

13   Daily, 6.5 to 7 million passengers take the train and 4.5 to 5 million use the bus network.

14   Reference to Suketu Mehta's *Maximum City*.

individual vehicles, although the congestion level is already very high. It is not unusual to spend two hours to travel the 35 kilometres that link the city centre to the international airport. It is likely that the saturation point will soon be reached which explains the wave of large-scale programmes in this field (Table 3.2). The figures on investment requirements in this sector vary from one source to another, but the metropolitan region's Business Plan estimated that 26.5 billion Euros needed to be invested between 2005 and 2011 for executing these projects (MMRDA and LEA, 2007). The MMRDA has planned a series of projects (new metro lines, two monorail lines, etc.) by 2031, which would call for investments of almost 300 billion Euros.

For other urban services, the situation is barely more satisfactory. Water supply is intermittent (five hours per day, according to the World Bank) and a large part of the population is not connected to the municipal water supply network. It is estimated that just 56 per cent of Mumbai's households have access to toilets linked to the main sewage system (World Bank, 2006). The situation is often grimmer – not only in the suburbs, where there are more slums, but also in the peripheries. In the Vasai-Virar area, Angueletou (2009, Chapter 6) has revealed the existence of a water mafia controlled by a local potentate, who has founded his own political party and controls water resources and access. This kind of control has been possible due to the porosity between private and public interests: thus, the president of the water tankers association (which supplies water to many inhabitants) is also a locally elected leader. Numerous studies and reports have underlined the variable access to supplies, depending on economic status and land ownership status, and the average consumption is estimated at 90 litres/hour/day or half the standard consumption rate (Shaban and Sharma, 2007). These figures reveal the inability to include poor and peri-urban populations in a hypothetically universal service.

The drainage and wastewater evacuation network is quite inadequate. For the five municipal corporations, the network provides services to only 54 per cent of the city in Mumbai, 17 per cent in Thane, 57 per cent in Navi Mumbai, 25 per cent in Kalyan-Dombivli, and 70 per cent in Ulhas Nagar and Ambernath. The other urban local self-governing bodies have no drainage network and there is no mention of wastewater management here (MMRDA and LEA, 2007, pp. 4–12). The Mumbai storm drain network is 70 years old. It is dilapidated and only covers the 'island city'. The others cities of the region, except for Navi Mumbai, have no effective network for draining rainwater, although the entire region, as the 2005 floods revealed, is extremely vulnerable to flooding when it receives exceptionally high rainfall during the monsoons.

The garbage collection department does not offer a better picture. In Mumbai, it is estimated that 73 per cent of household waste is sent to garbage dumps, which are themselves saturated, while discussions on new sites for dumping garbage are deadlocked. Lastly, those who live in Mumbai's residential areas generally do not have to face power cuts, but the overhead wire network is highly insecure in slum areas. In peri-urban zones, power cuts are a regular phenomenon, especially in summer, and the power generation deficit has been growing over the past few years, necessitating substantial investments in the relative short term.

Some explanations

The recurrent use of the term 'crisis' ultimately seems unsuited for a situation that has lasted a long time and will continue to prevail in the long term. The very real difficulty of implementing urban services expansion programmes cannot be brushed aside when settlements spring up before infrastructure can be built. Nonetheless, such an explanation is insufficient, particularly given that India has been experiencing relatively sustained growth for over ten years, which could have made it possible to upgrade urban infrastructure more quickly. Hence explanations have to be found elsewhere. These can be found in the fact that the direct administration model characteristic of infrastructure production and management all over India seems to have run out of steam and is marred by many limitations and even marginality, and also in the fact that local specificities make Mumbai a particularly difficult city to administer.

The ideal way of providing public services should be based on a universal service produced and controlled by a 'Weberian' kind of bureaucracy. Such an administration would be composed of high-level Indian Administrative Service officials at its helm along with technical bodies, essentially consisting of engineers. Official policies aim at expanding services by using cross-subsidy policies between types of use and user categories and by setting up special arrangements for slum-dwellers (shared connections). Regarding water for instance, 80 per cent of the income comes from industry which account for only 20 per cent of the total consumption. Thus, domestic rates are very low but have historically favoured the middle class which is already connected to the network, to the detriment of un-connected users. For the latter, supply is provided through shared connections, which are charged at low rates, but can create distortions[15] and do not preclude recourse to extremely expensive alternative supply strategies. These policies continue to be conceived on the basis of a technicist approach to needs as this involves merely a mechanical increase of networked services depending on the average estimated demand. However, this model has not led to the universalisation of services and access to services has become fragmented (Zérah, 2008).

Chronic under-investment provides only a partial explanation for this situation. A report submitted in 1993 on the storm drain network, for instance, was shelved due to lack of funding at a time when municipal finances were in a precarious state. The report was taken out of cold storage following the 2005 floods and serves as the

---

15   One of the first known distortions, mentioned in the related literature, concerns large user groups. Collective consumption being high, the lowest rate (for the lowest social strata) no longer applies and the unit price for water can be relatively high. Another distortion is the unequal sharing of bills between group members. Thus, Steinweg (2006) reveals that tenants are often forced to pay the total amount of the water bills of the shared connections to which they have access.

base of the BRIMSTOWAD programme (Table 3.2), underlining a mode of public action subject to the hazards of crises. This bears out the analysis of municipal budgets by Pethe and Lalvani (2006), which shows that the Mumbai municipality has a limited capacity for absorbing funds and under-invests despite the availability of resources. The authors also highlight the extremely low investment in slums, although these are the most deprived in terms of urban services.

Part of the explanation can be found in the complex connection between the provision of services and land tenure. Depending on the status of the land concerned, it is legally more or less possible to provide urban services. One main criterion distinguishes 'notified' slums (approximately 85 per cent) from those that are not: the latter cannot benefit from urban services and are usually located on public land belonging to the central government, the port authorities or the railways, or else certain private owners. For the others (48 per cent on private land, 21 per cent on state government land and 17 per cent on municipal land), the procedure for access to services differs. The owners (religious foundations, trusts or individuals) have to grant their permission for services to be extended, which is not the case for public land (WSP-South Asia, 2006). This situation therefore provides part of the explanation for the widely varying levels of services, depending on the particular slum, and raises the need for going beyond a simple analysis in terms of dual services that would reflect the legal or illegal status of neighbourhoods (coupled also with a perception of who is a 'citizen' or 'non-citizen' of the city).

In fact, there is not just a binary vision of the provision of services (access/non-access; formal/informal; legal/illegal) – there is actually a complex, mosaic-like gradation of services (Sharma, 1999, Zérah, 2008), more so since the importance of local political practices and the real role of elected representatives must be taken into account. The latter pressurise the administration to allocate urban services or finance certain infrastructure from the discretionary funds allotted to them.[16] With respect to a neighbourhood to the northeast of the city, De Bercegol and Desfeux (2007) have mapped out the variety of ways in which water is supplied, depending on the inhabitant's access to and bargaining capacity with the elected representatives and political parties present, as well as the informal mechanisms jointly produced by the lower echelons of the administration, elected representatives and inhabitants. Some condemn this nexus as clientelism and a paternalistic means of service delivery, but as suggested by some other authors, elected representatives play a crucial role as mediators for the majority of the people in their efforts to gain access to services (Benjamin, 2004). In this sense, they organise a vernacular form of access to services, based on a special relationship with certain groups – the reverse of a Weberian Universalist bureaucracy, but with a very colonial mode of operation, unconcerned about managing the diversity of Indian society.

---

16 Local elected representatives and Members of Parliament are allotted a yearly individual budget that they can use for development projects in their electoral constituency.

As far as public transport and housing is concerned, the peninsula offers very specific physical constraints. Moreover, in the 1970s, the construction of a business hub in Nariman Point, at the city's southern extremity close to the historic city centre, led to North-South flows that greatly restricted the transportation network. Mumbai is a strip of land measuring 63 km in length on which very little land is available. The strict limitations on making land available have been strengthened by extremely restrictive regulations. The first is the Floor Space Index (FSI) ceiling at 1.33. According to Bertaud, this has been decreasing since the 1980s, unlike the trend in all other coastal towns, particularly Shanghai. Added to this restriction is the Coastal Regulation Zone Act prohibiting construction on land that is less than 200 metres from the high tide line. Thirdly, the Urban Land Ceiling Regulation Act (ULCRA) of 1976 defining the ceiling on the sale of urbanisable lands has turned into a tool that has led to scarcity. The public sector has infrequently taken recourse to one of the elements of the legislation that allows the requisitioning of land for building public housing which has led to a freeze on land and proved to be yet another obstacle for the housing sector. The rapid (and chaotic) growth in the Vasai-Virar area in the 1970s can be explained by the fact that the ULCRA did not apply to the area. Fourthly, the Rent Control Act, which essentially concerns buildings in the city centre, has given rise to considerable distortions. By maintaining low rents, it has led to the blurring of property rights between landlords and tenants, leading to disincentives for renovating buildings. Many of these are dilapidated and even dangerous.

While this legislative arsenal has ensured the maintenance of genuine socio-economic diversity in the city-centre, the construction of public housing is far below what is needed. Real estate promoters and reformers, as will be seen later, have mobilised themselves against these laws restricting access to real estate. In practice, exemptions are possible, whether for increasing the FSI or de-notifying the use of a particular land. However, many of these exemptions are obtained through underhand means and covert arrangements between political leaders and promoters, approved by the administration, which once again reflects how flexible the norms are.

In conclusion, the direct administration model for the provision of services, based on norms (user needs, urban planning rules, etc.), and the public production of infrastructure is peppered with complex, more or less lawful, *ad hoc* arrangements. The collusion of interests, informal mechanisms, the role of brokers and touts in the various districts, pressure from elected representatives, bargaining and the capacity of local mobilisation of users change the rules of the game as well as procedures that have apparently been clearly enunciated. In addition, services are 'piloted' or steered along a parallel route via the budgets allocated to locally elected representatives and parliamentarians, as well as the clientelism or crony capitalism that characterise the political model of redistribution according to interest groups.

This is a complex mode of infrastructure production and management – one that is chaotic and varies greatly depending on the localities, while relying on a 'porous bureaucracy' (Benjamin, 2004). This gap between a macro vision of the city, seen in the context of the multitude and complexity of local arrangements and their relation to the political sphere would, on the face of it, convey the (false) image of a schizophrenic city. The infrastructure production model is not one of direct administration – although that is the model available to the inhabitants of residential districts (perceived as legal inhabitants and subject to local taxation) – but a hybrid model, shaped by daily local practices through which inhabitants whose rights are less well established negotiate minimal access to basic services. These two models coexist and are permeable at their borders; and while public action has been in the process of being reshaped since the early 1990s, one can only wonder about the unexpected effects of new policies. In fact, new paradigms of public action have been implemented at different speeds, depending on the sectors. As we shall discuss below, they are partly influenced by the recommendations made by international organisations and development professionals, hurriedly labelled as 'good governance'. Nonetheless, for a better understanding of the results and practices in Mumbai's case, the long detour via the ideal model and its hybrid reality appears necessary so as to study the way in which public policies are recast, by comparing the reality with the manner in which they were conceived.

New Paradigms of Public Action: A Slow and Disorganised Transformation?

New practices were grafted on to the 'direct administration model'. These cannot be called brutal or consensual reforms, particularly in the infrastructure sector and in terms of urban policies. It has more to do with the slow transformation of institutions, mechanisms for providing services and practices. Nevertheless, over two decades, the way in which infrastructure was conceived, produced and managed has changed and has led to a transformation in the way collective action is conducted in the city. The rising power of certain civil society actors and the mercantile world, which aspire to a certain form of urban modernity and quality infrastructure, has been coupled with the influence of the 'good governance' norms propounded by the World Bank which exerts a strong influence in Mumbai. The physical transformation of the city far outstrips the level of services provided, which needs to catch up significantly. Thus, these transformations cannot simply be analysed merely in the light of the growth of the supply of urban services. They have also reconfigured power equations in the city and engendered processes of restructuring space that lend themselves better to fragmentation.

The Private Sector's Place in Infrastructure Management

The private sector's role in managing urban services must be distinguished from public-private partnerships for building housing and new greenfield infrastructure projects.

Sub-contracting local public services

The Mumbai municipality's endeavours to delegate certain tasks to operators in the sectors of water, sanitation and solid waste management are far from being an unqualified success. As far as the sanitation and garbage disposal sector is concerned, the term 'privatisation' is used to describe the recourse to small local firms for collecting household garbage. In a certain sense, the term is a misuse of language. 'Privatisation', or even 'delegation' is, above all, aimed at conforming to a discourse on governance, whereas in reality, as shown by Hibou through examples from Africa (Hibou, 2006), it perpetuates a clientelist system of awarding public works contracts that has already been in force for decades. In the three wards in which the author conducted in-depth studies, the following aspects came to light. The recourse to the private sector consists of allotting sub-contracts to small private companies from the informal sector. In reality, it is a way of dealing with the freeze on staff recruitment in the public sector and the urgent need to extend services to the suburbs. The task of granting contracts was devolved to the sub-divisional level in order to facilitate management, simplify payment procedures and initiate a process of administrative decentralisation. What, then, have been the effects of this policy?

To a certain extent, an improvement in services has been observed, especially on certain routes where no form of garbage, waste and debris collection had existed previously. Nonetheless, there is insufficient monitoring and control of small companies. Moreover, administrative devolution, necessary given the size of the city, entails payment delays, which place new entrants in the public contracts market at a disadvantage. For others, devolution consolidates the proximity or even the collusion of interests between municipal employees, entrepreneurs and local elected representatives. Many of these small companies are locally-based fronts or the last link of a chain of companies that finally form an oligarchic structure of public works companies[17]. Hence, relationship channels and links between the formal and informal sectors, the political and the public, are structured at a level that might be described as infra-local. Incomes, resources and power circulate and are redistributed partially via public policies that ostensibly comply with international norms for transforming the public sector, but are actually locally re-appropriated and transformed. This chapter will deal with this issue later, with reference to participatory programmes, since in certain localities, private garbage collection and sanitation companies are also active in slums as 'community organisations'.

Lastly, sub-contracting does not help transform the service provision mechanism. It is not an efficient economic tool in the form that it is practised – the contracts fix the sum of equipment and labour costs for specified tasks and calculate a fixed

---

17 This information is obviously difficult to prove. Nonetheless, the qualitative interviews conducted at small companies clearly reveal evidence of tie-ups between the various owners of these small companies that trade contracts and favours. Other discussions with Mumbai-based researchers or actors appear to confirm the oligopoly of some companies with regard to profitable public contracts in the field of public works.

profit margin. There is no incentive for innovation, the improvement of working conditions or the use of more modern equipment. Ultimately, these companies maximise their profits by reducing salary overheads, which translates into informal employment and extremely tough working conditions (Zérah, 2009a).[18] The thinking on how innovative contracts could be drawn up would still appear to be at a limited stage. Within the framework of the programme for building toilets in slums – a module imposed by the World Bank as part of a vast project for the improvement of sanitation – contracts have been executed with an NGO and two private companies. The results of research on this programme (Yannic, 2003), which have been discussed elsewhere (Zérah, 2008), emphasise that the approach is, ultimately, one that remains quite typical of construction contracts. There is no motivation for companies to work in localities that are geographically difficult to access or demand longer investments in terms of communication and participation. All this leads to a form of 'spatial selectiveness'. Companies therefore prefer to work in localities they are familiar with and where they have full command over local governance issues.

When the municipality wants to develop a different form of engagement with the private sector, conceived as a strategy relying on management or concession contracts with companies capable of investing, the questions that arise are of a completely different nature. This kind of approach, which is much more in line with the reforms undertaken in many other countries, triggers strong resistance. This occurred in the water distribution sector, managed by the municipal board, which the administration wished to delegate to a private operator on two occasions in the past ten years. On the first occasion, the difference in investment estimates between the municipal board and the potential companies was so great that the call for tenders was not published at all. In 2004, the project was revived. An aid fund for poor or emerging countries[19] (PPIAF) agreed to finance a consultant whose mandate was to conduct a precise audit of the network and make technical and institutional recommendations for supplying water 24 hours a day in a ward of approximately one million inhabitants. But the project was immediately viewed as a Trojan horse for 'privatisation', and NGOs, Residents' Welfare Associations and community associations as well as RTI[20] activists rose up against it. This coalition

---

18   Garbage collectors most often work with bare hands, wear simple sandals and do not have suitable work uniforms. The situation is not much different in the public sector. It must be briefly recalled here that in the hierarchical system of Indian society's organisation into castes, these tasks are assigned to the lowest castes and the sanitation sector in India is organised on this basis.

19   The Public-Private Infrastructure Advisory Facility (PPIAF) is a fund created in 2000 at the initiative of the United Kingdom and Japan with the support of other industrialised countries and the World Bank. It supports studies and training and contributes to defining methods for better cooperation between the public sector and private companies for infrastructure management.

20   The 2005 Right to Information Act grants every citizen the right to ask for access to government administrative and institutional files.

secretly obtained a great deal of information through certain municipal engineers who were opposed to the project (Bawa, 2009). The consultations presenting the project, which were open to the public, sometimes turned violent. Finally, the municipality accepted the report's technical conclusions, but the institutional recommendations, which favoured a management contract, turned into a subject for internal debate. The local elected representative opposed them, but the administration nonetheless floated a call for tenders. This kind of constant friction between elected representatives and high officials gave rise to an atmosphere of defiance and the companies became apprehensive as they expected the project to be withdrawn or obstructed.

This example partially explains the limited commitment of the major operators in the urban services sector in India. The existing contracts are essentially service contracts (Navi Mumbai, Kalyan) for billing or taking metre readings. Partnerships for service management that call on major operators (national or international) ready to invest financially have remained marginal. The municipal authorities have turned mostly to small local operators, who maintain and reinforce local clientelist networks and allow public responsibilities to be delegated at a lower cost. But it is true that these networks are also a source of employment (though in conditions worse than those prevailing in the public sector) and an integral part of the informal economy at an infra-local level.

PPPs for new infrastructure: on the difficulty of building a market
Several major projects requiring considerable investment are being executed or planned in the form of public-private partnerships (PPP). The PPP model, whether for airport modernisation or metro projects, is now being encouraged by the central government. As there are several such projects, this chapter will examine two bridge construction projects more closely as they will help illustrate the varied challenges involved in public-private partnerships and the place of large projects in the city.

The two toll bridges[21] that will be presented stemmed from the desire to restructure the metropolitan transportation system. The Bandra-Worli Sea Link (BWSL), by opening up a new route, was aimed at unclogging a feeder between the southern area of the city and its western suburbs; it is a typical case of a classic construction contract. The Mumbai Trans-Harbour Link (MTHL) between Mumbai and Navi Mumbai helps make the connection between the two cities more fluid and make a district more accessible; it was originally supposed to be a BOT (Build, Operate and Transfer contract).

The Bandra-Worli Sea Link, or the classic problems of infrastructure projects
The bridge between Bandra and Worli was proposed as early as 1962 during the first regional development plan. Out of the eight lanes planned, four were finally opened in July 2009 and the last four in March 2010, ten years after the

---

21   The option of a parallel railroad for improving public transport options was abandoned in the case of MTHL.

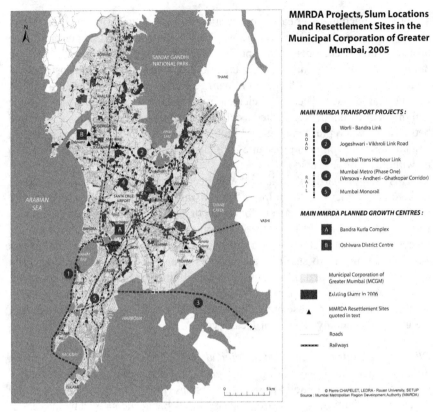

Figure 3.3   Map situating Mumbai Metropolitan Region Development Authority Transport Projects

official launch of the project. If one follows Prud'homme's (2005) categorisation, which defines four kinds of possible errors in infrastructure projects, the BWSL is a textbook case. Firstly, any big project is 'by nature' an evolving one (fresh assessment of needs, security and environmental restrictions, etc.) and ultimately deviates from the initial project. This 'substantive error' was coupled with a second problem – that of technical errors due to unforeseen circumstances. In BSWL's case, the two were combined. To preserve the navigable channel used by fishermen, the bridge's alignment and type of suspension had to be revised. This change necessitated importing expensive equipment from China, leading to cost escalation and a protracted dispute between the road development corporation and the project manager. In 2007, the latter halted work and demanded that the contract value be revised. It took several months for negotiations to be resumed and concluded successfully, following which construction was completed. In the end, the project costs soared from 67 million Euros to more than 275 million Euros (Leboucher, 2008), while toll tax collections are currently below estimates.

Thirdly, the economic errors that Prud'homme attributes to the general economic climate (cost escalation, errors in traffic flow estimates, etc.) cannot be explained away here by the downtrend in the economic context. In reality, the reasons for the massive jump in project costs and the distorted cost-benefit analysis can be found in the fourth kind of error, dysfunctional institutions.

Typically, public authorities overestimate benefits and underestimate costs, and companies anticipate the possibility of obtaining additional subsidies. The practice of floating invitations to tender is systematically used in India, but since procedures are often vitiated, the system adds to this distortion. Further, due to the complex relations between elected representatives and high-ranking officials, the latter underestimate costs to persuade political decision makers of the viability of the projects they envisage. On the other hand, companies turn opportunistic when they perceive a State to be weak and open to renegotiations, or with which they enjoy close relations. Added to this are delays due to the project approval structure, particularly environmental clearances, many of which have to be obtained from the central government.

In this case, as it took a long time to obtain the approvals and the construction of the bridge did not comply with the project's environmental norms, it could be considered an illegal structure, which added ammunition to the project's opponents' fire, and they took judicial and political recourse. As the fourth part of this article will show, the groups hostile to this project also contributed to extending the delays by blocking the construction of the bridge. This emphasises the difficulty the authorities face in building a stable and solid consensus on concrete projects as this bridge would take 47 years to be built!

The MTHL: lack of public control or corporate opportunism?
The failure of the MTHL, i.e. a PPP for the motorway bridge that was supposed to link southern Mumbai to Navi Mumbai, leads to questions about the relative absence of urban firms and the slow development of the infrastructure market. But before drawing any general conclusions, it would be necessary to review the details and background of the project.

The trigger was the saturation of the two existing links between Mumbai and its new city. The city of Navi Mumbai was growing fast and Raigad district, which already had an industrial zone, was to host Special Economic Zones (SEZ), the new international airport and new container terminals. This top priority, a 22-kilometre six-lane link, would have a long-term impact on the city's physical aspects. As in the case of the bridge discussed earlier (BWSL), this project too had been dragged from one report to another since 1962. It was extremely costly (1.3 billion Euros according to the 2004 estimates), required numerous environmental clearances and posed security hazards[22]. Consequently, it was only in the early 2000s that the project was officially announced. In 2004, a call for tenders was floated, to which six consortiums applied. Three of these were selected in July 2006 but only one

---

22   It passed close to the Bhabha Atomic Research Centre.

submitted a financial bid in February 2007. One of the consortiums eliminated in the first phase, led by Reliance Energy Limited (REL), filed a lawsuit in the Supreme Court. After a year of legal procedures during which the project came to a standstill, the Supreme Court ordered the Roads Development Corporation (MSRDC), the project's contracting authority, to re-include the consortium. The MSRDC had to float a fresh tender, which put four consortiums in the fray, including REL, headed by Anil Ambani, and the SKIL consortium, led by his elder brother, Mukesh Ambani. After all these twists and turns, the only consortiums to tender were the two headed by these two feuding brothers.

Reflecting the chaotic processes being described, a second detour through the history of an industry and a business family becomes necessary. The Reliance group, founded by the patriarch, Dhirubhai Ambani, had become the largest industrial conglomerate in India within a few years, with diversified interests: petrochemicals, metallurgy, telecommunications and power generation. After his demise, the war of succession to his industrial empire pitted his two sons against each other and the company was divided (Srinivas, 2005). A legal agreement distributed the different subsidiaries and defined non-competition clauses for certain sectors. Despite this, the two groups found themselves competing against each other for Mumbai's first metro line and this motorway bridge project.

With regard to the financial tender, the REL consortium proposed a concession period of seven years whereas the MSRDC projections estimated a return on investment at 25 years. On the other hand, the elder brother, Mukesh Ambani, who had acquired agricultural land in Raigad for building a SEZ and would directly benefit from the added value to the land once the bridge was built, made an equally unrealistic bid through SKIL, with a return on investment of over 75 years. REL's extremely low bid reflected Anil Ambani's determination to prevent the other consortium from winning the contract, at any price whatsoever. Moreover, the clash between the brothers was also accompanied by political rivalry. Anil Ambani cultivated relations with the Samajwadi Party,[23] contrary to Mukesh Ambani, who was extremely close to the Congress Party in Maharashtra and its Chief Minister. This proximity had led him to nurture the belief that the contract was his for the taking. But, given the vast differences and unrealistic bids, the Maharashtra government was obliged to cancel the bids and revert to the classic solution of public financing. This case certainly raises a number of questions with regard to the definition of public interest, when public authorities have been the victims and instruments of a fratricidal war between two industrial groups and two brothers who are also members of the Indian establishment.[24] The project cost estimates

23   He was elected to the Upper House of the National Assembly with the support of this party. The Samajwadi Party is a political party of socialist inspiration, mainly based in Uttar Pradesh. Its electorate is essentially composed of Other Backward Classes and Muslims.

24   This is not anecdotal. Recently, this fight assumed national proportions as Anil Ambani, battling out his elder brother on the purchase price of natural gas distributed by

have trebled since 2004 and from a Build Operate Transfer contract, it has turned into a Design Build Transfer contract, using solely public financing. Although these specific cases mainly highlight the particularly harmful collusion of interests between the industrial elite and the political world, one can also see how long public authorities take to develop the capacity to steer PPPs. Political arbitrariness combined with low skills in managing shortcomings and complexities result in the intervention of the courts, which act as decision makers whose decisions cannot be questioned. While the public sector did have some cards up its sleeve for negotiating a favourable contract, given the economic repercussions for the Raigad district, private groups have mostly shown how opportunistic they can be. Can this be explained by the absence of major urban firms or what Dominique Lorrain terms 'urban capitalism'? Projects involving firms in the construction and public works sector usually make it through the rough patches and the projects are executed, whereas those based on shared responsibility and financing do not seem to reach the expected conclusion without substantial financial support from the State. In terms of Lorrain's terminology, the two Reliance groups (one of which has won the first metro line contract) are at the peripheries of urban capitalism. These companies have little inclination towards urban projects and are only interested when the economic climate and public policies are in their favour (Lorrain, 2002: 18). The high commercial risks with regard to land acquisition or the right of way for metro projects add another constraint.

Ultimately, the Road Development Corporation (MSRDC) decided to build the bridge by itself (at a higher cost), but the urban development authority (MMRDA), which reports directly to the Ministry of Urban Development (ministerial portfolio held by the Chief Minister), by advancing the argument of the MSRDC's failures and fortified by its political support, won the right to build the bridge after several months of conflict and competition between public establishments, thus recalling the distortions possible in terms of the optimal allocation of resources in cases where elected representatives enjoyed high discretionary powers. Thus, even as industrialists appear to be investing in a project for Mumbai's transformation, as will be shown below, their actions would seem to be primarily directed towards real estate transactions and lobbying for increasing the regional government's investments. The development of a solid and stable form of even an 'Indianised' urban capitalism does not seem to be making any progress (or not quickly enough), although the JNNURM does seem to be supporting such a programme. The projects conducted and financed by the public sector, although subject to the typical delays, a lack of transparency and recourse to uncontrolled sub-contracting, seem to have a better track record in terms of reaching completion. Such is the case of the disputed but executed construction of 50 flyovers by the MSRDC.

Mukesh Ambani, directly accused the Minister of Petroleum and Natural Gas of furthering the interests of the elder Ambani. Due to this clash, the Minister of the Economy was compelled to intervene and numerous commentators expressed their outrage in the press at witnessing national interests being held hostage to a dispute between two industrial groups.

PPPs for the construction industry

In 1991, subsequent to innovations initiated a decade earlier, housing policies relied on new principles and the strengthening of market mechanisms. The challenge lay in building apartments, especially for reducing the percentage of the slum population. The tragic housing scarcity in Mumbai shows that it is partially incorrect to equate slums with poverty, here more than in any other city. The policy initiated therefore consisted of depending on public-private partnerships by increasing the floor space index (FSI) if a developer was selected to build housing instead and in the place of a slum. It was believed that placing additional square metres on the market – generated by hiking the FSI – would help subsidise housing for slum-dwellers. In this case, the developers' profits were limited to 25 per cent. In the final analysis, this programme has not really proved to be a success. In fact, the main change occurred in 1995 when the Shiv Sena-BJP coalition came to power after having campaigned partly on the theme of '800,000 free houses for the poor'. The principles of the previous policy were retained, but the ceiling on profit margins was done away with, the FSI raised and a part of the additional buildable square metres could be converted into the 'Transfer of Development Right' (TDR) – all this, only to encourage private developers. In exchange, the developers were to build apartments free of cost for the selected slum households and contribute to setting up a working capital to pay for the maintenance of the buildings. To support this policy, the SRA (Slum Rehabilitation Authority) was founded in 1995 and the new programme was christened the 'Slum Rehabilitation Scheme'. The main aspect of this policy was the creation of TDRs or Transfers of Development Rights, Mumbai being the pioneering city in this regard, with the policy being pursued by the Congress-Nationalist Congress Party government post-1995.

What does the TDR policy imply? Firstly, TDRs replaced the process of land acquisition by the public sector. In the beginning, a compensation mechanism had to be found for indemnifying the owners whose lands were required for the construction of urban services (schools, dispensaries, street widening), for the construction of which the municipality was unable to offer financial compensation. In such cases, the owner was compensated by the TDR, which stands for the right to build on a piece of land different from the land acquired, and in an area beyond the 'island city'. This principle, inspired by a policy implemented in the United States for preserving natural spaces and agricultural land threatened by urban expansion, delinks land from the use it is put to. Secondly, through this mechanism, the authorities believed that the 'island city' could be unclogged, as TDRs could not be used in the city centre. With effect from 1997, the policy was extended to slum rehabilitation programmes *in situ*, under the label 'Slum TDR', and later to six programmes on the rehabilitation of persons displaced by infrastructure projects.[25] These 'Slum TDRs' were a resounding success and are more numerous than the first generation.

25   For 'Slum TDRs' or *in situ* resettlement, the developer must obtain the agreement of 70 per cent of the households concerned. For the 'PAP TDRs' or Project Affect People,

Under this system, a developer acquires a slum or the SRA sometimes places land at its disposal. The SRA approves the proposed resettlement, issues the required permissions and controls the compliance of the building with existing housing norms. The building developer must resettle the inhabitants or displaced persons and can place the additional built-up square metres on the market or use the TDRs for other construction projects. These TDRs offer a twofold advantage: they are reasonably cheap to purchase and can be transferred to residential zones. These factors have therefore contributed to the development of an active TDR market that is extensively transforming the way the real estate market works. Further, the authorities can also be present in this market as the TDRs also apply to slums located on public land. In such a case, TDRs can be auctioned to building developers. This has also helped some institutions finance other projects. On paper, the policy is based on the idea of a win-win solution for the public sector, the developers and the inhabitants. It is also rapidly spreading to other actors, as in some resettlement projects, NGOs can use this mechanism for building houses.

In fact, the policy is playing a considerable role in the transformation of the metropolis and is being extensively studied to analyse its impact[26]. First of all, it has freed developers not only from the strict restrictions imposed by the Land Ceiling Act, but also from all the tedious procedures that went with it. As a result, the TDR policy, especially the 'Slum TDR', is a success that has led to the mushrooming of projects. Nonetheless, not all of it presents a rosy picture. For one, the allocation of space for housing is extremely uneven. While TDR holders can only concretise these virtual rights in the suburbs, they nonetheless opt for attractive and sought-after suburbs. Thus, Nainan shows how, of the 52,024 housing units built for resettling displaced households, 36,253 were in a single ward, where the prices per square metre were among the lowest in the city; at the other extreme of the scale, around 15 per cent of the TDRs built are in the posh localities of Juhu, Bandra and Santa Cruz (Nainan, 2008). This ultimately extremely simple mechanism for creating a market has brought about a process of urban restructuring and spatial segregation. Some wards have turned into areas to which slum inhabitants have been relegated, while others have attracted construction projects of a high standing. Secondly, this instrument was not accompanied by a consistent planning policy, either at the city scale, locality scale, or even at the scale of a group of buildings. This therefore translated into the 'delinking of construction from infrastructure' (Bertaud, 2004) and is partly the reason for the opposition expressed during the author's interviews with municipal engineers, who view the policy as a major restriction on infrastructure investments in some localities. The lack of planning, coupled with the scant restrictions imposed on developers with regard to minimal

---

the term used for persons displaced by infrastructure projects, this rule does not apply. TDRs can also be used in a third case, which is that of transit camps built for displaced persons while their housing is being built.

26   This section relies extensively on existing works. The changes in this sector are central to understanding Mumbai's transformation over the past two decades.

infrastructure, are contributing to the consolidation of intra-urban differences in the level of services. Finally, the policy is marred by the lack of decongestion or planning, as it merely provides an *ad hoc* process that developers take advantage of, among others.

It is said that 70 per cent of the TDR market is owned by the region's biggest developers.[27] The latter are taking advantage of the liberalisation of the realty market and using their influence on politicians in order to obtain favourable decisions, including the de-notification of certain land uses. For instance, the Maharashtra government amended the law on the reconversion of land on which erstwhile textile factories had been shut down, located in the heart of the city, to satisfy the real estate lobby. The amendment reduced the proportion of land reserved for public spaces and housing and led to a swift gentrification of the locality. The financial interests at stake prevailed over the legal recourse and protests were organised against this decision by the authorities, which was clearly not dictated by the public interest. Nonetheless, numerous well-established small-time local developers can still be found in this sector (Nainan, 2008). These 'artisans' of urban capitalism (Lorrain, 2002) form part of the integrated chain of actors that Nainan calls the 'building boomers' and in which the public sector is a stakeholder. In practice, the established cases of corruption, collusion between locally elected representatives, government officials and developers to serve their respective interests, regularly reported in the press, are at the heart of the way this segment of the realty market works[28]. There are various methods that are used to obtain the consent of 70 per cent of the slum households concerned in a project: financial incentives, the use of local intermediaries, the convergence of interests of locally elected representatives and developers, or even the clear threat of violence. As shown by Weinstein, an organised 'mafia' flourishes alongside the legitimate and powerful real estate sector, as market liberalisation, the lack of housing and land scarcity combine to make this sector a veritable El Dorado for raking in considerable illegal profits (Weinstein, 2007).

Lastly, unlike infrastructure programmes for utility networks, in which changes have taken place relatively slowly, the past 20 years have witnessed large-scale urban restructuring backed by the growth of the real estate market (despite a few years of falling prices). Profits from this sector have therefore contributed to a political consensus, as witnessed by the fact that the Congress-Nationalist Congress Party coalition failed to question the choices of the Shiv Sena-BJP government. Since realty and resettlement projects are locally rooted at the city district level, through local elected representatives, 'strong men' and local intermediaries, all political parties are able to take advantage of these policies

---

27   Information provided by a government official, during an oral presentation, who had participated within the MMRDA in the conceptualisation of the TDR policy.

28   For instance, when an enquiry committee was appointed for verifying the number of serious accusations made against the SRA, a part of the building and its files went up in flames.

and control the allocation of urban resources. To conclude, and viewed from a distanced, institutional perspective, the housing policies initiated over the past two decades in Mumbai make it possible to perceive the constant tension between the objective of urban performance and that of improving living standards. By seeking to use the private sector as a lever to fulfil a 'public interest' mission, these programmes that offer strong incentives to the construction sector, coupled with spiralling real estate prices, have finally produced relatively disappointing results as far as the improvement of housing for the deprived is concerned. Apart from the obvious distortions of the market, the number of housing units provided fell well below the targets set. According to Burra (2005), in 2005, ten years after the SRS programme was launched, 19,000 housing units were built and 80,000 were under construction – figures that are far below projections and needs. Furthermore, during periods of crisis, such a policy can be called into question. The reversal of the TDR market over the past few months and, therefore, the halt of numerous resettlement projects raises even more questions about Mumbai's 'TDR model', which is also being adopted in other Indian cities.

Participation in All Its Facets[29]

Among the new instruments of public action, the so-called 'participatory' practices have gained considerable ground. These involve the creation of new spaces of dialogue with users or the co-production of services (Ostrőm, 1996). Strongly encouraged by the World Bank, which supports community participation in the construction of toilets in slums and housing rehabilitation programmes, these practices are also the result of pressure from non-governmental organisations, the rising power of organised middle-class associations and, to a certain extent, the determination of certain progressive high-ranking officials.

Hence, there are many supporters of 'participatory action', although the logic behind their approaches may vary. Nonetheless, be it for the city of Mumbai or the metropolitan authority, the government has initiated many infrastructure programmes with a participatory dimension. Analysing several programmes, one wonders about their often contradictory logic and the way in which participation reshapes power equations in the city. Two main modes of participation can be distinguished. The first relies on NGOs, which play the role of intermediaries or bridges between the inhabitants and the authorities. The second is based on the direct participation of the inhabitants, organised either in the form of 'neighbourhood associations' – not so innocently called 'community-based organisations' in slums and 'residents' welfare associations' in residential areas. In the interests of clarity, the experiences of slums and residential areas will be dealt with separately.

---

29   This section draws on the argument proposed in an article on participation in Mumbai, published in the journal, *Development and Change*, see Zérah (2009a).

Participation mediated by NGOs

Two examples will be used to illustrate some of the problems related to the emergence of powerful NGOs in steering projects. The first, the Mumbai Urban Transport Project, was one of the projects aimed at improving the metropolitan region's transportation network (Table 3.2). The World Bank, which is funding 57 per cent of the total cost, has imposed a resettlement and rehabilitation plan for the 20,000 displaced households and traders (i.e. 100,000 persons). The plan includes an entire series of compensatory measures (acquiring housing with full ownership is one of the essential aspects for the households). The urban planning agency (MMRDA) is responsible for coordinating the project's technical execution, but two NGOs, recognised in Mumbai for their competence, were selected for assuming charge of the project's participatory aspects. They have been tasked with conducting household surveys, supporting the displacement and resettlement process, organising resettled communities and setting up information centres in each locality involved in a displacement project.

The second project, the Slum and Sanitation Programme, initiated in 1995, is a municipal scheme, once again negotiated with the World Bank as part of a large-scale programme for improving the sanitation system. At the World Bank's demand, flexible norms were defined so that NGOs (and not public works companies alone) could bid in response to invitations to tender for the construction of 35,000 toilets in slums. The contract stipulated that the municipality would support communication efforts in all the neighbourhoods and guarantee water and electricity connections to the toilet blocks. The NGOs or companies selected would build the infrastructure, carry through the social engineering process among the inhabitants and help in creating a community association. The project aimed at involving the inhabitants at each stage of the process. Ahead of construction, they had to participate in the design of the infrastructure and, especially, contribute to the capital cost (at least 70 per cent of the families had to agree to pay an advance). Thereafter, the neighbourhood association had to certify the completion of work, manage the infrastructure, decide on user fees and take care of accounting.

The contracts were awarded to two private local entrepreneurs and an NGO, SPARC (Society for the Promotion of Area Resources Centres), which was also one of the two NGOs selected for the transportation project (MUTP).[30] The presence of SPARC in all these projects is not just of minor interest. SPARC played a central role in several infrastructure projects as the organisation has strengthened its influence in deliberations over public policies and has emerged as the NGO representing the poorest of the poor (see part 3). More than as an NGO, SPARC describes itself as an 'alliance' between an NGO managed by members of the Indian elite (including former high-ranking officials), the charismatic leader of the National Slum Dwellers Federation and a network of women's committees well established in the localities. Historically, the alliance spearheaded several social movements in the 1970s, which conferred on it its legitimacy – for international

---

30   The second was SRS (Slum Rehabilitation Society).

organisations and international academic circles as well. Its involvement in numerous projects in Mumbai makes it possible to question the conditions under which NGOs intervene in public projects and their capacity to gain expertise over the long term. In other words, are they capable of influencing the process or are they simply a cog in the bureaucratic machinery?

Let us begin with the transport project (MUTP) and the resettlement of displaced persons. In order to establish compensation rights, which depend on the concerned slum dweller's arrival date in the slum,[31] a survey was conducted by SPARC. While the process as a whole was considered to be equitable, numerous complaints were made by some of the inhabitants and small traders (Tata Institute of Social Sciences, 2008:102), highlighting how difficult it was to do exhaustive work in such projects, possibly leading to the discrediting of NGOs. SPARC's ambiguous position is even more obvious when one looks into the process preceding resettlement. In some of the sites surveyed, the NGO representatives presented the MMRDA resettlement offer as an opportunity that it would be irresponsible not to seize. While the inhabitants wished to obtain more detailed information on the consequences of the rehabilitation process, the NGO – or more precisely, its local employees – sought to force them to accept the deal by giving them just a one-day deadline (Özel, 2007) and the residents were unable to distinguish between the NGO representatives and MMRDA employees. The NGO had then behaved almost like a sub-contractor for the metropolitan authority. The Slum and Sanitation Programme provides similar observations, with a tendency to outsource social intermediation (Sharma and Bhide, 2005). Wherever SPARC was well-established locally, i.e. it had accumulated experience and built a relationship of trust with the inhabitants, the results achieved were quite satisfactory (Yannic, 2003). The importance of such long-term engagement for the success of rehabilitation projects is also one of Nijman's conclusions (2008) in his study of the Slum Rehabilitation Society's practices. However, participatory public infrastructure projects have transformed the action of NGOs, which, by becoming full-fledged partners, shoulder a part of the responsibilities and are contractually bound to the public authorities. The obligation to produce results and contractual incentives *de facto* orient their actions towards the achievement of the technical objectives set, while less importance is given to the democratic process, which necessitates a long time for building a consensus. This situation is further aggravated by coordination problems between NGOs and municipal and metropolitan authorities.

From the public sector's viewpoint, working and collaborating with NGOs constitutes a major change. The Slum and Sanitation Programme (SSP) met

---

31   The cut-off date was before 1995, but it was pushed to a later year. It triggered off a political debate between those supporting its extension to 2000 and those who were against it, so as not to send an encouraging signal for migrations. This led to numerous exclusions when slums were displaced, as households that were unable to prove their arrival date before the cut-off year were not entitled to any compensation.

with considerable resistance from its engineers (Yannic, 2003). The complexity of administrative procedures and SPARC's refusal to fall in with the practice of reaching arrangements between private entrepreneurs and municipal employees slowed down both projects and payments. As a result, NGOs like SPARC now content themselves with bypassing the lower rungs of the administration to negotiate directly with the higher echelons of the administration, politicians and the World Bank. This *modus operandi* helps them solve problems, but in the long term, limits the learning of new practices and sharing expertise and, therefore, in the long run, also limits any deeper transformations in public and collective action.

Another point of discussion concerns the capacity of NGOs to be real intermediaries for local communities. One of the greatest expectations from so-called 'participatory' programmes is the social intervention work in neighbourhoods, which is supposed to enhance efficiency in the provision of service. However, numerous criticisms have been directed at SPARC's role in the SSP.[32] Sharma and Bhide (2005) argued that the association behaved like a typical private entrepreneur that was more concerned with building infrastructure rather than strengthening local organisational capacities, although it was for this very purpose that SPARC had been selected. Yannic (2003) compared SPARC to two other local public works companies involved in SSPs. She revealed SPARC's efficiency and success in localities where the women's committees were well established. In others, SPARC's performance was comparable to that of private contractors. In fact, one such contractor, through the recruitment of some social workers, succeeded in mobilising the local communities so that they could meet the programme criteria. It selected localities with a greater financial capacity and harnessed its knowledge to effectively navigate the maze of local administration; it ultimately fulfilled all its contractual obligations, although technical imperatives overrode the objective of community empowerment. From the viewpoint of the authorities, private entrepreneurs were also able to achieve a minimum level of participation while improving infrastructure when incentives were appropriately designed. That may be an instrumentalist vision of participation, but it is one that is encouraged by the authorities.

Furthermore, one of the arguments advanced by those in favour of strengthening the role of NGOs is their involvement in building arenas of public debate and spaces for democratisation. In the programmes that have been studied, once the infrastructure is built, the users' committee should become autonomous and represent the community before the municipal authorities. However, the results achieved do not meet these expectations. In the case of the Mumbai Urban Transport Project, the cooperative housing societies are yet to be established. In fact, this situation drew the attention of the World Bank Inspection Panel, which suspended the loan for a few months. After the resettlement process, a real estate transaction market (rent and transfer of allotted housing) sprang up and some

---

32   The criticism is not exclusive to the SSP. Although SPARC is often praised in international arenas, its action is considered to be extremely controversial in Mumbai by academic and activist milieus.

of the intermediaries turned out to be MMRDA employees, as well as those of NGOs (Tata Institute of Social Sciences, 2008:32). Similar abuses tainted the Slum and Sanitation Programme. Although the users' committees worked in some of the localities, a sub-contracting system with local actors, who managed the infrastructure like private firms, was also set up.

Several conclusions can be drawn. On the one hand, NGOs are accountable first and foremost to the authorities, as they are contractually bound to them. They give priority to technical imperatives and reduce social engineering to a minimum. In cases where a long history of work in localities and a relationship of mutual trust already exist, the participatory aspect of the programmes works. When that is not the case, the results are quite mixed for the inhabitants, but remain compatible with the authorities' utilitarian vision of participation. The fact that such participation is ultimately embedded in the pre-existing governance structures at the infra-local scale – often made up of networks of small local entrepreneurs, influential persons and local elected representatives capable of seizing the opportunities offered by the participatory programmes (or blocking them) – is not surprising. Nonetheless, the lack of attention to the realities of infra-local governance and the role played by local representatives limits the impact of programmes aiming at a greater proximity between the State apparatus and its users. Lastly, the limitations faced by SPARC reveal the great difficulty NGOs face in expanding their sphere of action and replicating their acquired expertise in localities where they have no roots.

Direct community participation
The Municipal Corporation of Greater Mumbai (MCGM), with the aim of working in greater proximity between the municipality and users, introduced the Slum Adoption Programme (SAP). It aimed at expanding and improving sanitary conditions in slums. To this end, garbage was to be collected from homes by a neighbourhood organisation that would then deposit it at a collection point agreed upon by the municipality. Each SAP programme covered 200 families (1,000 persons), who had to pay a nominal monthly amount for the service provided. All users' committees that fulfilled certain criteria (including the employment of people from the neighbourhood) could benefit from the programme. The CBO or Community Based Organisation would receive a grant-in-aid for a period of three years. As the municipality assumed that there would be an increase in the number of households ready to join the service over the years, the amount of the grant would be gradually reduced until the associations managed to balance their budgets. The management of the scheme was decentralised at the ward level. Ward-level officers selected the CBOs after consultations with the local elected representative and were responsible for disbursing the grants. The author's surveys during field work in three wards (Zérah, 2009b) and those of Desai and De Wit in other wards (2006) demonstrate that local elected representatives played a central role. The grant and renewal of contracts strongly depended on the intervention of the local elected representatives. They protected or favoured certain committees and could withdraw their support in the event of a clash. Sometimes, the local elected

representatives themselves literally 'adopted' the scheme without bothering with the intermediary role to be played by CBOs. Thus, when the author questioned a municipal councillor as to whether he was aware of the said programme, he boasted, 'Of course. I'm the one handling it'.[33]

The programme is structured by the informal relations prevailing between the local administration, elected representatives and the committee heads. The associations are dominated by the figure of the 'social worker', a term that describes residents of the neighbourhood involved in organising festivals or collective activities and who almost always have a political affiliation and/or serve as intermediaries for different parties. Sometimes, it is even the local leader. In some cases, these users' associations are actually companies participating in other municipal schemes and forging alliances to deploy human resources in different localities and various programmes, whether participatory or private. There are community associations that favour a certain form of democratisation (one that is, however, relative as far as the committee's internal composition is concerned) and which have succeeded in creating a breach in the paternalistic manner of running services in slums. Nonetheless, these committees are fragile as they are very largely financially dependent on administrative subsidies that are sometimes delayed.

Hence, the Slum Adoption Programme experience suggests that the participatory approach is continuing to be applied and is reshaping the prevailing clientelist relations, depending on the kind of relations (elected representative-residents, elected representatives-local administration), the type of locality, the prevailing political competition and the composition of the population. Contrary to the idealised vision of communities, community participation embedded in local politics does not lead to self-management, but to forms of recomposed power equations within communities. Community participation is often very like sub-contracts to private operators and it may rather be referred to as 'community privatisation'. In reality, participation appears to be one of the channels for circulating and allocating resources (both funds and employment) between the formal and informal spheres of governance.

Participation in residential areas
The injunction to participate is a product of the discourse on good governance, but also reflects the middle classes' rise to power after 15 consecutive years of sustained growth. The swift rise in incomes, the advent of international brands in the consumer market and the increasingly frequent and regular contacts with developed countries have transformed the aspirations of a section of the middle class and the elite for a modern, efficient city with quality services. These claims partly rely on the existing structure of neighbourhood associations that some municipal schemes contribute to transforming into instruments of public action.

Thus, in 1997, the Mumbai municipality decided to launch a new scheme in residential areas for collecting and sorting household waste. The enthusiasm of a

---

33   Interview conducted in February 2006.

high-ranking municipal servant for the successful beautification of a road by its residents with the administration's support, the saturation of dumping sites and the rapid increase in waste tonnage led to the launch of the programme, 'Advance Locality Management' (ALM). It was based on a simple principle: at the level of a street, building or group of buildings, the households would be collectively involved in organising the sorting of waste and in setting up a composting system. In exchange, the municipality would take care of cleaning the roads regularly and deal with the residents' grievances on a priority basis. The committees (or ALMs) were registered at the municipality but were not legal entities, unlike the co-operative housing societies from which they stemmed. The official count in 2007 was 648 committees, of which only 150 were truly very active (Baud and Nainan, 2008). For the very first time, this programme institutionalised a space for dialogue and cooperation for residential areas. Monthly meetings were held in each ward with the director of the local administration, municipal engineers and employees, and ALM representatives[34]. Although trivial problems and personal grievances were often aired, these meetings created a space for repeated interaction between users and the administration. This process contributed to creating a space of trust (or at least for reducing mutual mistrust between the two parties), the emergence of civil society leaders capable of laying down priorities and establishing dialogue, and the testing of municipal expertise by users, who became public action monitors, in a sense. In concrete terms, the service improved significantly in areas where ALMs abounded, were federated and carried weight in the administration. However, such a configuration only arose in localities with a specific history and identity (Christian and Parsi localities or urbanised former villages).

While there are relatively few active committees (ALMs), what are the reasons that lead them to play a significant role in urban governance by diversifying their activities to other utility networks (drainage, rainwater and electricity) (Zérah, 2009a)? Firstly, the representatives of these associations, because of their social origin, can deal with the local administration on an equal footing, directly approach government officials and carry weight in public works executed in their neighbourhoods. Although they sometimes face opposition in their locality, they emerge as legitimate representatives before the municipal authorities, indicating a growing activism, and receive extremely positive press coverage. More than one-thirds of the ALMs studied have registered Public Interest Litigations (PILs) and can draw on a vast network of knowledge for pooling together technical expertise and legal counsel. When the judiciary rules extensively in their favour, their influence is enhanced, although it may be disproportionate to their actual presence. Secondly, these associations are able to rise above the neighbourhood level. Due to their knowledge of local issues, they nurture organisations involved in cross-cutting issues (good governance, urban planning, heritage and environmental conservation) and form part of a growing civic network organised on the city and even national scale. Thirdly, their commitment to serving their interests

---

34   The absence of local elected representatives may be noted.

is, of course, also part of the explanation. These resident-activists come across as champions of public interest but, in reality, develop a discourse based on their rights as taxpayers. It is quite fascinating to see such association members veering towards a form of anti-parliamentarianism, cynical about the criminalisation of the political sphere, initiating dialogues with local elected representatives and being directly involved in the electoral process by presenting independent candidates. Will this politicisation process prove that it is impossible to extricate oneself from a society organised into interest groups? The interest group that neighbourhood associations and the federations to which they belong are attempting to build is sometimes ambivalent: praising the goal of modernising Mumbai while simultaneously opposing urban renewal projects when they may lead to the destructuring of certain areas; supporting public transport while pushing for the expulsion of street vendors and pockets of dwellings for the poor. But ultimately, it is about urging a vision of urban citizenship focusing on the idea of legality and of being taxpayers. The dissection of the concrete implications of 'participation' highlights the differentiated access to urban resources that it actually exacerbates. The opening-up of spaces for consultation and certain public policies have favoured the well-to-do classes and certain NGOs that are sometimes accomplices in urban restructuring, while the informal and clientelist networks in slums have managed to seize the tools of new urban governance, without, however, having any significant impact on the quality of urban services.

Reforming the Steering of Public Action

The inclusion of previously ignored actors in steering the city (housing and utilities) denotes the desire to restructure the conduct of public action. From the debates they arouse, the 'participation and privatisation' diptych is one of the most visible aspects of the overhauling of the public sector's working modalities, which nonetheless also takes other avenues. Three major directions can be traced in this process, forming part of the principles of the new public management system referred to in the early 1990s by Osborne and Gaebler (1992).

The first movement stemmed from the restructuring of a State that produced and supplied services, turning it *into a state that regulated* and provided suitable incentives for development. On Mumbai's scale, this intention was affirmed by the Government of Maharashtra, which would like the municipality's role to evolve into that of a facilitator (GOM, 2004). One of the reforms envisaged by the regional government was to transform the municipal water authority into a public sector undertaking, which would then be freed from numerous administrative procedures, particularly in terms of personnel management. However, in reality, changes in the regulatory framework are slow. In 2006, a water regulation authority was instituted for allocating resources and determining the tariff policy. A call for tenders for this purpose shortlisted several consultants whose work was influenced by good governance norms. But, as the disputes over tariffs show, even the system of steering utility networks by setting up depoliticised norms, to be developed within new and independent institutions, was unable to do away with the necessary political arbitration. More indirectly, public sector establishments increasingly imposed certain management modalities on the local urban authorities whose infrastructure they financed. In the water sector, small local authorities in the suburbs were encouraged to increase their tariffs, develop programmes for leakage detection and establish energy audits (Sangameswaran, 2009).

This is even more visible in the power distribution sector, whose reforms were given an impetus by India's central government. Two major milestones can be identified in its restructuring process. Firstly, the Electricity Regulation Commission Act was adopted in 1998. Its concrete outcome was the setting up of the Maharashtra Electricity Regulatory Commission, whose main function was to decide on tariffs on the basis of technical and economic criteria to encourage operator efficiency. The Electricity Act followed in 2003, introducing new principles for organising the sector. These two laws established and organised competition. In Mumbai, these legislative changes have had a real impact as public and private distributors co-exist, particularly two of the largest Indian consortiums, which compete for the market in the city's well-to-do suburbs: Reliance and Tata (Zérah, 2008).

The ongoing trend is that of the reduction of subsidies for the middle class and a regular increase in tariffs for stimulating investments in new production capacities. These tariff hikes have triggered protest campaigns – the latest, dating back to June 2009, was accompanied by acts of vandalism orchestrated by the Shiv Sena against Reliance. The protests spread among other political parties, including the local Congress branch, which highlighted a dispute between the municipality and the government, accused of having endorsed the hike. The establishment of regulatory agencies is directly inspired by the Anglo-Saxon model and its implicit objective is to (somewhat unsuccessfully) depoliticise debates on major utility networks.

Another path followed is *the modernisation of the bureaucratic machinery*. High-ranking officials, members of the IAS (Indian Administrative Service) have been the craftsmen and backbone of a powerful administration. They have formed a respected, elitist corps that has been at the heart of formulating and implementing public policies. Inefficiency, corruption and sheer waste have undermined how they are viewed by citizens, and government officials have been criticised and even discredited (Vaugier-Chatterjee, 2001). Consequently, the *aggiornamento* or modernisation of the civil service is regularly announced and several of the measures taken have been influenced by the new public management style, the 'best practices' disseminated by the World Bank and consultancy firms that have had a strong presence in the urban scenario since the mid-1990s. All this has offered new professional prospects to senior officials. They are no longer insulated from international experiences: seminars, conferences and study trips facilitate the dissemination of 'best practices' and open the doors to careers in the private sector or multilateral organisations. Several initiatives have been taken for Mumbai: the overhauling of budgetary practices with the changeover to a double entry accrual accounting system, the development of new tools with the help of information technology (online payment, procuring administrative documents), greater administrative devolution, a better interface with users in city districts, the establishment of interactive platforms with NGOs, the recruitment of social workers for participatory programmes and the simplification of administrative permissions for complying with municipal building bye-laws.

Nonetheless, these changes remain marginal and the functioning of administrations continues to be marked by inertia. The acceleration of critical reforms, such as the overhaul of the local fiscal system and land deregulation resulted from the strong pressure exerted by the federal state, which laid down the conditions for access to JNNURM funds for water, sanitation and storm drainage. That was the case with property tax reforms, for instance, planned for 2010, after years of dilly-dallying. Along with excise duties, property taxes are one of the two main sources of revenue for the municipality (around 30 per cent). Property tax calculations had introduced numerous distortions between old and new buildings, the island city and suburbs, and domestic and non-domestic use (Pethe and Lalvani, 2006). Despite a hike over the past few years, property tax potentials failed to be realised and the debate on the method of calculation included the change from a tax calculated on the capital value rather than its rental value and the standardisation of rates between suburbs and the city-centre. This controversy continued for several years without being settled and triggered local political disputes. For the city-centre, where the tax rate was low, local elected representatives were concerned by the electoral repercussions in the event of a hike and by the situation of tenants in buildings with frozen rents, organised into a powerful association. By contrast, certain municipal councillors elected from the suburbs started exerting pressure for reforms to be initiated, but the state government would regularly block them.

There was nothing out of the ordinary in this attempt to balance and mediate between pressure groups, but it could well happen that pressure exerted by the national government will finally settle this local debate. This also applies to the abolition of the Urban Land Ceiling Act, which Maharashtra was among the last to implement in 2007, and which should logically have led to the availability of new constructible lands in the market. Important municipal and metropolitan reforms are therefore remote-controlled by the central government, which has, however, declared the intensification of decentralisation to be one of the main challenges in urban reforms.

The *political decentralisation* undertaken in 1992 was conceived as an essential instrument not only in the democratisation process, but also for the transformation of public action. The institutional architecture envisaged for metropolises was based at three levels: the Metropolitan Planning Committee, the Municipal Council and the Ward Committee, in order to articulate the steering of metropolitan areas based on neighbourhood democracy. A decade and half later, the feedback has been quite mixed. As early as in 1999, a government ordinance had defined the Municipal Council's composition (two-thirds of the 45 members had to be local elected representatives, while the remaining one-third could consist of representatives from the government, the business world or civil society), but this is yet to come into being. Often announced, its establishment was supported by those with a long-term strategic vision, partly for reasons of the optimum management of the urban region. Such a council could take charge of the coordination of metropolitan projects, the metropolitan transport authority and strategic planning. Further, a Metropolitan Council would have elected representatives only from the region who would be directly concerned by its development. It would therefore be vested with the political legitimacy lacking in the MMRDA and would be less subject to arbitration by elected representatives of other districts. Without going into greater details, it would suffice to say that as far as the Municipal Council was concerned, the municipal representatives enjoyed very little power, except in specific cases (long-standing local presence, power initially developed outside political arenas, etc.). Nonetheless, the regular disputes between elected representatives and employees have not only highlighted the 'nuisance value' of Municipal Councillors (who can push for the transfer of an official), but have also revealed the gradual process of the emergence of enterprising local elected officials. Finally, the last rung of Ward Committees for instituting participatory democracy failed to work well. First of all, the Ward Committees were created as late as 2000 and brought together approximately 240,000 persons per ward, which is a rather large jurisdiction. Moreover, the decision-making powers and budgets allocated were too meagre for these committees to make their weight felt in the decisions made by the administration. To overcome this lacuna, the JNNURM issued directives for the regional governments to adopt a law on community participation. This model 'community participation law' would involve the establishment of neighbourhood committees in which the residents' representatives would be present alongside the local elected official. Discussions on the Metropolitan Council and Neighbourhood Committees were held and involved representatives from the business sphere, NGOs upholding a discourse on 'good governance', and Residents' Welfare Associations. The involvement of these players in the debate can be explained by the stakes involved in the distribution of members from the political world in these bodies and those from civil society, in the broad sense of the term. To the mistrust of decentralisation among political parties was added the lack of faith in local elected officials among certain categories of the population, which believed that they played a role in the 'criminalisation of politics' (Jaffrelot, 1998).

Hence, while it may be observed that several fronts had been opened for reshaping public action, the process did not uniformly apply to all sectors and all areas of action of the State's machinery. This simultaneously reveals an element of continuity, even resilience, in existing institutions, as well as the persistence of tensions between decentralising and centralising forces, illustrated by the terms and conditions imposed by the JNNURM or by the deregulation of the power sector. Do these consistent factors limit the apparent efforts being made for urban restructuring based on 'Vision Mumbai'?

Vision Mumbai: A Specific 'Growth Coalition' Model?

The concern over Mumbai's economic decline since the early 1990s, arising from the shrinking number of jobs in the manufacturing industry and the difficulty faced in attracting new investments, is noticeable. The city's image was tarnished by the terrible Hindu-Muslim riots in 1992. Furthermore, the decision of the Shiv Sena-BJP government to rechristen Bombay as Mumbai in 1995 aroused some anxiety among local industrialists. In 1993, McKinsey produced an initial report, underlining Mumbai's strengths in terms of becoming an international financial hub and, in 1995 industrialists close to the Mumbai Chamber of Commerce and Industry founded Bombay First, along the lines of London First. This think-tank looked towards Asia, especially Singapore and Hong Kong, in search of fresh perspectives for the city's future (D'Monte, 2002). But it was in the early 2000s that a collective vision was energetically revived for the entire metropolitan region. In 2003, Bombay First published a consultancy report for which McKinsey & Company had been commissioned, its objective being the elaboration of a strategy for transforming Mumbai into a world class city by 2013, drawing inspiration from Shanghai this time (Bombay First and McKinsey, 2003). The project involved identifying the hurdles and bottlenecks obstructing economic growth, along with the investments necessary for reviving the economy. The report was widely disseminated and the Government of Maharashtra, which was once again headed by the Congress since 1999, adhered to its recommendations.

The Contents of Vision Mumbai

Before taking a look at the governance mechanisms recommended by 'Vision Mumbai', let us begin with its contents. It is inspired by the manner in which Asian cities have created coalitions in order to induce growth – in other words, 'growth machines' (Logan and Molotch, 2007). The declared ambition is to 'Transform Mumbai into a world-class city with a vibrant economy and a globally comparable life for its citizens' (Government of Maharashtra, 2004: 11). The genealogy of this discourse with the image of the future of the global city is obvious. Vision Mumbai is well and truly a discourse on the city's global nature and attractiveness (Robinson, 2006), placing it at the same time within the framework of the reduction of urban poverty, an inescapable reality of the city. The diagnosis proposed is as follows: economic growth is being hampered by the lack of housing due to excessively restrictive land and realty market regulations, along with an infrastructure deficit. Consequently, colossal investments are required in these two sectors, as well as in productive capital and must be accompanied by the deregulation of the land market to make it possible to promote new buildable plots. For companies to (re)invest, it is necessary to bring about a transformation in the State's role, which must, first and foremost, make major public investments and create an atmosphere conducive to private initiatives (GOM, 2004: 21). Since the publication of the first 'Vision Mumbai' document, which identifies six main areas of action – economic growth, transport, housing, physical and social infrastructure, funding and governance – the content of the agenda has taken shape on the basis of new, internal or commissioned studies. As far as financing is concerned, the McKinsey report had estimated investment requirements at 40 million dollars approximately, which is close to the figures proposed by the 'business plan' commissioned by the MMRDA (MMRDA and LEA, 2007). But the estimate by World Bank experts is much higher and they have found the current low investment worrying, as revealed in the analysis of local finances conducted by the University of Mumbai (Prud'homme, 2007). The establishment of a funding structure dedicated to infrastructure is one of the solutions proposed to remedy the continued under-investment trend. It could also contribute to making public-private partnerships more systematic and lead to a new governance architecture for major projects. Nonetheless, the fund is yet to come into being and it is the JNNURM or regional government that mainly supports the financing of current projects. Yet, the experts financed by the World Bank in order to help implement 'Vision Mumbai' have laid emphasis on a strategy inspired by the Asian model, in which the 'city finances the city'. This approach combines the deregulation of the land market (abolition of the Urban Land Ceiling Act, amendment of the Rent Control Act) and a well-thought out increase in the FSI, concentrating on the main arteries and transport bottlenecks. This strategy could be used to guide the city's spatial transformation, while setting up clear and transparent land income collection mechanisms (impact fees or development charges), replacing the opacity characterising the TDR market's current operations (Bertaud, 2008). Leveraging the real estate market lies at the heart of the city's economic growth and would ultimately help finance infrastructure projects.

However, at this stage of the implementation of this supposedly grand vision of transformation, the key elements of reform – apart from the abolition of the Urban Land Ceiling Act – are still pending. As a result, infrastructure projects remain partly isolated from each other and are not being reassessed in keeping with the rapid transformation of the city and its daily flows (as can be seen, for instance, in the Bandra-Worli Sea Link, implemented on the basis of the initial reports, dating back to 1962). Thus, the recently created Metropolitan Transport Authority is nothing but a hollow shell (Zérah, 2009c). The Mumbai Vision, widely disseminated and supported by the English-speaking press,[35] involves the academic elite only marginally (unlike the examples given by Logan and Molotch), which reveals the paucity of data on the city's economy and social structure. After several years, the 'Vision' seems to have remained a roadmap, despite the World Bank having worked with the regional government to produce more analytical work that would help nurture this vision and not limit it merely to the piling up of more infrastructure projects (Table 3.2). Does this state of affairs

---

35   Hindustan Times, for instance, published a well-documented series on the content of Vision Mumbai (http://www.hindustantimes.com/news/specials/bombay/index.shtml) and provides regular follow-ups.

reveal that the Mumbai Vision is, first and foremost, a political instrument based on an exhortation to transform the city?

Emergence of a Kind of State-controlled 'Urban Regime'?

In order to answer this we need to focus on the Vision's governance structure. To do so, we have chosen to examine the instruments set up for steering the Vision and the actors involved in the process, while raising the question of whether or not a specific kind of urban regime is emerging. Mossberger and Stoker (2001) have identified several factors characterising the notion of an urban regime: the constitution of a stable group with access to institutional resources via formal or informal mechanisms, the inclusion of different groups with the aim of cooperating even if they do not necessarily share the same values, a certain stability in coalition groups, agreement on an action plan and the coordination of relations between the State and private interests, which is a central element of urban regimes (Stone, 1989).

Several initial conditions seemed to have been met for the emergence of an urban regime in Mumbai, embodied in Vision Mumbai. First of all, Vision Mumbai is an action plan with avowed goals and well defined projects. It is a programme for the physical transformation of the city through numerous projects, with an agenda composed of repeated interactions between the government and the industrial elite. In fact, the Government of Maharashtra's official report (GOM, 2004) takes up the one drafted by Bombay First (Bombay First and McKinsey, 2003), sometimes verbatim. However, Bombay First is a think-tank that has relied on the privileged relations between high-ranking officials and the industrial elite from its very inception. The idea of the think-tank emerged in 2002 at the Tata Department of Economics and Statistics[36], which a former government official had recently joined. The department initiated a series of meetings on Mumbai's future, as well as an international conference that would lead to the foundation of Bombay First. The proximity between decision-makers and the business community is being strengthened (even institutionalised) by the pursuit of Vision Mumbai.

For implementing it, the Government of Maharashtra appointed a Chief Secretary (Special Projects) who, with the support of the Cities Alliance[37], set up the Mumbai Transformation Support Unit (MTSU) in 2005. A support cell offering expertise, the MTSU gathered existing knowledge on the city and initiated new research for guiding policy formulation. It depends on government resources, but also includes a few actors from civil society and the academic world, and enlists the help of consultants. Besides this body, two follow-up committees were set up. The first was formed in 2004, bringing together representatives of the business world (industrialists, bankers) and civil society (artists, filmmakers), as well as two governmental organisations. SPARC put forward the interests of the poor

---

36   Interview conducted in October 2008 with one of the initiators of Bombay First.
37   www.citiesalliance.org

Table 3.2   Main infrastructure projects

Ongoing Projects

Mumbai Trans Harbour Sea Link Project (Estimated cost: € 1.38 billion)
Construction of a bridge linking Mumbai to Navi Mumbai. The project is running behind schedule despite repeated extensions of deadlines, and the modes of financing have kept changing (see details in Part 2)

Mumbai Urban Transport Project-I (MUTP-I) (Estimated cost: € 854 million)
Project supported and partially financed by the World Bank. The project aims at improving the railways, building new roads and improving the bus transport system. It requires the coordination of numerous agencies and involves the resettling of many displaced families

Mumbai Urban Infrastructure Project (MUIP) (Estimated cost: € 441 million)
Programme for the improvement and construction of roads, coordinated and financed by the MMRDA.

First metro line (Versova – Andheri – Ghatkopar) (Estimated cost: € 392 million)
A Special Purpose Vehicle (MMRDA, Reliance Infrastructure and Véolia Transport) was established for the construction of the first metro line, a large part of which is financed by the Reliance conglomerate.

Mumbai Sewage Disposal Project (MSDP) Stage-II Priority Works (Estimated cost: € 344 million)
Follow-up of a previous major project, partly financed by the World Bank, which included a community participation model for building toilets in slums

Brimstowad (Estimated cost: € 300 million)
The aim of this municipal project is to upgrade the storm drainage system. The JNNURM is partially funding this project.

Construction of a dam on the Vaitarna (Estimated cost: € 264 million)
Increase in water resources. Programme financed with the support of the JNNURM (central government).

Maintenance and widening of the Mithi river (Phase II) (Estimated cost: € 50 million)
Programme coordinated by MMRDA and MCGM

Projects Planned

Mumbai Metro Line – III (Colaba – Bandra) (Estimated cost: € 1.72 billion)

Redevelopment of Dharavi (Estimated cost: € 933 million)
A rehabilitation programme for Mumbai's largest slum, located at the juncture of the island city and the suburbs. Dharavi is home to more than one million people and numerous small enterprises. This is a highly disputed project and has been covered in numerous articles in the international press as well as the academic world.

Mumbai Metro Line – II – Charkop-Bandra-Mankhurd (Estimated cost: € 921 million)

Table 3.2   Main infrastructure projects continued

Mumbai Urban Transport Project II (MUTP-II) (Estimated cost: € 833 million)
This project is aimed at improving the urban rail network by easing the passenger load (extension of some lines, increase in the number of carriages) and improving access to stations, along with signalling. It mainly involves public financing (essentially the railways and MMRDA).

Construction of a new airport in Navi Mumbai (Estimated cost: € 794 million)

Monorail project planned by the MMRDA (Estimated cost: € 440 million)

in the committee, thereby consolidating its influence, and AGNI, a federation of various Residents' Welfare Associations, conveyed the voice of the 'middle class'. In reality, this Citizens' Action Group did little, met infrequently and had a limited influence on the process. Real influence lay with the 'Empowered Committee', established in 2006, which met regularly and tracked the progress of all the Vision Mumbai projects. The committee was composed of 17 government officials, 7 representatives of major industrial groups, as well as one from the bank specialising in real estate loans. This was indeed a forum in which 'a more or less stable group with access to institutional resources' (Mossberger and Stoker, 2001) gathered. To a certain extent, the committee was a modern avatar (though a less effective one) of the role that the nineteenth century industrial elite played in the establishment of local institutions (Ramanna, 2002) and the production of utility networks (Dossal, 1991). The group also shared certain values, strengthened by the links between high-ranking bureaucrats and the private sector. For instance, the Chief Minister's Chief Secretary, who has been working since 2004 towards implementing Vision Mumbai, left his public service job to join the recently created Tata real estate subsidiary, but she continues to participate in the committee with a different designation.

Finally, the notion of stability is central to the notion of an urban regime and it would appear that, despite the high degree of political competition, the conditions necessary for a certain continuity in public action have been met, with the successive re-election of the Congress-NCP coalition. The results of the May and October 2009 polls for the national and regional assemblies respectively gave the Congress another mandate, bringing stability and a 5-year vision for pursuing the Vision Mumbai agenda. For the Congress, conducting this exercise is a key instrument for intervening in the city to contain the Shiv Sena's influence (as much as that of its own political allies) at the metropolitan level, and also for intervening directly in a municipal space that is not under its political control. This is reflected in the constant rivalry between the State's urban planning agency (MMRDA) and the Municipality of Mumbai (MCGM), between the MMRDA and the roads authority (MSRDC, the minister in charge being from the NCP), or between CIDCO (City and Industrial Development Corporation of Maharashtra Ltd., which falls under the government) and the city of Navi Mumbai (an NCP fiefdom). The regional government receives the direct support of the central government, led by the Congress, given an impetus by the abundance of JNNURM funds and the personal commitment of the Prime Minister of the Indian Union.

What Mumbai's case reveals is clearly the marginalisation of the local component, despite its being central to 'growth machine' theories and urban regimes. The Mumbai municipality is a marginal actor in Vision Mumbai, which is mainly carried out by the federal state and industrialists whose corporate offices are located in Mumbai, not to mention the World Bank's advisory role[38] and the consultancy firms that contribute to shaping the reform agenda. Can it therefore be described as a stable coalition (or a kind of 'regional urban regime') – one that would have succeeded in forging a minimum consensus on the city's future despite keeping the local component (an essential aspect of the urban regime) at arm's length? Has this Vision mobilised people or led to some form of consensus about the future of the city in this complex and fragmented social reality? In other words, does Vision Mumbai reflect a real change in urban management or does it simply constitute political lip service?

Vision Mumbai: Not a Shared Political Project

Abundant forms of dissension

No project or measure in Mumbai has been free of protests. So there is nothing exceptional here, except perhaps the pluralistic and competitive structuring of the public space and political arenas; to this are added the recourse to new instruments, such as judicial procedures or the Right to Information. This situation multiplies the possibilities of intervention in the conduct of collective action and can create a real stumbling block or even confrontations between divergent interests.

The disputes over government urban restructuring projects also reveal the conflicts between different social groups. As confirmed by Harriss (2005) in Delhi's case, the modes of access to the State for the poor (slums and squatters) differ from those used in more established residential localities. The former have greater recourse to the 'strong men of the locality' and to visible protests (demonstrations, sit-ins) than the latter. If the dichotomy between 'political society' and 'civil society' enunciated in P. Chatterjee's (2004) theory is adopted, this situation can be explained by their status as those who are 'governed' and enjoy uncertain rights, which obliges them to live on the margins of legality (links with illegal services and housing, for instance) and which implies the constant negotiation of their rights via bargaining and reciprocity mechanisms with political circles.

---

38   The advisory role is quite informally structured. The World Bank does not finance the MTSU, but helps it in defining the research necessary for refining and specifying the content of public policies. To this end, it turns partly towards universities outside the Bank, which contribute as consultants. This role must be distinguished from the one the Bank plays in the MUTP transport project, funded up to 57 per cent by the Bank, which is therefore directly involved in the project and its implementation.

This disjunction with 'civil society' (and its legal inhabitants, whose rights are not questioned) is further strengthened by the new instruments of public action and the opportunities given to civil society to come forward as a legitimate interlocutor. At the local level, this translates into opposition to road widening projects or to the construction of commercial centres, or protests of the NIMBY (Not In My Backyard) type, but also, increasingly, into actions aimed at 'modernising' the city by supporting projects for expelling slums or lobbying for increasing restrictions on authorised areas for hawkers.

To this end, neighbourhood committees or associations use two effective instruments, apart from their clout, which is sometimes curtailed or even suppressed by the networks of political influence created by the inhabitants or poor labourers. The first is Public Interest Litigation or PILs, which authorise any physical or moral entity not directly a victim to lodge a complaint in the name of a group and refer it to the legal authorities. While this procedure was introduced for quicker and more equitable access to justice for all, it has turned into the preferred tool for organised members of the middle class and numerous non-governmental organisations today. Hence, more than one-third of the residents' committees interviewed had taken recourse to judicial procedures, as these often favoured them. Moreover, for obtaining information on government projects, activists, associations and NGOs use the Right to Information Act, 2005, which came into existence and owed a considerable part of its contents to a very broad, pan-Indian social movement (Baviskar, 2010). This law bestows on all citizens the right to demand access to certain kinds of administrative documents as well as annotations made by officials. Residents' Welfare Committees often use it to obtain information on the public works executed in localities – information that can be used as a means of opposition, for example, by questioning the way contracts have been awarded or the high costs of public works planned.

The opposition to the bridge between Bandra and Worli is at once emblematic of activism of the NIMBY or even protectionist type, but also expresses the eventuality of the confluence of interests between different groups. It calls for a more detailed examination. Three groups used the procedure for referring matters to the High Court: the two Residents' Welfare Associations of Bandra and Worli, as well as an environmental protection NGO, which opposed the construction of the bridge as it would alter sea currents and the fragile mangrove ecosystem, while leading to the shrinking of the mouth of a river. These PILs decelerated the bridge-building process just as much as did the strong criticism by the fishing community (almost 100,000 inhabitants), for whom the bridge would mean the end of access to their fishing areas. In keeping with the distinction Harriss and Chatterjee make, the fishermen's mobilisation took the form of protests and demonstrations, making use of its informal ties with a government minister who hailed from the same community. Hence, while the construction of the bridge started in June 1999, the fishermen started their protests on 9 July. A second demonstration – a larger one, including other associations – took place on 2 October, followed by the arrest of 400 protesters in November of the same year. As soon as the contract was signed, the first PIL was filed. It is this kind of accumulation of divergent interests that led to a de facto stalemate in the project, while the demands being made to regional authorities to realign the bridge fell on deaf ears, although the national Ministry of Environment and Forests more or less accepted it as a viable solution. This situation largely reflects the lack of prior public debate and consultations to discuss the project. And yet, the official advertisement procedures had been followed for the project, but were limited to a purely technocratic approach. Finally, the authorities were forced to change the bridge's alignment, resulting in a delay of several years and considerable cost escalation.

A second example, which will be briefly mentioned, reiterates the possibility of the formation of heterogeneous coalitions for opposing infrastructure projects. For instance, the resistance to the delegation of water distribution services in a particular ward also brought together a priori divergent interests (slum dwellers, Residents' Welfare Associations, municipal employees, water rights activists, etc.), while also highlighting the contradictions existing within some of the groups themselves (BAWA, 2009). Hence, AGNI – represented in the Citizens' Action Group – was in favour of a private operator for improving governance, but at the local level, its representatives were actively mobilised against the project.

So a complex matrix linking different issues builds up, depending on the scale at which problems occur, along with a certain degree of fluidity in the development of movements opposing the restructuring of the city. This complexity, amplified by the size of the city and the diversity of localities, is in itself subject to a profusion of latent conflicts ready to be triggered the moment a restructuring project is launched. Such discordant and diffuse forms of dissension, articulated at different levels of the city, undermine efforts made towards forging a consensus on the subject of Vision Mumbai, which limits and even disqualifies the relevance of the concept of a stabilised urban regime.

How can a minimum consensus be developed for steering collective action?
The lack of information and transparency in the conduct of major projects fuels the reactions of civil society, elected representatives (both local and regional) and opposition parties, which is what leads to such impasses or delays in projects underway, as in the case of the construction of the first metro line,. While the production and management of utility and service networks are precisely the sectors that give rise to questions about solving the problems of collective action, the definition of what constitutes public interest and the social compromises necessary, the inconsistent mechanisms of public debate and the clash of various interest groups appear, on the other hand, to be leading to a 'zero-sum society' (Thurow, 1980). Only a realisation of the social challenges involved in resettling persons displaced by major infrastructure projects – despite the numerous problems it brings in its wake – is an established fact and reflects the learning process of government organisations when they have to deal with concrete

problems and incentives for change (as with the World Bank's imposition of a resettlement module). Otherwise, Vision Mumbai has not had a 'trickle-down effect' on the manner in which projects are conducted by the municipality or para-governmental bodies, which have only marginally changed their operating style. These organisations are extremely reluctant to part with information or to open spaces for debate and are ill-equipped to understand the emerging challenges of the environment or the notion of risks. Numerous factors would still appear to be lacking for the creation of spaces for negotiation and deliberation.

Some of these could be set up fairly swiftly. But that brings us to think, first of all, about the paucity of data on the city – demonstrating the lack of interest on the part of senior officials in dealing with projects in the light of social realities. While these exercises for gauging the reality require careful handling, the meagre data (even baseline data) on the job market and its structure; the place, weight and location of informal activities; mobility and circulation issues; the housing sector and even local public finances have several consequences. They limit, for example, all attempts at a strategic definition of the city's economic future, as shown in the USAID-funded report (The Urban Institute, 2006). The latter not only highlights certain sectors in which Mumbai has a real comparative advantage, but also others, such as biotechnology, to which the entire project of the 'global city' should conform, but which have no roots in the region's economic structure. In fact, productive sectors that are embedded in the informal sector are neglected.

The broader question of forums for discussion and negotiations on major projects is a pricklier affair. How can an apparatus for public debate be set up in a society as pluralistic and competitive as urban Mumbai? Some may even add: is it even necessary and desirable? After all, the aim is not to nurture an idealistic or irenic vision of public debate. The creation of spaces for debate can be instrumentalised as a way of persuading the government or – as has been observed earlier in the case of some participatory processes – used by certain interest groups. Moreover, as demonstrated by the long time taken for the principle of participation in public debate to develop (and be enshrined in the judicial system) in the European Union[39], the establishment of such mechanisms can only be envisaged in the long-term, through the institutionalisation of procedures that would make a better definition of public policies possible. At the very least, a form of actual public debate on the functioning of existing procedures would help bring out some of the challenges that project designers would not have envisaged, or even engender acceptable solutions for project assessment so as to avoid the impasses that eventually lead to de facto changes in projects, as can be seen in the Bandra-Worli bridge case. Lastly, in addition to improving the city's economic performance and taking urban poverty into account, new challenges related to environmental issues (in the broader sense) and risk management will emerge as

---

39   Such as the Commission National du Débat Public in France or the mechanism of public audience in the UK and a number of European Directives that are applied in European countries.

factors defining public policies. Opening up discussions on the future of the city to a much larger number of actors can be one of the ways of taking these new issues into consideration.

Conclusion

The upgrading and building of new infrastructure are both the symbols and materiality of a modern and efficient global city. To attain this status, a series of major projects were presented as the backbone of a 'Vision Mumbai' that would transform India's economic capital. The analysis presented in this chapter, which concerns the institutional framework for the implementation of these projects and the introduction of new instruments of public action, forms part of a reflection on the place of institutions and practices over the long term. Thus, without wishing to gloss over the real changes made in governmental practices and urban society, this work also highlights the persistence of two rationales and modalities of access to the city. The first rationale is the process of the continuous institutionalisation of urban power through the establishment of organisations (municipal or regional) for planning and developing spaces and providing services for a section of the inhabitants. For the others, access to the city and negotiations on rights to the city are embedded in informal processes that are somewhat effective and are too quickly dismissed by describing them as 'clientelism', or even corruption. While efforts at transforming public action may not manage to catch up on the infrastructural backlog, they nonetheless have a significant impact on urban restructuring and power equations in the city. Participation is a tool that enables certain organised groups from the middle class to throw in their weight as legitimate and influential actors in urban governance, while the co-production of urban services in slums is shaped by the structuring of the social fabric. Housing schemes, based on partnerships with the real estate industry whose lack of transparency and adhocism has been brought out in this chapter, are perfect examples of the interpenetration of the logic of institutionalisation and the informal logic that upholders of reforms and those in charge of implementing them fail to take (or do not wish to take) into account, either in their planning or in practice. Mumbai is therefore the archetype of developing cities in which the complexity of interconnections and coordination between the formal and informal spheres is central to the access to and distribution of resources.

Another important aspect brought out through the study of large utility networks is the considerable difficulties public authorities face in controlling the public-private partnership mechanism. It is true that, given the few companies present in the urban sector and the often opportunistic behaviour displayed by them, the ability to steer projects involving private partnerships – both in terms of defining contractual conditions and project follow-up – is limited. The long time taken to learn how to manage PPPs, particularly in comparison with other Asian countries, can also be explained by the high political volatility and the difficulty of generating public interest in a fragmented society structured on the basis of competition between social groups (and their interests). This pluralism and diversity that characterises Indian society and its democracy therefore raise obstacles in a political system based on accommodating different rationales, which prefers managing disputes rather than seeking mechanisms for resolving them (Bardhan, 1984).

Thus, one of the questions raised in this chapter at the outset, concerning the ability to steer the city, needs to be raised once again. In other words, is the city of Mumbai governable and capable of producing a form of collective action? In various ways, Mumbai projects the image of a badly governed city. On the one hand, it appears to be governed at the wrong scale, thereby exacerbating the disjunction between institutional governance bodies and functional spaces (a municipality controlling just a limited part of the urban region and a government that is mainly concerned about the State and not the region). On the other hand, more than a vision with the goal of articulating the terms of the debate – i.e. how to reconcile a competitive city with an inclusive city and how to take tomorrow's challenges into account (environmental risk, climatic risk, etc.) – 'Vision Mumbai' is a pile of badly coordinated, badly conceived and badly implemented projects by engineers and high-ranking public servants, little inclined to examine project designs through the prism of social realities. The major urban projects envisaged by international experts and the industrial and administrative elite therefore often end up being disputed or even rejected, through all manner of protests, stemming from the very same urban elite that is nonetheless calling for modernisation, but demanding more open consultation processes. The strategy based on the growth model inspired by Asian cities and of the city financing the city is therefore being challenged and basically remains a political discourse, for the time being. Transforming the city at a forced pace is not conceivable.

Should one then conclude – joining the ranks of the numerous Cassandras and anxious observers – that Mumbai is in a crisis and that its decline is inevitable? After studying numerous indicators and given the volatile and deleterious political climate towards newcomers, it would be tempting to add one's number to the circle of pessimists. But, as initially stated in this chapter, shouldn't we once again highlight the importance of the long term and history in order to place the current 'crisis' in its context? While Mumbai is India's richest city, it is still a 'poor' city and has been so for decades. Similarly, decentralisation is a process that takes place over a time scale that differs from the time taken to schedule reforms. The presence of precarious housing and slums with deplorable living conditions will not be erased by imposed modernisation, but it is not inescapable. In fact, it is this very precarity that is at the heart of the functioning of a part of the city's economy, based on flexibility, the recourse to cheap manual labour and support services for the tertiary sector. Consequently, today's orientation and choices will structure the city's future. The seeds of future problems have already been sown: major urban projects encouraging the use of individual automobiles to the detriment of public transport (despite metro projects); slums and hawkers being relegated to the margins, reflecting the rejection of proximity and of the porosity of the use of the city, as well as the inability to take the real scale of urbanisation (i.e. the metropolitan region) into account. Rather than an accumulation of projects (some of which are necessary and useful), what is required is a transformatory vision that draws on the development of data at the metropolitan scale as a means for getting a better grasp on economic and social realities, as well as on local expertise, the outlines of which need to be defined so as to better gauge and deliberate on the challenges of the distribution of resources in the city.

References

Angueletou-Marteau, A. (2009). Accès à l'eau en périphérie: petits opérateurs privés et pauvreté hydraulique domestique. Enjeux de gouvernance dans les zones périurbaines de Mumbai, Inde. *Département d'Economie*. Grenoble: Université Pierre Mendès France.

Bardhan, P.K. (1984). *The Political Economy of Development in India*, Oxford; New York, NY: B. Blackwell.

Baud, I. and Nainan, N. (2008). 'Negotiated Spaces' for Representation in Mumbai: Ward Committees, Advanced Locality Management and the Politics of Middle-Class Activism. *Environment and Urbanization*, 20: 483–99.

Baviskar, A. (2010). Is Knowledge Power? The Right to Information Campaign in India, in Gaventa, J. and Gee, R.M. (eds) *Citizen Action and National Policy Reform: Making Change Happen (Claiming Citizenship: Rights, Participation and Accountability)*. London: Zed Books.

Bawa, Z. (2009) K-East WDIP Case Study. 'The voice of city dwellers in urban governance. Participation, Mobilisation, and Local Democracy – Comparing Indian / South African debates'. Centre de Sciences Humaines and Department of Civics and Political Sciences, Mumbai University.

Benjamin, S. (2004.) Urban Land Transformation for Pro-Poor Economies. *Geoforum*, 35: 177–87.

Bertaud, A. (2004). Mumbai FSI Conundrum: The Perfect Storm: The Four Factors Restricting the Construction of New Floor Space in Mumbai. http://alain-bertaud.com/AB_Files/AB_Mumbai_FSI_conundrum.pdf.

Bertaud, A. (2008). Options for New Alternatives for Development Control Regulation and Justification for Increasing FSI. (Power point presented on 3 April, Mumbai).

Bombay First & McKinsey (2003). Vision Mumbai. Transforming Mumbai into a World-Class City. Mumbai: Bombay First.

Burra, S. (2005). Towards a Pro-Poor Framework For Slum Upgrading in Mumbai, India. *Environment and Urbanization*, 17: 67–88.

Chatterjee, P. (2004). *The Politics of the Governed. Reflections on Popular Politics in Most of the World*, New York: Columbia University Press.

D'Monte, D. (2002). *Ripping the Fabric: The Decline of Mumbai and its Mills*, New Delhi; New York: Oxford University Press.

De Bercegol, R. and Desfeux, A. (2007). La gestion du service d'eau par réseaux de groupes d'usagers. Etude de l'accès à l'eau dans un bidonville mal desservi par la municipalité de Mumbai. *Institut d'Etudes Politiques de Rennes*. Mumbai, Rennes : Centre de Sciences Humaines et Institut d'Etudes Politiques de Rennes.

Desai Al, P. and De Wit, J. (2006). Slum Adoption Program – SAP in Mumbai – An Analysis. IDPAD Seminar on 'New Forms of Urban Governance in Indian Mega-Cities'. New Delhi.

Dossal, M. (1991). *Imperial Designs and Indian Realities: The Planning of Bombay City, 1845–1875*, Bombay: Oxford University Press.

GOM (2004). Transforming Mumbai into a World-Class City. First report of the Chief Minister's Task Force. Mumbai: Government of Maharashtra.

Hansen, T.B. (2001). *Violence in Urban India. Identity Politics, 'Mumbai', and the Postcolonial City*, Delhi: Permanent Black.

Harris, N. (1995). Bombay in the Global Economy, in Patel, S. and Thorner, A. (eds) *Bombay, Metaphor for Modern India*. New Delhi: Oxford University Press.

Harriss, J. (2005). Political Participation, Representation and the Urban Poor, Findings from Research in Delhi. *Economic and Political Weekly*, XL: 1041–54.

Heuzé, D.G. (2007). La violence et la ville: le cas de Mumbai durant les deux dernières décennies du XXe siècle La ville en Asie du Sud. Analyse et mise en perspective, *Purusartha*, 26, 255–306.

Hibou, B. (1998). Retrait ou redéploiement de l'Etat. *Critique Internationale*, 1, 151–67.

Jaffrelot, C. (1998). *La démocratie en Inde religion, caste et politique*, Paris: Fayard.

Kennedy, L. and Zérah, M.-H. (2008). The Shift to City-Centric Growth Strategies in India. Perspectives from Hyderabad and Mumbai. *Economic and Political Weekly*, XLIII, 110–17.

Klein, I. (1986). Urban Development and Death: Bombay City, 1870–1914. *Modern Asian Studies*, XX, 725–54.

Kothari, R. (1964). The Congress 'System' in India. *Asian Survey*, 4, 1161–73.

Leboucher, P. (2008). Infrastructures à Mumbai. Etude de quatre projets d'aménagement: Bandra Worli Sea Link, Mumbai Trans Harbour Link, Mithi River Upkeep, Brimstowad. Delhi: ENTPE-Centre de Sciences Humaines.

Logan, J.R. and Molotch, H.L. (2007). *Urban Fortunes: The Political Economy of Place*, Berkeley, CA: University of California Press.

Lorrain, D. (2002). Capitalismes urbains: la montée des firmes d'infrastructure. *Entreprises et Histoire*, 30: 7–31.

Markovits, C. (1995). Bombay as a Business Centre in the Colonial Period: A Comparison with Calcutta, in Patel, S. and Thorner, A. (eds) *Bombay: Metaphor for Modern India*. New Delhi: Oxford University Press.

Mehta, S. (2004). *Maximum City: Bombay Lost and Found*, New York: Alfred A. Knopf.

MMRDA (2003). Population and Employment Profile of Mumbai Metropolitan Region. Mumbai: MMRDA.

Modi, R. (2009). Resettlement and Rehabilitation in Urban Centres. *Economic and Political Weekly*, XLIV: 20–22.

Mossberger, K. and Stoker, G. (2001). The Evolution of Urban Regime Theory: The Challenge of Conceptualization. *Urban Affairs Review*, 36: 810–35.

MMRDA & LEA International Ltd (2007) Business Plan for Mumbai Metropolitan Region. Draft Final Report. Mumbai: Mumbai Metropolitan Region Development Authority

Nainan, N. (2008). Building Boomers and Fragmentation of Space in Mumbai. *Economic and Political Weekly*, XLII: 29–34.

Nijman, J. (2008). Against the Odds: Slum Rehabilitation in Neoliberal Mumbai. *Cities*, 25: 73–85.

Osborner, D. and Gaebler, T. (1992). *Reinventing Government: How the Entrepreneurial Sspirit is Transforming the Public Sector*, Reading, MA: Addison-Wesley Pub. Co.

Oström, E. (1996). Crossing the Great Divide: Coproduction, Synergy and Development. *World Development*, 24: 1073–97.

Ozel, D. (2007). Mumbai Urban Transport Project (Mumbai, Inde) : Les politiques de réhabilition et de relogement. Pour une nouvelle éthique de développement? Paris: Institut France d'Urbanisme.

Pacione, M. (2006). Mumbai. *Cities*, 23: 229–38.

Pethe, A. and Lalvani, M. (2006). Deciphering the Code of 'Mumbai' Budgets. *Workshop on Actors, Policies and Urban Governance in Mumbai*. Mumbai University.

Pinto, D.A. and Pinto, M. (2005). *Municipal Corporation of Greater Mumbai and Ward Administration*, New Delhi: Konark Publishers Pvt. Ltd.

Pinto, M. (2000). *Metropolitan City Governance in India*, Delhi: Sage.

Prud'Homme, R. (2005). Infrastructure and Development, in Bourguignon, F. and Pleskovic, B. (eds) *Annual World Bank Conference on Development Economics: Lessons from Experience*. Washington DC: The IBRD/ The World Bank.

Prud'Homme, R. (2007). Seven Notes on Mumbai's Growth and How to Finance It. Notes for the World Bank and the Mumbai Transformation Support Unit ed. Unpublished.

Ramanna, M. (2002). *Western Medicine and Public Health in Colonial Bombay, 1845–95*. Hyderabad: Sangam Books.

Robinson, J. (2006). *Ordinary Cities: Between Modernity and Development*, London; New York: Routledge.

Sangameswaran, P. (2009). Neoliberalism and Water Reforms in Western India: Commercialization, Self-Sufficiency, and Regulatory Bodies. *Geoforum*, 40: 228–38.

Sassen, S. (2001). Global Cities and Global-City Regions: A Comparison, in Scott, A.J. (ed.) *Global City-Regions: Trends, Theory and Policy*. Oxford: Oxford University Press.

Scott, A.J. (ed.) (2001). *Global City-Regions. Trends, Policy, Theory*, Oxford: Oxford University Press.

Shaban, A. and Sharma, R.N. (2007). Water Consumption Patterns in Domestic Households in Major Cities. *Economic and Political Weekly*, 42: 2190–97.

Sharma, K. (1999). *Waiting for Water*. Mumbai: Society for the Promotion of Area Centres.

Sharma, R.N. and Bhide, A. (2005). World Bank Funded Slum Sanitation Program in Mumbai. Participatory Approach and Lessons Learnt. *Economic and Political Weekly*, 40: 1784–9.

Shaw, A. (1999a). Emerging Patterns of Urban Growth in India. *Economic and Political Weekly*, 34: 969–78.

Shaw, A. (1999b). The Planning and Development of New Bombay. *Modern Asian Studies*, 33: 951–88.

Srinivas, A. (2005). *Ambani vs Ambani: Storms in the Sea Wind*, New Delhi: Lotus Collection, Roli Books.

Steinweg, T. (2006). *Different Perceptions of Accountability and Performance in Mumbai's Water Sector*. Amsterdam: University of Amsterdam.

Stone, C. (1989). *Regime Politics, Governing Atlanta, 1946–1988*, Lawrence, KA: University Press of Kansas.

Tata Institute of Social Sciences (2008) Impact Assessment of Resettlement Implementations under Mumbai Urban Transport Project (MUTP). Mumbai, Prepared by Tata Institute of Social Sciences for the Mumbai Metropolitan Region Development Authority (MMRDA).

The Urban Institute (2006). Economic Growth of the Mumbai Metropolitan Region. Washington DC: USAID and the Urban Institute.

Thurow, L. (1980). *The Zero-Sum Society: Distribution and the Possibilities for Economic Change*, New York: Basic Books.

Urban Age (2007). Urban India: Understanding the Maximum City. London, Berlin: The London School of Economics and Political Science and the Deutsche Bank.

Vaugier-Chatterjee, A. (2001). Du cadre d'acier au cadre de bambou: grandeur et décadence de la bureaucratie indienne, *Autrepart, Numéro Spécial édité par M. Raffinot et F. Roubaud: les fonctionnaires du Sud entre deux eaux: sacrifiés ou protégés?*, 20: 161–76.

Vora, R. (2009). Maharashtra or Maratha Rashtra? in Jaffrelot, C. and Kumar, S. (eds) *Rise of the Plebeians? The Changing Face of Indian Legislative Assemblies*. New Delhi: Routledge.

WSP-South Asia (2006). The Mumbai Slum Sanitation Program: Partnering with Slum Communities for Sustainable Sanitation in a Megalopolis. New Delhi, Water and Sanitation Program-South Asia.

Weinstein, L. (2007). Mumbai's Development Mafias: Globalization, Organized Crime and Land Development. *International Journal of Urban and Regional Research*, 32: 22–39.

World Bank (2006). India. Water Supply and Sanitation. Bridging the Gap Between Infrastructure and Service. Background Paper: Urban Water Supply and Sanitation. New Delhi: The World Bank.

Yannic, N. (2003). The Slum Sanitation Programme in Mumbai: a community-participative approach: at what conditions co-production of sanitation services can achieve higher sustainable operation and maintenance by the communities through construction of social capital? *M. Phil Thesis*. Paris X-Nanterre.

Zérah, M.-H. (2008). Splintering urbanism in Mumbai: Contrasting Trends in a Multilayered Society. *Geoforum*, 39: 1922–32.

Zérah, M.-H. (2009a). Participatory Governance in Urban Management and the Shifting Geometry of Power in Mumbai. *Development and Change*, 40: 853–77.

Zérah, M.-H. (2009b). Reforming Solid Waste Management in Mumbai and Hyderabad: Policy Convergence, Distinctive Processes, in Ruet, J. and S. Tawa Lama-Rewal (eds) *Governing India's Metropolises: Four Case Studies*. Delhi: Routledge.

Zérah, M.-H. (2009c). Une 'Vision Mumbai' pour transformer la ville ou la difficulté à (re)penser la gouvernance métropolitaine. EchoGéo, 10, http://echogeo.revues.org/index11389.html.

Chapter 4

Governing Cape Town: The Exhaustion of a Negotiated Transition

Alain Dubresson and Sylvy Jaglin

The 'miracle' of the political agreement concluded at the beginning of the 1990s between the ruling National Party and Nelson Mandela's African National Congress (ANC) committed South Africa to a post-apartheid transition that aimed to consolidate representative democracy and to construct a liberalised economic order integrated into the world economy (Saul, 2001; Webster and Adler, 1999). This transition, which can be described as negotiated by the country's elites (Bond, 2005) or as resulting from 'elite pacting' (Marais, 1998; Beall et al., 2005), relied on the implementation of a new, hybrid mode of regulation (Wilkinson, 2004). Created through a deal between the ANC, the trade unions and white employers' circles, this combined neo-liberalism with redistribution, in order to respond to the dual imperative of stimulating strong growth by opening up to the global market at the fastest possible pace *and* of reallocating resources in favour of those who had been victims of the old racist regime.

In the urban political order, the creation of metropolitan governments has been consubstantial with this compromise. On the one hand, this creation process has adhered to the theses of competitive regionalism, which views the strengthening of regional institutions as a necessary adaptation of the state's spatial structures to neo-liberal globalisation (Scott, 2001; Brenner, 2004). In this movement towards political rescaling, metropolises have become a benchmark scale: privileged spaces of the new accumulation regime, they gain increased responsibilities and regulatory capacities. On the other hand, this policy has also espoused the theses of a neo-progressive metropolitanism that is preoccupied with a more equitable distribution of resources. Combining debates on the shape of the city, political fragmentation and redistribution mechanisms, this international intellectual trend has helped to propagate discourse on a metropolitan governance that involves fiscal integration, unification of services and spatial planning (Rusk, 1993; Downs, 1994; Orfield, 1997; Savitch and Vogel, 2000). Although it has been inspired by these various currents, the specific form taken by South African metropolitan governments is primarily a political response to concrete local problems such as dismantling urban apartheid, homogenising service delivery, land-use planning, building infrastructure, local economic development, unified taxation, environmental protection, and so on. Just as Jonas and Pincetl have demonstrated 'the variety of New Regionalisms' through the example of California (Jonas and

Pincetl, 2006), we must stress the originality of the institutional responses brought to bear on the metropolitan question in South Africa – responses rooted in the region's urban configurations.

Those who conceived the project for a new South African society viewed big cities as the heart of its economic, social and cultural development. The transition to democracy set up a system of local government in six such cities that is sometimes described as one of the most autonomous in the world (Cameron, 1999): this was both part of the political search for a new urban citizenship (Gervais-Lambony, 2003) and part of a wide-ranging reshaping of public policy that should have led, at all scales, to 'a new post-apartheid spatial order' (Rogerson, 1998). The success of the administrative and territorial reorganisation process could by no means be taken for granted;[1] yet it did succeed, and three distinct types of local authorities have emerged: Municipalities, Districts – which surround them, and with which they share responsibilities – and Metros.[2]

Defined by the 1996 Constitution as one of the three spheres of government (along with the national and the provincial), the current eight metros[3] have a large autonomy and protected executive, regulatory power within a jurisdictional territory where they are able to provide true local government, legitimised by democratic election.

They are also vested with local 'developmental duties'. Embodying the dual imperative of efficiency and equity,[4] the concept of 'developmental local government'[5] remains a hotly debated and still vaguely defined topic (Swilling, 2006; Pieterse and van Donk, 2008) – though it generates normative prescriptions from central government. Metropolitan municipalities have to mobilise specific planning tools and coordinate their development policies with those of the other two spheres of government. A mixed[6] type of local governance is imposed on them from above; they are required to rely on one 'vision' of the economic future, on public-private partnerships and on a strategy negotiated with private firms and residents' 'communities'. The metropolitan

---

1   On political and administrative restructuring, the process of decentralisation at the national scale and reconcentration at the local scale and the issue of local power, see Cameron, 1999; Gervais-Lambony, 2004.

2   Selected on the basis of criteria laid down in The Local Government: Municipal Structures Act, No. 117 of 1998.

3   Buffalo City (East London), City of Cape Town, eThekwini (Durban), Ekurhuleni (East Rand), Mangaung Municipality (Bloemfontein), Nelson Mandela Bay Metropolitan Municipality (Port Elisabeth/Uitenage/Despatch), City of Tshwane (Pretoria), City of Johannesburg.

4   'Equity' here means spatial equity (equality of access to services) and social equity (redistribution to disadvantaged individuals and groups in order to improve their well-being).

5   Embodied in the preamble to Municipal Systems Act, No.32 of 2000.

6   'Mixed' or 'partnership' governance refers to mechanisms and processes that coordinate a wide variety of actors (in the public, private and not-for-profit sectors) in the aim of building cooperation to achieve collectively negotiated objectives.

government scale is also presented as pertinent to the effective promotion of local economic development (Rogerson, 1997; Maharaj, 1999; Nel and Binns, 2001). The implementation of 'local economic development' is intended to promote good local linkages between economic growth and urban integration, and this multidimensional concept has become a recurrent theme at the international scale. Rarely defined in the specialist literature, it is not based on any solid, stable body of theory (Freund and Lootvoet, 2005), but it was very quickly appropriated by South Africa's political elites.

So the democratic revolution and the building of the 'rainbow nation', carried forward by Nelson Mandela's government and based on principles of restitution, redistribution, equity and affirmation of rights, gave birth to an ideal of urban integration that aimed to break with the legacy of apartheid. This integration was supposed to be an organic combination of spatial equity (compacting the city by making it physically denser, introducing mixed-use development and equalising access to urban resources), social equity (redistribution, solidarity, guaranteeing a minimum subsistence income for everyone) and political inclusion (democratisation, decentralisation, participation).

Cape Town is South Africa's legislative capital and capital city of the Province of the Western Cape, as well as the country's second city in terms of population (3.7 million in 2011) and its second economic centre; today, it is the heart of an emerging metropolitan region that includes six other municipalities[7] – a region with a total population of four million and a per capita GDP higher than that of the metropolitan regions of Mexico City or Istanbul[8] (OECD, 2008). As South Africa's 'Mother City' and 'an up-and-coming global city' (Gibb, 2007), it belongs to the Beta category but is considered as a 'not intensive globalization' city in the GaWC 2010 classification.[9] With an estimated GDP of R250 billion in 2010 at current prices (WCG, 2012; per capita equivalent: R67,567 – about €7,432[10]), Cape Town has 7.2 per cent of the total population of South Africa – but about 11 per cent of national GDP. However, the local economy is less globalised than that of Johannesburg and, to sum up the situation (Vacchiani-Marcuzzo, 2008), its opening to the international market is growing but remains limited; and although Cape Town has captured R35.3 billion of foreign direct investment (FDI) from 2003 to 2011 (Wesgro, 2012), these are highly concentrated in property, call centres and tourism, and they provide about 10 per cent of gross fixed capital formation.

As in the other South African metropolises – but in an original way as far as the literature on big cities is concerned (Lefèvre, 2009) – the current central debate is about neither administrative fragmentation nor the search for an optimum size that would reconcile functional space and institutional territory; this is because the

---

7   Stellenbosch, Drakenstein, Swartland, Saldanha Bay, Theewaterskloof, Overstrand.

8   According to the OECD (2008), the region's 2007 per capita GDP was US$15,250 adjusted for purchasing power parity.

9   Source: The World According to GaWC 2010, (www.lboro.ac.uk/gawc/).

10   In 2010, 1 rand = €0.11.

political and territorial unification embarked upon in 1996 was completed in 2000 by the creation of a unified metropolitan municipality, or 'Unicity'. Instead, debate focuses on the new metropolitan institutions' capacity to drive change, defined principally in terms of integration. If we accept, following North, that the rules of the game are institutions with a 'shared beliefs' dimension and that the players are organisations and individuals that themselves have certain mental models (Chabaud et al., 2005; North, 2005), then two questions arise. Over the long term and in the way they function in practice, do the new institutions favour decisions that promote integration? To what extent do they match the behaviours and representations of local officials or, more dynamically, to what extent do they favour learning processes that help to construct a shared representation of an integrated, post-apartheid urban society? From the point of view of urban change analysis, therefore, our interest lies in understanding whether the creation of a metropolitan government, which crystallises a fundamental break with the past, will be enough to bring Cape Town's local urban policies out of institutional path dependencies.

In the late 1980s, under the apartheid regime, Cape Town was a legally and politically segregated city, institutionally fragmented but functionally integrated by networked public services and through the employment market. The metropolis of the 2000s is institutionally and politically integrated, but residential desegregation there remains weak, poverty and socio-economic polarisation remain very high and the apartheid legacy penalises the poor townships and so still divides the city. For many South African researchers, urban integration has begun to look like a 'cruel mirage' (Pieterse, 2007: 25), and most of them refer to a 'crisis' or a 'tragedy' of governance: the idea that public planning and development policy has failed still dominates.

Nowadays, discourse on the city is changing, both in Cape Town and in South Africa as a whole, moving from 'a particularistic expression of the imperative of overcoming apartheid to a more generalised aspiration for urban innovation led by a developmental state' (Boraine et al., 2006: 260); it seeks ways and means to make the city viable and acceptable for everyone within the context of globalisation – an 'inclusive city'. The debate has thus shifted from examining the content of public policies towards investigating disjunctions between different scales of governance (horizontal and vertical) and between scales of governance and levels of regulation, as well as questioning the relevance of the metropolitan government level as a regulatory scale in the globalised economy. Why has Cape Town's local government only partially managed to promote urban integration, given that it possesses true institutional and technical competencies, real financial room for manoeuvre and a wide range of local development tools and that its successive leaders have always attempted – at least until 2006 – to prioritise pro-growth and pro-poor policies?

In order to try and understand the successes, limitations and failures that have been recorded, we shall focus first on the creation of local public policy capacity, conceived in order to react to the challenges identified. Then we shall describe the inability to control the shape of the city, how the social cost of urban sprawl is detrimental to poor citizens, and the financial pressures involved in managing the city. Finally, we shall discuss the idea that urban change can be driven and regulated at the metropolitan scale, through an examination of conflicts in governance and of the contradiction between what was expected from the political plan for integration and the reality of the municipality's regulatory capacity.

Building Municipal Capacity and 'a Top Corporate Governance City'[11]

Territorial and Institutional Metropolitanisation: 'One City, One Tax Base'

Before 1996, the present-day metropolitan territory of Cape Town was divided into 61 administrative units. There were 19 'white' local authorities, of which some administered the 29 management committees of townships reserved for 'coloureds', six local councils for the 'white semi-rural' areas and seven 'Black Local Authorities' (BLAs);[12] the last were administrations created for the townships assigned to black populations and they were directly answerable to the old provincial administration.[13] In 2000, in a move away from the unfortunate legacy of pre-1996 administrative atomisation under the apartheid model, the single (Uni)City of Cape Town (CoCT) (Figure 4.1) was set up; nowadays it is divided into 105 electoral wards, in which councillors are elected for a five-year term (105 directly elected and 105 nominated through a form of proportional representation), and 23 sub-councils.

Territorial integration amidst political instability
In Cape Town, the transformation of the public policy framework – a transformation that was supposed to increase the efficiency and performance of territorial administration – took a singular turn because of the configuration of the local political arena. The instability of elected coalitions has characterised the political landscape since 1996. During the so-called 'institutional transition period' (1996–2000), the provisional system of local government ('two-tier government') set up after the May 1996 elections included six Metropolitan Local Councils. These were temporary municipalities, run by parties involved in or deriving from the old apartheid regime – the New National Party (NNP) and the Democratic Party (DP); the then Cape Town Council was the only exception – it

---

11   CoCT, 2004.

12   The use of the 'race' categories of apartheid ('black', later 'black African', 'white', 'coloured', 'Indians', 'Asians') obviously does not imply any adherence to the ideology that gave rise to the classification, nor to the political regime that used it. These categories are still employed in demographic surveys.

13   To these we might add the defined service areas managed by the Regional Services Council, which spanned the territories listed.

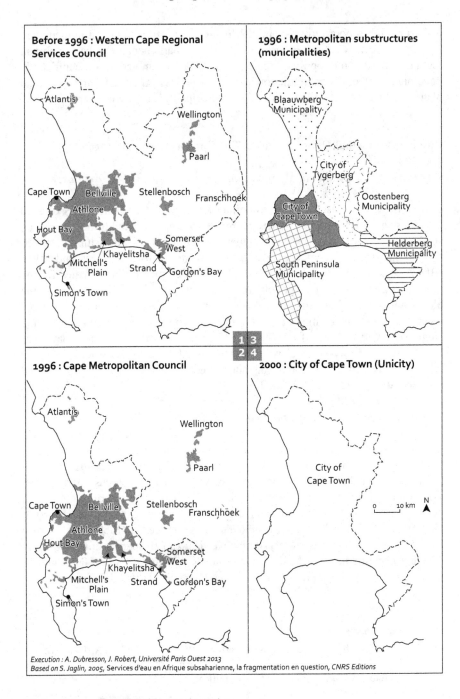

Figure 4.1   The Unicity construction

was administered by the ANC. Overall responsibility for these six municipalities lay with a horizontal structure: the Cape Metropolitan Council (CMC).

At the end of the transition period, the DP and the NNP united to form the Democratic Alliance (DA) in order to win the December 2000 municipal elections; this meant that they governed the new, unified metropolis for two years – a unique situation among South African metropolises – as well as the Province of the Western Cape. In October 2002, this alliance broke up and a new political coalition was formed between the ANC and NNP members[14]. The 2004 provincial elections validated – even established – this strategy: the ANC obtained the majority of votes, but since it did not have the majority of seats it had to govern the Province with the NNP. At the end of July 2004, the latter's leading national officials moved to sign their own death warrant by joining the ANC.

In the March 2006 local elections, the DA was again returned to power in the City, but its position was weak: its leader, Helen Zille, was elected Mayor by a coalition of parties, gaining just 106 votes as against 103 for the outgoing Mayor. Bitter clashes between the ANC and the DA were arbitrated by small parties and by the Independent Democrats, an assortment of politicians whose unpredictable behaviour led them into alliances and inter-alliances that were frequently ephemeral. From the time when it took office, therefore, the new multi-party local government was riddled with internal rivalries and incessant jockeying for position, which was destabilising at the local, provincial and even national scales; and it was not until the end of the last floor-crossing window – during which two new political parties were created – that a coalition led by the DA was finally confirmed in power on 21 September 2007.

The 2009 provincial elections may have marked a pause in this endemic political instability (Wilkinson, 2004). The DA won these elections by a wide margin; Helen Zille was elected Premier of the Province in May 2009; the new Mayor of Cape Town, Dan Plato, elected shortly afterwards, received 119 votes to his opponent's 66 and so in theory he has slightly greater room for manoeuvre than his predecessor. Moreover, since the 18 May 2011 municipal elections, the DA-led coalition has been reinforced: the DA alone got 135 seats, the ANC 73 and the Mayor, Patricia de Lille, has a solid majority. However, the years of instability and the clear 'racialisation' of voting behaviour during the last elections – evidenced by localised voting within the municipal territory – have left a deep mark on political relationships. The ANC itself was torn apart by antagonistic forces and a violent internal struggle that led to the implosion of the Provincial branch in 2009 and fuelled the creation of a dissident party, the Congress of the People (COPE). Nowadays, therefore, the political arena – the context in which

---

14   NNP members made use of the practice of 'floor-crossing', which is permitted by law and allows an elected representative – during given periods known as 'floor-crossing windows', which open during the second and fourth years of a five-year term of office – to change sides but keep his or her seat without going back to the electorate.

the management arrangements that constitute local governance are drawn up – is far from a peaceful place.

Functional integration: a plan of action and a set of tools for unified municipal government

Local institutional reform also originated from a 'modernisation' of the municipal apparatus, inspired by the principles of transparency, responsibility and efficiency extolled by New Public Management (Watson, 2002), the influence of which had already become perceptible during the 1980s. This modernisation applied to both the local executive and the administration.

The merging of the transition municipalities was accompanied by a reform in the way that the new local executive was run. This attempted to combine democracy and efficiency by offering the elected majority the choice to create either a 'mayoral committee' around the mayor or an 'executive committee'. The first scenario was a more personalised form of power, with the mayor, the deputy mayors and their secretariats having the exclusive right to draw up policy documents and by-laws to put to the council vote; in the second variant – apparently more transparent – the preparation of documents would be confined to a specific committee with all the political parties represented according to their respective proportions on the council. In Cape Town, because of the fluctuating balance of power and the fragility of coalitions, the mayoral committee solution has prevailed since 2002. Although it is viewed as less participative and democratic, it is also perceived as more efficient.

Administrative restructuring was more complex and slower than foreseen. It was hampered by technical and social difficulties in creating uniform rights and duties for public servants. For example, it was necessary to create a single system of employment regulations for some 30,000 municipal workers, who were governed by 26 different sets of regulations, at the same time as reducing the number of municipal employees to about 22,000 by 2009. Despite the fact that erratic human resources management resulting from affirmative action and clientelist battles between successive coalitions brought a certain amount of conflict into this restructuring process, a unique metropolitan administration was created in less than ten years – a challenge that was not easy to meet.

In terms of municipal policy tools, most efforts were focused on local finances and urban planning. The initial stage involved setting up separate management structures within each of the six former transition administrations, whose individual systems were first aligned and then merged when total financial integration took place on 1 July 2004. This process was accompanied by a spectacular modernisation of information-gathering and data-processing systems. The use of a great many different systems had been sustained or initiated in 1996 within each temporary municipality, but none of these was able to meet the needs of the new Unicity. Their alignment relied on the adoption of an integrated management software package (also known as 'enterprise resource planning', or ERP)[15]. Its use was decided before the 2000 elections and implementation started in the following year: it aimed to harmonise standards and the collection, capture and control of data indispensable to public financial management (human resources management, management of equipment, management of municipal real estate, for example). The application of shared standards and procedures thus enabled the replacement of the 112 old systems and their 72 interfaces. Since then, all operations have been processed using ERP and brought together in one place. The current system handles 1.7 million transactions a day, 3,000 simultaneous connections and, on the basis of a new fibre-optic network[16], ensures that information is cross-linked and circulated between all municipal services.

Although there has been a lot of evidence from municipal employees about the problems raised by deploying this system, the issue for local decision-makers has been not just to demonstrate their technical and organisational prowess but also (as in many other spheres) to give a dazzling demonstration of 'capacity' – in this case, their capacity to conform to the dominant norms of managerial excellence. Through this investment, the municipality certainly wanted to bring its processes up to standard, increase the reactivity of its services and listen more to its users. It is very difficult to assess the results without data and without hindsight, but their ambivalent aspects are hardly likely to differ significantly from those obtained by other studies, which analysed firms (Segrestin, 2004). Yet the municipality also wanted to write its name on the honour roll of well-managed cities and, on this second point, it entirely succeeded. The merger process was viewed as a model and later applied by the Tshwane Metropolitan Municipality (Pretoria); and the Cape Town experiment was rewarded in 2004 when it won the 'International Smithsonian Institute/Computerworld Honours Prize for the most significant IT project'.

However, the consequences extended well beyond this impact on reputation. Although we cannot go too far in the direction of technical determinism, it is difficult to ignore the 'cognitive framing effects' introduced by ERP (Segrestin, 2004) or to dissociate the major directions of post-apartheid rationalisation in municipal organisation from the ERP matrix. This tool both enabled and justified a redefinition of conditions for running local administration – and brought it more easily into line with the new national rules and with international best practices. It also allowed the old Fund Accounting System to be abandoned and a new public accounting system to be introduced – GAMAP (Generally Accepted Municipal Accounting Practice), which is in line with international standards, assessment rules and performance and became compulsory for South African municipalities from 1 July 2005. Above all, it enabled cities to come into line with the budgetary reform introduced by the Municipal Finance Management Act, No. 56 of 2003 and its 44 implementing regulations, which has completely changed local authorities' financial practices.

---

15   A software package developed by SAP, a major player in the business services sector.

16   This network was constructed by the municipality to meet its internal communication needs; its excess capacity is resold to licensed service providers.

This law redefines the roles of political and administrative functions and clarifies the differences between them. It distinguishes, on the one hand, the political function of the Mayoral Committee, which is responsible for making fundamental choices, setting priorities and presenting results to the Municipal Council from, on the other hand, the management function of the City Manager, who is responsible for putting major choices into practice and accountable for this implementation under specific evaluation criteria that are subject to annual audit. Above all, the Municipal Finance Management Act introduced far-reaching budgetary reform by establishing and imposing mechanisms to develop a strategic framework for the budget process, based on the concept of performance and so linking expenditure to results. It requires that this framework should be the outcome of multiple negotiations with the other spheres of government, 'communities', sub-councils and ward committees, and that each year a budget document should be presented to the public for comments, four months before the council vote.

The same basic principles hold good for urban planning and development, for which the essential tool at the municipal scale is the 'Integrated Development Plan' (IDP) – a title that refers to both a process and a product. The concept of an integrated plan is based on two considerations: the need to drive cross-disciplinary activities by combining various national sectoral policies at the local scale and the extreme complexity of implementing an urban planning approach that has to integrate – in one place – all the dimensions of local development. Therefore the IDP has been designed as a negotiation process allowing the municipality to fulfil its constitutional obligations as an agent of integrated local development while adapting them to local realities, identifying problems and choosing priorities (Parnell and Pieterse, 2002). In order to do this, a great deal of discussion must be undertaken with all the main players: the private actors (both market and non-market) and officials from the two other spheres of government – not only those responsible for planning at their respective scales but also officials from certain urban development programmes that operate at the local scale[17]. Therefore the whole range of national and regional planning and development priorities must be laid out at the local level by establishing a Spatial Development Framework (SDF) that coordinates with national and provincial schemes, and this framework must be included in the IDP. So the latter is also a document that sets out the municipality's short-, medium- and long-term objectives and the resources to be mobilised.

Shortly before its 2006 electoral defeat, the old coalition had approved the Economic and Human Development Strategy (EHDS), which was based on the aspiration for a 'good city' (Parnell and Boulle, 2008) and advocated comprehensive urban management. After coming to power, the new coalition brought the IDP objectives, the budgetary strategy and Cape Town's economic

---

17   For example, the production of subsidised housing by the public authorities was a prerogative of the provinces until March 2011, and the Presidency has its own major urban programmes (in Cape Town, the Urban Renewal Programme is directed at the townships of Khayelitsha and Mitchell's Plain).

development plan (CoCT, 2007a) into line and adopted a second-generation five-year IDP (IDP 2007–2012). From this point of view, there has been improved integration of the various components of urban planning. Progress in integrating the development aspect should follow from adoption of the new SDF in May 2012; this sets out planning objectives on the basis of intra-urban districts and replaces the document drawn up during the transition (CoCT, 2009b). Its implementation now relies on the new Land Use Management System (LUMS) and on the new Cape Town Zoning Scheme which unifies the former 27 different zoning regulation schemes and came into effect on 1 March 2013.

This outcome – functional integration – is concomitant with a change of municipal strategy since March 2006. Until then, IDPs and annual budgetary commitments clearly showed that the metropolitan government, whichever political coalition was in power, was attempting to maintain an even balance between 'pro-growth' and 'pro-poor' policies. From 2006, priority has been given to infrastructure and amenities ('infrastructure-led economic growth'), especially because the organisation of the International Federation of Association Football (FIFA) World Cup in 2010 led to major works involving a total cost estimated at around R10 billion. So in the current IDP, the three major priorities are to create a favourable environment for economic growth, to develop infrastructure and services and to develop public transport. The investment budget, in which almost two-thirds of expenditure is devoted directly to infrastructure and amenities, was increased fourfold, going up from R1.5 billion in 2005–2006 to R5.5 billion in 2009–2010, just before the World Cup. Outlay has been sustained following that major event, (R5.9 billion for 2012–2013, R5.4 billion in the provisional budget for 2013–2014). Solidarity with poor citizens has been maintained through public provision; the central idea of the EHDS, stressing the need to reduce tension between economic performance and redistribution,[18] has not been disowned; but the strategic document's change of name[19] and the budget reorientation are evidence of normalisation in the treatment of poverty, reflecting the conditions of Cape Town's competitiveness and urban growth in a context of globalisation.

Running Large Technical Systems

The metropolitan government inherited the principle of running direct utility services (electricity, water and sanitation, waste) from earlier municipal organisations, and has preserved it. In the current CoCT organisation chart, these utilities are managed by three separate departments within the Utility Services Directorate (Table 4.1).

---

18   'Council's position on the tension between growth and poverty reduction is clear – that the size of the cake must be grown, whilst sharing the cake more equitably'. (CoCT, 2006: 9).

19   In October 2009, the EHDS was rechristened the 'EDS', confirming the elimination of the 'human' dimension (CoCT, 2009a).

Table 4.1   Municipal organization chart (2013)

City Manager Deputy City Manager	Directorates	Departments
	Community Services	City Parks; Sport and Recreation; Library and Information Services
	Economic, Environment and Spatial Planning	Economic and Human Development; Planning and Building Development Management; Development Facilitation; Infrastructure Development Coordination; Spatial Planning and Urban Design; Environmental Resource Management
	Finance	Treasury; Revenue; Expenditure; Supply Chain Management; Property Valuations; Budget; Shareholder Management; Housing Finance and Leases; Inter-service Liaison
	Health	Clinics and Environmental Health; Specialised Health
	Transport, Roads and Stormwater	IRT Implementation; IRT Operations; Transport; Roads and Stormwater; Strategic Support
	Corporate Services	Strategic Human Resources; Personnel Services; Employment Equity; Information Systems and Technology; Specialised Technical Services; Customer Relations and Administrative Services
	Human Settlements	Informal Settlements; Existing Settlements; New Settlements; Housing Land and Forward Planning; Strategy, Support and Co-ordination
	Safety and Security	Emergency Services; Metro Police; Law Enforcement and Security; Traffic Services; Specialised Services
	Utility Services	Electricity Services; Water and Sanitation; Solid Waste Management; Service Authority; Service Regulation and Logistics
	Social Development	
	Tourism, Events and Marketing	

The Deputy City Manager has line responsibility for Chief of Staff, Strategic Policy Unit, Executive Support, Legal Services, Governance and Interface, Integrated Strategic Communication and Branding, Integrated Development Plan, Expanded Public Works Programme and the probity functions of Internal Audit, Forensic Services, Integrated Risk Management and the Ombudsmans Office.

This horizontal integration within the municipal apparatus is similar to the kind of integration operated by a multiservice government corporation. Despite efforts during the 2000s to make the various skills involved 'autonomous' and to clarify cost allocations between the different services by establishing increased financial autonomy for each of them ('ring-fencing'), for the CoCT this integrated organisation remains a source of large economies of scale (shared services, integrated invoicing, mutual exchange of information on 'consumers' and cooperative consumer monitoring) and of intersectoral cross-subsidies, principally funded by income from the electricity service.

In fact, electricity distribution, introduced to South Africa by municipal governments in the late nineteenth century, forms the backbone of this integrated system (SACN, 2007), both financially and functionally. Representing about a third of municipal operating budgets, it provides a substantial part of everyday Treasury flows. Most, if not all, municipalities enjoy large financial surpluses from their electricity distribution activities, which they use to subsidise the provision of other services. Generally referred to as a 'contribution', the amount varies considerably from one municipality to another, ranging from 5 per cent of total revenue to over 40 per cent in some cases (Fowles, 2004). In Cape Town, this contribution remained stable at around 10 per cent in the 1980s and early 1990s, before rising to 13 per cent in 1997 and almost 15 per cent in 2003–2004,[20] so that, with contributions from water revenues, it has been able to play the role of a balancing item at times of financial pressure. Finally, electricity is more than a source of income: it is also essential to the management of revenues and to controlling arrears, since cities – notably Cape Town – have developed a 'creative' way of using intelligent electricity prepayment meters to manage payment for other services (Plancq-Tournadre, 2004; SACN, 2007).

The 'modernisation' of this municipal system has been carried through on the basis of the idea that metropolitan centralisation, in itself, promotes a combination of efficiency and equity. In the early 2000s, this rested on three pillars: integrating supply systems within a single metropolitan administration; redirecting public investment flows towards the townships; and adopting a single tariff structure enabling costs to be recovered.

Integrating the supply. In spite of various trials and tribulations, the processes of integrating and homogenising old local structures are now on the way to completion. They required major legal and technical innovations, with ERP implementation serving as a catalyst for the more general ambition to standardise information. Other, less spectacular efforts were also needed in order to carry this unification across into users' everyday lives. So, for historical reasons, four technically different (electricity) prepayment meter systems were in use in Cape Town, with uneven performance and separate, mutually incompatible marketing networks. Therefore customers could only buy their electricity from a limited

---

20   Since then, it has been brought back to 10 per cent at the request of the national energy regulator.

number of suppliers. Initially envisaged for 2007, the integration of the four systems onto a unified platform came into effect in June 2009, and since then customers have been able to buy their prepaid electricity from any one of 403 distribution stations within the municipal boundary. They can also purchase it over the Internet or by mobile phone.

On the other hand, provision of the electricity remains divided between a municipal operator (originating from the merger of earlier direct municipal distributors) that buys electricity in bulk from Eskom – a national state-owned enterprise – and Eskom itself, which distributes about a quarter of the electricity sold in the metropolis. In 2009, of some 785,000 consumers, 580,000 were served by the municipal operator and 204,000 – mainly industries and domestic consumers in Cape Flats – by Eskom (CCT, UTS 06/06/09).[21] As a result of this division, the proportion of poor consumers (defined as households consuming less than 150 kWh/month) is much higher in the districts served by Eskom. The disparities linked to this split between supply areas should have been governed by a service agreement between the City of Cape Town (the organising authority for the local service) and Eskom (the supplier). However, these provisions were not implemented; and the objective of unifying the conditions of service (tariffs, service levels, electrification programmes) has been postponed until the electricity distribution industry is restructured nationally – a change that is taking a long time to materialise.

Investments. Rationalisation and modernisation of municipal services, which has sometimes seemed to stand in contradiction to the expectations of the 'developmental local state' (McDonald and Smith, 2002), has nevertheless been accompanied by significant investments and by revision of tariffs to a 'fairer' basis. Schemes for investing in technical networks have three points in common: they give priority to meeting the infrastructure backlog in the townships, they extend existing capacities in order to meet demand and they include an increasing proportion of programmes designed to bring amenities to informal districts.[22] The CoCT has three main sources of finance: 'development contributions'[23], the Municipal Infrastructure Grant (MIG)[24] and its own funds. The first of these are mainly levied on major urban development operations; the amount is negotiated with private-sector actors, who can also pay off their 'contributions' by directly financing infrastructure (CCT,

---

21   These data are from the municipal archives. Throughout the rest of this chapter, they are indicated by the following type of reference: (CCT+TSI/UTS/FIN+date); they are available online from the City of Cape Town's official Council web site: http://www. capetown.gov.za/en/CouncilOnline/Pages/default.aspx

22   Marked by the adoption, in May 2007, of a municipal Informal Settlement Plan (MCA Africa, 2006).

23   These are taxes levied, under Section 42 of the Land Use Planning Ordinance 1985 (LUPO) and a 2004 Municipal Interim Policy (MC 45/11/04), on property deals and rezoning applications that impact on demand for services.

24   A blanket subsidy granted by the national government to local authorities for investments in support of their programmes to improve essential services.

UTS 18/09/09). The Municipal Infrastructure Grant is an incentive to develop infrastructure programmes that benefit poor households by improving services and creating jobs. Finally, the CoCT finances a significant proportion of investment in infrastructure from its own funds and through borrowing.

These investments have primarily benefited electricity distribution, enabling a near-universal service to be achieved despite institutional fragmentation. About 200,000 new connections were installed in ten years, and the 2011 official[25] rate of electrification in the metropolis is 96.3 per cent (compared to 86 per cent in 1995). The costs of this progress have been largely met from the national budget, through the Integrated National Electrification Programme, while some of the extensions intended for major urban development operations have been financed by the private sector through development contributions. The municipal budget has borne the remaining financial outlays required to meet both the backlog and the boom in demand for electricity, which grew by 50 per cent in the Western Cape over ten years (1994–2005) (MCA Africa, 2006).

Parallel efforts have been agreed in the water and sanitation services, this time with two clear priorities: to upgrade existing infrastructure in the townships (for example, the Water Leaks Repair Programme and the Fixit Project have enabled repair of water networks,[26] installation of meters and mending of leaks in over 23,000 old council houses) and to provide additional capacities, notably in the increasingly densely populated working-class districts (construction of additional treatment units in Cape Flats and Athlone). Detecting leaks and reducing peak consumption – combined with aiming to conserve water resources – have been worthwhile because they have helped to defer the big investments required to increase production capacity. Most of the financial strain has been taken by the municipality, with support from the national budget through the Municipal Infrastructure Grant.

Finally, expenditure on waste management has increased spectacularly, although there is a gap between priorities in terms of service – extending and upgrading service delivery in townships and informal settlement areas – and the actual allocation of resources. In reality, resources have been granted for modernisation of landfill sites and to replace the fleet of vehicles, and it was these priorities that absorbed most of the budget between 2001 and 2005 (MCA Africa, 2006).

Therefore investment effort has privileged the creation of uniform service standards at the metropolitan scale – to the advantage of the most deprived spaces – and has attempted to support growth, both in the corridors of prosperity (notably in the north of the city) and in the vast housing developments intended

---

25   The uncertainty relates to the rate of connection in informal settlements, where the continuous influx of population requires ongoing, unspecified redefinition of the amount of investment required.

26   Including relocation under the public highway of water mains that had formerly been buried, for the sake of economy, under the 'private' parts of plots of land earmarked by the apartheid authorities for municipal apartment buildings.

for poor sections of the population (such as the N2 Gateway project). Although there are no longer any backlogs in providing facilities to planned districts, they still remain in the informal districts, where some 117,000 households are served by free public drinking fountains and have access only to unsatisfactory individual sanitation systems (CCT, UTS 06/06/09).

Tariffs. Convergence in tariffs and taxes is the third vector of this unification at the metropolitan scale. Apart from the principle of a single tariff structure, the approach imposed has been to reconcile cost recovery (Jaglin, 2003; McDonald and Smith, 2002) with social equity, notably through the provision of 'free basic services'. Thus, water tariffs are used to introduce several mechanisms to promote solidarity: between old districts and new extensions, through geographically based cross-subsidies; between big and small consumers, through a progressive five-band tariff; between households and large business account holders, through a surcharge of 7 per cent on commercial tariffs to subsidise an allowance of 6m³ a month free of charge for every household – a policy introduced nationally in 2001. This approach was more difficult in the electricity sector, because of the presence of two operators. Although the old municipal tariffs were based on a single tariff structure,[27] this does not apply in the townships served by Eskom, where tariffs are still coordinated at the national scale and defined on the basis of a different schedule. At first, consumers in the townships were deprived of the free electricity allowance because of a dispute between Eskom and the municipality, but in 2004 they were brought into line with other consumers, with the CoCT paying for free units provided by Eskom. In contrast, policies for the electrification of informal housing remain an area of discrimination between consumers. In making new connections to informal settlements conditional on obtaining a ministry subsidy, Eskom lags behind the municipality's proactive policy.

Over these first years of the metropolitan government, therefore, the priority was to set up a framework that would favour the spread of spatial equity in terms of both quality and tariff. True to the municipality's political project, this approach was also driven by municipal engineers, many of whom presumed that the only acceptable mode of achieving integration would be to extend the standards and rules for a universal infrastructure service to the whole metropolitan area – a model that, in the past, had underpinned the expansion and management of services in affluent districts. Although they censured it for its slowness and its neo-liberal bases, 'progressives' defended the principles of this approach to unification, since they objected to any differentiation in the service offer as tending to reproduce the inequalities created by apartheid (Bond et al., 2000; Smith and Hanson, 2003).

---

27   Domestic 1, over 800 kWh/month; Domestic 2, between 400 and 800kWh/month: subsidised tariff with no standing charge; Lifeline Tariff, under 400kWh/month: billed at Domestic 2 but with 50kWh granted free of charge.

Solidarity With the Poor Through Public Provision

Social reorientation of services

Whereas at first the emphasis had been on institution-building, from 2002 there was a noticeable policy reorientation, with social assistance measures being established to help the most vulnerable sections of the population. This solidarity was expressed in particular by the decision not to 'privatise' water services – an approach that had been considered under the previous City Council (McDonald and Smith, 2002) – and by the reorientation of local policy towards providing housing and essential services as well as supplying informal settlements with basic amenities.

These social concerns also had an increasingly marked impact on tariff structuring. From this point of view, the introduction of the 'Total Municipal Account' (TMA) represents an interesting initiative (Marsden, 2003a). Based on the idea that a large proportion of households in payment arrears are for all practical purposes insolvent, this approach accepts that only a comprehensive, intersectoral solution can improve the monitoring and treatment of household indebtedness. So, each financial year, a consultative committee[28] is entrusted with modelling the impact of taxation and tariff policy on the Total Municipal Account, for different districts and types of household; the results are then used by the municipality as a tool for steering and communication.

Apart from cross-subsidies and the policy of providing essential services free of charge, various mechanisms have been introduced to progressively limit the poorest people's bills for municipal services. For the water service, an additional band was created and the tariffs for the first three bands were reduced in order to take into account the needs of poor families who cannot manage to keep their consumption within the free basic allowance. The CoCT's Integrated Water Leaks Repair Strategy takes a comprehensive approach to the indebtedness of poor households who are behind in their payments to the municipality and handicapped by poor quality fittings that lead to a large number of leaks (Smith, 2006). Within this framework, the arrears of 7,500 households covered by the scheme were written off in November 2007[29] (CCT, UTS 10/11/07). A minimal sanitation service has been instituted free of charge. Substantial exemptions from refuse collection charges have been granted, according to the property value of a given home. As far as the electricity service is concerned, in order to limit the subsidies budget while still helping the poorest users, from 2005 the municipality targeted the free service solely to consumers billed on Domestic Tariff 2[30] and using less than 400 kWh a month.[31] A 2004 survey in Khayelitsha had given a positive

---

28   TARPAC: the Tariff and Rates Policy Advisory Committee.

29   This was on condition that they managed to limit their monthly consumption to less than 10kl for a half-year period.

30   See Note 27.

31   Fixed at 450 kWh/month in 2005, the Lifeline Tariff ceiling was lowered to 400 kWh/month in 2007–2008, although this is still higher than the 150 kWh recommended in

assessment of the impact of a free service on this kind of consumer. It estimated the amount of electricity for a household's minimum needs at about 150kWh/month: although the monthly free allowance of 50kWh is not enough to cover this minimum, it nevertheless reduces the average price per kWh by a third and, at this consumption level, makes electricity an energy choice that is both more affordable and more attractive (Lloyd et al., 2004).[32] In fact, this survey also showed that a growing number of households in Khayelitsha were switching away from paraffin towards full electrification for domestic use, while half the households connected to the electricity network reported that they had been using more electricity for more purposes since the extension of the free service to Eskom customers (Lloyd et al., 2004). It remains the case that poor households devote 10 per cent to 15 per cent of their monthly income to energy purchases (excluding transport) and that in Khayelitsha this can even be as high as 20 per cent (Annecke et al., 2005) – and therefore they still remain in fuel poverty.[33]

The metropolitan Indigent Policy: going beyond a universal service to a more comprehensive anti-poverty strategy

In order to take a more comprehensive approach to serious poverty, in 2001 the metropolitan authorities adopted another tool, the 'Indigent Policy', in the aim of reducing indebtedness among the poorest households by easing their tax and tariff burden. In theory, this measure should have made it possible for many households to bring their payments to the municipality down to zero, but because it was based on a narrow concept of social assistance and a notion of encouraging responsibility among poor people that is very far removed from the realities of life in the townships, it was made contingent on conditions that restricted its impact. For example, households had to register, with written supporting evidence, on a list of beneficiaries (or 'indigent rolls') and renew this registration every three months; or they might be required to make an arrangement to pay off arrears that could sometimes be considerable (Plancq-Tournadre, 2004).

The ruling ANC-NNP alliance promised change, and in October 2002 it announced a six-month moratorium on disconnections and evictions, followed a few months later by a new Indigent Policy (Van Ryneveld, 2003), which was later amended and strengthened by the multi-party coalition.

This social policy expresses solidarity with underprivileged citizens, and so promotes the equity that is now considered necessary to strengthen the

---

the National Guidelines.

32 In Khayelitsha in June 2004, the average expenditure of a household with electricity was R96.40 a month compared to R99.20 a month for a household without electricity (the cheapest paraffin then cost R2.90/litre and electricity 50c/kWh minus the free 50kWh/month) (Lloyd et al., 2004: 16). If the cost of frequent fires, air pollution and respiratory diseases linked to the use of paraffin in the home were taken into account, the difference would of course be very much greater.

33 Defined by the 10 per cent threshold.

competitiveness of a metropolis. So, in the 2011–2012 municipal budget, all properties valued at less than R200,000 were exempted from municipal taxes (185,000 households) and provided with a basket of free services including weekly household refuse collection, 50 kWh of electricity, 6 m^3 of water and 4.2 m^3 of sewerage. In addition, all owner-occupier households living in properties valued at under R300,000 receive an allowance of R38 a month.[34] Lastly, households with incomes under R3,000 a month can apply to be registered on the indigent rolls in order to benefit from the tax exemption and the monthly R38 allowance.[35] The last measure aims to extend the benefits of this social policy to non-owner-occupier households, as long as they make themselves known to City Hall (232,000 'indigent' households were registered in 2011). Indeed, reaching the 'invisible poor', who miss out on benefits and free services because of the unregulated nature of their land tenure, remains one of the main social policy issues (Parnell and Boulle, 2008). Finally, assistance is granted to low-income retired people and to people with disabilities (21,000 people in 2012).

Challenges to Integration: The Limitations of Municipal Policy

So a substantial part of the municipality's energy and resources is mobilised towards the objective of integration, with convincing results in spheres where public control has been well established over a long period. The counterpoint to this is that an inability to control the shape of the city or the social cost of urban sprawl and the financial pressures arising from extending the older service model to the whole municipal territory challenge the metropolitan government's capacity to promote equitable, sustainable change – and challenge it on more than one front.

Polycentric Sprawl: When the Shape of the City Slips from the Politicians' Grasp

Cape Town's metropolitan territory[36] extends over almost 2,500 km^2, and the geomorphological characteristics of the site (Figure 4.2), the specific nature of the local ecosystems and the particular land uses mean that it is far from totally urbanised. Table Mountain (highest point: 1,080m above sea level) and the peninsula's secondary mountain chains – which stretch for 50 km – dominate the

---

34   This 'monthly indigent grant' corresponds to the provision of 4.5 m^3 of extra free water and 3.15 m^3 of collected wastewater.

35   So, in 2010–2011, the Municipality devoted R1.1 billion (5 per cent of the total budget) to funding free services and tax reductions for poor households.

36   2,499 km^2 according to SACN (2006), a fact confirmed by Robert Cameron (personal communication). According to the municipality, the surface area is 2,461 km^2. After the boundary adjustments that took place in 2000, the surface area was perhaps not calculated by the same methods as those used by the Demarcation Board. On the territorial divisions, see Cameron (2006).

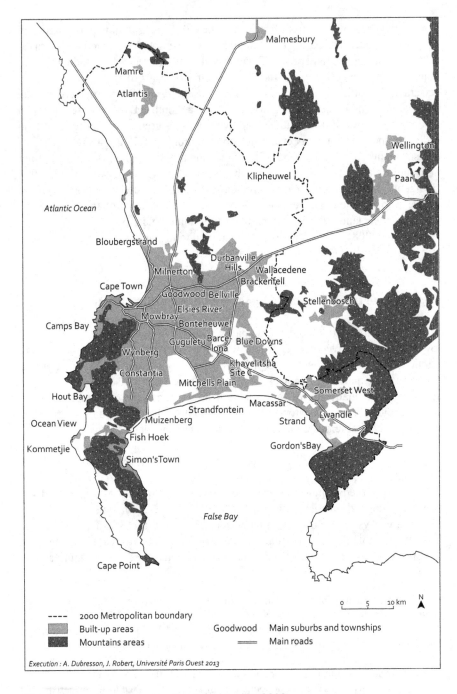

Figure 4.2   Cape Town urbanized area in 2008

ocean shoreline with the very steep – in places, vertical – slopes of their powerful escarpments. Because of its unusual ecological features, the 'Cape Floral Region' is one of the world's sanctuaries of biodiversity and, since 2004, has been the smallest 'hot spot' listed by UNESCO as a World Heritage Site. About 9,600 individual species have been counted there, of which 70 per cent are endemic and unique, including those of the *fynbos* biome. 'Natural' ecosystems, which cover a total of 970 km² in the mountains, on the plain[37] and along the 294-km coastline and were exploited under the apartheid regime, are now the object of conservation policies keenly supported by rich Capetonians; the activities of numerous ecological associations have led to the designation of areas where no building is permitted.[38] To these 'protected' areas can be added agricultural land that is still under cultivation (including fine vineyards in Constancia, the Durbanville foothills and on the eastern fringes of the municipal territory), security zones surrounding the Koeberg Nuclear Power Station (defined by two radiuses of ten and 20 km around the plant) and noise abatement zones adjoining the international airport.

Despite these restrictions, the expanse of the city has sprawled in spectacular fashion since the 1980s. Between 1985 and 2005, the physically urbanised area increased by 40 per cent.[39] It grew by seven km² a year between 1977 and 1988, but over the period 1985–2005 the increase reached an average of 12 km² a year; by 2010, there were probably about 820 urbanised km². This polycentric sprawl marks a break with the old, semi-concentric growth pattern (Wilkinson, 2000).

Migration inflows centred on poor Cape Flats
The metropolitan territory had a population of about three million at the turn of the millennium, and has reached 3.7 million according to the 2011 national Census results (StatSa, 2012). As in the other big South African cities, Cape Town's demographic growth has slowed down[40] because of the general fall in fertility, the relative downturn in immigration and the impact of the AIDS pandemic on mortality. But the rate of population growth has unexpectedly increased from 2001 to 2011 and the former projections (+ 0.5 per cent a year from 2011 to 2016, then to + 0.2 per cent, Dorington, 2005) could have underestimated the effects of new black populations in-migrations flows.

Two essential quantitative factors must be underlined. Firstly, from 1996 to 2005, 700,000 new citizens have had to find accommodation space in the city and about 300,000 more are expected to try and do so between now and 2021. Secondly, although migrations of coloured populations have fallen, internal

---

37   Almost 1,500 species are confined to the sandy Cape Flats plains.
38   So 430 km² are formally protected, and there are now 24 nature reserves covering 147 km².
39   This includes 55 new suburbs, nine new shopping malls and two new industrial zones.
40   To be more precise, + 2.9 per cent a year from 1970 to 1996 (SACN, 2006), + 2,2 per cent from 1996 to 2001, + 2,6 per cent from 2001 to 2011.

migration of disadvantaged black populations, coming especially from the rural areas of Eastern Cape and flows of refugees from Somalia, Congo and Zimbabwe (60,000 to 80,000) have accelerated the urbanisation of poverty. Unlike other big South African cities, Cape Town certainly does not have a majority of black citizens, but their relative proportion is increasing and they are the poorest. In the 2001 Census, 'black Africans' made up 31.2 per cent of the total population (9 per cent in 1960), coloured people 46.1 per cent, white people 21.2 per cent and Indian/Asian people 1.5 per cent. In the 2011 Census, black people form 38.6 per cent of the total population, with 42.4 per cent coloured people, 19.3 per cent white people, 1.4 per cent Indian/Asian and 1.9 per cent 'other'; according to current projections 2021, coloured people could remain the most numerous.

Combined with the previous apartheid model of social engineering, this predominance of coloured populations suggests why the educational and skills levels of the non-white workforce in Cape Town are higher than national averages, while poverty is lower.[41] It also helps to explain why public local development policy intended to promote a form of 'catch-up' by encouraging integration is directed at the Cape Flats townships, especially Khayelitsha, where a large proportion of black citizens were assigned residence by race-based town planning policies and where current migrations converge. Finally, this particular population feature influences not only the composition and the behaviour of the electoral bases of opposing local – or locally represented – political forces, but also their shifting strategies of alliance or confrontation.

Changes in the production base and new economic centres of gravity
Cape Town's urban sprawl also results from a rapid alteration in the city's production base, the increasing importance of flexible accumulation and the consequent changes in the economy's spatial dimensions. This transformation at the local scale cannot be dissociated from major national macroeconomic choices, in particular the 1996 adoption of the Growth, Employment and Redistribution strategy (GEAR), which – in line with neo-liberal orthodoxy – advocates opening up to competition in national and international markets, the 2006 implementation of the Accelerated and Shared Growth Initiative, which tries to create a better balance between growth and redistribution while still accelerating the process of opening up to the global economy, and the New Growth Path adopted in 2010.

Although now relatively diversified, the production base is still dominated, as ever, by services[42] – and, above all, it works for the national market. However, over some 20 years, the bases of accumulation have changed: manufacturing industry remains important but there has been a rapid shift towards a financial and a high tech service economy that is more open to the outside. Post-Fordist restructuring

---

41   In Cape Town, populations classified as 'coloured' used to benefit from 'labour preference', in particular in public administration.

42   In 2010: FIRE 34,2 per cent of urban GDP, Wholesale and retail trade 16,3 per cent, Manufacturing 14,3 per cent.

(Crankshaw, 2012) has affected legacy industries in different ways (a crisis in the textile industry; vitality in agribusiness and agro-food processing, which is the leading export sector) and various key growth sectors have developed (oil and natural gas, automobile components, yacht building and repair, new information and communication technologies including e-business and call centres, the film industry). Tourism is expanding rapidly,[43] as is the 'FIRE' ('finance, insurance, real estate') sector, based on the headquarters of powerful insurance groups (Old Mutual, Sanlam, Metropolitan Life) and major retail groups (Shoprite, Woolworth, Pick N'Pay, Ackermans, Truworth, Foshini).

Four strong trends characterise the location of private investments in production within the metropolitan area (Turok, 2001, Sinclair-Smith and Turok, 2012). First, up to 2001, a number of services eased rapidly away from the Central Business District (CBD) towards high-income suburban areas, although the CBD has been very vigorously revitalised since then. Second, dispersal away from existing nodes of centrality has accelerated. This is based on new uses of the urbanised space: the change of use of buildings along main roads in wealthy areas and the spread of business parks and office buildings integrated into private property development schemes that promote small mixed-use complexes on rezoned land. Third, a clear 'northern drift' marks the fact that this is the favoured location for major investments (R10 million +), to the detriment of the poor South-East where the informal economy is growing rapidly. Fourth, certain spaces are becoming more specialised, with service nodes increasingly positioned in specific market segments. At a bigger geographical scale, we should note that nodes and corridors (Figure 4.3) are increasingly differentiated from one another, in part because specialized clusters are appearing in them, and that some corridors – like the historic Voortrekker Road – have been marginalized by megaprojects situated very close to them. These strong tendencies have two spatial consequences.

Firstly, the production of added value is concentrated in wealthy areas. In 2007, almost 60 per cent of the city's production came from the city centre districts (CBD, Foreshore, Waterfront: 22.1 per cent), the Bellville node and the Durbanville corridor (12.1 per cent), the Koeberg corridor with its adjacent shopping and leisure centres (9.7 per cent), the Claremont node and the Main Road corridor (7.3 per cent). These productions bases are linked by intra-urban freeways to the two major logistical hubs – the international airport and the port. The airport, situated 22 km from the city centre, is the country's second airport, with traffic of 8.5 million passengers in 2011 and 14 million expected in 2015. Several times winner of international competitions,[44] it has benefited from major works, with the construction in 2003 of a new international arrivals building (cost: R120 million; capacity: one million passengers/year) and then a new 21,000 m² central terminal

---

43 On average six million visitors from 2008 to 2011, of whom 1.8 million came from abroad.

44 It was Skytrax 'Best Airport in Africa' from 2001 to 2005, and then in 2011 and 2012.

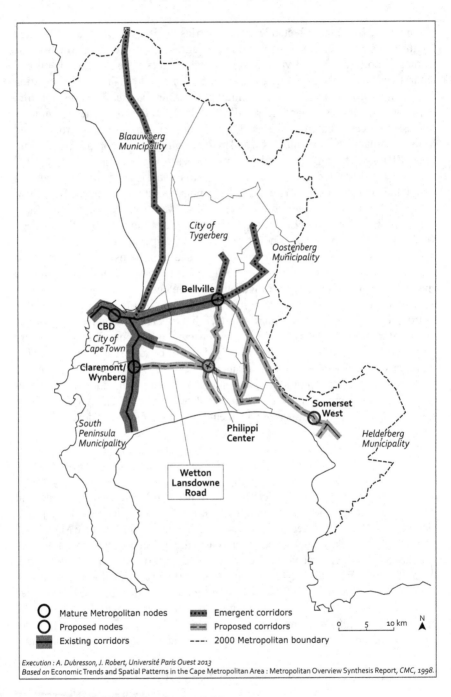

Figure 4.3   MSDF nodes and corridors

completed in November 2009 (R1.2 billion). The port, because it is so far from the Province of Gauteng, the heart of the South African economy, and because of competition from the more versatile ports on the Indian Ocean coast (not only Durban, Port Elisabeth and East London, but also Maputo in Mozambique), has only modest traffic – nine to ten million tonnes/year, of which 70 per cent is general merchandise. However, its role as a hub for oil and natural gas is important[45] and the Western Cape agribusiness industries (wines, fruit and vegetables) export from it. In total, almost a quarter of South African goods traffic passes through the logistical system of the Cape Town urban region, which combines the two ports at Cape Town and Saldanha, the airport, oil pipelines, the rail network and two main freeways (OECD, 2008). In this context, the Port of Cape Town is benefiting from a 5-year modernisation programme launched in 2008 (R5.4 billion); this aims to double its traffic, in particular container traffic, which should rise from 740,000 to 1.4 million TEUs (20-foot equivalent units) by 2013 thanks to a new Super Post-Panamax reception terminal for container ships.

Secondly, premium spaces have rapidly emerged within wealthy areas, arising from the new spatial dimensions of the economy and strengthened by both the implementation of 'City Improvement Districts' (CIDs) – inspired by US 'Business Improvement Districts' (BIDs) – and major preparatory works for hosting the 2010 FIFA World Cup. The CBD has been regenerated (Pirie, 2007): cumulative investments there are estimated at R12.5 billion from 2000 to 2006, and in 2009 there were hopes of almost R30 billion more between 2006 and 2012 (CoCT, 2009a). The city centre's tourism and financial services functions have been maintained or even increased, and economic diversification has been promoted: ICT/business-process outsourcing, call centres, creative and cultural industries (CCID, 2012). The east side regeneration (The Fringe) has been launched for hosting the 2014 World Design Capital event. In 2012, the total amount of rentable office space in the central city reached 785,000 m², the CBD concentrated 33 per cent of Cape Town Class A offices and the current value of the 8,500 recorded properties was estimated at R21.7 billion. The private sector has invested about R2 billion in Claremont since 2000, and CID officials talk about a 'Claremont Renaissance'.[46] Big multifunction complexes, drawing on models from around the world, have sprung up in or near wealthy areas; these include the Waterfront (Ferreira and Visser, 2007), originating from the development of 60 ha around the old port basins, purchased in 2006 for R7 billion by the Lexshell consortium[47]

---

45   In addition to the crude oil supplied to the oil refinery at Milnerton, 1/3 of crude oil export flows from the Atlantic coast of Africa and 1/4 of those from the Middle East pass near Cape Town, where maintenance, repair and provisioning of tankers are carried out, as they are for offshore drilling platforms situated in South Africa's coastal waters off Mossel Bay in the Western Cape, where methane reserves are exploited.

46   See Claremont Developments, www.skyscrapercity.com/showthread.php?p=12363287

47   Lexshell is held by Istihmar PJSC (Dubai), London & Regional (United Kingdom) and a group of black South African investors.

and bought in 2011 for R9.7 billion by a South African group of investors[48], the International Convention Centre,[49] and Century City, a large enclosed area constructed around a canal and including a shopping centre (Canal Walk), an amusement park, an office park, hotels and protected nature reserves, beyond and around which gated residential housing estates have been built (Kalaora, 2002) and are now sprawling.

Public housing choices and extension of the urban area

Sprawl also results from national choices in relation to housing model. Access to housing is not only a political priority, as set out in the ANC's first programme (the Reconstruction and Development Programme, or RDP) and in the Housing White Paper published in 1994, but also a fundamental right, enshrined in the 1996 Constitution and confirmed by the Housing Act of 1997.[50] In order to tackle the shortage, a major national programme involving the production of 1.5 million housing units in five years was launched. However, what matters is the model chosen, rather than the efforts made to produce housing.

Negotiated at a National Housing Forum where numerous public sector, private sector and not-for-profit sector actors met – including the Urban Foundation, a private-sector institution that is a powerful local vector of neo-liberal thinking – this model was one variant of a hybrid mode of regulation that privileged public-private partnerships and mixed governance. Central government ignored the rental solution, which had too many connotations of apartheid – and anyway, where there were segments of the housing market that could be tackled in this way, the private and cooperative sectors were already doing so. Instead, it concentrated its efforts on promoting increasingly widespread private ownership, first of all by pursuing framework improvement programmes (the People's Housing Process, or PHP) directed towards working-class self-advancement, then by speeding up the sale of public housing stock in the townships, and finally by democratising funding for first-time buyers. So, in 1995, on the income criterion (under R3.500 a month) alone, 86 per cent of South African households had access to the Housing Subsidy Scheme, intended for first-time buyers (Plancq-Tournadre, 2006; Royston, 2002).

Aiming to normalise the situation of people excluded from formal housing, the implementation of a public model of individual low-density housing relied on a partnership between a proactive state, whose role would be to incentivise and

---

48   The new owners are Growthpoint Properties, the country's largest listed property investment company, the Government Employees' Pension Fund and the Public Investment Corporation.

49   CTICC is a publicly owned facility (R1.4 billion invested); it takes about 50 per cent of the market share of conventions hosted in Africa in 2012.

50   In 1994, the national housing shortage was estimated at 1.2 million units and, according to the 1996 Census, 13 per cent of the total population (one million households) were occupying land which had no services or where services were still in the process of being laid on.

facilitate, private enterprises producing working-class housing and 'communities', which were meant to participate in designing projects that would affect them. The innovation lay in the entirely subsidised nature of the urban development offering: houses built on individually defined plots of land, fully equipped with networked water, sanitation and electricity services, were offered for owner-occupation.

Two modifications subsequently brought this initial model into line with international orthodoxy. The first, in 2002, was an overhaul of the funding system, making it obligatory for all beneficiaries to play a part in financing – already the practice in PHP programmes. The principle of making access to a loan conditional on the recipient's financial participation was systematised, except for households defined as indigent.[51] It introduced the notion of placing responsibility on households, in the expectation that this would strengthen their sense of ownership. The second change took place in 2004. The national Cabinet approved a new housing development plan and the Housing Minister unveiled the 'Comprehensive Housing Plan for the Development of Integrated Sustainable Human Settlements', better known under the title *Breaking New Ground* (BNG). The central objective was to eradicate insecure informal settlements through *in situ* rebuilding operations and/or – where rebuilding was complicated or impossible – by relocating households. The second modification involved a change of approach, moving from simple delivery of clustered residential units to producing integrated spaces, supplementing the previous package with social amenities and economic infrastructure. In this way, it was thought, the development of functional, sustainable neighbourhoods would be guaranteed.

In fact, in Cape Town as in other big cities, the outcomes of this public model of low-density individual housing that would create peripheral, monofunctional districts ran counter to the model's objectives. First of all, the legacy of the way residential space had been organised was reproduced and perpetuated. In order to build on a large scale and at low cost, both the municipality and private developers exploited public land reserves located on the distant Cape Flats. Private land available at market prices in central or pericentral areas was too costly to purchase; in addition, the municipality of Cape Town owned less land than the Province and less than some other public and parastatal entities, such as the South African Defence Force or the Transnet Group, with which it often came into conflict. One of the rare opportunities adjoining the city centre was the vacant space of the old District 6, razed to the ground under the apartheid regime; but complex restitution proceedings were ongoing, and poor people could not gain access to the few houses built there. To this public model was added, for more profitable demand segments, a private supply dominated by big development groups and almost exclusively based on the model of an individual house located in the centre of a plot of land, whose size increased in line with income: so 20 per cent of private properties monopolised 41 per cent of the area of residential land. The combination of

51   In 2002, income under R800/month, then income under 1,500 in 2004.

these two models[52] considerably increased the consumption of space. From 2005 to 2008, building plans submitted were primarily for single dwelling houses (85 per cent to 88 per cent), while town houses (10 per cent to 14 per cent) and blocks of flats (1.5 per cent) were less sought after. Average population density in relation to the whole built-up area remains low (about 40 people/ha) and, in 2008, 95 per cent of residential space was classified by municipal planners in the low-density category (11 dwelling units/ha).

Second, allocation procedures and conditions did not ensure sufficient production of housing to meet the backlog and to satisfy new demand; the housing shortage has increased continually since the 1990s. Assessed at 150,000 units in 1998, it reached 300,000 in 2007, and was estimated by the municipality at 400,000 in 2011. Since 2005, the rate of new applications has been in the order of 18,000 to 20,000 a year, while the production of public housing – taking all categories together – has been very erratic: only once between 2001 and 2006 did it exceed 5,000 housing units/year, and it did not reach 10,000 units until 2008. Consequently, illegal informal settlements have proliferated within or near townships remote from the city centre. In 1994, there were about 28,000 housing units in the shanty towns; by 2008, according to the municipality's estimates, there were about 117,000 and by 2011 about 130,000 (CoCT, 2012). According to the 2011 Census, 219,000 households live in informal housing (20.5 per cent of the total of households), of which 77,000 in informal dwelling and backyard shacks[53] and 144,000 in informal settlements. Then, with the average household sizes of poor urban dwellers (Black people: 3.25; Coloured: 4.42), between 711,000 and 968,000 Capetonians live officially in informal housing, and the reality is probably one million.

Failure of the first Metropolitan Spatial Development Framework (MSDF)
The MSDF, adopted in May 1996, was an attempt to control the shape of the city through spatial planning. It was based on the idea of the compact city – an alternative to apartheid town planning that would enable the opportunities the city offers to be made accessible to the majority of residents – and it set out a systematic, positive vision promoting integration. Watson has made a noteworthy study that covers the history of how it was drawn up and the issues and the failures of urban planning during the transition period (Watson, 2002). The MSDF was based on four key elements: defining 'nodes of centrality' to be strengthened or created at the heart of areas inhabited by poor populations; defining multifunctional 'corridors' whose purpose is to be connected to nodes, thus allowing an integrated spatial model to be set up; establishing a Metro Open Space System, or MOSS;[54]

52   On average, the subsidised sector generates 60 per cent of annual newbuilds and the market, 40 per cent.
53   Dwellings constructed from sheet metal and other recovered materials, situated behind formal housing.
54   A system for defending and preserving open spaces within the metropolitan territory, where no building is permitted.

controlling spatial growth by identifying 'urban edges'. The objectives set out have not been achieved, the dynamics of functional integration between nodes and corridors has apparently not got underway (or, at least, only to a very limited extent), urban sprawl has not been curbed and the legacy of inequalities within the structure of the city remains.

According to the analyses put forward, the ineffectiveness of the MSDF arises from the fact that either it has not been applied or it cannot be applied. The first argument relates to failures of both vertical and horizontal governance during the transition period, to the political conditions of the political and territorial merger, to rivalries between the six former temporary municipalities and to the institutional fragmentation that then marginalised and isolated planners within an organisation that proved to have no internal synergies (Watson, 2002; Dubresson, 2005). The second argument (that, even when applied, the MSDF was not efficient) relates to a debate about the conceptual bases of an attempt at spatialised public regulation.

Watson (2002) expressed two major criticisms. Firstly, controlling the location of private investments, especially in favour of areas of poverty, was a chimera. It was neither realistic nor realizable to legislate on this topic while the spatial behaviours of businesses – two thirds of which were SMEs – were increasingly marked by flexibility, mobility and competing on the basis of physical externalities. Secondly, this lack of understanding of the current structuring of the economic space reflects a closed mode of thinking, in which spatial planning remains sectoral and specialised. We should add that thoughts of equalising access to waged employment by prioritising business locations also merit examination. The jobs created by investments do not automatically go to nearby residents, particularly in a context where the educational and occupational standards of disadvantaged populations are very low and where the problem of their basic training is far from being resolved.

So the MSDF was part of an attempt at spatial regulation whose conception and principles originated in the national sphere, and it was often in contradiction to the new spatial dynamics of the economy and to land and property market actors' strategies. Therefore the MSDF did not play the role of a general reference framework, recognized as such by all the parties, and its bases were mistaken. Of the four key elements, only two were relatively uncontested: first, the creation of a boundary or 'urban edge' in order to protect agricultural land (in particular, the nearby vineyards), fragile ecosystems and peripheral spaces and aiming to encourage the city's internal densification, and second, the identification of the MOSS. The Democratic Alliance, which controlled the City Council until October 2002, launched a process for revising the MSDF; efforts were made by both subsequent coalitions to pursue this and it is now complete. The whole question is whether the new SDF (CoCT, 2009d), which advocates strategic planning less focused on zoned territorial control and privileges the implementation of integrated programmes, is better able to promote urban change to the benefit of the most disadvantaged citizens.

The Social Costs of Sprawl

In addition to the continued extension of the city's surface area – which runs counter to compaction – the effects of segregation and marginalisation must be taken into account. People to whom subsidised housing is allocated belong to the same strata as far as monetary income is concerned – and often to the same 'racial group' – as residents who settled there earlier. In addition, the fact that aid being passed through developers is spread so thinly has led to a reduction in per-unit subsidies, which in turn has resulted in lower-cost production and low-quality building. Since between half and two thirds of the maximum amount of subsidies has been absorbed by the costs of bulk service extensions, the core houses are small in size (just one or two rooms plus bathroom: 40–50 m² at best, 15–25 m² in most cases), often of mediocre architectural merit and sometimes less well provided with amenities than the 'matchbox houses' in the old townships. Moreover, the absence of businesses forces employees and jobseekers to make long daily journeys to areas where there is work. Transport costs place a heavy burden on household expenses and penalise the most disadvantaged households, who can access the formal labour market only with difficulty.

Therefore, in contrast to the concentration of added value in the city's wealthy areas, there has been no change in the economic isolation of Cape Flats, where the two largest townships, Khayelitsha (which houses black Africans) and Mitchell's Plain (where most residents are coloured), are located. Thus, Khayelitsha has at least 12 per cent of the city's total population, but provides only 0.7 per cent of its formal GDP. There is very little data available as to the value produced by informal activities, which are said to provide 12 per cent of the city's total GDP (Parnell and Boulle, 2008). One of few certainties is the increasing power of gangs and of the criminal economy. The literature on organised crime shows that integration into the market sphere of people excluded from the official waged labour market is in large part achieved through the criminal economy – a rational survival response in Cape Flats, and one which introduces millions of Rand into circulation and is said to provide about 120,000 jobs (Standing, 2003 and 2005).

This reproduction of social division in the urban space is illustrated by the distribution of citizens according to the socio-economic status index of households (Figure 4.4).[55] It is true that there are small pockets of poverty spread all over the urbanised space, but poor areas are mainly concentrated in the South-East, where the coloured and black populations remain largely confined. There are few examples of desegregation, and the main lines of racial segregation have not changed in two decades. Combined with distance from production spaces, this geographical concentration of poor people has disastrous consequences. First, and

---

55   The index is an arithmetic mean of the percentage of households with income under R19,300/year, the percentage of 'adults (20+) with highest educational level < matric', the percentage of the economically active population that is jobless and the percentage of those working who are in unskilled jobs.

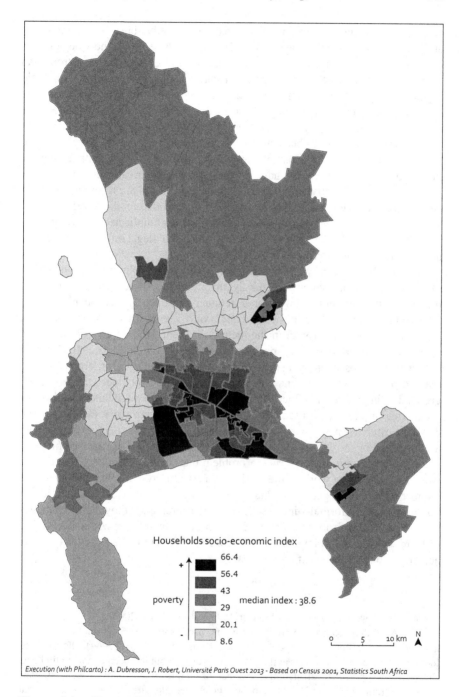

Figure 4.4   Households socio-economic index in 2001

despite the efficiency of social networks that bring together businesses, employees and jobseekers (Crankshaw and Goetz, 2010), it reduces their knowledge of job opportunities as well as their access to jobs located elsewhere in the metropolitan territory. Second, it helps to maintain disparities in urban planning. Apartheid regulations placed limitations on trade and economic activities in the black townships. Of course, these regulations have been abolished, but in fact the economic potential of disadvantaged areas remains very low. When the land in a given district has never been formally registered, it cannot be bought or sold through official banking channels; when connection to high-voltage lines is impossible, potential investors have no access to the electrical energy needed for industrial or artisan activities; because large areas of land are rarely available in densely populated townships, any form of zoning intended for the development of shopping centres or even production installations is complicated. Therefore it is always very difficult for people living in townships and illegal informal settlements to play a full part in the formal urban economy.

This is all the more worrying because, at the metropolitan scale, indicators of growth and employment are hardly favourable to these people. Moreover, the end of the apartheid-administered economy and accelerated opening to the international market have had clear effects on Cape Town's economic vitality. The rate of economic growth in the metropolis went from about + 2 per cent a year in the late 1980s to + 4.1 per cent on average from 2000 to 2010. But if it is to integrate jobseekers and significantly reduce unemployment, growth should reach 6 per cent or 7 per cent a year, or create 40,000 jobs per year. Although growth has improved, it is fluctuating and not vigorous enough, and it is also less productive of jobs than it used to be (so-called 'jobless growth'); in addition, the new jobs offered – particularly in services – are inaccessible to poor citizens who are unskilled or too low-skilled and very often, in the case of older employees, victims of economic restructuring, a problem that applies especially to coloured women who used to work in the textile industries. Between 1995 and 2004, the number of jobs in waged employment fell,[56] while the number of insecure jobs – both formal and informal – increased, as did measured unemployment.[57] Statistics show a growth in formal jobs since 2005: in 2011, there were about 1.3 million of them and the unemployment rate fell to 23.9 per cent (29.2 per cent in 2001) according to the official definition.

---

56   There were 727,000 waged jobs in 1995 and 715,000 in 2004.

57   According to the 'narrow' definition used since 1996 to measure *official unemployment*, an unemployed person is someone of working age (15–64) who has been looking for a job for four weeks at the time of questioning but has been unable to find one. Between 1995 and 2004, calculations show that the number of unemployed people in Cape Town rose from 175,000 to 275,000 and the official unemployment rate from 17.2 per cent to 23.4 per cent on average. Disaggregated by 'group', it was particularly high within the black and coloured populations, with rates of 62 per cent and 36 per cent respectively.

However, at the scale of the last two decades, this relative statistical improvement remains fragile and – since Cape Town has not been spared South Africa's recession resulting from the international financial crisis triggered in late 2008 – has not in any way helped to stem monetary poverty, measured by the yardstick of the Household Subsistence Level (HSL), or social polarisation. In 1996, the monetary income of 19 per cent of households was below the HSL (<R12,000/year); by 2001, the figure had risen to 32 per cent (<R20,000/year) and by 2005, to 38 per cent (CoCT, 2009f). In 2011, 47 per cent of households had a monthly income of R3,200 or less – and even this is merely an average that mask intra-urban disparities (87 per cent of Black African and 54 per cent of Coloured households had a monthly income of R3,600 and less). Poverty and social polarization (Cape Town's Gini coefficient was 0.57 in 2010) contribute to the heterogeneity of the population: according to Swilling (2006), 16 per cent of households now belong to the urban elite and 31 per cent to the middle class, while 51 per cent of the population fall into the working-class or the poor categories (Table 4.2).

Table 4.2   Social stratification of Cape Town's residential spaces

Residential groups	Key characteristics	Number of households	% of households
Silver spoons	Elite, largest consumers, getting richer	54,630	7
Upper-middle class	Established, mature, conservative, professionals, gated	68,129	9
Sub-total		*122,759*	*16*
Middle suburbia	Tight budgets, mid-level jobs, bargain hunters, big spending on educating children	77,380	10
Community nests	Mixed, Afro-cosmo, shifting, small spaces, stylish, café culture, dense	17,564	2
Labour pool	High density family neighbourhoods, stable jobs, secondary education, struggling	42,404	6
New bonds	New SA families, youngish, targets of the developers	101,638	13
Sub-total		*238,986*	*31*
Township living	Old places, few jobs, youth culture, soul of the new SA, buzzy, vulnerable	80,980	11
Towering density	Teetering, high hopes, few options, the educated leave as soon as possible, limited reinvestment	170,752	22
Dire straits	Old places, overcrowded, services collapsing, high unemployment, decaying	26,108	3
Below the breadline	Shack settlements, desperation, insecurity	111,770	15
Sub-total		*389,610*	*51*

Source: Swilling, 2006: 34.

Studies devoted to the townships draw a catastrophic picture of poverty, with three quarters of households in some districts living below the poverty line (de Swardt et al., 2005). Although inequalities are less racially determined than in the past, they are no less profoundly divisive of Cape Town's heterogeneous society, which is no less polarised than South African society as a whole (Aliber, 2003; Terreblanche, 2004); and despite the consolidation of a middle stratum that includes black and coloured Capetonians, the prospect of a rapid reduction in disparities is improbable.

Reproducing Technical and Management Models under Financial Pressure

The spread of integrated networked services and the introduction of a universal connection standard have served the objectives of post-apartheid governments by redressing earlier discrimination (Jaglin, 2004; Jaglin, 2005); but, as the financial pressures of the mid-2000s showed, they have taken place in conditions that have not allowed a sustainable guarantee of infrastructure management and maintenance.

So, in 2003, the CoCT was confronted with a major cash crisis. This was because, in order to finance its policy, it had drawn on its financial reserves and also expanded cross-subsidy mechanisms: the contribution made by electricity surpluses to the general budget reached almost 15 per cent in 2003–2004, while the water contribution rose from under 11 per cent in 2001–2002 to almost 19 per cent in 2003–2004 (Marsden, 2003b). Because of this drain on its receipts, the Directorate of Utility Services soon experienced difficulties guaranteeing not just investments for extension and renewal but also spending on infrastructure maintenance. In 2006, it had to cancel a budgeted Capital Renewal Reserve[58] and postpone all its major projects (CCT, TSI 09/09/06), while insufficient liquid assets meant that it could not properly guarantee the maintenance and replacement of existing amenities. The municipality has now equipped itself with new tools for monitoring its finances, including monthly reports that have clearly revealed two recurring factors undermining municipal services.

The first is the worsening volume of arrears (R3.157 billion in April 2009) (CCT, FIN 18/06/09) and of bad debt provision. Despite the creation of a Multidisciplinary Debt Management Task Team, a tougher debt control policy and the installation of technical devices to limit consumption (instead of simply disconnecting a supply), the problem remains.

The second factor is worrying under-investment in local infrastructure (SACN, 2006). In the electricity network, this under-investment explains various kinds of deterioration that, since 2006, have led to serious disruptions in electricity supply – though it is true that these have been amplified by failures on the part of the national operator. The delay in the programme to refurbish and replace the old network, which was highlighted in a 2006 technical audit by the national

---

58 Funds for upgrading and replacing infrastructure, provided from operating budget surpluses produced in previous financial years.

regulator, is explained both by the lack of necessary investment (estimated at R1.6 billion) and by the shortage of skilled labour in the sector, which is in part linked to the slow, complex process of administrative restructuring: 'Despite the increasing reliance on the use of contractors due to skills shortages, the maintenance is on average 12 months behind schedule and growing' (CCT, UTS 06/06/09: 124). In the city centre, various types of infrastructure (substations, the underground high-voltage and medium-voltage network) are functioning at the limits of their capacity and have sometimes gone beyond their useful asset life: various refurbishment and strengthening schemes are in progress or planned, at a cost of R160 million.

There are also signs of obsolescence in the water services – in particular, an increase in the number of mains pipe bursts: 4,000 in 2006–2007, more than 6,000 in 2007–2008 (CCT, UTS 15/04/07; CCT, UTS 06/06/09). In many districts, the water networks and the sewers have reached or gone beyond their useful asset life: in 2006, 31 per cent of the pipe infrastructure was over 50 years old, 22 per cent had reached the end of its useful asset life and 11 per cent was predicted to reach that point in the next ten years (CCT, TSI 19/08/06). A recent evaluation estimates the book value of the water and sanitation network at R2.6 billion (30 June 2008) and the cost of replacing it at R26.1 billion – that is, ten times as much (CCT, UTS 06/06/09). An Asset Management Programme is underway, aiming to improve the municipality's infrastructure maintenance strategy.

So the bases on which integration policy in the sphere of networked services could succeed are somewhat fragile. Blaming management errors explains neither the rapidity nor the timing of financial deterioration in a municipal organisation whose management excellence has received recognition. Its causes must be sought in a deeper gulf between conditions and capacities for implementing the political objectives of integration. For the City Councils of the first post-apartheid decade, being politically proactive was the key factor in a policy that consisted of applying the conventional model of services on a universal basis. By 'conventional model', here we mean a system for producing services aiming to satisfy individual needs through a standardised service offering delivered via networked infrastructure. With high fixed costs and large economies of scale, the development of such services relies on creating universal access that allows 'mass' consumption, which is less costly to produce because demand is undifferentiated. In apartheid cities, which were tools of peripheral Fordism, this model was developed in order to satisfy demand from white populations and to facilitate reproduction of a black and coloured labour force that was fixed by quota according to the needs of the local employment market. Although apartheid Cape Town was a segregated city, it nevertheless had a high level of functional integration through public service networks, a population mostly provided with disposable income through contracted employment and, although there were no shared social practices, a form of objective 'solidarity' within the urban economic system (Jaglin, 2001).

In the early post-apartheid years, there was no debate about the social and technical arrangements underlying the conventional model of services, nor about their adaptation to the conditions of urbanisation that resulted from the lifting of migration controls and changes in the labour market, marked both by a growing diversity of increasingly individualised urban practices and by the persistence of ethnic and cultural differentiations and the intensification of micro identities. However, it is gradually becoming apparent that enduringly varied demand from users with contrasting consumption profiles – in unstable family or occupational situations, with uncontrolled or even illegal land tenure – cannot be met through the routinised, standardised procedures of planning and management used in the conventional service. Thus, centralisation of the municipal system creates blockages and bottlenecks in service delivery to rapidly growing poor areas where the annual influx of new arrivals actually requires the opposite: flexible, reactive planning and decision-making procedures. At the levels of consumption offered by the conventional infrastructure, the principle of cost recovery is incompatible with the poorest households' ability to pay, so that costly information campaigns have to 'train' them to use technologies that allow them to restrict their own levels of demand (Smith, 2006). As Swilling emphasises, 'limited household incomes mean residents need to be protected from service systems that will be a constant drain on their finances' (Swilling, 2006: 33).

Therefore the attempt to bring the conventional service into general use is taking place at a time when its relevance is being called into question by the post-apartheid trajectory of Cape Town's urban society, tormented by poverty and increased informality, as is evidenced both by the outstanding payments owed by those poor people who are included in the network and by the exclusion of an 'irreducible' proportion of households, who remain outside the networks despite the adoption of relevant social policies.

However, this situation has had some impact, and two changes in the late 2000s provide evidence of the gradual adjustments that have resulted from it. First, the municipal system has tried to find the potential for flexibility that it has lacked up to now, by concluding contracts with decentralised private providers – formal and informal, market (local businesses) and not-for-profit (community organisations). Second, its thinking about informal settlements has changed. Viewed as temporary, these used not to be taken into account in the service offering; but in 2003, the municipality accepted that the rate at which new housing was being delivered would not allow it to eradicate informal settlements and, in 2007, it adopted a Municipal Informal Settlement Plan that emphasises a political desire to provide basic services to all citizens of Cape Town, whatever their living conditions.

Taking into account these different factors and this new environment, the CoCT has gradually designed diversified supply arrangements and differentiated levels of service: basic services for informal settlements, partly subcontracted to informal operators; standard services in planned districts; 'improved' services, on a contract basis, in areas that are prepared to pay a premium for them (Marsden, 2003c). This diversity now covers a continuum of situations that vary depending on the services but provide evidence of a desire to abandon the conventional model in favour of a service offering that is more concerned with contemporary conditions of belonging to and in the city (Jaglin, 2008).

Forms of Governance and Forms of Regulation Amidst Conflicts and Mismatches

Municipal institutions have been transformed and the actors – both individual and collective – have partly changed, but despite the democratisation of access to resources and urban amenities, the reproduction of inequalities and exclusion mechanisms is still a source of tension and a cause of violence. Institutional change seems to be able to move beyond collective beliefs and practices, partly because of the upheaval of the end of apartheid and the proactive political behaviour that accompanied it. In fact, the form of governance that prevails between the three spheres of government has struggled to adapt to the challenges of urban development, as has governance between those spheres and the private sector actors. The cooperative mechanisms of horizontal and vertical forms of governance are exposed to the partisan logics of public administrations, constrained by the nature of private capital and its elites and ill-equipped to face the logics of the informal sector; so they have remained weak, even ineffective.

Institutional Integration Under Pressure

By creating a prolonged, uncontrolled situation of disorder, local government reforms and the more general reforms affecting the running of the public sector have acted as a drag on the municipality's capacity for action.

First of all we would like to stress the reduction in the power of influence enjoyed by local council officers and the increase in that of the political authorities. Under apartheid, only the 'white local authorities' were true operational entities equipped with resources and competencies. They were managed by a council secretary assisted by departmental officials, since the elected council members were most often lay people and dependent on the opinions and advice of the secretary and the heads of technical services, who played a disproportionate role in formulating policies (Cameron, 2003). In Cape Town, this was still a very marked characteristic in the early 2000s, when service reforms, for example, were influenced by engineers and local council officers and where the operational structures of the six transition municipalities (with the exception of the quickly merged posts of department heads) remained in place until 2004. But the coming to power of an ANC-led coalition in October 2002 and the adoption of a Mayoral Committee gradually increased the political authorities' power of influence and the personalisation of municipal power.

Next we wish to emphasise that the reorganisation of municipal departments has led to the loss of about 6,000 posts since 2001; at the same time, many replacements have been made within the administration through the vigorous application of affirmative action and appointments linked to employment equity, with a great deal of pressure placed on senior managers. Thus, a number of officials responsible for planning were replaced or transferred to other posts, and many experienced, highly qualified professionals resigned or retired in the two or three years following the change of political regime. Long-term uncertainty and the 'transformation fatigue' often experienced by employees subjected to incessant reorganisation have aggravated the problem (Edmunds, 2006).

These organisational and budgeting issues were tackled more energetically when Helen Zille came into office in 2006. The newly elected Mayor then reported a serious staffing crisis and a loss of the skills, knowhow and expertise based on ties and networks that were not formalised but had oiled the wheels of vital horizontal relationships, both internal and external to the municipal apparatus – a loss that has still not yet been made good. Between March 2006 and March 2007 the new ruling coalition had to fill 1,780 skilled posts (project heads, engineers, technical officers) as a matter of urgency. The process of making a fresh start on managing not only visible but also 'invisible' public policy steering instruments (Lorrain, 2004) has been underway since 2006. First of all, professional competence rather than skin colour has been reaffirmed as the criterion for recruitment, and budget provision has been made to create posts that will attract skilled personnel. Next, coordination between departments and departmental adaptability have both been improved: timescales for implementing major projects fell from 15 weeks in 2006 to 6.5 weeks by the end of 2008, and timescales for rezoning, granting building permits and tendering have also been reduced. Finally, the infrastructure-led growth policy and the spectacular expansion of the investment budget have been supported by financial rationalisation. Better mobilisation of resources (94 per cent of the budget was spent in 2007–2008, as against 60 per cent in 2003–2004) and rigorous management – approved by a favourable ('unqualified'[59]) audit and, from 2007 onwards, by a positive international agency classification (an AA credit rating, the best of any of the South African metropolises) – enabled the launch[60] of three programmes for the issue of municipal bonds[61] to raise money for the City's External Finance Fund, intended to supplement resources allocated for investments. These programmes also made it possible to propose provisional budgets of R21.9 billion in 2011–2012, R.30.3 billion in 2012–2013 and R31.7 billion in 2013–2014. The municipality's adaptability and the results achieved

---

59   The term 'unqualified' means that application of the evaluation criteria has not revealed any major financial management problem.

60   Through the Bond Exchange of South Africa.

61   June 2008, R1 billion, with an over subscription of almost 300 per cent; June 2009, R1.2 billion; March 2010, R2 billion.

were recognized and rewarded at the international scale in 2008, when Helen Zille was voted the world's best mayor.

The Ups and Downs of Mixed Governance

A firm hand in steering municipal public policy is especially crucial where the public sector actors are involved in numerous partnerships with the private sector. The symmetry or asymmetry of relations between the municipality and market forces influences the way the city is structured.

City Improvement Districts: the risks of entrepreneurial urban planning
A good example of this is provided by the current 22 CIDs. The rules of the game for CIDs are codified in a municipal by-law dating from 2004, updated on 1 July 2012, and the municipality monitors the mechanism (Dubresson, 2008). But in practice, the key personalities, the competencies, the differences in know-how, the antagonisms, the alliances and the balance of power at any given moment between the political, administrative and technical elites and the private sector businesses (with each of these groups being far from homogeneous) carry more weight than the legislation. The issue of the CIDs' autonomy – like that of the Cape Town Partnership (CTP)[62] – and of their ability to influence the way the city is structured is important because they not only manage additional services within defined intra-urban areas but also promote economic growth by catalysing and spearheading large-scale urban renewal programmes. Of course, their activities conform to the content and the letter of the 2004 and 2012 by-laws, but the problem is knowing to what extent these programmes are determining – and even carrying out – municipal urban planning choices within their respective areas of action; and this illustrates the risk of disguised privatisation of urban development through the formation of intra-urban 'shadow states' (Mitchell, 2000: 444).

This risk arises primarily from the entrepreneurs' capacity to organise themselves in order to produce dominant representations, based on their own interests, and to impose them during negotiations, in the context of fluctuating relationships with the City Council. Describing the birth of the CTP, Nahnsen demonstrates that, by the end of the institutional merger process, it had won this representational battle and that it 'guides the decision-making of the City Council and promotes itself as the management agent of the City of Cape Town, developing 'partnership based

---

62   An intermediate body between municipal level and CID level, the CTP was launched in July 1999 by a coalition of public-sector and private-sector institutions, including the old Cape Metropolitan Council, the old City of Cape Town, the Provincial Government, the Cape Town Regional Chamber of Commerce and Industry, the South African Property Association (SAPOA), the Cape Town Heritage Trust, Cape Town Tourism, Business Against Crime, the City Community Patrol Board and the Cape Town Business Forum. This mixed coalition of locally powerful actors aims to revitalise the economic base and to promote the regeneration of the CBD.

management solutions' to the problems of the central city' (Nahnsen, 2003: 147). In the many upheavals that marked the transition to the Unicity, the CTP appears to have been a coherent force that managed to impose the entrepreneurs' vision – for example, by giving priority to the northern rather than to the eastern part of the CBD. This has led some observers to wonder whether it is the CTP that really governs Cape Town (Hooper, 2004). Even though it does not have the financial and legal resources that are available, for example, to New York's Times Square Business Improvement District, its strong capacity for intervention makes it powerful. Since the arrival of a new official at its head in April 2003, clear trends can certainly be observed, with increasing openness to the public sector actors. It is still the case that successive major urban renewal programmes for the city centre have been devised and launched by the CTP – including the most recent one, which favours the eastern section of the city centre – and that it has considerable ability to apply pressure, based on its indisputable technical knowledge. But a distinctive, completely new financial basis has now been added to this activism: in 2007, for the first time since its creation, the CTP obtained agreement for municipal funding to the tune of R18 million over three years.

In Claremont, the local CID has also changed its role in terms of the operations it carries out: from acting as a facilitator and catalyst for private investments by improving services and promoting the area, it has moved to become the contracting authority responsible for a public infrastructure, mobilising its own private resources. According to an agreement signed in January 2006, the municipality took on responsibility for building the new combined transport station (buses and taxis situated next to the railway station), at a cost of R24 million, while the CID has entirely financed the Claremont Boulevard construction works (R22 million), which will significantly reduce traffic congestion on Main Road – already a very long-standing unsolved problem. The stated objective is an ambitious one: with some vehicle traffic and all informal trading removed, Main Road should be regenerated as a mainly pedestrian area, lined with public parks and linking two 'bits' of the city that are currently separated. Even though it may be overridingly determined by the needs of the private sector, this type of partnership co-production can lead to the production of new, pure public goods that are localised yet freely accessible to everyone, and this is the case with the new road. But at the scale of the metropolitan territory, the geography of these arrangements is not neutral; the CIDs have disparate tax bases, and those that are capable of mobilising large resources could become producers of increasingly self-financed infrastructure and amenities, thanks to skilfully negotiated compromises with the municipality. Repeated requests for loosening of constraints and demands for management autonomy – intended to counter the current regulation of the CIDs, which is viewed as too bureaucratic in nature – are moving in this direction.

Therefore we cannot evade the question of the political – or, to be more precise, of whether it is legitimate for CIDs to intervene in the structuring and use of the urbanised space. Indeed, they are not democratic institutions, since the only voters are people who own property there, yet they manage service surpluses and are involved in projects that affect all those who live in their areas and even beyond. It is not enough to talk about the CIDs' compliance with the legislation, nor to refer to the 'participation' of property owners in the local development of their areas or to the good civic awareness flagged up by all CID officials. More important are their relationships with politicians and with intra-urban scales and representative democratic bodies. In given areas, there is a legitimacy arising from universal suffrage, directly at the scale of the wards (whose boundaries, however, do not always match the CIDs') and indirectly at the scale of the sub-councils. Yet, although personal relations – even overlapping functions – do exist between elected representatives and CID members, the latter's officials can design and implement their projects without necessarily discussing them with politicians and, above all, without being accountable for them. In fact, they have appointed themselves privileged intermediaries between citizens and the municipality, as is shown by the many forums organised under their aegis. This is probably where the most significant opportunity for increased autonomy lies: a political and symbolic order can be legitimised under cover of technical and management activities described as 'apolitical' but which in reality are instruments of power, and this process can help to produce such an order. In Cape Town, this is nothing new: 'elite-bias' had already been highlighted in relation to the operation of forums and of the Unicity Commission during the municipal merger phase (Pieterse, 2003).

CoCT and private investors: partnerships slow to develop at the metropolitan scale
Since 2000, all the ruling coalitions have stressed the imperative of economic growth and of promoting Cape Town as a 'world-class city', which presumes effective linkages between the objectives of the metropolitan government and those of private businesses. Yet, beyond the personal relationships forged between politicians, members of the municipal administration and businesses (and unlike Durban, for example: Freund and Lootvoet, 2005), relations between employers' organisations and the municipality have only belatedly been formalised, and the municipal administration is not viewed by the business world as very efficient.

The structure of the formal private sector production base is heterogeneous: 93 per cent of businesses are small in size[63] but supply 50 per cent of total added value and 40 per cent of formal jobs. Very few firms or small entrepreneurs have a relationship with the municipal bodies in charge of local economic development. Most of them are unaware of the documents drawn up by the municipality in that sphere, or view them as bureaucratic and irrelevant. Many small employers are critical of the way the municipality is run, in particular of tendering procedures that marginalise them or even push them out altogether. RED Doors – devolved information agencies that support business start-up or expansion projects and skills training intended to make it easier for SMEs to access municipal procurement

---

63 22 per cent are categorised as 'small' (with between ten and 50 jobs) and 71 per cent as 'very small' (fewer than ten jobs).

opportunities and to encourage young entrepreneurs[64] – handle only a few hundred requests a year. Employers' organisations, whether sectoral or not (Cape Town Regional Chamber of Commerce and Industry; Afrikaanse Handels Instituute[65]), primarily represent big firms, whose managers are not really concerned about public policies on spatial planning and urban integration[66] – and when they are, disapprove of the municipality's desire to influence the location of businesses (Rasamijao, 2005). In 2007, only 25 per cent of Cape Town entrepreneurs considered that local government policy really did anything to support them, 45 per cent viewed it as of not much use (12.5 per cent) or very little use (22 per cent), while 40 per cent thought it was neutral in economic terms; the municipality's ability to react to the demands of business was judged to be rather weak (Wolpe, 2007). Since 2008, however, the municipality's image has improved.

The various annual forums, which are specialised by sectoral niche and organised by – or with the support of – the municipality, are good promotional marketing tools, but they do not play an intermediation role. When it comes to drawing up the economic section of the IDP, this is a matter of trade-offs inside the sphere of local government rather than of real negotiations with business. On 24 April 2007, at a symposium with the evocative title 'Business meets the City' organised by the Cape Town Regional Chamber of Commerce and Industry, the then Mayor, Helen Zille, said: 'We [...] lack a one-stop interface between the City and business that will make things easy for entrepreneurs and investors. We want to introduce such a facility into the municipality'.[67] Since the demise of the Western Cape Economic Development Forum, which debated the MSDF project in the mid-1990s, there has been no instrument facilitating exchange between the municipality and businesses, and administrative structures such as the Business Area Management Branch have not been very effective.

Under these conditions, it is understandable that, in mobilising the CID tool, private sector businesses are not motivated solely by the need to improve the running of certain services and to control transaction costs; their approach also aims to build specific, stable relationships with the municipality. On this second point, however, only the Cape Town Partnership Business Forum, created in 2001, has played an effective role (although one limited to the CBD), with annual meetings of its 37 members representing the biggest city-centre firms, the organisation of regular seminars and debates on municipal policy and the publication of reports and a monthly electronic newsletter; it also systematically lobbies the three spheres of government, facilitated by Cape Town's status as South Africa's legislative capital. It is easy to understand, therefore, why the CTP is one of the few organisations to enjoy good visibility in the business world

---

64 Young Entrepreneurs Network forum.

65 The Afrikaner Chamber of Commerce.

66 In 2004, 82 per cent to 89 per cent of company directors – depending on the sector – were unaware of the existence of the MSDF.

67 CoCT, Media Release No. 116/2007, 24 April 2007 (www.capetown.gov.za/press).

(Rasamijao, 2005) and why it is generally looked on as a model to be followed. But it was not until 19 September 2006 that the CTP launched the Cape Town Business Areas Network, with the municipality's support, as a forum for all businesses in the metropolitan region. Another coalition at the metropolitan scale may have been gestating since the 2007 launch of two different private sector initiatives. The first, Accelerate Cape Town, was created by 23 big businesses – a number that had grown to 36 by 2010 – and is devoted to developing an economic vision towards 2030, one which is shared by all the public- and private sector actors involved; the second, the Cape Town Property Developers' Forum, is an attempt to establish an instrument for tackling problems that arise between the municipality and land and property developers.

These two initiatives are taking place in a context where Cape Town's 'brand-image performance' is declining and even failing. First of all, the new black economic elite has a negative perception of the city. It seems to them very unwelcoming, dominated by strange or even alien social models and codes, and an expensive place to live. Even though salaries are lower than in the Province of Gauteng, access to responsible jobs and partnerships with local businesses can be difficult – so they see a move there as representing 'career suicide' rather than success, and they prefer Johannesburg or even Durban. In 2009, the results of a survey of black executives whose representations characterised Cape Town as a 'racist city' were at the centre of a fierce media controversy. Yet the theme of Broad Black Economic Empowerment (BBEE) plays an essential role in the strategy and communication of businesses and, according to officials from Accelerate Cape Town, the difficulties encountered in attracting and retaining black managers and skilled white-collar workers were the root cause of Shell moving its headquarters and both BP and Old Mutual shifting some of their management activities from Cape Town to Johannesburg in 2008. Whatever the firms' motivations, these moves ring alarm bells. Second, if Cape Town is to play in the league of 'secondary global cities' – if that is its objective – the city needs to redefine its image, to go beyond its earlier, highly conventional associations with beaches, Table Mountain, holiday properties and retirement homes for the British, and to project itself differently in the future. Nowadays, this means showing how, starting from the production niches defined in the last IDP, Cape Town can be promoted as a competitive 'entrepreneurial city', an idea that is increasingly mobilised in private and public discourses and which – given the investments made (Haferburg et al., 2009; Swart and Bob, 2009) and the media coverage of the event – might have been facilitated by the city's playing host to the FIFA World Cup (11 June to 11 July 2010). Thus, the recent Western Cape Economic Development Partnership, launched on 26 April 2012 and packing 40 key organisations could become a new type of collaborative leadership driving the step-change in Cape Town economy.

Formal-informal: impossible to come to any arrangement?
In Cape Town, as in other South African cities, the boom in the informal economy poses the municipality formidable problems with mediation, with mediators

and with developing shared objectives, in two spheres in particular – passenger transport and the activities of small traders. The models that prevail in formalising mixed governance between the municipality and formal private sector actors cannot be applied to informal economic activities, of which there are many in Cape Town: from this point of view, the city remains an emerging-country metropolis.

Passenger transport (Wilkinson, 2008) is characterised by a duality that arises from and is reinforced by the legacy of socio-spatial segregation. First, the majority of those who use collective forms of transport are poor Capetonians – when they are able to pay (when they are not, they walk); second, for the most part, those who have average or high incomes use private vehicles. Users of public modes of transport (train, bus) which are already not very practical, are further penalised by the lack of comfort and safety and the length of journey times. Proportionate to their incomes, costs are relatively higher for them than for the wealthy and the rising middle classes using their private vehicles. In September 1998, the first document issued as a result of 'Moving Ahead' – a planning process initiated in 1995 to prepare the first post-apartheid transport plan for the Cape Town metropolitan area – offered a vision of an efficient, equitable, universally accessible metropolitan transport system.

A decade later, after numerous attempts at planning (some of which ran concurrently), the quality and the efficiency of services provided by the three primary modes of collective passenger transport have fallen. Exacerbated by a shift in use from the public system to private systems (minibuses), vehicle traffic congestion during rush hours has risen spectacularly. Road accident and road death statistics are among the highest in the world, and the police are no longer managing to enforce observance of the Highway Code. Even after years of national and provincial directives attempting to promote change in transport systems, there has been no reconstruction of Cape Town's system. The permanent conflict between the Province and the Municipality over control of the work finally led the CoCT to make a unilateral announcement, on 3 December 2008, that it would create its own Municipal Transport Authority by the end of 2009, finally established in October 2012. On top of this, there is the influence of associations of private minibus owners, sometimes controlled by gangs, who are trying to take over the most lucrative bus stations and routes by means of frequent violent attacks on passengers and bus drivers.

The organisation and the regulation of private collective transport – let alone its integration into a restructured system – raise enormous difficulties. The recapitalisation programme[68] is limited by the strategies of small private transport

---

68   This programme, which should have begun in 2000, was finally launched only in October 2006. It involved promoting the scrapping and replacement of dilapidated vehicles; a subsidy of R50,000 per minibus was paid to owners with an operating licence, who could take old vehicles to regional agencies. The objective was to replace most of the 127,000 16-seater minibuses (2003 figures) with 18- or 35-seater vehicles. The minimum cost of replacing a minibus is estimated at R250,000.

providers; it is very difficult to persuade them, or to force them, to take part in a system that differs radically from their existing one. Any attempt to negotiate is made very difficult by the fragmentation in informal transport, the violence that governs conflicts between competing associations and the savage opposition of private transport providers to the new Integrated Rapid Transit system (the IRT, christened 'MYCiTi' in March 2010), which was set up for the FIFA World Cup and prefigures the medium-term development of a separate bus network. It remains very difficult to work out management compromises on the urban transport front. Certainly the implementation of the National Land Transport Act (2009) could finally clarify the institutional deal: from June 2011 onwards, the CoCT will manage state bus and rail transport subsidies directly and, in 2013–2014, integrated municipal management will be put in place, based on a single rail-bus ticket. However, the arrangements made for the duration of the FIFA World Cup between the CoCT and a trade union umbrella organisation are fragile: the minibus owners are still very hostile to the IRT system, and the strikes and violence that took place since 2011 bear witness to their determination.

As far as small traders are concerned, the situation is more varied, because they are less organised in terms of associations capable of mobilising and acting at the municipal scale. On the one hand, a number of street dealers are recent migrants, among them foreigners from other African countries who have fled civil wars or are attracted by a higher level of income; on the other hand, the strategic issues vary according to the products involved. This atomisation has allowed the CoCT to gradually implement its Informal Trade Policy (CoCT, 2009e). Small traders who are scattered about in fixed locations and street peddlers who move around are now subject to measures that group them, settle them in one place and involve them in the tax system at various intra-urban scales. So the city centre's 1,400 informal traders have been confined to certain streets, where spots are reserved for them, or else grouped together in four markets. However, the tough negotiations that took place in 2006 around the redevelopment of the Grand Parade show that the days of authoritarian action to drive people out of wealthy areas have given way to negotiated normalisation. In some CIDs, informal labour has been accommodated in the form of partnerships between SMEs, unemployed residents and local development committees.

In poor areas, normalisation is much more difficult or even impossible to implement, especially when it comes to *shebeens*. First of all, these informal township drinking establishments carry a strong symbolic charge because of their social, economic and political function during the apartheid years. Second, the control of alcohol distribution is a significant financial and social issue. Thousands of illicit *shebeens* (sources suggest there are 20,000 to 30,000 in the Province, most of them in Cape Town) fuel a high level of alcoholism, which is reported to be responsible for 59 per cent of violent deaths in Cape Town, the highest rate of any of the country's major cities. 80 per cent of crimes are attributed to combined consumption of alcohol and *tik* (methamphetamine). In 2008, the Province passed the Western Cape Liquor Act, which restricted sales licences, strengthened police controls and, especially, prohibited the sale of alcohol on residential land; this has provoked the classic reactions to alcohol prohibition, and the municipality is not managing to stem these. Similarly, it has failed in its attempts to group artisans together in business zones and is having to face up to evasive strategies, as micro entrepreneurs constantly move around inside the city in order to escape control and taxation, since invisibility is their guarantee of survival.

These blocks on dealing with collective passenger transport, drinks distribution and small artisan businesses do not just reflect dysfunctions or difficulties in horizontal governance, but also relate to the problems of multilevel government.

Vertical Governance and Multilevel Government

The political capacity to create and sustain sufficient financial solidarity efforts is a major problem confronting South Africa's multilevel system of government. Redistributive approaches are based on the premises that increased solidarity can and must be financed through the national budget and/or local taxpayers and users. Yet the political compromise on which such approaches are based in democratic South Africa – a compromise arising from 'elite pacting' and the rhetoric about post-apartheid 'reparations' that has accompanied it – is reaching the point of exhaustion just as major societal problems, particularly in the metropolises, are gradually being redefined in terms of overarching issues such as economic globalisation. While the need for social transfers is constantly being reaffirmed, both in Cape Town and at the national scale, it is very difficult to discern the main lines of a new 'social pact' justifying these efforts, beyond a general discourse – in which, for example, the CTP and the municipality engage – warning against the risks of a highly unequal society and again placing equity at the heart of development. On the one hand, this discourse is no substitute for local debates on issues of urban cohesion and its cost; on the other hand, it has not won over public opinion and, in the eyes of an increasingly doubtful public, is not enough to legitimise the content and extent of redistribution. Although it continues to be taken for granted that redistribution must be to the benefit of the poorest, both those who were excluded by apartheid and more recent victims of economic changes, its justification now lacks a unifying 'grand narrative' to give meaning to the bargaining and lobbying that directs the allocation of resources.

This uncertainty about sharing efforts and competencies gives rise to numerous problems in relations within the world of multilevel administration. So, at the national scale, the degree of solidarity to which metropolitan areas should be entitled remains problematic and debated (Whelan, 2004), with the South African Cities Network (SACN) interpreting government policy as the expression of a more general refusal to view urban change as a shared responsibility with financial involvement by all three spheres of government (Boraine et al., 2006). In Cape Town, local technical officers have many times drawn the municipal executive's attention to the fact that the amounts received from the government (via the Equitable Share allocation) are not sufficient to provide sustainable funding for the policy of free services, justifying, for example, an argument with the National Treasury about the sum granted to the city in 2009.[69]

The difficulties encountered in tackling the issue of housing in Cape Town also illustrate the dysfunctions of vertical governance. As far as conditions and methods for access to land were concerned, the legal abolition of apartheid legislation was a fairly simple political act. Drawing up a real-estate site inventory, checking titles to ownership or use and integrating them into a single land-registration system was a far more complicated process. Before a new housing policy could be launched, identification of state, provincial and municipal property assets had to take place, an operation that was not complete even in 2009; as central government was still not in a position to map and assess its own property, most of the provinces and current municipalities were still struggling to define theirs.

Before the 1996 Constitution, municipalities were responsible for the production of public housing in South Africa. The Housing Act of 1997 privileged the spheres of central and provincial government. The former determines national policy and draws up the institutional and financial framework, while the latter manages national programmes and must support municipalities in fulfilling their housing duties. Municipalities must devise, plan, coordinate and facilitate appropriate housing development. The emphasis is on their intermediary role – as a mediator facilitating the two other protagonists' policies and activities, in particular by providing the necessary infrastructure. Nevertheless, the Housing Act does offer them the possibility of intervening as a direct actor in producing housing, since it allows them to be 'accredited' as managers of national schemes; in this sense, municipalities can encroach on the prerogatives of provincial housing departments.

Legislation on the respective areas of competence of the provinces and municipalities is imprecise (responsibility for zoning, for example, is ambiguous), and areas of overlap tend to be interpreted locally. Therefore, as the clientelist dimension of housing has become an essential fact of politics, control over work in this area has been increasingly disputed between the two spheres of government. Conflicts in this area between the Municipality of Cape Town and the Provincial Government of the Western Cape – including during periods when the same party, either the DA or the ANC, was at the head of ruling coalitions in both spheres of government – have been sharpened by the fact that the balance of power over land is highly unfavourable to the local sphere of government and by the fact that the Land Use Planning Ordinance (LUPO), which dates from 1985, has been in force until February 2012. The municipality, which needs to provide 8,750 ha of land, has not – or hardly at all – managed to mobilise land reserves held by the Province or by state-owned enterprises; so it is limited to acting on an ad hoc basis in order to meet its obligations. In the absence of available funds, it has put plots of land situated in industrial zones up for sale, aiming to encourage economic activity in order to supplement the budget for buying vacant private land. Meanwhile, the

---

69   National Treasury, Response to unfounded claims by the City of Cape Town of unfair allocations to the City by the National Treasury, 20 February 2009.

LUPO, which has been repealed and replaced by the provincial Western Cape Land Use and Planning Bill on 15 February 2012, has been exploited by all the protagonists in turn, according to the specific issues involved. So, in 1999, the Government of the Western Cape challenged the LUPO as an apartheid law in order to prevent the MSDF being applied, contributing to the latter's 'top-down' defeat; in 2005, the ANC Mayor deployed it in order to counter extension plans for the Waterfront; in 2008, a fierce conflict saw the Province and the Municipality in opposition over rights to land that had not been developed by June 2007 – a deadline set by the Province, which had extended deadlines enshrined in the LUPO.

These conflicts were made worse by administrative blocks relating to the award and transfer of funds from the central sphere: budgets granted late, insufficient sums committed by the Province, all kinds of interference in the selection of the people to whom housing would be allocated (an issue that was already tricky because of competition between citizens defending their own 'priority entitlements'[70]). The success of housing policy has also relied on the success of partnerships that were supposed to mobilise private companies to negotiate with 'communities' in order to reach accord between the actors about the social aspects of a given project – with access to public funding conditional on this agreement. The private sector's response to this appeal has been poor and 'community participation' has rarely worked, since the issue is one that involves a great deal of conflict between individuals. One emblematic example is that of the major N2 Gateway project (Smit, 2008). Arising from an intergovernmental cooperation initiative for the production of integrated urban neighbourhoods, this project aimed to restructure insecure informal settlement areas situated on either side of the N2 freeway and, in some cases, to relocate the populations living there. According to initial estimates, 15,000 housing units should have been built by June 2005; now, 25,000 are supposed to be built. During the first phase, the attempt at intergovernmental cooperation failed and the municipality was dismissed from its role as the responsible contracting authority. Management of the project was transferred to a public body that functioned commercially, whose market logic led to the de facto exclusion of Capetonians with incomes below the HSL – i.e. 85 per cent of the 15,000 households involved. Since then, the public body has suffered financial collapse, the excluded poor have rebelled (a number of them have refused to be moved to a temporary relocation area situated on the outskirts of the city at a distance of some 15 km) and 'backyarders' living in the townships near this major project have invaded the apartments, claiming the prior legitimacy of their housing entitlement.

However, the CoCT and the government of the Western Cape signed an agreement in 2012, which cuts red tape and speeds up delivery housing, by

---

70   This is because, even on adjoining plots of land or in neighbouring districts, citizens define themselves in competing categories – 'the haves and the have-nots', 'insiders and outsiders' – with the result that it is very difficult to give real content to the often fantasy notion of 'community'.

empowering the CoCT to manage and administer all housing projects which it has been credited to perform within its municipal boundaries.

Various episodes in the restructuring of electricity distribution and the failure of the regionalisation experiment in Cape Town provide further illustration of the way in which multilevel governance has ground to a halt. In the 2000s, the main elements of the electricity distribution industry in South Africa were Eskom, the national integrated company, and municipal distributors (still over 400 in 1998; 187 by 2005). This fragmented form of national organisation was viewed as the source of the system's inefficiencies and inequalities. Restructuring, on the agenda since the 1990s, aimed to create viable regional entities that would merge and take responsibility for the activities carried out by Eskom and the municipalities (Eberhard, 2003). Its principal justifications related to funding electrification, 'rationalising' tariffs and improving both the performance and the quality of services (Gaunt, 2008). The institutional scheme proposed in 2001 was based on the creation of six Regional Electricity Distributors (REDs) offering more or less equivalent tariffs and services.

In 2002, while electricity restructuring was still under discussion, the CoCT, governed by an ANC majority, agreed to take part in a Presidential pilot project and entered into a Service Delivery Agreement with RED1, a municipal entity defined as a pilot company owned by the City and licensed by the national electricity regulator (NERSA). RED1 started operating on 1 July 2005, with a remit to provide the electricity service for the whole area under municipal jurisdiction, both in parts served directly by the municipality and in Eskom's parts. However, its policy options remained limited because of Eskom's reticence. As a municipal entity, RED1 was subject to the Municipal Systems Act and the Municipal Finance Management Act, whose requirements are not identical to those of the Public Finance Management Act that governs state-owned enterprises such as Eskom. On the basis of legal objections, Eskom did not transfer any assets to RED1, despite signing the temporary operating agreement (Gaunt, 2008).

In parallel, central government thinking on national reform led, in October 2006, to a new restructuring scheme based on six wall-to-wall REDs, this time created as public entities.[71] It would have solved some of the problems raised by Eskom, but this time the decision posed symmetrical difficulties for the municipalities. The CoCT, whose Mayor at the time was from the opposition to the ANC, claimed that this decision – by changing the nature of the entity involved and thus the governance of a undertaking and of a service both previously controlled by the municipality – changed the direction of the restructuring process and made this new arrangement unacceptable (PMG, 2007). 'Quite simply and unambiguously, we say we are not interested in transferring our staff and assets into a public entity' (Ian

---

71   In the public entities model – where the national government and ESKOM would hold a minimum of 51 per cent of the capital – CoCT, which had been the sole shareholder in the RED municipal entity, would have had to make compromises with the other shareholders.

Nielson, Mayoral Committee Member for Finance, quoted in *Mail & Guardian*, 4 January 2008). The CoCT applied to the regulator for cancellation of all agreements, revocation of RED1's distribution licence and the entity's return to City Council control – which in fact meant that RED1 was wound up in December 2006.

This Cape Town episode reveals the weaknesses of vertical governance in a sector whose restructuring, at first viewed as a national reform that would be sectoral in nature, had a strong impact on municipalities, which demanded more consultation (Aristi, 2004). Thus, the big cities asserted that restructuring of the electricity sector did not necessitate its 'demunicipalisation': 'City departments are already large enough to achieve the benefits of economies of scale. The current RED proposals will introduce fragmentation at city level, so that efficiency gains in electricity distribution will be offset by efficiency losses in the cities, notably in billing and collection, customer relationships, cashflow, and debt-raising and servicing' (SACN, 2007: 83). Equally, the municipalities claimed that an electricity distribution service's responsibilities to its consumers would be better guaranteed in the municipal system, which is subject to electoral sanction, than in the arrangements of the future regional entities. They also challenged the idea that specialised organisations dedicated to electricity distribution alone would necessarily be more flexible and free of constraints than the local public sector. They emphasised that, in contrast, energy planning and urban planning are closely interdependent and that a strong relationship between cities and electricity undertakings can facilitate this integration within the perspective of a more environmentally friendly energy policy (SACN, 2007). They also argued that it had not been established that the REDs would be more attentive to consumer needs, notably those of the poor, whereas municipalities take a cross-cutting approach to all local services that enables them to make economies of scope and innovations in the handling of poverty and indigence (Gaunt, 2008; Jaglin, 2008). Finally, this restructuring model was perceived by the big cities as instituting a system of geographically based cross-subsidies that would benefit small towns, or even the less well-equipped REDs, so that there would be fewer resources available for cross-subsidies within metropolitan spaces (Gaunt, 2008) – as the CoCT hammered home: 'The City sets charges at a realistic level and generates a surplus from electricity which is used for a number of social subsidies. [...] It is this subsidy funding that the City wants to protect' (PMG, 2007).

In the end, in December 2010, the government abandoned its restructuring plan and so the big cities had won the argument; the CoCT was delighted, since, by retaining control over the electricity distribution service – an important factor in its competitiveness – it also preserved its capacity for action in other areas that depend in part on the resources it generates by selling electricity. In electricity distribution, the national actors have failed to impose their view on the CoCT but in electricity generation, local initiatives are still restricted by the national legal framework and by system of energy innovation (Jaglin, 2014)

Scales of Governance and Levels of Regulation

One of the beliefs conveyed by the concept of 'developmental local government' is that urban change may be not only stimulated and spearheaded at the metropolitan scale but also regulated there. Yet in certain strategic areas, the limits of municipal policy arise from weaknesses in governance (notably vertical governance) and, even more, from mismatches between scales of government/governance and levels of regulation, with the local sphere finding itself disadvantaged and powerless in the face of the processes that have overtaken it.

Despite the many convulsions of a change that has combined 'immediate, widespread impact' with – in this case, concomitant – 'gradual change', the municipality of Cape Town has solid institutional and technical skills at its disposal; however, these have not been sufficient to ensure that its planning and development policy has been effective – or to move the city's transformation in the direction of economic, social and spatial integration. In Cape Town, as in all the world's big cities, controlling a complex constellation of management arrangements and of enmeshed programmes is obviously complicated. Yet the role of local authorities in steering the city remains all the more controversial because there is no automatic match between scales of governance and levels of regulation and because not everything is open to regulation by public institutions, however efficient these are. So the CoCT's local policy comes up against strong trends that run counter to its objectives – and over which it often has little hold.

Capital accumulation and supra-metropolitan forms of regulation
Like all urbanised spaces, Cape Town's space is now characterised by a rise in flexible accumulation, labour market change, the increasing insecurity of waged employment and growth in the informal economy. In these four areas, the CoCT cannot act as 'more than a mere master of ceremonies' (Freund and Lootvoet, 2005: 68). Although it may have its finger directly on the pulse of the overall level of business and trade, the metropolitan authority is not in a position to influence structural change in its economic base, which comes about through market forces; at most, it can support structural change or try to adjust it, using its room for manoeuvre in order to make its own territory more attractive. But it remains subject to major national trends, such as the fall in per capita infrastructure investment since the late 1990s (Fedderke, 2008) and the negative consequences of this at the local scale, which are illustrated by the crisis in delivering electricity services; equally, it has not been able to avoid the slowdown in national growth since 2007 – or the 2009 recession.

Conversion to neo-liberalism and political rescaling have certainly opened up opportunities for autonomous action at the local scale, but these opportunities remain overridingly determined by choices made at other levels of regulation. Tools of public regulation – such as major monetary choices involving the rand and trade, sectoral incentive policies, the level of protection afforded to a given activity and the setting of wage levels – are the preserve of central government or negotiations at the national level. For example, attempts to curb the collapse in production and industrial jobs in the textile industry, linked to the massive influx of Chinese products, cannot be made at the policy scale of the CoCT, and maintaining production of vehicle spare parts (catalytic converters) in Cape Town depends on external demand. And when it comes to market forces, choices relating to firms' investments and strategies do not come within the remit of the local scale – or even the national one. Moreover, the way South African capitalism is organised is unusual. In 1994, six conglomerates[72] represented 84 per cent of capitalisation of the Johannesburg Stock Exchange (Cling, 2000). Since then, these big firms have engaged in complex processes of mergers and acquisitions or of breaking up either vertically or horizontally – sometimes followed by reintegration, including that of the Rupert empire in 2009.[73] A number of South African firms contribute to the capitalisation of foreign stock exchanges, and some have their company headquarters outside the country. These major manoeuvres on the part of white capitalism (see Southall, 2010) – about which the BBEE can do nothing – are outside the CoCT's scope. Even its capacity to engage in activities that could transform Cape Town into an 'entrepreneurial city' remains weak.

This mismatch between the institutional scale of metropolitanisation and the levels at which economic dynamics are formed and regulated is obviously not specific to South Africa, but it weighs all the more heavily on local governments' public policy because the essential task of that policy up to now has been to build economic and social integration – which, as far as investments and private sector jobs in Cape Flats are concerned, it is not managing to do. First, incentive measures to encourage small entrepreneurs within the townships through supporting small business start-up and development have had only modest results up to now – and these have been very uneven between the different townships. Second, the ambiguities and dysfunctions of vertical public governance do not facilitate linkages between different investment plans; and this combination of handicaps rebounds negatively onto the image of poor areas and their potential for change.

Intrametropolitan dynamics: 'heterogenisation' versus integration

It is chosen forms of solidarity, rather than organic ones, that shape the metropolitan territory. First and foremost, there are the enclosed, confined residential spaces of the middle and upper classes, supported by the implementation of a security-oriented form of governance that tends towards isolation. For the time being, this governance and the secured spaces remain under the control of municipal legislation, with the CoCT having fended off a threat – supposed or real – of local secession by Durbanville, a wealthy district in the north of the metropolitan area

---

72　Anglo American, SA Mutual, Sanlam, Rembrandt, Anglovaal, Liberty Life.

73　The commercial empire founded by Anton Rupert (1916–2006), formerly Rembrandt, based in Stellenbosch, near Cape Town, split into two companies into 2000; it was reconstituted as a multisectoral conglomerate with the support of national and foreign banks and firms.

(Morange and Didier, 2008). Furthermore, on 1 February 2008, the CoCT adopted measures against 'gated communities'. But the secure pockets that already exist do nothing to strengthen public spaces or to help create a social bond and, by shifting a number of security problems into Cape Flats, they strengthen the illegal economy and the criminalisation of poor areas.

Indeed, illegal activities proliferate in the main black and coloured townships, where the unemployment rate can be as high as 61 per cent for people aged under 30 and where wage earners, often on low incomes, are increasingly subject to job insecurity. Not all these activities are controlled by organised gangs, but there has been physical violence against official public transport and against modern types of legal trading in Nyanga, as well as xenophobic violence – including an attempt, launched in May–June 2008, to drive out foreign traders who come from elsewhere in Africa, which meant that about 20,000 individuals had to be moved, with 8,000 temporarily accommodated in municipal facilities. New attacks in August 2010 have shown that there is still a great deal of tension in poor areas. These areas are also the object of gang warfare for control of the drugs trade (ecstasy exported to the United States; amphetamines distributed in South Africa) and of some collective passenger transport routes. About 280 gangs, involving 80,000 to 100,000 individuals, were identified by the CoCT in 2001,[74] and all the literature (Salo, 2004; Jensen, 2008) shows that their activities have intensified since then, with the appearance of Nigerian and Chinese organised crime syndicates.

In terms of regulation, there are two possible interpretations. The gangs, which are themselves divided in a context of producing and declaring compound identities (Daniels and Adams, 2010), provide their own form of governance and of regulation, and thus have territorialised Cape Flats. By sharing out the townships or sections of townships, they have multiplied the number of infra-urban frontiers and therefore they are contributing to the fragmentation of the urbanised space. Conversely, ties – which Standing (2005) has described as 'strategic associations' – between the political elite in power during the transition (or part of this elite) and the gangs form a system of reciprocal exchanges based on the corruption-protection-elections triptych, and this in turn forms part of a composite mode of regulation at the metropolitan scale.

Whatever one's analysis of these trends, the treatment of Cape Town's heterogeneity is a central planning and development issue that has hardly been tackled – and so remains unresolved. Unification of the city has led to thinking first and foremost in terms of metropolitan scale; but nowadays it seems that local government must also deal with localised forms of performance, varied intra-urban trajectories and micro differentiations within the city.

---

74 *Cape Flats Renewal Strategy*, Executive Committee, CoCT, 15 May 2001.

Conclusion

Two decades after the legal abolition of apartheid, the municipality of Cape Town is still having to face up to significant problems inherited from racial urban planning and amplified by the arrival of poor migrants in Cape Flats, by insufficient economic growth and job creation, by multiple instances of withdrawal into enclosed residential spaces and by increased crime. This 'local development government' is also faced with mismatches between scales of governance and levels of regulation, as well as with a lot of difficulties in terms of horizontal and vertical forms of governance. From this point of view, the post-apartheid transition has led to a normalisation of the problems that need to be tackled, since mismatches and problems in governance are common to all authorities in Northern as well as Southern metropolises. As elsewhere, the Cape Town experience shows, on the one hand, that local, proactive, enterprising public policy is not enough to stimulate the desired change and, on the other hand, that a number of problems relating to political rescaling remain unresolved, as the literature criticizing 'ideological' visions of metropolitan governance underlines (Mitchell-Weaver et al., 2000; Jonas and Pincetl, 2006).

These facts seemed to support theses of urban convergence in neo-liberal globalisation (Cohen, 1996). Indeed, everywhere, urbanised spaces and urban dwellers are shaped by conflicting forces; the tension between competitiveness and solidarity works to the advantage of competitiveness; spatial and social heterogeneity grows, fuelled by the ways actors are structured at infra-urban scales that sometimes bring increased autonomy. However, this does not dispense with the need to investigate both the role of specific local features in globalisation (Cox, 2004) and the particular nature of Cape Town, especially its elites and its practice of mixed governance.

Can it be left to the local elites to promote an act of collective imagination (Wilkinson, 2004) and invent a growth coalition, an original urban regime, based on shared beliefs and integrating redistribution? At the moment, this seems doubtful. The history and heterogeneity of private businesses located in Cape Town and the low extent to which the current political and economic elites overlap does not make it easy either to form or to build up a 'coalition' that would bring a shared representation of urban economic development. A first attempt to put one together – in order to bid for the 2004 Olympic Games (Hiller, 2000) – was followed by the creation of Accelerate Cape Town by some big private sector firms; this forum promotes Cape Town's future as an 'entrepreneurial city', but it is both too recent and too narrow to make any rapid alteration in an established situation. Hosting the FIFA World Cup, on the other hand, could have contributed to a significant change in favour of competitiveness. It still remains for the municipality to build its relations with black Capetonians (Smith, 2009). More broadly, ordinary citizens are not very involved in planning and development decisions that affect them: since 2000, the political elites, of whichever party, have remained very mistrustful of 'communities' – a rhetorical category, to which they rarely try to appeal except during election campaigns. They have certainly rejected private governance as far as implementation of their constitutional obligations is concerned; but, bogged down in a cumbersome form of cooperative public governance, they have in fact facilitated the proliferation of partnerships with the main private sector actors in wealthy areas – though they have not managed to extend these to the city's disadvantaged spaces and citizens.

Since it takes a variety of different forms at infra-urban scales, this mixed governance has been the object of divergent analyses. For some, it provides evidence of a rapid neo-liberal alignment to external models, even a 'Californianisation' of Cape Town (Robins, 2003: 87), and of a move away from the ideals of integration – a move that is emphasising physical divisions within the city and accelerating its fragmentation, so that in the end the current urban macro structure is well suited to the spatial dimensions of flexible accumulation. For others, the way Cape Town is changing is more ambiguous. A hybrid of two forms, its mixed form of governance is not in itself the determining factor in tearing the city apart; on the contrary, it might be the key to a progressive form of management – if the metropolitan government can deploy an innovative vision that brings together social justice and the shape of the city, can make use of its regulatory tools and can combine them with those of the province and central government in order to counter the forces of dislocation and curb their effects (Boraine et al., 2006; Pieterse, 2007). Its aim should be to avoid disconnection between successful spaces and spaces of poverty within the metropolitan territory thanks to new patterns of thinking (Swilling, 2010). Even then, the achievement of the universal right to the city (Parnell and Pieterse, 2010) – which cannot depend on the metropolitan government alone – will have to play an integral part in a political project that makes sense both for the city dwellers who benefit from redistributive policies and for those who finance them. However, things have now reached the stage where the 'elite pacting' that founded democratic South Africa has been exhausted and many questions are being raised about the concept of 'developmental government'; so it still remains to draw up a new social contract and to develop a new unifying narrative.

References

Aliber. M. (2003). Chronic Poverty in South Africa: Incidence, Causes and Policies, *World Development*, 31(3): 473–90.

Annecke, W., Gillespie, B., Dobbins, A., Sebitosi, B. (2005). *An Assessment of PNES Customer Satisfaction and the Contribution of Electricity to the Quality of Life of Households in Khayelitsha, South Africa. Cape Town,* Unpublished report for Electricité de France (EdF).

Arist,i J. (2004). *The Electricity Service in Cape Town: A Multi-perspective Analysis,* Marne-la-Vallée, ENPC (projet de fin d'études).

Beall, J., Gelb, S., Hassim, S. (2005). Fragile Stability: State and Society in Democratic South Africa, *Journal of Southern African Studies*, 31(4): 681–700.

Bond, P., Dor, G., Ruiters, G. (2000). Transformation in Infrastructure Policy from Apartheid to Democracy: Mandates for Change, Continuities in Ideology, Friction in Delivery. In M. Khosa (ed.), *Infrastructure Mandate for Change*, Pretoria: HSRC Publishers, 17–48.

Bond, P. (2005). *Elite Transition: From Apartheid to Neoliberalism in South Africa*, Pietermaritzburg: University of KwaZulu-Natal Press.

Boraine, A., Crankshaw, O., Engelbrecht, C., Gotz, G., Mbanga, S., Narsoo, M., Parnell, S. (2006). The State of South African Cities a Decade After Democracy, *Urban Studies*, 43(2): 259–84.

Borel-Saladin, J., Crankshaw, O. (2009). Social Polarization or Professionalization? Another Look at Theory and Evidence, *Urban Studies*, 46(3): 645–64.

Brenner, N. (2004), *New State Spaces: Urban Governance and the Rescaling of Statehood*, New York: Oxford University Press.

Cameron, R. (1999). *Democratization of South Africa Local Government. A Tale of Three Cities*, Pretoria: J.L van Shaik, Academic.

Cameron, R. (2003). Les relations politique-administration: le cas de la ville du Cap, *Revue internationale des sciences administratives*, 69(1): 55–74.

Cameron, R. (2006). South African Local Government Boundary Reorganization. In U. Pillay, R. Tomlinson, J. du Toit (eds), *Democracy and Delivery. Urban Policy in South Africa*, Cape Town: HSRC, 76–106.

Cape Town Partnership, (2006). *The Cape Town Central City Partnership. A Profile*, Cape Town: Cape Town Partnership.

Cape Town Partnership, (2008). *Central City Development Strategy*, Cape Town: Cape Town Partnership.

Central City Improvement District (CCID), (2012). *The State of the Cape Town Central City 2012*, Cape Town: CCID.

Chabaud, D., Parthenay, C., Perez, Y. (2005). Evolution de l'analyse northienne des institutions: la prise en compte des idéologies, *Revue économique*, 56(3): 691–704.

CoCT, (2004). *City of Cape Town Sustainability Report: Phase 1 Draft Set of Indicators*, City of Cape Town: CSIR, Report No. ENV-S-C 2004–055.

CoCT, (2006). *City of Cape Town Economic and Human Development Strategy. Part I: Context and Framework*, Cape Town: City of Cape Town, Revised May 2006.

CoCT, (2007a). *5 Years Plan for Cape Town. Integrated Development Plan (IDP), 2007/8–2011/12*, Cape Town: City of Cape Town.

CoCT, (2007b). *State of Cape Town 2006. Development Issues in Cape Town*, Cape Town: City of Cape Town.

CoCT, (2008). *City Statistics*, Cape Town: City of Cape Town, www.capetown. gov.za/censusinfo/CityStatistics.

CoCT, (2009a). *Review of the Economic Development Strategy (previously EHDS), draft, October 2009*, Cape Town: City of Cape Town, Economic, Social Development and Tourism Directorate, Economic and Human Development Department.

CoCT, (2009b). *5 years plan for Cape Town. Integrate Development Plan (IDP) 2007/8–2011/12. Executive summary 2009–2010 Review*, Cape Town: City of Cape Town,

CoCT, (2009c). *Labour Force Trends in Cape Town. September 2005 to September 2007*, Cape Town: City of Cape Town, Strategic Development Information and GIS Department.

CoCT, (2009d). *Cape Town Spatial Development Framework. Technical Report, draft for comment*, Cape Town: CoCT/CitySpace Planning Cape Town.

CoCT, (2009e). *Informal Trading by-law, 20 March 2009*, Cape Town: City of Cape Town.

CoCT, (2009f). *State of Cape Town 2008. Development Issues in Cape Town*, Cape Town, City of Cape Town.

Cling, J.-P. (2000). *L'économie sud-africaine au sortir de l'apartheid*, Paris: Karthala.

Cohen, M. (1996). The Hypothesis of Urban Convergence: Are Cities in the North and South Becoming More Alike in an Age of Globalization? In M. Cohen, A. Ruble, J. Tulchin, A. Garland (eds), *Preparing for the Urban Future. Global Pressures and Local Forces*, Washington DC, Baltimore: The Woodrow Wilson Center Press, The Johns Hopkins University.

Crankshaw, O., Goetz, D. (2010). *The Mechanisms of Labour Market Spatial Mismatch: A Realist View*, Cape Town: UCT, African Centre for Cities, Papers, February 2010, *africancentreforcities.net/papers*

Crankshaw, O. (2012). Deindustrialization, Professionalisation and Racial Inequality in Cape Town, *Urban Affairs Review*, 48(6): 836–62.

Daniels, D., Adams, Q. (2010). Breaking with Township Gangsterism: The Struggle for Place and Voice, *African Studies Quarterly*, 11(4): 45–57.

De Swardt, C., Puoane, T., Chopra, M., Du Toit, A. (2005). Urban Poverty in Cape Town, *Environment and Urbanization*, 17(2): 101–11.

Dorington, R.E. (2005). *Projections of the Population of the City of Cape Town 2001–2021*, Cape Town: City of Cape Town.

Downs, A. (1994). *New Visions for Metropolitan America*, Washington DC: Brookings Institution and Cambridge, MA: Lincoln Institute of Land Policy.

Dubresson, A. (2005). Métropolisation institutionnelle et spatialités économiques au Cap (Afrique du Sud), *Revue Tiers Monde*, 181: 21–44.

Dubresson, A. (2008). Urbanisme entrepreneurial, pouvoir et territoire. Les City Improvement Districts au Cap. In A. Dubresson, S. Jaglin (eds), *Le Cap après l'apartheid. Gouvernance métropolitaine et changement urbain*, Paris: Karthala, 183–215.

Dubresson, A., Jaglin, S. (2008). (eds), *Le Cap après l'apartheid. Gouvernance métropolitaine et changement urbain*, Paris: Karthala.

Eberhard, A. (2003). *The Political, Economic, Institutional and Legal Dimensions of Electricity Supply Industry Reform in South Africa*, Stanford, CA: Center for Environmental Science and Policy (Working Papers Series).

Edmunds, M. (2006). Can Cape Town Survive Another Change of Guard? *Mail & Guardian Online*, (accessed 21 November 2006 at www.mg.co.za/printPage. aspx?area=/insight/insight_national&articleId=28868).

Fedderke, J. (2008). Capital Formation in South Africa. In J. Aron, B. Kahn, G. Kingdon (eds), *South African Economic Policy under Democracy*, Oxford, New York: Oxford University Press.

Ferreira, S., Visser, G. (2008). Creating an African Riviera. Revisiting the Impact of the Victoria and Alfred Waterfront Development in Cape Town, *Urban Forum*, 18: 227–46.

Fowles, P. (2004). The Future of Municipal Electricity Distribution in South Africa, Communication To Industrial & Commercial Use of Energy Conference 2004, http://active.cput.ac.za/energy/web/icue/papers/2004/17_P_Fowles.pdf

Freund, B., Lootvoet, B. (2005). Où le partenariat public-privé devient l'instrument privilégié du développement économique local. L'exemple de Durban, Afrique du Sud. In A. Dubresson et Y. Fauré (eds), *Décentralization et développement local: un lien à repenser*, *Revue Tiers monde*, 181: 45–70.

Gaunt, T. (2008). Electricity Distribution Industry Restructuring in South Africa: A Case Study, *Energy policy*, 36(9): 3448–59.

Gervais-Lambony, (2003). *Territoires citadins. Quatre villes africaines*, Paris: Belin.

Gervais-Lambony, (2004). Mondialization, métropolisation et changement urbain en Afrique du Sud, *Vingtième Siècle, Revue d'Histoire*, 81: 57–68.

Gibb, M. (2007). Cape Town, a Secondary Global City in a Developing Country, *Environment and Planning C*, 25(4): 537–52.

Haferbug, C., Oβenbrügge, J. (eds), (2003). *Ambiguous Restructuring of Post-apartheid Cape Town: The Spatial Form of Socio-political Change*, Muenster: Lit Verlag.

Haferburg, C., Golka, T., Selter, M. (2009). Public Viewing Areas; Urban Interventions in the Context of Mega-events, in U. Pillay, R. Tomlinson, O. Bass (eds), *Development and Dreams. The Urban Legacy of the 2010 Football World Cup*, Cape Town: HSRC Press, 174–99.

Harrison, P., Huchzermeyer, M., Makeyiso, M. (2003). *Confronting Fragmentation. Housing and Urban Development in a Democratic Society*, Cape Town: UCT Press.

Harrison, P., Todes, A., Watson, V. (2008). *Planning and Transformation. Learning from the Post-Apartheid Experience*, RTPI Library Series, London, New York: Routledge.

Hiller, H. (2000). Mega-events, Urban Boosterism and Growth Strategies: An Analysis of the Objectives and Legitimations of the Cape Town 2004 Olympic Bid, *International Journal of Urban and Regional Research*, 24(2): 449–58.

Hooper, P. (2004). The Tail that Wags the Dog, that Bites the Poor: Cape Town Response, *Interfund, Partners in Development*, 5(1): 169–76.

Jaglin, S. (2001). Villes disloquées ? Ségrégations et fragmentation urbaine en Afrique australe, *Annales de géographie*, 619: 243–65.

Jaglin, S. (2003). Service d'eau et construction métropolitaine au Cap (Afrique du Sud): les difficultés de l'intégration urbaine, *Revue française d'administration publique*, 107: 433–46.

Jaglin, S. (2004). Consumérisme, co-production et territorialisation dans les services d'eau en Afrique: vers une démocratization marchande du management local ?, In R. Le Duff, J-J. Rigal (eds.), *Démocratie et management local. 1ères rencontres internationales*, Paris: Dalloz, 325–51.

Jaglin, S. (2005). Métropolisation institutionnelle et services urbains au Cap: l'équité en question, *Annales de la Recherche Urbaine*, 99: 60–71.

Jaglin, S. (2008). Gouvernement technique au Cap: services en réseaux et intégration urbaine. In A. Dubresson, S. Jaglin (eds), *Le Cap après l'apartheid. Gouvernance métropolitaine et changement urbain*, Paris: Karthala, 119–55.

Jaglin, S. (2014). Urban Energy Policies and the Governance of Multilevel Issues in Cape Town, *Urban Studies*, 51(7): 1392-1412, Published online 13 September 2013. http://usj.sagepub.com/content/early/2013/09/13/0042098013500091

Jensen, S. (2008), *Gangs, Politics and Dignity in Cape Town*, Chicago: University of Chicago Press.

Jonas, A., Pincetl, S. (2006). Rescaling Regions in the State: The New Regionalism in California, *Political Geography*, 25: 482–505.

Kalaora, L. (2002). Centres commerciaux et flux urbains. Etude de cas: Century City en Afrique du Sud, *Flux*, 50: 63–6.

Lefèvre, C. (2009). *Gouverner les métropoles*, Paris L.G.D.J., Lextenso éditions.

Lorrain, D. (2004). Les pilotes invisibles de l'action publique: le désarroi du politique ? In P. Lascoumes, P. Le Galès (dirs), *Gouverner par les instruments*, Paris: Presses de Science Po, 163–97.

Lloyd, P. et al. (2004). Improving access to electricity and stimulation of economic growth and social upliftment. Paper presented at the Eskom/IETA/WBCSD Workshop, Midrand, South Africa, 27–29 July, Available at: www.erc.uct.ac.za/recentpub.htm

Mabin, A. (2006). Local Government in South Africa's Larger Cities. In U. Pillay, R. Tomlinson, J. du Toit (eds), *Democracy and Delivery: Urban Policy in South Africa*, Cape Town: HSRC Press.

McDonald, D. (2008). *World City Syndrome. Neoliberalism and Inequality in Cape Town*, New York, London, Routledge.

Maharaj, B. (1999). Local Economic Development in South Africa Cities: Searching for a New Approach. In P. Gervais-Lambony, S. Jaglin, A. Mabin (), *La question urbaine en Afrique australe*, Paris: IFAS-Karthala, 243–57.

Marais, H. (1998). *South Africa: Limits to Change. The Political Economy of Transformation*, London/Cape Town: Zed Books/UCT Press.

Marsden, M. (2003a). *Trading Services Tariffs for 2003/04*, Cape Town: CCT, 571–641 (Exco Minutes 21 May 2003).

Marsden, M. (2003b). *Trading Services Infrastructure: Implications of Capital Budget Cutbacks: Risks and Risk Management*, Cape Town: CCT, 1374–99 (Council of CCT Minutes 27 August 2003).

Marsden, M. (2003c). *Establishment of Internal Business Units in Trading Services: A Mechanism for Equitable, Affordable and Sustainable Services*, Cape Town: CCT,. 265–84 (Council of CCT Minutes 27 August 2003).

MCA Africa, (2006). *Capital Investment Patterns in Cape Town 2001–2005. Part 2: Analysis and Interpretation of Infrastructure Investment*, Cape Town: MCA Africa, May.

McDonald, D., Smith, L. (2002). *Privatizing Cape Town: Service Delivery and Policy Reforms Since 1996*, Johannesburg, MSP, Occasional papers Series no. 7.

Mitchell, K. (2000). The Culture of Urban Space, *Urban Geography*, 21(5): 443–9.

Mitchell-Weaver, C., Miller, D., Deal Jr, R. (2000). Multilevel Governance and Metropolitan Regionalism in the USA, *Urban Studies*, 37(5–6): 851–76.

Morange, M., Didier, S. (2008). Gouvernance sécuritaire dans les quartiers riches du Cap (1996–2006). Temporalités et échelles de la normalisation post-apartheid. In A. Dubresson, S. Jaglin (eds), *Le Cap après l'apartheid. Gouvernance métropolitaine et changement urbain,* Paris: Karthala, 217–49.

Nahnsen, A. (2003). Discourses and Procedures of Desire and Fear in the Re-Making of Cape Town's Central City: The Need for a Spatial Politics of Reconciliation. In Haferburg, C. and Oβenbrügge, J. (eds), *Ambiguous Restructuring of Post-Apartheid Cape Town: The Spatial Form of Socio-Political Change*, Muenster: Lit Verlag, 137–56.

Nel, E., Binns, T. (2001). Initiating 'Developmental Local Government' in South Africa: Evolving Local Economic Development Policies, *Regional Studies*, 35(4): 355–70.

North, D.C. (2005). *Understanding the Process of Economic Change*, Princeton NJ: Princeton University Press.

OECD, (2008). *Cape Town, South Africa*, Paris: OECD, Territorial Reviews.

Orfield, M. (1997). *Metropolitics: A Regional Agenda for Community and Stability*, Washington D. C., Brookings Institution Press, Cambridge MA: Lincoln Institute of Land Policy.

PMG, (2007). *Minerals and Energy Portfolio Committee: Future of Regional Electricity Distributors: City of Cape Town*, Parliamentary Monitoring Group: 28 February 2007, www.ameau.co.za/library/restructuring

Parnell, S., Boulle, J. (2008). Utopie urbaine et gouvernement local. La stratégie de développement économique et humain au Cap. In A. Dubresson, S. Jaglin (eds), *Le Cap après l'apartheid Gouvernance métropolitaine et changement urbain,* Paris: Karthala, 251–72.

Parnell, S., Pieterse, E. (2002). Developmental Local Government. In S. Parnell, E. Pieterse, M. Swilling, D. Wooldridge (eds), *Democratising Local Government. The South African Experiment,* Cape Town: UCT Press.

Parnell, S., Pieterse, E. (2010). The 'Right to the City': Institutional Imperatives of a Developmental State, *International Journal of Urban and Regional Research,* 34(1): 146–62.

Pieterse, E. (2003). Problematising and Recasting Vision-Driven Politics in Cape Town. In Haferburg, C. and Oβenbrügge, J. (eds), *Ambiguous Restructuring of Post-Apartheid Cape Town: The Spatial Form of Socio-Political Change,* Muenster: Lit Verlag, 157–88.

Pieterse, E. (2007). Tracing the 'Integration' Thread in the South African Development Policy Tapestry, *Urban Forum,* 18(1): 1–30.

Pieterse, E., van Donk, M. (2008), 'Developmental Local Government: Squaring the Circle Between Intent and Outcomes'. In M. van Donk, M. Swilling, E. Pieterse, S. Parnell (eds), *Consolidating Developmental Local Government: Lessons from the South African Experience,* Cape Town: UCT Press.

Pieterse, E. (ed.), (2010). *Counter-Currents: Experiments in Sustainability in the Cape Town Region,* Johannesburg: Jacana Media.

Pirie, G. (2007). 'Reanimating a Comatose Goddess': Reconfiguring Central Cape Town', *Urban Forum,* 18(3): 125–51.

Plancq-Tournadre, M. (2004). Services d'eau et d'électricité au Cap ou comment la sortie d'apartheid fabrique des débranchés, *Flux,* 56–57: 13–26.

Plancq-Tournadre, M. (2006). Du droit au logement à la précarisation immobilière? Le cas du Cap en Afrique du Sud, *Autrepart,* 39: 111–27.

Rasamijao, L. (2005). *Rapport d'enquêtes auprès de 101 entrepreneurs au Cap,* Nanterre, Gecko, université Paris X-Nanterre.

Robins, S. (2003). Global Warnings: Urban Governance in the Cape of Storms, in Haferburg, C., Oβenbrügge, J. (eds), 2003, *Ambiguous Restructuring of Post-Apartheid Cape Town: The Spatial Form of Socio-Political Change,* Muenster: Lit Verlag, 87–114.

Rogerson, C. (1997). Local Economic Development and Post-Apartheid Reconstruction in South Africa, *Singapore Journal of Tropical Geography,* 18: 175–95.

Rogerson, C. (1998). Restructuring the Post-Apartheid Space Economy", *Regional Studies,* 32(2): 187–97.

Royston, L. (2002). Security of Urban Tenure in South Africa: Overview of Policy and Practice,. In A. Durand-Lasservce, L. Royston (eds), *Holding Their Ground,* London: Earthscan, 165–81.

Rusk, D. (1993). *Cities Without Suburbs,* Baltimore, MD, Johns Hopkins University Press.

SACN, (2006). *States of the Cities Report 2006*, Braamfontein: South African Cities Network.

SACN, (2007). *State of City Finances Report 2007*, South African Cities Network (http://www.sacities.net/2007/oct24_finance.stm).

Salo, E. (2004). *Negociating Gender and Personhood in the new South Africa. Adolescent Women and Gangsters in Manenberg, Township of the Cape Flats*, Stellenbosch: Department of Sociology, Stellenbosch University (New Social Forum Seminar Series).

Saul, J. (2001). Cry for the Beloved Country: The Post-Apartheid Denouement, *Monthly Review*, 52(8): 1–51.

Savitch, H., Vogel, R. (2000). Metropolitan Consolidation versus Metropolitan Governance in Louisville, *State and Local Government Review*, 32(3): 158–68.

Scott, A., (2001). *Global City-Regions. Trends, Theory, Policy*, Oxford: Oxford University Press.

Segrestin, D. (2004). Les ERP entre le retour à l'ordre et l'invention du possible, *Sciences de la société*, 61: 3–15.

Sinclair-Smith, K., Turok, I. (2012). The Changing Spatial Economy of Cities: An Exploratory Analysis of Cape Town, *Development Southern Africa*, 29(3): 391–417.

Smit, W. (2008). Le grand projet N2 Gateway: une exclusion des pauvres. In A. Dubresson, S. Jaglin (eds), *Le Cap après l'apartheid. Gouvernance métropolitaine et changement urbain*, Paris: Karthala, 23–44.

Smith, L. Hanson, S., (2003). Access to Water for the Urban Poor in Cape Town: Where Equity Meets Cost Recovery, *Urban Studies*,. 40(8): 1517–48.

Smith, L. (2006). *State Conflict vs Cooperation with the Civil Society Through Water Demand Management Approaches. A Comparison Between Cape Town and Johannesburg, South Africa*, Paper presented at the Unesco workshop on Water conflicts, Paris, 20–21 November 2006.

Smith L. (2009). The Limits to Public Participation in Strengthening Public Accountability: A Reflection on the 'Citizens' Voice' Initiative in South Africa, In *The Voices of the Poor in Urban Governance: Mobilization, Participation and Politics in South African Cities, CORUS Workshop 23–25 November 2009*, Cape Town: UCT, pag. mult.

Southall, R. (2010). South Africa 2010: From Short-Term Success to Long-Term Decline?, In J. Daniel, P. Naidoo, D. Pillay, R. Southall, *2010: Development or Decline? New South African Review 1*, Johannesburg: Wits University Press.

Standing, A. (2003). *The Social Contradictions of Organised Crime on the Cape Flats*, Pretoria, Institute of Security Studies.

Standing, A. (2005). *The Threat of Gangs and Anti-Gangs Policy. Policy Discussion Paper*, ISS paper, 116, August 2005.

Statsa (Statistics South Africa), (2012). *Census 2011. Statistical Release (PO 301.4)*, Pretoria: Statistics South Africa.

Swart, K., Bob, U. (2009). Venue Selection and the 2010 World Cup: A Case Study of Cape Town, In U. Pillay, R. Tomlinson, O. Bass (eds), *Development and Dreams. The Urban Legacy of the 2010 Football World Cup*, Cape Town: HSRC Press, 114–30.

Swilling, M. (2006). Sustainability and Infrastructure Planning in South Africa: a Cape Town Case Study, *Environment and Urbanization*, 18(1): 23–50.

Swilling, M. (ed.), (2010). *Sustaining Cape Town. Imagining a Livable City*, Stellenbosch: Sustainability Institute, Sun Press.

Terreblanche, S. (2004). La démocratie post-apartheid: un nouveau système élitiste? *Afrique contemporaine*, 2: 25–56.

Turok, I. (2001). Persistant Polarisarion Post Apartheid? Progress Towards Integration in Cape Town, *Urban Studies*, 38(13): 2349–77.

Vacchiani-Marcuzzo, C. (2008). Quelle place pour Le Cap dans la mondialization? Stratégies spatiales des IDE et dynamique urbaine », in A. Dubresson, S. Jaglin (eds), *Le Cap après l'apartheid. Gouvernance métropolitaine et changement urbain*, Paris: Karthala, 157–82.

Van Ryneveld, P., Muller, D., Parnell, S. (2003). *Indigent Policy: Including the Poor in the City of Cape Town's Income Strategy*, Cape Town, CCT.

Watson, V. (2002). *Change and Continuity in Spatial Planning: Metropolitan Planning in Cape Town Under Political Transition*, London and New York: Routledge.

Webster, E., Adler, G. (1999). Toward a Class Compromise in South Africa's 'Double Transition': Bargained Liberalization and the Consolidation of Democracy, *Politics & Society*, 27(3): 347–85.

Wesgro, (2012). *City of Cape Town. District Fact Sheet*, Cape Town: Wesgro.

Western Cape Government (WCG), (2012). *Regional Profile. City of Cape Town*, Cape Town, WCG, Provincial Treasury, Working Paper.

Whelan, P. (2004). *Local Government and Budget*, Cape Town, Idasa (Occasional papers).

Wilkinson, P. (2000). City Profile. Cape Town, *Cities*, 17(3): 195–205.

Wilkinson, P. (2004). Renegotiating Local Governance in a Post-Apartheid City: The Case of Cape Town, *Urban Forum*, 15(3): 213–30.

Wilkinson, P. (2007). Reframing Urban Passenger Transport Provision as a Strategic Priority for Developmental Local Government. In M. van Donk, M. Swilling, E. Pieterse, S. Parnell (eds), *Consolidating Developmental Local Government: Lessons from the South African Experience*, Cape Town: UCT Press.

Wilkinson, P. (2008). 'Moving Ahead'? La difficile transformation des systèmes de transports urbains au Cap. In A. Dubresson, S. Jaglin (eds), *Le Cap après l'apartheid. Gouvernance métropolitaine et changement urbain*, Paris: Karthala, 87–117.

Wolpe, R. (2007). *Investment Constraints in Cape Town, Presentation to the City of Cape Town, 5 April 2007*, Cape Town: Wesgro, Wolpe Development Stategies.

List of Abbreviations

ANC: African National Congress
BBEE: Broad Black Economic Empowerment
BLAs: Black Local Authorities
CBD: Central Business District
CID: City Improvement District
CMC: Cape Metropolitan Council
CoCT: City of Cape Town
CTICC: Cape Town International Convention Centre
CTP: Cape Town Partnership
DA: Democratic Alliance
DP: Democratic Party
EHDS: Economic and Human Development Strategy
ERP: Enterprise Resource Planning
HSL: Household Subsistence Level
ID: Independent Democrats
IDP: Integrated Development Plan
INEP: Integrated National Electrification Programme
LUMS: Land Use Management System
LUPO: Land Use Planning Ordinance
MOSS: Metro Open Space System
MSDF: Metropolitan Spatial Development Framework
NNP: New National Party
PHP: People's Housing Process
RDP: Reconstruction and Development Programme
RED: Regional Electricity Distributor
SACN: South African Cities Network
SDF: Spatial Development Framework

Chapter 5

Santiago de Chile
Prototype of the Neo-Liberal City:
Between a Strong State and Privatised
Public Services.

Géraldine Pflieger[1]

Introduction

After the coup d'état of 11 September 1973, marked by the attack on the La Moneda presidential palace and the death of the socialist President Salvador Allende, one of the first political acts of the junta led by Augusto Pinochet was to dissolve all municipal councils in the country on 19 September, before banning political parties and dissolving Congress during the days that followed (Valenzuela, 1977). The coup d'état destroyed not only national and local democracy but also the link between the state and the nation, placing the state in the hands of a military power with little legitimacy. With no democratic legitimacy to draw upon, the military government chose to rationalise its exercise of power by instituting a moral, religious and security-oriented order and by early support for market liberalisation, promoted by 'the Chicago boys' and the big industrial lobbies. This policy was resolutely directed towards economic growth and state retreat from functions such as social policy or redistribution. The Chilean state gradually delegated its legitimate power of intervention to market mechanisms, 'the feeling of belonging was fractured,

1   I would like to offer my warm thanks to the incumbents of the City Chair (*Chaire Ville*) at Sciences Po Paris, Dominique Lorrain and Frédéric Gilli, for inviting me to take part in this exciting research project on Governing Big World Cities and for offering me the opportunity to carry out the field research that has underpinned the writing of this chapter. My sincere gratitude goes to the members of the Chaire Ville network for their comments and advice during the collective discussion of two earlier versions of this contribution: Alain Dubresson, Charlotte Halpern, Sylvy Jaglin, Marie-Hélène Zérah and Bernard Hourcade. My warm thanks also go to Regina Witter, doctoral student at EPFL, for the quality and precision of her comments and suggestions. Finally, I am grateful to my partners at the Catholic University of Santiago de Chile, in particular Maria-Elena Ducci, as well as to all those experts and local actors who gave up their time for me.

and the relationship between the individual and the market substituted for that between the nation and the state [...]' (Castells, 2006: 118).

In 2010, Santiago de Chile, whose metropolitan area is home to 40 per cent of the country's population, remains a city politically and formally marked by the dictatorship, which imposed strict free market precepts on spatial development from 1979 onwards. The trauma of the dictatorship, the establishment of a society functioning in a more sophisticated manner and fears about destabilisation of democracy, newly restored in 1989, have all helped to maintain the old development principles as well as the growth coalitions that have supported them – and this despite changes of government and the fact that a centre-left political coalition ruled the country between 1990 and 2010. Today, Santiago de Chile is a prototype of the neo-liberal city, with governance shared between privatised public services and strong regulatory activity on the part of the state. There are few limits on urban expansion, but property developers and new residents pay a steep price for it. Since the 1960s, the construction lobby has put steady pressure on the Ministry of Housing to extend the limits of urban growth and to provide high-quality infrastructure to service it; high urbanisation costs and property developers' cherry-picking strategies contrast with the situation of low- to middle-income households stuck in social housing, repaying the building costs over a lifetime. The state is highly present in the metropolitan spatial development: it exercises a strong regulatory and monitoring function. However, it does not manage to entirely disguise the social, infrastructural and environment imbalances caused by a type of urban expansion on which the only check is market mechanisms.

Since it is a metropolis with no heavy industry, historically the Chilean capital's economic and urban development was not organised around a coalition between the state and the industrial sector. In fact, the main industry in Chile is located outside Santiago Metropolitan Region, in the north of the country: copper mining represented 23 per cent of national GDP in 2007. In consequence, Santiago has long been an administrative capital. Its recent economic development, between 1970 and 2000, has been based on the tertiary sector, banks, volume retailing and distribution, property and, lately, finance. Since the mid-1990s, thanks to its economic stability, the Chilean capital has become the main development hub for finance and the headquarters of multinational firms for the southern cone of Latin America. Organisations representing the construction, public works and property development sectors have sustained residential development and the development of new business districts. Since the 1960s, analyses of urban development policies for the Chilean capital have highlighted the structuring dimension of the relationship between the construction and property sectors and central government. Although this bipolar picture of urban power may appear caricatured and outdated to a European reader, it seems quite obvious and transparent to Chilean citizens, observers and urban actors. The fact that very little power is decentralised to municipalities, the absence of any metropolitan authority and the near non-existence of urban social movements until the mid-2000s all prevent us from drawing a more complex picture or discerning the emergence of the complete system of actors that is typical of a contemporary metropolis.

In this context, this chapter will discuss three questions:

- What are the scope and the limits of a form of governance based principally on state policy rather than on decentralised authorities?
- What is the respective place of private sector and public-sector actors? What is the function of the Chilean regulatory state at the urban scale?
- What is the place of instruments for steering technical networks and public services in a context of fully-fledged privatisation?

It will look simultaneously at the political and technical steering of the Chilean metropolis, the political institutions as such and the institutional arrangements implemented to deal with urban complexity (North, 1990), in order to try to grasp the continuities and discontinuities in the government of Santiago (Le Galès and Lorrain, 2003).

The first part is devoted to a presentation of Santiago de Chile's metropolitan context in 2010. There follows a historical, problem-based analysis in four phases, representing the four key moments in the institutionalisation of urban power in the capital, to which the current system of government is heir. These four successive phases focus on four specific priority issues (or problems) for public policy, whose resolution dominates the decision-making process: housing, supplying drinking water and electricity, developing road infrastructure and, more recently, modernising the public transport network. Tackling these four problems through public policy has meant renegotiating approaches to urban development and creating new instruments for intervention by the state as planner. The current government of the Chilean capital has inherited institutional rules and instruments devised at each of these key moments, which have not been challenged or fundamentally reformed. More precisely, these four stages of institutionalisation are:

- between 1973 and 1981, the imposition of powerful, centralised government by a state whose principal objective was to respond to the housing crisis, using force to tackle issues of informal urban growth. This initial phase established the basis of a powerful state, with compartmentalised ministerial policies and very little decentralisation.
- between 1979 and 1995, the implementation of reforms privatising public services (water and electricity) in order to enable the expansion of networks and support the policy of liberalising land use. In response to lack of capacity for urban expansion, the second phase led to the foundation of a solid growth coalition that brought central government into association with the construction and property development sector lobbies.
- between 1994 and 2005, the development of state regulation at the metropolitan scale in order to ensure linkages between urbanisation and

road provision and to tackle congestion problems. The intention was to support private investment in highway infrastructure (concessions and toll roads) and to develop new instruments for conditional urban development in order to increasingly apply the principle of 'user pays'.

- since 2005, the chronic weakness of regional and municipal government together with the rebirth of neighbourhood movements have increasingly challenged the urban development model driven forward by the state since the early 1980s. With the crisis of governance in public transport and the rise of local opposition to urban development projects, the growth coalition has to deal with internal and external contradictions. The question of whether existing institutional arrangements should be overhauled is being asked on all sides and highlights the possibility, in the medium term, of far-reaching changes to methods of governing the capital.

From the military government's seizure of power until recently, the story of Santiago de Chile as a city followed the major historical trends of spreading privatisation reforms, market liberalisation and then public-private partnerships. Notably under the influence of the World Bank, the Inter-American Development Bank and free market thinkers, Chile has been a favoured testing ground for neo-liberal reform – since well before the fall of the Berlin Wall which marked a pivotal moment in the dissemination of these principles throughout the world.

Santiago de Chile in 2010

Santiago de Chile, founded in 1541 by the Spaniard Pedro de Valdivia, is located on a vast plain 80 km long and 35 km wide, bounded by the Andes cordillera to the east and, to the west, by the coastal chain that separates it from the Pacific Ocean and from Valparaiso, around a hundred kilometres away. In 2002, Santiago Metropolitan Region had six million inhabitants, or 40 per cent of the national population, living in an urbanised space of some 60,000 hectares. (See Table 5.1)

As regards the *economy*, according to the Central Bank of Chile, Santiago Metropolitan Region's GDP represented 42 per cent of national GDP in 2005. (See Table 5.2)

Chilean GDP is mainly distributed across three sectors. First, the copper mining industry, located in the north of the country, represented 18.6 per cent of GDP in 2008. The second largest sector is financial services (16 per cent of GDP), followed by manufacturing industries with 13 per cent (food, machinery and equipment, chemicals and refining). The Chilean capital is the fifth largest economic hub in Latin America, after Mexico City, Buenos Aires, Sao Paulo and Rio de Janeiro. 79 per cent of Santiago's GDP comes from the tertiary sector,

Table 5.1   Changes in population, density and employment in Santiago Metropolitan Region

Province	Population 1982	Population 1992	Population 2002	Population 2007 (estimate)	Area km²	Population density 2002 people/km²	Jobs 2002 2nd quarter	Jobs 2005 2nd quarter
Santiago	3,694,939	4,311,133	4,668,473	4,903,020	2,030.5	2,299.4	–	–
Cordillera	132,275	277,687	522,856	621,041	5,528.3	94.6	–	–
Chacabuco	57,022	90,640	132,798	155,205	2,076.1	64.0	–	–
Maipo	207,874	293,021	378,444	425,697	1,120.5	337.8	–	–
Melipilla	95,708	118,802	141,165	150,538	4,065.7	34.7	–	–
Talagante	130,279	166,654	217,449	234,747	582.3	373.4	–	–
Total	4,318,097	5,257,937	6,061,185	6,490,248	15,403.4	393.5	2,299,120	2,526,140

Sources: Author's table from INE data

Table 5.2   Growth and trends in Santiago Metropolitan Region's GDP as a share of national GDP

	1960	1985	1997	2005
Regional GDP/share of national GDP (%)	44.7	45	50.1	42
		1960–1985	1985–1997	
Growth in regional GDP (%)		2.7	8.2	

Source: Author's table from Central Bank of Chile data

with 26 per cent accounted for just by financial and intermediary services. 78 per cent of national financial GDP is concentrated in the Chilean capital alone (Central Bank of Chile, 2001). Numerous multinational companies have located their headquarters for the southern cone of Latin America in the city: HP, Proctor and Gamble, IBM, Nestlé, Intel, Motorola and Yahoo. So, since the 1980s, Santiago de Chile has attained world city status (Parnreiter, 2005). Its economy has become progressively more integrated into development dynamics via its exports and thanks to free trade agreements signed with the United States, the European Union and APEC (Asia-Pacific Economic Cooperation).

The *territorial* organisation of Chile is extremely centralised. The country is divided into 13 regions which in 2010 comprised 54 provinces. In addition, the sectoral ministries appoint regional secretariats (SEREMI) in each of the 13 regions. Santiago Metropolitan Region covers six provinces and 52 municipalities. Only municipal councillors and mayors are elected by direct universal suffrage. Regional Governors (*Intendentes*), who run regional authorities, and Governors, who are in charge of provinces, are all appointed by the President of the Republic (who is elected by universal suffrage).

Within this vast Metropolitan Region, the metropolitan area of Greater Santiago (*Gran Santiago*) covers 37 municipalities, consisting of the 32 municipalities of the Province of Santiago and five municipalities in adjacent provinces. It is organised around a modest historic colonial centre located in the north of the Municipality of Santiago. To the east, this centre gives way to affluent districts with high-rise residential and business developments in the municipalities of Providencia, Las Condes and Vitacura, which emerged in the 1950s and whose development has continued up to the present day with the building of new skyscrapers. Further away to the north-east, on the slopes of the cordillera, rise the tiers of rich neighbourhoods and new gated communities with their own open-air shopping centres and dedicated private infrastructure (roads and highways, schools and green spaces). To the north, beyond the Manquehue hills, vast schemes were launched in 2002 to build a private city in the Chicureo Valley, intended for the middle and upper classes. The southern and western quadrants have historically been the location of informal settlement districts and later, social housing, essentially in the

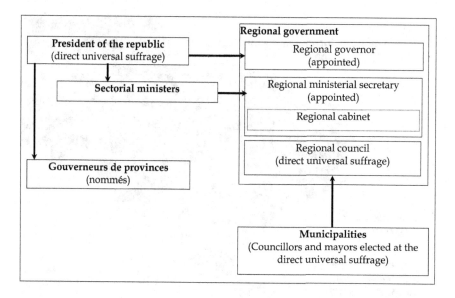

Figure 5.1   Regional territorial organisation
Source: Author's chart

form of small houses or group housing developments, built between the mid 1960s and today. These terraced houses were built in accordance with the principle of social home ownership, thanks to subsidised loans. Finally, to the south and east, in the part of the metropolis that stretches between the municipalities of La Florida, Puente Alto and Maipú and along the Valparaiso highway, residential areas have recently been undergoing redevelopment directed towards the middle classes.

As Figure 5.2 shows, Santiago de Chile is characterised by a high level of *social differentiation*, the legacy of past planning policies. The map provides evidence of extreme segregation, since the gap between average incomes in the lowest- and highest-ranked municipalities is almost a factor of ten (an average of €489 per month in the municipality of La Pintana, €4450 in Lo Barnechea). However, as Francisco Sabatini (2001) emphasises, the scale of residential segregation within Santiago de Chile is tending to become more subtle. Following the logic identified by Douglas Massey (2005) – according to which residential segregation is primarily driven by the desire of the more affluent to secede – the residential trajectory of the upper-middle or upper classes is based on more diffuse separation strategies. They do not necessarily live in the areas that are richest in terms of income but in the gated neighbourhoods being built all over the metropolis, in the middle class municipalities of Maipú, Quilicura or Puente Alto, as much as in the wealthy Municipality of Las Condes.

The metropolis continues to experience sustained *urban development*, which follows the classic form resembling the sails of a windmill, along major routes. It

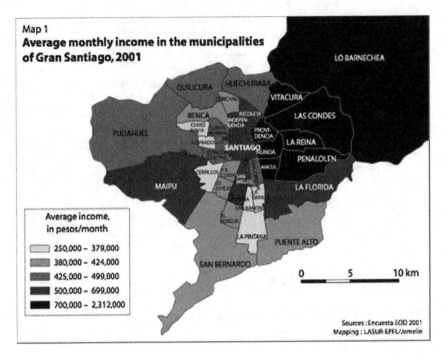

Figure 5.2   Average household income, by Greater Santiago municipality, 2001

testifies to the rate of urbanisation during the second half of the twentieth century, which took the metropolis from a population of 980,000 in 1940 to 5.2 million in 1992 and from an urbanised area of 11,000 hectares to 50,000 hectares over the same period. The highest rates of growth were observed during the 1940s and 1950s, with annual population growth of 4.1 per cent. During the 1990s, the annual growth rate remained at 2.6 per cent. Under the effects of urban sprawl, the density of the urbanised area dropped from 96 people per hectare in 1992 to 85 in 2002.

Infrastructure policies to keep the rapidly expanding metropolis functioning were rather slow to develop, but accelerated strongly during the 2000s, as far as urban highways and the metro system were concerned.

With the support of public-private partnerships, the capital's *highway system* has been noticeably strengthened by the opening of 120 km of highways between 2004 and 2006, including new east-west corridors, a significant part of the ring road to the south and west and new south-east and north-east access roads. The most important element of this new infrastructure is the Costanera Norte Kennedy urban highway, mainly tunnelled under the Mapocho River and linking the business districts in the east of the metropolitan area directly to the international airport. The total investment made in the 2000s was nearly €2 billion euros. The metropolitan area now boasts 215 km of urban highways, all equipped with electronic toll collection and tariffs charged by the kilometre.

In parallel, a marked acceleration in building rapid transit *metro* lines can be observed from the 2000s onwards; this was instigated by President Ricardo Lagos, who today still has a reputation for contstruction projects. The first two metro lines were opened in 1975 and 1978 and were built by a Chilean-French consortium. Following some limited extensions during the 1970s and 1980s, the metro network was still of modest size in 2001, with a 40 km network of three lines. With the extension projects launched in the late 1990s and the 2000s (all opened between 2002 and 2006), the network increased by 42 km, with the new southbound Line 4 being more than 30 km long. Total investment in the metro was €1.7 billion euros. With the extension of Line 1 eastwards and Line 5 to the west, by 2010 the Santiago Metro had reached a total length of 104km.

As regards the *bus network*, from the end of the 1970s, Santiago de Chile saw complete deregulation of the sector. Since 1988, private bus companies have been able to offer their services freely on existing or new routes. Competition between small bus operators has led to a gradual decline in the quality of service: overcapacity of supply, a deteriorating active fleet, a congested public transport system and fare increases. Following numerous attempts to reregulate the sector during the 1990s, the government undertook a total modernisation of the system by creating a truly integrated network in 2007, through the Transantiago Plan. However, implementation of the reform faced severe difficulties in financing the sector, as well as failures of coordination between the different ministries responsible. As Santiago is Chile's first city, the major crisis in public transport considerably weakened the new President, Michelle Bachelet, who had been elected in 2006; it forced the resignation of her Minister of Transport and led to more than three years of parliamentary debates on the conditions for financing public transport.

In parallel, since the mid-1990s, an increase in purchasing power has resulted in *widespread car ownership* and an explosion in the number of motor vehicles on the road. Stable from 1977 to 1991, the average number of cars per household rose from 0.36 to 0.56 between 1991 and 2001, the date of the last household survey (source: EOD survey). Over the same period, the modal share of journeys made by car went up from 14.6 per cent to 27.4 per cent, while that of buses and shared taxis fell from 47.1 per cent to 30.4 per cent, and that of the metro from 6.7 per cent to 5 per cent (Source: EOD survey 1991, 2001).

1965–1981. From Housing Crisis to Crisis of Democracy: The Brutal Institutionalisation of State Power

The contemporary political history of the metropolis begins with the housing crisis. Beginning in the 1950s and up to the 1973 coup d'état, this crisis demonstrated the inability of both the property market and the state to propose alternatives to accelerating informal urbanisation. The housing crisis was central to the presidential campaign that brought Salvador Allende to power in 1970, supported by a broad left-wing coalition. However, the Popular Unity Government quickly found itself confronted by stark contradictions between its limited capacity for governmental intervention in the field of housing and the unceasing development of informal districts. The difficulties the Allende Government met when confronted by housing problems were to considerably weaken the democratic regime and offer a pretext for the military junta to take power. The effects of the 1973 coup d'état and Augusto Pinochet's coming to power included the strong institutionalisation of state power in the urban sector (a ban on informal urbanisation that was never circumvented; support for an essentially private sector-based social housing policy; dislocated local government), which remains to this day one of the dominant features of government of the Chilean capital.

Housing Crisis and Mounting Contradictions

Before Augusto Pinochet came to power, the Chilean state had been faced with sustained informal urbanisation but, over more than 20 years, had been unable to find any solutions to the crisis. In 1950, there were around 350,000 people living in informal housing in the central area, while on the periphery of the metropolis there were 79,000 people in this type of housing (out of a total Greater Santiago population of 1,350,000) (Icaza and Rodriguez, 1988). It was during the 1950s that the first illegal land occupations were established in the south of the city. In its first stage, informal settlement developed in several forms: division of old blocks of flats into smaller housing units (*conventillo*); sharing of one apartment by several families (*allegado*); setting up of informal encampments by migrant workers and sometimes even by political groups such as the Communist Party (*callampa*); and construction by the state of emergency housing projects (*población*). Between 1959 and 1963, the centre-right Government of Jorge Alessandri swept away some of these informal districts. It rehoused 20,000 families in permanent housing located in the municipalities where the shanty towns had been set up, thus confirming the trends towards residential segregation that had been accelerating over the previous ten years or so. In 1960, still under the Alessandri presidency, a new master plan was implemented to 'limit the anarchic and uncontrolled urbanization of Greater Santiago'. The Intermunicipal Regulatory Plan for Santiago (*Plan Regulador Intercomunal para Santiago*, or PRIS) set a limit on growth for the first time and froze some agricultural land in order to mark out a green belt around the urbanised area. However, this policy did not have the expected impact, and the creation of shanty towns continued.

On a political level, informal working-class districts were central to Chile's partisan – and class-based – conflicts of the 1960s. The housing crisis can be partially attributed to the Chilean Chamber of Construction (Cámara Chilena de la Construcción, or CCC), which then – as now – exerted a great deal of influence on national housing policy (Cheetham, 1971). The construction lobby conducted a strategy of cherry-picking while maximising returns on properties built, thus excluding a large majority of Chilean households. At least, this was the interpretation of the left-wing parties and extreme-left movements that gained strength during the second half of the 1960s (Castells, 1973). In 1965, the Christian Democrat Government of Eduardo Frei created the Ministry of Housing. The new Ministry launched *Operación Sitio*. Fifty-two thousand families were rehoused on the far periphery of the metropolis. Plots of land were offered to families and self-help housing was then supported by grants of materials. These newbuilds often had no access to water and so the quality of the housing stock remained unsatisfactory.

From official informal districts to encampments, these marginal districts became fertile ground for radicalisation by Chilean social movements, ranging from associations close to the Socialist Party (PS) and Communist Party (PC), which were to form the Popular Unity campaign that brought Allende to power, to revolutionary left groups. This was because the housing crisis was actually an endogenous urban crisis: the proportion of rural immigrants was on average lower in informal districts than in the rest of the metropolitan area, proof that the development of shanty towns was not due solely to rural exodus (Castells, 1973). In 1967, with the public-sector budget crisis – linked to the increase in external debt – the Christian Democrat Government revised its ambitions and drastically reduced support for social housing construction. The Communist Party supported the land seizure by 648 families in March 1967 and faced up to repression by the forces of law and order. The PC then organised committees of the homeless in many districts within the metropolitan area, in order to exert pressure on the Ministry of Housing, and if necessary to launch new land occupations. These occupations were mostly carried out by poorly-housed people living in overcrowded accommodation *(allegados)* or in very small apartments *(conventillo)*. The creation of new encampments and new squats is to be attributed more to militant action than to inexorable pressure caused by immigration and rural exodus. From this point of view, the Chilean movements of the 1960s are close to present-day movements for the right to housing (Mayer, 2000). In Santiago, between 1967 and the 1970 presidential elections, confrontations between the forces of law and order and *pobladores* movements intensified. From 1968, group protests were stepped up, following the line of the revolutionary left (Movimiento de Izquierda Revolucionaria) and openly calling for armed struggle, with slogans such as 'a house or death' and 'from seizing land to seizing power'. In March 1970, in the Municipality of La Florida in the south of the city, the PS and PC united to create a new camp under the name of 'Popular Unity', taken from the name of the governmental alliance that was to bring Salvador Allende to power. Between 1969 and 1970, the number of new encampments *(campamentos)* increased from 35 to 103 (De Ramón, 1990), with names such as New Havana, Che Guevara or Lenin. The presidential campaign was fought on the housing issue and the informal districts were used as campaigning and electoral bases by left-wing parties. Some neighbourhoods were managed by Popular Unity Committees (CUP) which worked directly for the success of the left-wing alliance (Castells, 1973).

From Housing Crisis to Crisis of Democracy

Popular Unity's electoral programme promised that 100,000 housing units would be built every year. But just the new occupations incited by left-wing movements during the presidential campaign had involved 60,000 families. In addition, the 1970–1971 emergency housing programme faced opposition from the CCC, which did not support a policy directed towards small-scale construction and small businesses. The CCC initiated a boycott of social housing programmes, and not a single house was built during the first six months of the new government. In spite of an agreement reached with the CCC and the relaunching of construction – at a rate of 40,000 housing units per year between 1970 and 1973, as against fewer than 21,000 between 1967 and 1970 under the Frei Government – the housing shortage was still making itself strongly felt. From early 1972, land occupations began again – even under the influence of Popular Unity parties, despite their being in power. This in fact accelerated the phenomenon without managing to resolve it or even to limit it. In 1971 alone, 72 new encampments were set up. In 1972, there were a total of 275 informal districts, with 83,000 families (Paquette, 1998). Between 1972 and September 1973, demonstrations in the encampments gained in intensity under the influence of the revolutionary left, which was increasingly breaking with Popular Unity policy. Outflanked on his left, Salvador Allende also found himself confronted by a truck drivers' strike which was later revealed to have been supported by the CIA. His whole policy of nationalising the copper mining industry and moving towards centralised economic planning was widely denounced by national (wholesale/retail trade and the property sector) and international economic lobbies. The government, thoroughly destabilised, was confronted by an impossible climate and insurrections on all sides. It was in this context that the military junta took power by force in September 1973.

With the coup d'état and the assumption of power by the military government, the creation of new encampments was permanently halted. The first political act of the junta was to reduce local government to zero because it was seen as presenting a risk of political challenge. Electoral registers were destroyed, elections were banned, left wing parties dissolved and civilian courts transformed into military tribunals. Hundreds of mayors and municipal councillors elected under Popular Unity were arrested (Valenzuela, 1977). A few days after the coup d'état, all mayors and municipal councillors in the country were dismissed from office: from then on, General Pinochet appointed all mayors. He maintained in post all mayors belonging to his National Party and appointed new ones to previously communist and socialist town halls. On the centre-right, the number of Christian Democrat mayors fell from 91 to 70; only Christian Democrats close to the new government were appointed. Twenty-nine members of the armed services became mayors.

By law, the new mayors were attributed all the decision-making prerogatives previously devolved to municipal councils. However, although in theory mayors were given increased power, in practice they had no autonomy. All tax revenues were gathered in by the state, which then redistributed funds to municipalities. All municipal personnel were given the status of central government civil servants. Urban government became a driver for transmitting governmental power, following a military-type command chain. In particular, governors of provinces were given powers which extended to municipalities and they could monitor and countermand decisions taken by mayors, who were their subordinates. In practice, governors could even extend their meddling into the details of municipal organisation, such as the appointment of heads of district committees, especially in municipalities in the provincial capitals.

Table 5.3   Distribution by party of mayoral offices, before and after the coup d'état

Party	Before 11 September 1973	After 11 September 1973
Opposition to Allende's Popular Unity		
Christian Democrats	91	70
National Party	48	79
Others	15	20
Allende's Popular Unity		
Socialists	60	0
Communists	36	0
Radicals	20	0
Left Christians	4	0
Others		
Independents	12	81
Armed services personnel	0	29
Total	**286**	**286**

Source: Author's table based on data from Valenzuela, 1997

Brutal Institutionalisation of State Power in the Urban Sphere

Having halted the creation of new informal districts, in 1979 the military government embarked on a policy to bring the shanty towns down by force. Between 1979 and 1986, 246 shanty towns were razed and 150,000 people displaced and rehoused. Although the government's stated objective was to prevent the risks of flooding to encampments located near watercourses and to restore illegally occupied sites to their owners, in fact rehousing residents of these districts provided an excuse to clear the shanty towns out of wealthy municipalities

(Larrain, 1994). The municipalities receiving the rehoused families were almost all located in the north and south of the metropolitan area, where land was cheapest (La Pintana, Renca, Puente Alto, La Granja, Cerro Navia and San Bernardo). By concentrating financially insecure households in the poor southern municipalities and permitting substantial appreciation in land values in wealthy municipalities, this policy of eradicating shanty towns had the effect of increasing the already high level of segregation in the metropolitan area.

Palliative measures were proposed, and some social housing units were built in the form of owner-occupied apartments or small houses, purchased with the aid of a subsidy. Programmes inspired by free market thinking abandoned the policy of supplying public housing initiated by Allende and instead focused on a policy of supporting demand. Social housing units for lower-income groups represented 45 per cent of new housing production between 1985 and 1990 and 15 per cent of newbuild housing was deported by the housing subsidies programme (Paquette, 1998).

Finally, some shanty towns located in poor municipalities benefited from a rehabilitation programme known as 'rooting' (*radicación* – implying an alternative process to 'eradication'), which was funded by the Inter-American Development Bank. In this case, families were given a deed of ownership (Larrain, 1994) and a basic one-room home with mains drainage, piped running water and electricity was built for them.

The policy of eradicating shanty towns and rehabilitating informal districts was conducted at a turning point in Pinochet's economic policies. A new discourse was promoted, one that nuanced the ultra free market paradigm that had officially guided government policy since 1975. As Rodrigo Hidalgo emphasises (2004: 231):

> The military regime attempted to promote a new discourse to describe its development model; the adjective 'social' was added to 'market policy' in order to establish the concept of a social market policy.

Improving the sanitation standards of housing and providing essential services represented a central argument used by the military regime to justify the razing of particular shanty towns, in an attempt to mask the purely authoritarian and segregationist character of this type of intervention, as well as its effects in terms of anomie and the breakdown of residents' social networks (Lafoy, Torres Rojas et al., 1990; Ducci, 1997). And – from a less social and more neo-liberal perspective – the state's policy focus on supplying poor households with access to urban infrastructure could be presented as recentring government regulatory activity relating to public safety and public health. So the state abandoned its function as the builder of social housing in order to restrict public policy to delivering vital public amenities and services (Lafoy, Torres Rojas and Munoz Salazar, 1990).

The state's reassertion of control over cities was the last act in a long housing crisis which had crystallised the whole of the national political debate during the 1960s. The inability of successive governments to resolve the housing crisis

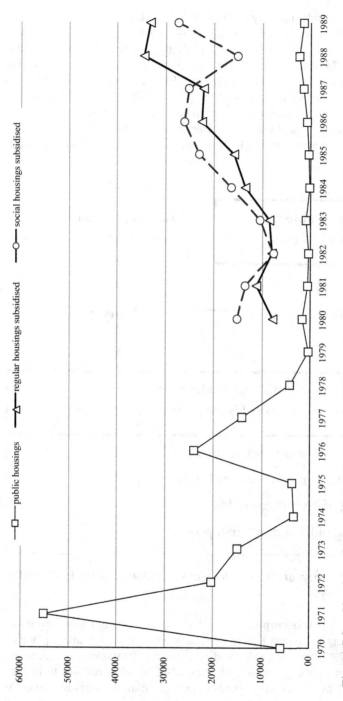

Figure 5.3   **Number of housing units built or subsidised by the state between 1970 and 1989, under the military dictatorship**

Sources: Author's graph from INE data on building permits (cited in Paquette, 1998)
Key to Figure 5.3
Nombre de logements = Number of housing units

Legend (top):
- ☐ public housings
- △ regular housings subsidised
- ○ social housings subsidised

intensified the demands made by the radical left, which was drawn to the idea of armed struggle. At the same time, these movements used land occupation in wealthy municipalities as their main mobilising instrument. When the newly-elected Popular Unity Government also proved unable to resolve this issue, the housing crisis turned into a profound crisis of democracy. As Figure 5.4 clearly shows, one of the symbolic markers of the period 1975–1980 was the creation of formal institutions to control urbanisation and local authorities by the central state. This choice was – and still is – a direct consequence of the military coup, which has played an overwhelmingly dominant role in the recent history of urban policies in Chile.

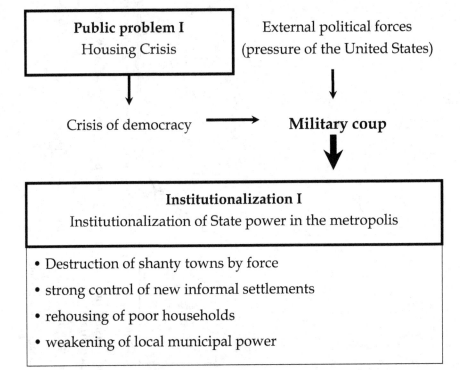

Figure 5.4   Overview of the first phase of institutionalization, 1965–1981

Having dealt with housing problems by force, from the early 1980s the military government began to change course towards more free market urban planning policies. The 1980s were to be devoted to major regulatory reforms and to the modernisation of utilities. The essential aim of these measures was to liberate urban growth. Having set up a state-present, centralised administration, the government provided itself with instruments that would promote the creation of a powerful growth coalition.

1979–1995. Water and Electricity Reforms Serving Urban Expansion

The new urban development policy embarked upon in 1979 did not limit itself to eliminating informal urbanisation. It had the parallel aim of providing the metropolis with the legal means and the infrastructure necessary for its expansion. Under the influence of the military government's US advisers, a policy of urban expansion was gradually imposed, solidifying a growth coalition between the state and the construction industry. This policy was based on reforms liberalising the electricity sector and recasting the financing conditions for water distribution services, stimulated by the World Bank. The first objective of these reforms was ideological in nature and aimed to trial methods of enabling state retreat from sectors that had previously been viewed as natural public monopolies. The second objective was to back the policy of urban growth by stepping up delivery of public services to areas zoned for urbanisation.

The urban government regime established in Santiago de Chile is a perfect fit for the growth coalition model formalised by Logan and Molotch (2007). A growth coalition is formed by actors who have a direct interest in growth – landowners, property developers and the construction industry – in association with actors who have an indirect interest: the public authorities and the major public services (Ducci, 2004). Within this framework, the public authorities have two key functions: they foster urban expansion by modifying development plans in order to enable new building and to create income from ground rent; they also create viable sites for urban development by building water, electricity and road infrastructures.

The Theoretical Virtues of Liberalising Land Use

One of the symbolic markers of Chilean development policy has been the quest for unfettered urban growth. After the Pinochet Government came to power, this desire for freedom in land use took shape over several years. It became established by the late 1980s, and has gone unchallenged ever since.

As early as the 1960s, the first PRIS had set an initial, though theoretical, limit on urban development – a limit that was never respected and came to symbolise an entirely ineffective institutional rule. The state itself built social housing outside the city boundaries, where land was cheaper, and it regularised informal encampments on the periphery of the city. In parallel, private developers carried through projects beyond the city boundaries in the north-east of the metropolitan area. In 1975, a first decree attempted to contain urban growth in order to meet two objectives: preservation of agricultural areas and densification of urban areas. The principle of limiting urban development at that time might appear to run contrary to the military government's free market perspective, but:

> A great deal of agricultural land on the rural periphery is being used up, which weakens our capacity to manage urban infrastructure and affects the city's ecological balance. Moreover, peripheral urbanization requires constant, highly expensive extensions to drainage, road and communication networks. (Ministry of Housing, 1977, cited *in* Petermann, 2006)

A new city boundary was established, integrating urbanisation that had taken place since the 1960s and adding an extra 700 ha for future urbanisation. This new city boundary applied until 1980, particularly because of the fall in construction of social housing.

However, in 1979, with the promulgation of the new National Urban Development Policy (*Política Nacional de Desarrollo Urbano*, or PNDU), the military government changed its philosophy, under the influence of liberal economists from the University of Chicago. It revised the 1960 PRIS, with three flagship measures:

- removing the former boundaries on areas considered suitable for urbanisation;
- more than doubling the surface area available for urbanisation projects, from 35,000 to 100,000 ha; and
- introducing tax relief on land and property deals.

The official objective of this was, firstly, to force land prices down and to support owner-occupation. This policy was drawn up by Miguel Kast, an economist with a University of Chicago degree and the main promoter of liberal economic policy in Chile. As Director of the Office of National Planning (Oficina de Planificacion Nacional, or Odeplan), Kast promoted a discourse that unambiguously favoured the free market and unfettered urban growth:

> Allowing cities to grow horizontally benefits housing users, it's cheaper, it's what people want, and the farmer can get a better price for his land. Land is an unlimited resource and it's the job of the market to define the optimal size of the city and land use. (Remarks published in 1979, cited in Hidalgo, 2004, p. 226)

For Arnold Harberger, also a University of Chicago economist and the originator of the 1979 planning policy, the cost of services and infrastructure should not pose a problem for the liberalisation of land use:

> The costs of expanding services in central areas in order to supply a million extra residents are much higher than the costs of providing the same services

to a million people living in the area zoned for urbanization. (1979, cited in Petermann, 2006)

In reality, the 100,000ha available for urbanisation did not correspond exactly to an area of undifferentiated costs for urban growth. The 1979 decree actually created two zones: (1) an urban zone, within which urbanisation was permitted and where the public authorities were obliged to invest in order to make sites viable and provide them with amenities and public services, and (2) an urban expansion zone, where private sector urban development was permitted but where the state had no obligation to build infrastructure (Petermann, 2006). The urban zone remained relatively limited, since it corresponded exactly to the area that had already been urbanised before 1979; the state did not guarantee that it would provide any amenities outside this perimeter.

Urban Growth Limited by Infrastructure

In practice, the effects of this liberalisation of land use were quite limited. Outside the urban area, there was relatively little urbanisation during this period. At the start of the 1980s, the complete liberalisation of the land market and the idea of 'Santiago without boundaries' represented more a statement of economic faith than a reality. This slow pace of growth can be put down to three factors: (1) the production of social housing by the public sector, located on the southern periphery of the metropolitan area, was by and large abandoned from 1978 onwards; (2) from 1982, economic crisis and recession severely limited investment in property; (3) the infrastructure constraints that acted as a drag on urbanisation in the urban expansion zone came to block urbanisation in general.

In spite of the fact that urban development was barely sustained between 1980 and 1985, new districts were built by private developers in the north-east quadrant of the metropolitan area, within the perimeter of the 'urban expansion zone'. Outside the official city boundaries from 1960 to 1979, these outlying districts – in the municipalities of Vitacura, Las Condes and Lo Barnechea – enjoyed a great deal of social, symbolic and countryside capital derived from their geographical location. Since it was on the edge of the metropolitan area, private water distribution companies gradually expanded in order to supply the zone. Lo Castillo, for example, which had been founded in 1947, had just a few hundred consumers in the early 1950s, nearly 7,000 in 1968, 42,000 in 1983, 65,000 in 1994 and 107,469 in 2005 (1968, 1983 and 1994 data from Daniere and Gomez-Ibanez, 1994; 2005 data from SISS). In the early 1980s, after the delineation of the new 'urban expansion zone', two additional companies were created to service new urban development in the Municipality of Las Condes – the Manquehue Drinking Water Company Ltd (Empresa de agua potable Manquehue Ltda, known as 'Aguas Manquehue') and the Villa Los Dominicos Drinking Water Company Ltd (Empresa de agua potable Villa Los Dominicos Ltda, or EAPVLD) (sources: INECON in Icaza and Rodriguez, 1988: 13–18). With a very high connection charge (around ten times higher than that of the public-sector operator) (Icaza and Rodriguez, 1988), private suppliers were effectively controlling land use by slightly increasing the costs of building in these areas. Although the connection charge enabled property developers to pursue their cherry-picking strategy, in return the developers had to support their private drinking water distributors by absorbing operating deficits for water distribution. During the 1980s, a large number of private distributors were unable to operate on the basis of the water tariffs set by the state. However, the three operators in the north-east of the capital did not go bankrupt because they enjoyed cross-subsidies from property developers, through the return on ground rents.

The following table (Table 5.4) shows the marked inequalities in drinking water consumption between the Metropolitan Sanitation Works Company (Empresa metropolitana de obras sanitarias, or EMOS) (233 litres per person per day) and Aguas Manquehue, which serves the affluent north-eastern districts and records an average consumption of 800 litres per person per day. Consumption patterns have, incidentally, changed little over 25 years: in 2007, the average consumption of Aguas Andinas (ex-EMOS) users was 212 l/p/d, while Aguas Manquehue users were still consuming, on average, 864 l/p/d.

Outside the districts built by the private sector in the north-east of the metropolitan area, the pressure exerted on land by infrastructure has not led to the fall in prices expected by those who championed liberalisation of land use; on the contrary, land prices rose markedly during the 1980s, both in the urbanised zone and in the urban expansion zone. Reforms to the electricity sector and later to the drinking water sector were motivated by two objectives: the first was ideological in nature, since the World Bank had made the granting of loans conditional on state retreat from operating public services; the second objective was related to urban planning, aiming to strengthen infrastructure investment capacity and to support urban expansion.

Privatisation Serves Urban Growth

Privatisation of the electricity sector occurred during a second wave of privatisation, between 1985 and 1989, and remains one of the foremost experiments in electricity-sector deregulation and privatisation in the world. Before 1978, the metropolitan region was managed by the Central Interconnected System (Sistema Interconectado Central, or SIC), with production divided between two enterprises, Endesa (70 per cent) and Chilectra (30 per cent), while the transmission grid and distribution were entirely in the hands of Chilectra. From 1978, preliminary restructuring of the sector was carried out: regulation of the sector was the responsibility of the National Electricity Commission (Comisión Nacional de la Electricidad). Between 1978 and 1984, the market was deregulated and unbundling of the sector began: Chilectra was split into three companies, one for production and transmission (Chilgener) and two for distribution (Chilmetro and Chilquinta). In 1986 and 1987, these three companies were privatised, as was Endesa

Table 5.4 Classification of drinking water distributors in Greater Santiago in 1985

Service	Status	Area served	Service characteristics				
			Population served	Number of customers	Average consumption (l/p/d)	Length of water network (km)	% population served
EMOS	Autonomous entity under public law	33 of the 34 municipalities (except Maipú, and sectors of Las Condes, Cerrillos and Central Station)	3, 550,000	644,000	233	6,000	88
EAPAM	Municipally owned company	Maipú + large part of Cerrillos + one sector of Central Station	240,000	48,927	244	475	5.9
EAPLOC	Private sector company	Large part of Las Condes	236,000	42,305	690	636	5.8
EAPVLD	Private sector company	Las Condes sector	6,584	1,013	850	35.5	0.2
Aguas Manquehue	Private sector company	Las Condes sector	1,664	306	800	16.2	0.03
Total			4,034, 248	736,551	262	7,162.7	100

Sources: Author's table using INECON 1985 data (cited by Iacaza and Rodríguez, 1998: 13–18)
Distributors:
EMOS: Metropolitan Sanitation Works Company (Empresa metropolitana de obras sanitarias)
EAPAM: Maipú Drinking Water and Sewerage Company (Empresa de agua potable y alcantarillado de Maipú)
EAPLOC: Lo Castillo Drinking Water Company Ltd (Empresa de agua potable Lo Castillo Ltda)
EAPVLD: Villa Los Dominicos Drinking Water Company Ltd (Empresa de agua potable Villa Los Dominicos Ltda)
Aguas Manquehue: Manquehue Drinking Water Company Ltd (Empresa de agua potable Manquehue Ltda)

in 1989. This privatisation followed the model known as 'popular capitalism': the government offered shares to employees, pension funds, the general public and other traditional investors, with the aim of diluting ownership of the companies.

The reform did not have the principal objective of raising the household connection rate. In fact, connection rates to electricity services had been relatively high in Santiago Metropolitan Region since the 1970s. The issue of service delivery to the poorest and/or most peripheral areas was less acute than for other Latin American cities. According to surveys of family budgets carried out by INE between 1988 and 1998, classifying all metropolitan households according to income, even among the poorest 10 per cent, only 7 per cent (or nearly 10,000 out of about 1.3 million households reportedly living in Greater Santiago) had no access to the service in 1998 (Matthieussent, 2003). Rather than trying to extend the service to more users, the privatisation and deregulation of the electricity sector had two other objectives:

- strengthening investment in order to improve the quality of service to customers, given the ageing of the network and the increase in demand resulting from urban expansion;
- reducing the public-sector deficit by cutting back government funding to state-owned enterprises in deficit.

Modernisation of the electricity sector occurred at the same time as a rise in the standard of living for Chileans. Between the early 1990s and the early 2000s, average electricity consumption went up from 100 kWh to 200 kWh per month (Matthieussent, 2003).

In contrast, urban issues represented a more significant determining factor for the modernisation of the water sector than they did for the electricity sector. Plans for reform of water and sanitation services were drawn up in 1988 and ratified in 1989, shortly before the fall of the military government (Shirley et al., 2000). There were serious problems with financing the state-owned enterprise EMOS: it was only just in profit between the early 1980s and 1987, self-financing tariffs were below the long-run marginal cost and the rate of return on total assets was only 2.7 per cent. According to the World Bank, EMOS' weak cash position together with limited access to borrowing – given the Pinochet Government's drastic public debt reduction policy – explained EMOS' under-investment in maintaining its systems and expanding mains drainage networks. EMOS' former head[2] has pointed out that, in 1987, 20 per cent of the network of pipes had exceeded its 30-year usable life; and the same 1986 World Bank audit estimated the need for investment in network maintenance and expansion for the period 1987–1989 at €118.6 million. But only €24 million were actually invested.

In this context, interviews carried out during the 1990s by Shirley et al. (2000) with the CCC mention that, from the mid-1980s, property developers strongly

2   Raquel Alfaro, Head of EMOS 1990–1996, interviewed 5 August 2003.

supported the military government's ambition to privatise EMOS. The property and construction sector anticipated new contracts resulting from an increase in investment capacity and possible real estate developments.

Apart from the property lobby, the 1989 reform benefited another prominent supporter – the World Bank. According to the former head of EMOS, Raquel Alfaro, in the Pinochet era, beginning in 1986, the World Bank made the granting of any new loan conditional on structural reform of EMOS. Thanks to this reform, from 1989 and especially between 1990 and 1994, the company was able to obtain a World Bank loan of €60 million, whereas the first (1980) loan had been limited to €26 million.

With the General Sanitary Services Law (*Ley general de servicios sanitarios*) of 30 December 1988, regional water distribution companies became limited companies under private commercial law and were made subject to new regulatory restrictions, while performance criteria were strengthened and the tariff model overhauled. First of all, in order to separate the policy regulation and management functions – for which the Ministry of Economic Affairs continued to be responsible until privatisation in 1999 – from the technical, economic and tariff regulation functions, a new independent authority, the Superintendency of Sanitary Services (Superintendencia de Servicios Sanitarios, or SISS), was created by Law No. 18.902 of 1990. SISS was given the classic powers of a regulatory authority: setting tariffs, monitoring technical standards, awarding concessions and effluent quality control. Next, attention turned to tariffs, where the price-setting process was thoroughly revised. The new self-financing model also applied to the company's development projects. Independent experts were to define the cost structures of a fictitious company, incorporating all the theoretical operating and investment costs of providing water and sanitation in the Greater Santiago region. This model company was then set in competition with the costs presented by EMOS, with the latter's development plan taken into account. SISS was to act as final arbiter of costs, generally coming down somewhere between those calculated by the experts and those published by the operator. Prices were then fixed for a period of five years. This tariff-setting formula strongly encouraged and continues to encourage investment, because any new asset – such as a wastewater treatment plant or new sewers – are integrated into the business model, which means that tariffs automatically follow the investments actually made by the operator.

Following the application of this model and with considerable price increases, EMOS' investment capacity markedly improved. In just one year (1989–1990), the average price of water in Santiago had already increased by 50 per cent; and by the end of 1998, the average price practically doubled (Gómez-Lobo and Contreras, 2003). Deducting World Bank loans, investments made by EMOS using its own funds rose from €4.8 million a year for 1987–1989 to nearly €17 million in 1990, €27.2 million in 1991 and an average of €34 million a year between 1992 and 1996 (€ constant prices, reference year 1996) (Shirley et al., 2000). This tariff reform enabled EMOS to speed up the rate at which areas not already covered by mains drainage were being connected. In addition, the new World Bank loan was intended exclusively to finance the regional sanitation system improvement programme.

The definitive adoption of the new regulatory framework some months before the fall of the Pinochet Government represented a stroke of luck for the new democratic government: it was able to blame this unpopular reform on the previous regime while enjoying its positive effects in terms of performance and economic efficiency. So, benefiting from both the increase in tariffs and the strengthening of business performance, the state as shareholder received more than €63 million in dividends between 1990 and 1994 (Shirley et al., 2000). In 1999, the privatisation of just 51 per cent of EMOS's shares, sold to a consortium consisting of Aguas de Barcelona, Agbar (Spain) and Suez (France), brought in €819 million for the state.

Economic and Environmental Efficiency, Social Inefficiency

Following a phase of massive investments in making first drinking water and then mains drainage networks universally available (Pflieger, 2008), the priority of the Chilean water and sanitation sector at the turn of the new century was the investment that remained to be made in treatment plants. In 1996, the national wastewater treatment rate was only 16.7 per cent, with a government objective of treating 100 per cent of wastewater by 2010 (Oxman and Oxer, 2000). The 1999 privatisation of EMOS and the 2000 tariff revision (for the period 2000–2005) committed investments of €886 million, of which €600 million (67 per cent) were for wastewater treatment. The investment plan was completed in 2009 when the Los Nogales plant in the north of the metropolitan area came into operation. The tariff-setting system gradually enabled optimal approaches to eco-efficiency objectives.

However, this strengthening of economic and environmental performance was achieved at the cost of big tariff rises from the second half of the 1990s onwards – and these were not without consequences for social equality of access to services. In 2003, 4 per cent of customers (about 30,000 consumers) had more than three months of payments outstanding to the company. Aggravated by a strong social segregation at the scale of the metropolitan area, the geography of indebtedness adds to social inequalities (Pflieger and Matthieussent, 2008). Between June 2002 and June 2003, the cumulative amount of unpaid water bills increased by 20 per cent, before stabilising between June 2003 and June 2004: Average indebtedness per inhabitant increased by 10 per cent (author's calculations from Aguas Andinas data). On the other hand, the proportion of customers with payments more than three months in arrears remained relatively stable (4.5 per cent in 2002, 4.15 per cent in 2003 and 4.4 per cent in 2004). It was the amount owed that increased, rather than the number of debtors. From 1990 onwards, the Chilean model of water management had provided arrangements to subsidise poor households in order to limit the social effects of price rises. However, the strongest criticism of the subsidy system arose from its significant failures in targeting aid. The Chilean model was limited by the fact that the principal eligibility criterion for these subsidies was absence of debt to the distribution company.

Neither the management reforms of the water and sanitation sector launched in 1989 nor the privatisation and deregulation of the electricity sector between 1982 and 1985 challenged network cohesion in tariffs or quality of service (Pflieger, 2008; Pflieger and Matthieussent, 2008). These results run counter to the 'splintering urbanism' thesis, according to which liberalisation would inevitably give rise to greater differentiation between levels of service delivery, both socially and spatially (Graham and Marvin, 2001). The reforms enabled a marked improvement in services: the gradual elimination of shared electricity meters; provision of universal mains drainage; then, from the early 2000s, the widespread, ongoing introduction of wastewater treatment. On the other hand, the economic model of self-financing and capital efficiency excluded nearly 5 per cent of the water sector's potential customer base, even before issues of creditworthiness and social inequality of access were taken into account.

Beyond the objectives of strengthening the economic, financial and environmental performance of public service enterprises, the reforms were intended to support urban expansion, which had been severely reined in between 1980 and 1985 (Figueroa, 2004). Between 1982 and 1992, and especially after 1985, the number of housing units increased by 35.6 per cent (INE, 1982 and 1992 censuses). This growth was also supported by an upsurge in the Chilean economy. The boundary of the 1985 urban zone was widely breached, not only to the north-east but now also to the south and south-west. The main promoter of this

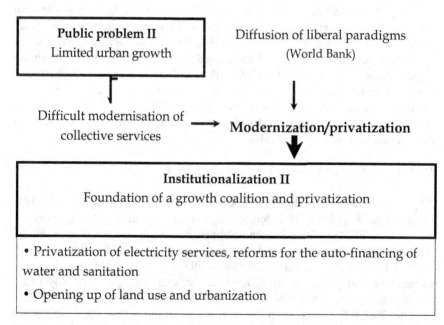

Figure 5.5 **Overview of the second phase of institutionalization, 1979–1995**

urban growth was the private sector, although some social housing developments supported by the state also took place outside the area zoned for urbanisation.

1994–2005. Urban Sprawl Up Against the Limited Development of Road Infrastructure

From the early 1990s, freed from its infrastructural constraints, the liberalisation of land use really began to produce effects. However, with the return of urban growth, the government quickly found itself confronted by two major challenges to urban management: urban sprawl on a chaotic model, poorly coordinated with road transport; and the growing congestion of road networks and public transport. At the beginning of the 1990s, the Chilean capital's arterial road system was underdeveloped and poorly maintained. In 1993, according to the Ministry of Public Works (Ministerio de Obras Públicas, or MOP), the condition of a third of the network was deficient. At the same period, the number of motor vehicles on the road was exploding, as was the modal share of journeys made by car, without the state being able to satisfy the growing demand for infrastructure.

At one point tempted by the idea of a denser city, the government – in particular, the Minister of Public Works – chose to base the development of the metropolis on two principles: new urban developments should be tied to major road infrastructure; travel within the metropolis should be facilitated by a vast programme of urban highway construction. This approach, based resolutely on building large-scale amenities, set Santiago on the road to a form of modernity much closer to the functionalist ideas of the 1960s than to the return to restrictive planning observed in Europe and the United States in the 1990s. Although the chosen option may seem anachronistic with growth objectives that entailed major consumption of space and energy, the methods used were in fact typical of the decade (public-private partnerships, concessions). The state shed its skin and emerged as a different kind of urban regulator acting on infrastructure: this time its intention was not to free up urban growth, but to determine its direction.

Highway Projects Drive Complete Liberalisation of Land Use

Although the state's inability to control urban growth was recognised, the new Metropolitan Regulation Plan for Santiago (*Plan Regulador Metropolitano de Santiago*, or PRMS) of 1994 again attempted to set limits on expansion. Under the successive Christian Democrat Ministers of Housing and Urban Planning, Alberto Etchegaray and Edmundo Hermosilla, the 1994 PRMS attempted to increase the average density of the metropolitan area and support the polycentric development of the metropolis that had already been envisaged by the 1960 PRIS (Poduje, 2006). However, as in the past, the government was unable to control land use, which remained a prerogative of the municipalities. Several real estate projects were in fact launched on former agricultural sites whose designated use was changed shortly before the Plan came into effect, and this meant that attempts to stabilise urban expansion came to nothing.

Faced with this immediate overspill, less than three years after the PRMS was promulgated, the Ministry of Housing and Urban Planning (Ministerio de Vivienda y Urbanismo, or MINVU) decided to amend the Plan in order to allow massive extensions in the north of the region. This decision put an end once and for all to the ambition to exercise strict control over urban expansion. However, it did not mean that the state was to disengage from urban regulation. On the contrary, from the mid-1990s onwards, it implemented new steering instruments.

This regulatory change took place under the influence of urban megaprojects initiated by private developers in the north of the metropolitan area, in the Province of Chacabuco. This 15,000-hectare agricultural area was free of any kind of state control and was not included in the 1994 PRMS. In fact, a loophole in the legislative apparatus (resulting from a desire to support the development of agricultural areas in the south of the country) allowed agricultural spaces to be urbanised on condition that they were divided up and marketed as individual plots of land. Until 1994, Chacabuco Province was of little interest to property developers because it is separated from the metropolitan area by a chain of mountains (Manquehue, Gordo). So although urban growth was possible, there was a lack of road infrastructure linking developments to the metropolitan area.

In 1994, the socialist future President Ricardo Lagos became Minister of Public Works and immediately launched a vast plan of highway construction through private concessions; these highways were opened in 2005–2006, under his presidency. The plan made provision for, among other things, the construction of the North-east Access Road (*Acceso Nororiente*) which directly links the agricultural plain of Chicureo, in Chacabuco Province, to the affluent districts in the east of the metropolitan area by a 21-km highway with four tunnels. At the same time, the developers of the vast private sector projects in Las Condes and Lo Barnechea began building a completely private access highway, which bypasses the metropolitan area to the north and directly connects their districts to the Chicureo Valley (the Camino Pie Andino[3]). Because so many private sector or public-private partnership highway projects were instigated, pressure on land in the Chicureo Valley grew. Faced with the prospect of urban development of this agricultural space, which was now authorised by law, MINVU decided to amend the 1994 PRMS in order to provide a minimum degree of monitoring and to support the projects. These 15,000 ha in the Chicureo Valley were incorporated into the area zoned for urbanisation. Since the 1994 Plan comprised 70,945 ha in total, of which 15,000 were available for urbanisation projects, the addition of an extra 15,000 ha in Chacabuco Province had the straightforward effect of doubling the area open to urban development. From this point on, debate would centre on

---

3   Renamed Camino Juan Pablo II (John Paul II) in 2005: http://teletrece.canal13.cl/t13/html/Noticias/Chile/218399Iimprimirq1.html

conditions for financing the new urban growth and would give rise to principles for conditional urban development.

Towards Endogenous Financing of Urban Growth? Highway Concessions and Conditional Urban Development

In 1994, Ricardo Lagos, at that time Minister of Public Works, brought in Marcial Echenique, a Chilean who is Professor of Land Use and Transport Studies at the University of Cambridge, to draw up principles for developments in the metropolis. In his paper (1996), Professor Echenique called for an extended city, structured by its road transport corridors, with real estate projects at a distance from the centre of the metropolitan area but functionally connected to it. These principles required considerable highway infrastructure, and therefore the professor and the minister collaborated on a plan for the rapid development of new urban highways under private concessions:

> Chile faces major infrastructure challenges if it is to continue to grow economically. The greatest challenges are in urban areas, especially in Santiago. In order to overcome problems of lack of infrastructure capacity, significant intervention will be required on the part of the state in order to regulate public-sector and private sector activity in the land and transport markets in a coherent way. These markets are interrelated, and therefore should be dealt with together. The state must also intervene in prices in the land and transport markets in order to improve the efficiency of the system and internalize the externalities generated by market agents, for both supply and demand. Finally, it is necessary to have a coherent policy for public and private investment (through concessions) to increase infrastructure capacity while lessening entrepreneurial risk. (Echenique, 1996, p.24, translated from the Spanish)

The first innovation in the 1990s was the development of *urban highways under private concession arrangements*. In 1991, the Concessions Law authorised their use in the road, airport and port sectors through build-operate-transfer (BOT) procedures. The concession system enabled the state to get round its lack of investment capacity for construction and, in particular, for maintenance of the metropolitan road system. Concessions offer some flexibility in the way highway projects are financed, because different proportions of road-toll tariffs and public subsidies can be set in order to achieve balanced recovery of costs. Between 1995 and 2000, €11 billion were invested under concession arrangements, of which €4.2 billion were for interurban highways and €2 billion for Santiago's urban highways (Engel, Fischer et al., 2001). In the Metropolitan Region, the concessions granted were for three major systems: the North-South system, the East-West system on the northern boundary of the city of Santiago (known as the Costanera Norte) and the Américo Vespucio system which includes the North-East Ring Road and the

Southern Ring Road. The North-East Access Road, whose planning triggered the urban megaprojects in Chacabuo Province to the north, should also be mentioned.

In 1998, the first urban highway concession to be put out to tender was the Costanera Norte (East-West system). It still remains the most controversial of the deals struck at this time. The initial quotation for the project was €153 million, of which 85 per cent was to be financed by electronic toll collection (Engel, Fischer and Galetovic, 2001). However, opposition from residents' groups along the line of the highway, together with environmental demands, caused a rise in project costs from €153 to €327 million. Intense controversy flared up between those tendering and the Ministry, even before the call for tenders went out. Potential tenderers decided to renegotiate the terms and conditions of the concession arrangements for four reasons: costs were higher than initially assessed; legal risks were significant because of the opposition from residents; risks of non-payment of electronic tolls had been underestimated; traffic transfer to alternative, toll-free routes had not been taken into account. From the point of view of the tendering companies, these factors represented significant risks to the project's profitability. The CCC brought pressure to bear for higher financial guarantees from the state; it threatened that all its members would boycott the tender procedure, unless the rules of the competition were amended. The Ministry of Public Works at first chose to resist, and put out the call for tenders. However, only one company responded – not a member of the powerful CCC – and the procedure was cancelled. In May 1999, the Ministry decided to adjust the financing arrangements for the project and agreed to commit €68 million in direct subsidies to finance project support costs and environmental offsets (provision of a wildlife corridor and of pedestrian links across the highway). In addition, the Ministry chose to guarantee minimum levels of traffic not – as before – on the basis of real traffic flows, but on the number of vehicles actually paying the toll (Engel et al., op. cit.). These new guarantees meant that the expectations of tendering companies could be met and led to the success of the second call for tenders.

The Chilean construction sector exerted pressure for systematic strengthening of public-sector guarantees even before the concessions were put out to tender. In return, the Chilean capital benefited from considerable amounts of private sector investment. The extent of the urban highways network in the metropolitan area increased markedly, from 95 km to 215 km within a decade. The quality of service offered noticeably improved and today provides the capital with a level of road accessibility equivalent to that of cities in the United States.

The development of highway concessions also symbolised MOP's new power from the mid-1990s onwards. Thanks to this system, it now had a decisive instrument and the financial means with which to structure the metropolitan space according to a logic of building large-scale amenities. Although it continually had to adjust its relationship with the private sector, the Ministry now had the final say on new highway routes, which became the principle engines of development projects.

Table 5.5   Highway concessions in Santiago de Chile

Company name	Project	Concession	Investors
Sociedad Concesionaria Autopista Central SA	North-South System 61 km Opened: Dec. 2004	€400 million 30 years launched: July 2001	Abertis (Spain): 50%, Skanska (Sweden): 50%
Sociedad Concesionaria Costanera Norte SA	East-West System 42.5 km Opened: April 2005	€423 million 30 years launched: April 2002	SIAS (Italy): 45%, Atlantia (Italy): 45%, Mediobanca (Italy): 10%
Sociedad Concesionaria Vespucio Sur SA	Ring Road, southern section 24 km Opened: Dec. 2005	€298 million 30 years launched: Dec. 2002	Atlantia (Italy): 51%, Acciona (Chile): 49%
Sociedad Concesionaria Vespucio Norte Express SA	Ring Road, northern section 29 km Opened: Jan. 2006	€320 million 30 years launched: April 2001	ACS (Spain): 46.5% Hochtief (Germany): 45.5% Cofides (Spain): 8%
Sociedad Concesionaria Tunel San Cristobal SA	Vespucio-Costanera Norte ring road link 4 km Opened: July 2008	€87 million 32 years launched: Feb. 2005	ACS (Spain): 50%, Hochtief (Germany): 50%
Sociedad Concesionaria Autopista Nororiente SA	North-East Access 22 km Opened: March 2009	€125 million 40 years launched: Sept. 2003	Itinere (Chile): 100%

Sources: Author's table from COPSA-Concesiones viales de Chile data

The second institutional innovation was the *implementation of the concept of conditional urban development*. The 1979 PRIS had introduced the principle that the costs of any new infrastructure entailed by developments outside the urban zone should be borne by the property developers. In order to support this principle, and with the prospect of the Chicureo Valley megaproject developments, in 1996 the government instituted the well-known 'conditional urban development zones', or ZODUCs. These operated on the following principles:

- zones must cover an area of at least 300 ha;
- 5 per cent of the area must be for medium- or high-density housing (300 to 500 people per ha);
- the rest of the zone must have a minimum average density of 85 people per ha;

- the zones themselves must finance the entire infrastructure needed to reduce the city-scale environmental and urban impacts of their development (roads, treatment plants).

The first ZODUC projects sprang up in the mid 2000s. These were the very first development phases of a private city in the north of the metropolitan area, potentially covering 15,000 ha. The proposed properties were detached houses in gated neighbourhoods of different types, with different offers targeting households ranging from the middle classes to the affluent, and also including golf courses, shops and private schools.

In 2003, the principle of conditional urban development was extended to a large part of Santiago Metropolitan Region by means of Conditional Urban Development Projects (Proyectos con Desarrollo Urbano Condicionados, or PDUCs). PDUCs were subject to the same financing and development conditions as ZODUCs, with three additional constraints: PDUCs had to include 30 per cent of subsidised housing, of which 12 per cent would be social housing; they also had to self-finance schools, health services, green spaces and sports facilities; finally, they must be built in tranches, each with a minimum of 3,000 residents. On the other hand, the restriction relating to density was made more flexible: the requirement for a certain proportion of medium-density housing within a project was abolished; and the average of 85 people/ha was made more flexible, with tolerance of +/- 15 people/ha. With ZODUCs and PDUCs, the state authorised the creation of veritable private towns, monitored through planning-requirement checklists worthy of post-War France: one town square for every 500 residents, one football pitch and one public transport stop for every 3,000 residents, a police station, a fire station and a gym for every 10,000 residents.[4]

Endogenous financing of infrastructure is a relatively innovative arrangement for urban megaprojects; but Chile was attempting to take things to their logical conclusion and apply the free market, user-pays principle to peri-urban development projects. However, part of the additional cost for subsidised or social housing was indirectly financed by the state. Moreover, in practice, implementation of the principle of conditional urban development is subject to fierce negotiations between property developers and the state.

Debate Over Financing the Collective Costs of Urban Growth

The most complex task for MOP was to define the cost of the environmental and infrastructural impacts of the two ZODUCs in Chacabuco Province. The planned urban megaproject was for 110,000 housing units, or 400,000 people (Poduje, 2006). The Ministry estimated that 75 per cent of journeys generated by

---

4   Interview with Javier Wood Larrain, Head of the Department of Urban Development and Infrastructure, MINVU SEREMI, Santiago Metropolitan Region, Santiago de Chile, 16 June 2009.

the project would be towards the central area and so would require the extension of highway infrastructure. The bill presented by MOP to the 14 property companies involved in the ZODUCs and the priority development zones was €265 million. This amount might seem reasonable in comparison with the anticipated €285 million appreciation in the value of the land for the two ZODUCs (Chicureo and Chamicero), without taking into account the other development zones. However, the property developers refused to take on the total cost of these works, claiming that the highways would also benefit future development projects in the north of the metropolitan area (Poduje, 2006). After eight months of negotiations, MOP decided to reduce the volume of road infrastructure to be built in compensation for development of the ZODUCs. The €265 million investment initially provided for fell to €93 million, of which €34 million would be paid by the state. In the final calculations, the companies accepted responsibility for all secondary infrastructure within and close to the development zones, as well as the costs of community facilities for their zone; on the other hand, they contributed little to the development costs of the highways built to link their zone to the centre of the metropolitan area.

The example of the Chacabuco urban megaprojects illustrates the profound contradiction that emerged at the very heart of the growth coalition at work in Santiago. The debate on self-financing of the collective costs of urban growth does not just illustrate the difficulty the state experienced in introducing regulation mechanisms; it also highlights the muffled controversy between private sector representatives themselves over the conditions extending the user-pays principle. On this point, representatives of the construction industry, property developers and Chilean free market think tanks were divided. For the Association of Property Developers (Asociación de Desarrolladores Inmobiliarios, or ADI),[5] any new urban project must include all the externalities within its costs, in particular the costs of extending infrastructure, whether within the part of the city already urbanised or for peripheral urbanisation. Although ADI is convinced of the beneficial effects of urban growth, it maintains that this must be financed by future residents, even if this increases building costs. For the director of ADI, who was also President of the Association of Highway Concession Holders (Concesiones de Obras Publicas de Infraestructura Publica, or COPSA), the developers' role is to market functional districts by ensuring that they have satisfactory levels of amenities and road infrastructure. This view is shared by the think tank Libertad y Desarrollo ('Liberty and Development'), which is close to the right-wing UDI party (Unión Demócrata Independiente). The think tank rehearsed classic free market arguments, maintaining that any attempt to place limits on growth – 'smart growth' – entails distortions in the market and pushes land prices up.[6] On the other hand, it is clearly assumed that the costs of urban expansion should be entirely borne by future residents:

---

5   Interview with Vicente Domínguez Vial, Executive Director of ADI, Santiago de Chile, 16 June 2009.

6   Libertad y desarrollo (2009) 'Regulación Urbana y el Crecimiento Inteligente de las Ciudades', *Temas Públicos* 911, 3 April, p. 2.

When people decide where they are going to live they take on all the costs, both direct and indirect, implied by this decision. In other words, they take on the true cost involved. In this way, and on the basis of their own preferences, they take a decision about where to live, whether this in an apartment in a densely populated area or in a house with a garden in an area of less density. In both cases, they must take on all the infrastructure costs that this decision entails.[7]

This point of view is not shared by the CCC, which distances itself from ADI. This difference has something to do with the make-up of the CCC. Although all members of ADI are members of the CCC and are represented on its board, 80 per cent of the Chamber's members are in the building industry and defend its interests. For the CCC, the rise in construction costs represents risks to the growth and competitiveness of the sector. The CCC maintains that the infrastructure costs of urban development should be borne through taxation. The Chamber represents a community which encompasses more than just property developers.

On the other hand, beyond the debate on the nature of the costs to be borne, all property lobbies and free market think tanks are agreed on denouncing the lack of transparency in current methods of attributing infrastructure costs to new projects. For the CCC or for ADI the calculation methods are both discretionary and lacking in transparency. It is true that MOP's prevarications over the size of the bill presented to the developers of the Chacabuco megaproject, which in eight months fell from €265 million to €59 million, offered no guarantee of transparency. In contrast, arbitration opened the way to bargaining which is now becoming customary for the negotiation of private megaprojects.

Since 2004, the Ministries of Housing and Public Works have been negotiating fiercely with the operators responsible for three PDUC projects, all located in the west of the city in the Municipality of Pudahuel, close to the airport and along the highway to Valparaiso. These three projects (Urbanya, Enea and Ciudad Lo Aguirre-Praderas) amount to an area of 1800 ha and a projected population of 200,000 inhabitants.

The current debate on the development costs of road infrastructure are a curious echo of the controversies in the late 1990s around the ZODUC projects. Moreover, MINVU and MOP do not share the same point of view:[8]

- MINVU believes that the developers of the three PDUCs should take on the financing of the secondary road infrastructure that serves the zones and some highway junctions;

---

7   Libertad y desarrollo (2009), op. cit. Quotation translated from the Spanish.

8   Interview with Javier Wood Larrain, Head of the Department of Urban Development and Infrastructure, MINVU SEREMI, Santiago Metropolitan Region, Santiago de Chile, 16 June 2009.

- MOP's view is that the developers should, in addition, finance all the costs of extending the existing highways that could absorb the daily flow of 50,000 additional vehicles towards the centre of the metropolitan area.

MINVU's position is similar to the compromise reached during negotiations over the ZODUC projects: developers do not have to bear the cost of extending highway infrastructure that will be used by future residents of other districts that may be developed. For their part, property developers assert that the cost of building secondary infrastructure is in itself much too high for the project to remain economically viable.

At the time of writing, these negotiations have yet to reach a conclusion, but they raise two problems: the divergence in the two Ministries' points of view exemplifies the difficulty of accommodating the sectoral interests of the state, which are not arbitrated by a coordinating body; this fragmentation of state activities weakens the state's capacity for negotiation with private sector operators and undermines the credibility of regulation. Of these two highly autonomous Ministries, MOP carries more weight because of its capacity to agree or turn down construction of the road infrastructure needed to connect the new districts.

Negotiations between MOP and the private sector take place regularly and there is no evidence that MOP is systematically susceptible to the expectations of the property development sector, as the current interminable discussions about the three PDUCs in the west of the metropolitan area demonstrate. This is not the only example of a trial of strength between MOP and private developers. In June 2006, the Chilean entrepreneur Horst Paulmann, who is active in the retail and distribution sector, decided to build the tallest skyscraper in Chile – and in South America – in the district of Providencia. This tower, designed by New York architects Pelli Clarke Pelli, who have been responsible for several skyscrapers in Asia, was intended to rise to a height of 257m and to include a shopping centre, two supermarkets, a hotel, cinemas and parking for 4,500 cars. Works were commenced with the blessing of the socialist President then in office, Ricardo Lagos[9], who was present when the first stone was laid. However, Horst Paulmann's plan had never anticipated the volume of traffic generated by a facility of this size nor the need to build bridges and new access roads to the tower. In the developer's mind, the financial costs of upgrading road provision should be met by the state. In the event, negotiations with MOP did not reach a successful conclusion, since the Ministry was reluctant to commit public funding or launch new public-private partnerships in order to support the development of this private sector commercial megaproject.[10] The project was halted in 2010, in the context of the financial crisis.

---

9   In 2006, President Ricardo Lagos gave honorary Chilean nationality to the entrepreneur Horst Paulmann, a German citizen resident in Chile since 1949.

10   Interview with Maria-Elena Ducci, Professor of Urban Studies, Catholic University of Santiago de Chile, 8 June 2009.

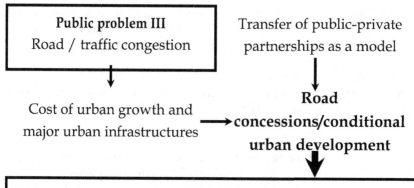

Figure 5.6   Overview of the Third Phase of Institutionalization, 1994–2005

By developing highway concessions, the state devised a way of supporting an investment of more than €1.3 billion during the 2000s, which would be almost entirely financed by road users over the next three decades. In contrast, the implementation of conditional urban development instruments was more controversial; opposition from within the government itself damaged the credibility of the state's attempt to assign the real collective costs of urbanisation to operators. Equally, negotiations with developers over the tens of millions of dollars being demanded from them took place without any systematic calculation of the costs of zoning, risk management, rainwater drainage, waste management or highway maintenance.

However, although debates about road development costs were fierce, ADI, the CCC and the state actually all agreed that cost integration should centre on technical networks and arterial road infrastructure. Development of public transport remained optional and was to be paid for by local passengers, according to demand. The new private towns built on the periphery of the metropolitan area had no obligation to connect to its main public transport network. The inevitable inference is that the capital's bus network remained a forgotten issue for the urban management instruments created from the early 1980s onwards.

2005–2010. Weaknesses in Regional Government: The Failure of Transantiago and Growth Management Issues

Since the mid-1990s, Santiago de Chile, like almost all major cities in the world, has been the object of the classic debate around the conditions for implementing good metropolitan governance – legitimate, intersectoral, regional in scale and comprehensive. As in all such cities, the debate – tinged as it was with a normative vision of a functional optimum – led to the promotion of solutions such as election of a Super Mayor (*Alcalde Major*), election of regional councillors by universal suffrage, political and fiscal decentralisation to the scale of the region and the creation of a Greater Santiago. However, the circulation of various models proposed by the movement for metropolitan reform has, in more than ten years, never led to any recasting of regional power.

As this chapter has attempted to show, the Chilean capital is directly administrated by central government and by the Office of the President of the Republic. However the strong centralisation and the sectorisation of urban policies have their limits. The failure to implement the public transport modernisation plan, Transantiago, reveals this. Starting in the mid-2000s, the capital saw growth management issues emerge as a public policy problem, in the direct form of congestion problems and more broadly in the form of the debate on living conditions, urbanity and modes of accessibility. Since the second half of the 2000s, the metropolis has seen the emergence of new urban social movements that challenge central government and, at times, municipalities.

Metropolitan Regional Government: A Regional Governor Trapped Between Ministries, the Presidency and Municipalities

In Santiago de Chile, power remains in the hands of the central state, in spite of the reforms – described as 'regionalisation' – undertaken by the military government in 1974. Devolution has essentially consisted of separating decision-making processes, which remain more than ever in the hands of the government, from executive or implementation activities, which are devolved to the regional level. The regionalisation process has transformed the previous 25 provinces into 13 regions, including Santiago Metropolitan Region. The new administrative boundaries were ratified by the 1980 Constitution. In 1991, following the return to democracy, regional reform laid down the conditions for indirect election of regional councillors by the elected municipal councillors from each municipality, with the region continuing to be governed by a regional governor appointed by the President of the Republic.

Although it has been the focus of numerous debates, the structure of regional government remains unchanged to this day. Caught between the power of the President's Office, the sectoral ministries and their devolved administrations and the pressure from regional politicians, a regional governor has very little autonomy.[11] From the central government point of view, the regional governor is under the direct control of the Presidency of the Republic, which does not hesitate to use its power of dismissal. Thus, regional governors often remain in post for less than a year or two before being replaced. The reasons for removal from office are frequently connected with decisions taken by the regional governor, since these must never go beyond the guidelines set by the Presidency. Recurrent debates around the possible election by universal suffrage of a Santiago Regional President often present this solution as some kind of utopia, given the considerable weight that a Regional President would have vis-à-vis the Presidency of the Republic, at the head of a territory that brings in 42 per cent of national wealth.

Not only are the regional governor's activities firmly supervised by the Presidency, but he also has to compete with the devolved services of ministries, the most powerful of which are MINVU and MOP. Thus, while the Regional Governor of Santiago manages a budget of only €105 million a year, total central government investment in the region amounts to €1.4 billion. Regional ministerial secretariats each have their own budget, directly allocated by their supervising ministry, and the regional governor has no power to influence the amounts allocated. In the same way, when it comes to PDUCs, the secretariats of MINVU and MOP directly negotiate the financial compensation claimed from property developers, with no intervention from the regional governor's office. These examples demonstrate the extreme sectorisation of state activities in the regions.

Under Presidential control, largely short-circuited by devolved ministry services,[12] the regional governor is also subject to clientelist pressure from regional councillors. The latter are elected by municipal councillors along party lines, and their sole function is intensive lobbying of the regional governor in order to achieve priority for health, education, waste management and urban security subsidies on behalf of the municipal councillors who elect them.[13] If they fail to obtain financial support from the regional governor, regional councillors have a real power of veto because of their ability to block spending. The regional governor is obliged to continuously build up for himself the political resources needed to govern, through deals cementing alliances with a majority of regional councillors, sometimes of opposed political persuasions. This distribution of power results in a recurring practice of 'interscale clientelism' between regional government and municipalities, which is typical of strongly centralised states.

---

11   Interview with Arturo Orellana, Senior Adviser to Álvaro Erazo, Regional Governor of Santiago Metropolitan Region, Santiago de Chile, 10 June 2009.

12   Interview with Marcelo Farah, Technical Adviser, SECTRA, 8 June 2009.

13   Interview with Arturo Orellana, Senior Adviser to Álvaro Erazo, Regional Governor of Santiago Metropolitan Region, Santiago de Chile, 10 June 2009.

The Limited Power of Local Politicians

The principal brief of elected municipal councillors is to go out and obtain the maximum number of subsidies for their municipalities from the central and devolved state. This position results from the gap between the weak fiscal powers of municipalities and their election by universal suffrage, which makes them answerable to voters and encourages them to chase results. It also reveals the incomplete nature of the decentralisation process put into effect when democracy was restored in 1990.

In 1990, democratisation went hand in hand with minimal decentralisation of decision-making. The motivations of the new centre-left coalition were, on the one hand, to reintroduce local elections and, on the other, to remove mayors and municipal councillors appointed by Augusto Pinochet from office. However, since the 1991 and 1992 reforms, no significant decentralising change has been observed in Chile. This stability can be attributed primarily to successive governments lacking the will to decentralise. Ministers of Public Works, in particular, have promoted a centralisation of power that seemed to them to guarantee efficient, rational use of public funds in undertaking large-scale infrastructure projects (Maroons, 2006).

It is hardly news that several projects for strengthening the power of the municipalities have been discussed on numerous occasions over the last 20 years without ever reaching a conclusion. Since 1998, supporters of stronger regional councils have come together to form a National Council for Regionalization and Decentralization (Consejo Nacional Para la Desentralización y Descentralización de Chile, or CONAREDE). Demands for regionalisation have indeed been taken up by the national executive, but a first attempt to introduce the election of regional councillors and of a regional president by direct universal suffrage, proposed by President Lagos in 2002, was rejected by the Congress and the Senate. This idea was later taken up again by President Michelle Bachelet (2006–2010), but nothing ever materialised.

The position of Chilean municipalities is the legacy of a centralising tradition whose roots go back long before the military coup – to the early twentieth century, when a powerful state was established and took pains to considerably weaken the power of prominent local individuals. Through studying the pre-dictatorship period, Valenzuela (1977) showed that, in the context of this centralisation, Chile's local politicians have always enjoyed the position of power broker between their electorate and the state, relying directly on party channels to assert their interests. However, since the return to democracy, this position as broker has become steadily more marked as municipalities have acquired – or appropriated – new spheres of interest. For a councillor beginning a political career, the position of mayor is much more desirable than that of member of parliament, even though the mayor has little autonomy in the allocation of funds from central government. In particular, the local level has become the place where right-wing party élites are renewed, and this underpinned the first change of power from Left to Right since democracy was restored – when Sebastian Piñera was elected President of the

Republic in January 2010. Mayors, whether from Right or Left, have gradually adopted the role of advocate of the municipal cause – a role they can easily convert into electoral support.[14]

Mayoral leadership powers have increased with their acquisition of new briefs that have been devolved to the municipalities. Besides the functions of distributing the public health and education budgets (a legacy of the Pinochet Government's municipal reforms), municipalities have acquired new spheres of interest, shared with the state, in drugs policy or activities promoting employment and learning. From the point of view of transfer of power to the municipalities, the model promoted is not one of devolution but of delegation (Mardones, 2008). From the 1990s, the state has been involved in a process of contractualisation with the municipalities, who have been given additional powers and state funding to take on clearly-defined tasks within the framework of a project specification drawn up by the state. In new spheres such as training or drug prevention, municipalities have become the state's sub-contractors; this delegation of power relates mainly to executive action and not to decision-making or the steering of public policy.

This position as service provider for the state should not mask the marked inequalities between different municipalities' capacity to intervene, particularly for basic areas of competence such as development of public spaces, schools or public safety. Inequalities between municipalities go back to the reforms initiated by the dictatorship. In 1981, the municipal reform initiated by the military government aimed to create new municipalities and redefine the boundaries of existing ones. The stated objective was to create institutional territories which would be socially and economically homogenous, in order to ensure the effective distribution of social assistance and educational funding. Municipal boundaries have not been altered since then, resulting in a pattern of municipalities that are highly specialised from a residential point of view. Differentiation between municipalities can be seen even in the quality of public spaces and more recently in the field of security policies. Stronger mayoral leadership has resulted partly from the development of municipal police forces which, however, do not fall under their remit. In wealthy municipalities, the availability of unarmed police represents a significant factor in satisfying expectations about living conditions. Unequal capacity to invest in the sphere of the living environment in the broader sense (schools, security, public spaces) accentuates the segregation process, as those residents who are in a position to move house deploy foot-voting strategies (Tiebout, 1956).

Transantiago – Example of a Crisis in Intersectoral and Regional Regulation

Between 2006 and 2009, the major crisis in Santiago's public transport system revealed the whole set of tensions confronting the Chilean capital's system of

---

14 Interview with Rodrigo Mardones, Assistant Professor of Political Science, Catholic University of Santiago de Chile, 9 June 2009.

government, marked as it was by centralisation, sectorisation and the low level of autonomy enjoyed by local government, whether municipal or regional.

As has already been mentioned, during the 1990s the debate about the effects of urban growth focused unanimously on the problem of highway congestion and the need to upgrade road provision for the metropolitan area as a whole. Property developers were asked for financial contributions. The user-pays principle was introduced through highway tolls. The concessions system enabled provision to be upgraded, while limiting the level of risk to which companies were exposed. Apart from the sizeable development of the metro network in the 2000s, the bus network remained the forgotten issue for the growth coalition between the state and the property sector that had sustained the capital's urban development for nearly 30 years.

The low level of state involvement in bus networks had its origins in the process of liberalising public transport launched in the mid-1980s. After the implementation, in 1983, of the principle of freedom in setting fares, complete freedom of entry to the public transport market, without any restriction or need for authorisation, was decreed in 1988. The Santiago Metro remained the only exception to the rule; having been administered directly under MOP management between 1974 and 1990, it has been managed by a state-owned limited company since 1990.

In this context of market liberalisation, the capital was faced with a constantly increasing bus fleet and with congestion of the main public transport corridors. Moreover, competition did not translate into lower prices but the exact opposite: overcapacity and the lower passenger load for each bus caused prices to rise. With the restoration of democracy, the sector was re-regulated from 1990 onwards. By granting concessions for individual routes, the state was able to partially control the number of buses on the roads, in order to limit congestion and pollution. However, during the 1990s, public transport was faced with major contradictions (Figueroa, 2004). First and foremost, as far as the local urban dynamics were concerned, liberalisation of land use led to the capital's continued sprawl. This transformation of the city was concomitant with sustained economic growth, which enabled a rise in the standard of living of affluent groups and the middle classes and increased access to automobiles. Demand for all modes of public transport continued to fall (metro, buses, shared taxis): this fall in the number of users fed and was in turn maintained by fare increases – ticket prices rose from €0.28 in 1998 to €0.47 in 2004. Before the Transantiago Plan came into effect in February 2007, the entire supply of public transport consisted of a fleet of buses totalling 8,000 vehicles owned by nearly 2,500 individual businesses.

In 1995, a first project to reform the public transport sector failed for lack of institutional support, and it was not until the second Urban Transport Plan (2000) that policy objectives were actually set out, affirming the need to modernise public transport, rationalise car use and develop alternative modes of transport. In order to steer implementation of the Plan, which was perceived as institutionally sensitive, an Interministerial Commission under the direct authority of the Presidency of the Republic was set up. It was chaired by the Minister of Public Works and made up of the Minister of Housing and Urban Development, the Transport Under-Secretary, the Director of the National Environment Commission, the Regional Governor of the Santiago Region, the Executive Secretary of the Interministerial Secretariat for Transport Planning and the Chairman of the Board of Directors of the Metro (Figueroa and Orellana, 2007). This Commission was given responsibility for steering 'Transantiago' – the plan to reshape provision of bus transport.

Following the importation of European models ('heavy' metro or rapid transport systems) it was now the turn of Latin American models to provide international examples – Bus Rapid Transit or the Curitiba (Brazil) model. The project's objectives were inspired by transport experiments carried out in Curitiba and Bogotá: improving the quality of service provided by public transport and maintaining (or even increasing) its modal share through the creation of a real network, reducing the number of operators (from 3000 micro-businesses to 15 operators) and buses (from 8,500 to 4,500, including 1,800 new buses), and providing an articulated structure for urban development. Transantiago was designed as an integrated system. It is based partly on the existing 'heavy' metro system and partly on a hierarchy of bus networks and the creation of trunk routes and local mini networks. The public-private partnership envisaged was comparable to the one in Bogotá, with private sector operators working under concession arrangements for each service area or bus route. Implementation of this complete change in the organisation of public transport took more time than expected. It finally came into effect overnight, early in the morning of 10 February 2007. However, from the first day of operation, the new system was faced with a major crisis, which lasted for more than a year. The 15 operators felt that they had not had the time they needed to equip the buses with the new payment systems; the new stops and roadway upgrades had not been completed; drivers did not know the routes; users were completely disorientated by the new network, the longer journey times and the fact that they now had to make connections between bus lines as well as between the new bus routes and the metro. Rapid growth in use of the metro, which was now accessible simply by paying a surcharge, led to heavy congestion. Strikes by drivers and protests by users proliferated.

Apart from the difficulty of designing the system and the consequences of implementing it too quickly, the Transantiago crisis demonstrated above all the institutional shortcomings in management of the project (Figueroa and Orellana, 2007). The fact that an Interministerial Committee was responsible for steering the reform had not led to strong coordination of public policies but to a dilution of responsibilities for public transport. Oscar Figueroa and Arturo Orellana (2007, op. cit.) have focused on the lack of an organising authority for transport at the metropolitan scale. Coordination could have been strengthened by creating a French-style transport authority reporting to the regional government. However, this option was not chosen. The project was steered by an interministerial body, the Urban Transport Planning Secretariat (Secretaría de Planificación de Transporte, or SECTRA), and this was not given the strong backing of or a

direct line of responsibility to the powerful Ministry of Public Works,[15] as might
be the case for highway projects. For example, MINVU funds intended for the
creation of new bus stops were, in the end, not paid. Difficulties also arose from
the complete disconnect between centralised ministerial steering of the project
and the municipal authorities that had to directly implement a reform with strong
territorial impact. Although Transantiago involved coordinating intersectoral
and interterritorial actions and public-sector and private sector actors, the
implementing institutions remained deeply embedded in a centralised mode of
governance, fragmented at sectoral level.

A parallel problem was that the sums of money committed by the state to
reform the bus system were extremely low. The reforms carried out in Curitiba
and Bogotá were 30 per cent or 40 per cent financed by the state, whereas, at the
outset, Transantiago had only a 10 per cent subsidy from the public purse. The
new infrastructure, new stations, bus stops, roadway redevelopment and the active
fleet all suffered directly from the low level of public investment. In April 2007,
two months after it opened, the Transantiago Plan had already generated a deficit
of €21 million, and the government was obliged to make a direct cash injection
of €70 million into the system, plus a €133 million loan (Mardones, 2008). In
December 2007, the Bachelet Government asked the lower house of parliament,
the Chamber of Deputies, to grant financing of €101 million for the year 2008. The
debate around public support for public transport contrasts with the unanimous
support enjoyed by the highway development programme. Although the €68
million subsidy for the Costanera Norte highway project in 1996 had encountered
little opposition, the granting of an equivalent subsidy for the bus network caused
widespread controversy. The right-wing think tank *Libertad y desarrollo* had
expected the project to fail and was saying so as early as January 2007:

> The need to increase provision is a sign that the system will collapse as soon as it
> starts up, and the inclusion of a $US 60 million subsidy is proof that the system
> will not be self-financing if fares are not raised.[16]

In fact, after lively debates in both chambers, the additional sum of money was
never voted through by parliamentarians, and Transantiago's debt continued to be
mopped up by the state, through grants of extraordinary funding voted through on
a half-yearly basis. It was only on 5 September 2009, after more than two years
of parliamentary negotiations, that a law was passed to set up a national public
transport subsidy system in order to provide Transantiago and all the country's
other public transport systems with stable public funding.

The unanticipated crisis of the Transantiago Plan stands as an episode that
reveals the state's lack of capacity to constitute itself as a collective actor in

---

15   Interview with Lake Sagaris, President of Ciudad Viva, 8 June 2009.
16   Libertad y desarrollo, 2007, 'Transantiago: Promesas Incumplidas', Temas
Públicos, n°804, 5 janvier, p 9. Translated from the Spanish.

order to guarantee the smooth running of the metropolis (Le Galès, 2002), despite its proven, long-standing expertise in public-private partnerships. The main stumbling-block for the Transantiago Plan arose from two deficiencies in coordination within the public sphere itself:

- defective coordination between ministries represents a serious dysfunction in the state's policy in the regions and only serves to confirm the fragmentation of devolved state services between MINVU and MOP, which has already been observed in the sphere of urban planning;
- the failure to integrate municipalities into the process of completely restructuring the bus network, even though the issues raised lie at the heart of urban community management.

This crisis highlighted the drawbacks of extreme sectorisation of state involvement. In addition to revealing strictly institutional failings, the Transantiago example shows that the state did not manage to change the growth coalition's direction or objectives with a view to gaining a firmer grip on the congestion resulting from growth. The internal crisis of the growth coalition over public transport issues was accompanied by an external challenge to the capital's development model. Twenty years after the return to democracy, protests – however faint – are emerging, and conflicts and urban movements are helping to bring Santiago de Chile into the ranks of contemporary metropolises.

In the Margins of the Growth Coalition, the Renewal of Urban Movements

Neighbourhood movements, despite being very dynamic during the 1960s (Castells, 1973), were completely crushed after the 1973 coup d'état. Following the trauma of the dictatorship, Chilean social movements were very gradually pieced together again. In the urban sphere, it was not until the 2000s that a few scattered initiatives emerged, two of which deserve our attention: the *Ciudad Viva* ('Living City') association in the old Bellavista neighbourhood and NIMBY-type opposition ('not in my backyard') in the affluent Municipality of Vitacura.

Ciudad Viva symbolises the first type of movement that can be observed in Santiago: citizens' groups that are essentially self-managing and participatory. The movement was set up in 1993 through the re-founding of the Bellavista neighbourhood committee, which had been very active in the 1960s but was subsequently dissolved by the military government. This neighbourhood is located in the north of the Municipality of Santiago, on the right bank of the River Mopocho, at the foot of San Cristobal hill. It is characterised by French- and Spanish-style baroque architecture and for several decades has been home to artists and craftspeople. In the late 1990s, the district experienced increased pressure on land: whole areas were acquired by property developers and there were real prospects of comprehensive clearance and renewal. The neighbourhood movement developed in this context. In 1997, its eco-committee became the principal opposition movement to the concessionary Costanera Norte highway,[17] leading a group of 25 community associations from districts on the right bank of the Mapocho, along the route of the proposed highway. The group won environmental off-sets in the form of anti-pollution measures and the development of public spaces. During the 2000s, it managed to obtained modifications to a real estate project in the heart of the neighbourhood, which in the end was transformed into a vast restaurant and bar district, the Patio Bellavista, developed by renovating historic buildings. Since these first successes, *Ciudad Viva* has mobilised in favour of alternative development projects at the metropolitan scale. In the early 2000s, the association worked for the modernisation of the bus network and the implementation of a Bus Rapid Transit system. In 2003, it organised a visit by the former Mayor of Bogotá, Enrique Peñalosa, initiator of the *Transmilenio* project, and this eventually led to the Transantiago Plan coming into effect in 2007.

In the second half of the 2000s, Ciudad Viva embarked on a campaign to promote cycling. It benefited from the unprecedented commitment of the Regional Government to develop a network of cycle paths throughout the metropolitan area. The Regional Government – which, as we have already seen, has very little power to coordinate sectoral ministries and their regional representatives – developed new fields of action in areas for which no authority had previously taken responsibility: the cycle network, the development of metropolitan green spaces (the Green Santiago plan – *Santiago Verde*), recycling (also promoted by *Ciudad Viva*). The Regional Government, with no direct powers over infrastructure research, innovation or policies, concentrated on the 'soft' regional development factors of leisure and the environment.[18] The models imported were a world away from the metropolis's current mode of development, with the implementation of measures inspired by pedestrian or transit city projects in Germany or by cycling-inclusive planning in the Netherlands. The *Vélib'* experiment in Paris also has a following in Santiago and it is one of the initiatives currently being considered by the Regional Government. For the first time, a citizens' association has achieved direct collaboration with government authorities.

Ciudad Viva also networks with another neighbourhood association, which is active in the historic Barrio Yungay, a district in the western part of the Municipality of Santiago. Like *Ciudad Viva*, this association is involved in various local community activities (festivals and exhibitions), heritage conservation and advocacy planning. In 2009, the argument for citizen participation was also the moving force behind fierce opposition to the new urban planning law, from urban movements such as the *Defendamos la Ciudad* collective ('Let's Defend the City'), which takes a more oppositional stance than *Ciudad Viva*. In the wake of *Defendamos la Ciudad*, there are now some 38 neighbourhood organisations and groups of architects, including 'Neighbours for the Defence of Barrio Yungay'

---

17   Interview with Lake Sagaris, President of Ciudad Viva, 8 June 2009.

18   Interview with Hector Olivo, Cycling-inclusive Policy Expert, Santiago Metropolitan Region, 12 June 2009.

and a powerful citizens' network in the Municipality of Ñuñoa, in the east of the metropolitan area. Protests have focused on failure to implement any citizen participation process for urban projects. An open letter of November 2008 to President Bachelet called for withdrawal of the new law, declaring:

> We demand the immediate withdrawal of the Draft Amendment to the Law on Urban Planning and Construction, as regards urban planning, because of the arbitrary process to which this project has been subjected, such as the gross errors and omissions contained in this text, drawn up by MINVU in conjunction with professional business associations in the construction industry and property sector, which is evidently contrary to the criteria of the common good necessary for any new legislation.[19]

This opposition managed to block the legislative revision process in the name of participation. In fact, Santiago's movements have gained in strength and, for the first time, have provided external criticism of the growth coalition. Within the current typology of the urban social movements that can be observed in the world's great cities (Mayer, 2000), groups such as *Ciudad Viva* or *Defendamos la Ciudad* are situated midway between movements that favour decentralised decision-making (participation and empowerment) and protests against the socio-territorial impacts of metropolitanisation and globalisation (local environmental conservation, neighbourhood defence and anti-gentrification movements). These defensive movements also go beyond the strictly NIMBY-type opposition movements that they may, at first sight, seem to resemble (Trom, 1999), and they frequently promote wider issues, campaigning to keep lower income populations in their neighbourhoods, for cultural development or for environmental justice.

However, the Chilean capital has seen the parallel development of strictly NIMBY-type movements, especially in the very affluent municipalities in the east of the metropolitan area. In March 2009, in the wealthy Municipality of Vitacura, the *Salvemos Vitacura* association ('Let's Save Vitacura') succeeded in obtaining the first referendum on a local proposition ever launched in Chile. Voter turnout was 70 per cent, and 70 per cent of voters rejected the plans put forward by the Municipal Council, which was led by a Mayor belonging to the right-wing party *Renovación Nacional*. The Mayor's plan involved increasing the maximum permitted height of buildings in town-house neighbourhoods to four, five or six storeys and of blocks of flats along the River Mapocho to a range of seven to 12 storeys. The opposition that led to the local referendum lasted more than four years and considerably weakened the otherwise powerful position of the Mayor of this wealthy municipality. In another example, in the middle-class Municipality of Peñalolen, the residents of an eco-community – made up of opulent houses built

---

19 'Solicitan a Bachelet que retire del Senado modificación a la Ley de Urbanismo elaborada por el Minvu'. 24 November 2008. Translated from the Spanish. http://www.defendamoslaciudad.cl, accessed 25.2.2011.

to the most advanced ecological standards – opposed the siting of a social housing neighbourhood nearby, on the grounds that its high density posed a risk to the nature of the landscape and the local environment. In contrast, in the Municipality of La Cisterna, the poor residents of a social housing district dating from the 1960s mounted opposition to the siting nearby of one section of the ambitious Portal del Bicentenario housing and business development project, which was being steered through by the state.

The spread of NIMBY protests and the success of the first local referendum at Vitacura have begun to worry the CCC, which is fearful of the contagion spreading to other municipalities and perceives a potential brake on the development of high-rise schemes on the most sought-after sites in the metropolitan area.[20] Moreover, over the last two years, ADI has begun to look at approaches to wider consultation upstream of urban development projects.[21]

Since the early 2000s, the government authorities have been confronted by the limitations of a form of urban development based mainly on motor vehicle accessibility. The difficulty of modernising the bus system has highlighted the state's inability to coordinate its sectoral activities, rethink its logic of building large-scale amenities and strengthen its relationship with municipalities in the sphere of urban management. The debate on the financing of public transport has also highlighted the reluctance of national politicians to commit public funding in support of broader accessibility policies, which would run counter to a well-rooted tradition of private sector financing of urban growth. In addition to this internal dissent, there has been a rise in external criticisms from new urban social movements and NIMBY-type protests. Although the emergence of new urban movements reflects a certain normalisation of local democratic debate – 20 years after the fall of the military government – it also demonstrates that central government and the private sector have still not found methods of overhauling the growth coalition and the growth model. The principal challenge facing public-sector and private sector actors nowadays is how to take into account the spatial and social effects of urban growth. They have not yet found institutional and political ways of responding to these new issues.

Conclusion

Santiago de Chile's development model, oriented towards extensive *and* intensive growth, has been sustained by a powerful growth coalition bonded together since the 1980s by a public policy based on liberalising land use, modernising technical networks and upgrading road provision. Since the 1960s, the role of property sector and construction sector representatives (ADI and the CCC) has

---

20   Interview with Maria-Elena Ducci, Professor of Urban Studies, Catholic University of Santiago de Chile, 8 June 2009.

21   Interview with Vicente Domínguez Vial, ADI, Santiago de Chile, 16 June 2009.

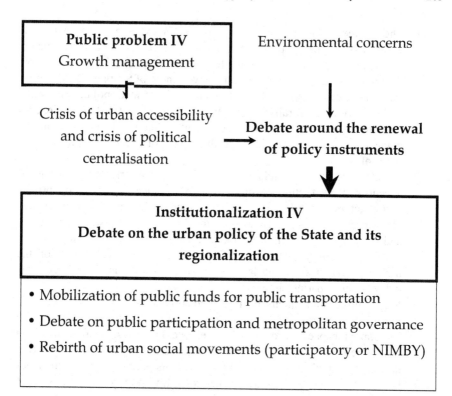

Figure 5.7   Overview of the current phase of institutionalization, since 2005

been evident at all the key stages in the evolution of urban policies: the brake on social housing construction policy under the Allende Government, the backing for a policy of social home ownership under the military government, the support for policies to liberalise land use and promote privatisation of public services during the 1980s and the activities favouring stronger public-sector guarantees for highway concessions. However, their relationship with the state has not been the smoothest: it has been punctuated by debates, trials of strength and, indeed, conflicts around issues of infrastructure provision for newly urbanised areas and of internalising the collective costs of urban development.

Viewed from the angle of this book's inquiry into modes of government for big metropolises and into the respective roles of formal governance mechanisms – ranging from central state intervention to the creation of metropolitan or intermunicipal authorities – and informal institutionalised arrangements, the metropolis of Santiago de Chile presents an original combination of several specific features:

1. The degree of decentralisation of power is extremely low. All urban policies – on spatial planning, housing, urban transport, infrastructure and technical networks – are directed by devolved state institutions. More than in most capital city regions, the government of Santiago is marked by the prominence of state intervention. There is no metropolitan governing body. There is a centralised form of power that does what is required for economic success but leads to significant difficulties in the institutional management of conflicts linked to the effects of growth – particularly in times of crisis.

2. Chile, a centralised and intensely free market-oriented state, gives a central place to the steering of large technical networks by private sector actors. Confidence in private sector management is nevertheless accompanied by tight regulation of the involvement of water, electricity and telecommunications network companies, which are held in check by the regulatory state. In particular, the rapid development of the highway system since the late 1990s has been sustained by large-scale public–private partnerships.

3. Regionalised and intensely regulated private sector management of technical networks sustains the growth of the metropolis through an investment capacity worthy of developed countries. This secures the economic performance of the metropolitan area. Instruments for steering networks or flexible institutional arrangements between public authorities have solved wastewater treatment, road transport and waste storage problems, thus enabling the avoidance of health and environmental crises. Moreover, the new instruments of conditional urban development are creating another option for governing the metropolis. Having given up trying to control urban expansion, the state is attempting to make the private financing model for new urban developments shoulder the costs of developing infrastructures such as schools, shops and even personal transport, all of which are indispensable to their smooth running.

4. The joint effectiveness of state policy and the network companies' activities has been most limited in the field of urban public transport. Since the early 1980s and the complete market liberalisation of its bus networks, Chile has experienced significant difficulties in steering public transport provision. Recent difficulties in the public transport sector reveal a major lack of any institutionalised arrangements that might be able to manage the effects of growth at the scale of a metropolis with a population of six million.

5. The second area where economically liberal, state-present governance in the Santiago region has shown its limitations is in the loss of political and social cohesion at the scale of the metropolis – a consequence of difficulties in providing political backing for private sector urban expansion and of the marked social specialisation of the different municipalities. In spite of recent initiatives to strengthen social rights, instigated by former President

Michelle Bachelet, redistribution at the territorial scale is not on the agenda. Even more, the private city that is being created to the north and west of the metropolis, beyond the built-up area and existing public transport networks, is increasing the differentiation and the fractures between inframetropolitan spaces.

List of Interviews

Raquel Alfaro, Head of Metropolitan Sanitation Works Company (Empresa metropolitana de obras sanitarias, or EMOS) 1990–1996, 5 August 2003.

Ana-Luisa Covarrubias Perez-Cotapos, Transport Expert, Libertad y Desarrollo think tank, 15 June 2009.

Vicente Domínguez Vial, Executive Director, Association of Property Developers (Asociación de Desarrolladores Inmobiliarios, or ADI), Santiago de Chile, 16 June 2009.

Maria-Elena Ducci, Professor of Urban Studies, Catholic University of Santiago de Chile (Pontificia Universidad Católica de Chile), 8 June 2009.

Marcelo Farah, Technical Adviser, Urban Transport Planning Secretariat (SECTRA), 8 June 2009.

Bettina Horst, Urban Issues Expert, Libertad y Desarrollo think tank, 12 June 2009.

Rodrigo Mardones, Assistant Professor of Political Science, Catholic University of Santiago de Chile (Pontificia Universidad Católica de Chile), 9 June 2009.

Alfredo Rodriguez, General Secretary, SUR Social Studies and Education Corporation (SUR Corporación de Estudios Sociales y Educación), 16 June 2009.

Hector Olivo, Cycling-inclusive Policy Expert, Santiago Metropolitan Region, 12 June 2009.

Arturo Orellana, Senior Adviser to Álvaro Erazo, Regional Governor of Santiago Metropolitan Region, Santiago de Chile, 10 June 2009.

Lake Sagaris, President of the Ciudad Viva (‹Living City›) Association, 8 June 2009.

Lucas Sierra, Researcher, Centre for Public Studies (Centro de Estudios Públicos), 15 June 2009.

Javier Wood Larrain, Head of the Department of Urban Development and Infrastructure, MINVU Regional Secretariat (SEREMI), Santiago Metropolitan Region, Santiago de Chile, 16 June 2009.

Bibliography

Castells, M. (1973). Movimiento de pobladores y lucha de clases en Chile. *Revista EURE*, 3(7): 299–340.

Castells, M. (2006). *Globalización, desarrollo y democracia: Chile en el contexto mundial.* Santiago: Fondo de Cultura Económica, 164.

Cheetham, R. (1971). El sector privado de la construcción: patrón de dominación. *Revista EURE*, 1(1): 125–48.

Daniere, A.G. et Gomez-Ibanez, J.A. (1994). *Infrastructure Services in Chile: A Spatial Analysis.* Irvine: University of California Irvine, Harvard University, 35.

De Ramón, A. (1990). La población informal. Poblamiento de la periferia de Santiago de Chile, 1920–1970. *Revista EURE*, 16, (50): 5–17.

Ducci, M.E. (1997). Chile: el lado oscuro de una politica de vivienda exitosa. *Revista EURE*, XXIII, (69), julio.

Ducci, M.E. (2004). Las batallas urbanas de principios del tercer milenio. In De Mattos, C., Ducci, M.E., Rodriguez, A. et Yanez Warner, G. (eds), *Santiago en la globalizacion: una nueva ciudad ?* Santiago: SUR Corporacion, 137–66.

Echenique, M. (1996). Algunas consideraciones sobre el desarrollo de la infraestructura en Chile. *Estudios Públicos*, 62: 5–28.

Engel, E., Fischer, R. et Galetovic, A. (2001). El Programa Chileno de Concesiones de Infraestructura: Evaluación, Experiencias y Perspectivas. In Larrain B., F. et Vergara M., R. (eds), *La Transformación Económica de Chile.* Santiago, Chile: CEP, 202–45.

Figueroa, O. (2004). Infraestructura, servicios publicos y expansion urbana en Santiago. In De Mattos, C., Ducci, M.E., Rodriguez, A. et Yanez Warner, G. (eds), *Santiago en la globalizacion: una nueva ciudad ?*. Santiago: SUR Corporacion, 243–72.

Figueroa, O. et Orellana, A. (2007). Transantiago: gobernabilidad e institucionalidad. *EURE – Revista latinoamericana de estudios urbano regionales*, 33(100): 165–71.

Gómez-Lobo, A. et Contreras, D. (2003). Water Subsidy Policies: A Comparison of the Chilean and Colombian Schemes. *The World Bank Economic Review*, 17(3): 391–407.

Graham, S. et Marvin, S. (2001). *Splintering Urbanism.* London: Routledge, 479.

Hidalgo Dattwyler, R. (2004). La vivienda social en Santiago de Chile en la segunda mitad del siglo XX: actores relevantes y tendencias espaciales. In De Mattos, C., Ducci, M.E., Rodriguez, A. et Yanez Warner, G. (eds). *Santiago en la globalizacion: una nueva ciudad ?* Santiago: SUR Corporacion, 219–41.

Icaza, A.M. et Rodriguez, A. (1988). *Estudio de caso, Santiago de Chile.* Santiago de Chile: Centro de investigaciones SUR, 61.

Lafoy, P.D.L.F., Torres Rojas, E. et Munoz Salazar, P. (1990). Satifaccion residencial en soluciones habitacionales de radicacion y erradicacion para sectores pobres de Santiago. *EURE*, XVI(49): 7–22.

Larrain, P. (1994). Néolibéralisme et ségrégation socio-spatiale à Santiago du Chili. *Cahiers des Amériques Latines*, 18: 103–12

Le Galès, P. (2002). *European cities. Social conflicts and governance.* Oxford: Oxford University Press, 352.

Le Galès, P. et Lorrain, D. (2003). Gouverner les très grandes métropoles ? *Revue française d'administration publique*, 2003/3(107): 305–17.

Logan, J.R. et Molotch, H.L. (2007). *Urban Fortunes: The Political Economy of Place*. Los Angeles: University of California Press, 413.

Mardones, R. (2006). Descentralisación y transición en Chile. *Revista de ciencia política*, 26(1): 3–24.

Mardones, R. (2008). Chile: Transantiago recargado. *Revista de ciencia política*, 28(1): 103–19.

Massey, D.S. (2005). *Strangers in a Strange Land : Humans in an Urbanizing World*. New York: Norton Publishers.

Matthieussent, S. (2003). *Mutations urbaines et service* électrique à *Santiago du Chili*. Mémoire de DEA Mutations urbaines et gouvernances territoriales: Institut Français d'Urbanisme – Ecole Nationale des Ponts et Chaussées, Marne-la-Vallée, 76 + annexes.

Mayer, M. (2000). Urban Social Movements in an Era of Globalisation. In Hamel, P., Lustiger-Thaler, H. et Mayer, M. (eds), *Urban Movements in a Globalising World*. London; New York: Routledge, 139–57.

North, D.C. (1990). *Institutions, Institutional Change and Economic Performance*. New York: Cambridge University Press, 152.

Oxman, S. et Oxer, J.P. (eds). (2000). *Privatización del sector sanitario chileno. Análisis de un proceso inconcluso*. Santiago de Chile: Ediciones Cesoc, 387.

Paquette, C. (1998). Grille de présentation de la métropole de Santiago du Chili. *Atelier international 'Métropoles en mouvement', CNRS programme 'villes/ réseau socioéconomique de l'habitat'*. IRD/PUCA/IUED, 16.

Parnreiter, C. (2005). Tendencias de desarrollo en las metrópolis latinoamericanas en la era de la globalización: los casos de Ciudad de México y Santiago de Chile. *EURE*, 31(92): 5–28.

Petermann, A. (2006). Quien extendio a Santiago ? Une breve historia del limite urbano, 1953–1994. In Galetovic, A. (ed.), *Santiago. Donde estamos y hacia donde vamos*. Santiago de Chile: Centro de estudios publicos, 205–30.

Pflieger, G. (2008). Achieving Universal Access to Drinking Water and Sanitation Networks in Santiago de Chile: An Historical Analysis 1970–1995. *Journal of Urban Technology*, 15(1): 19–51.

Pflieger, G. et Matthieussent, S. (2008). Water and Power in Santiago de Chile: Socio-spatial Segregation through Network Integration. *Geoforum*, 39(6): 1907–21.

Poduje, I. (2006). El globo y el acordeón: planificación urbana en Santiago 1960–2004 In Galetovic, A. (ed.) *Santiago. Donde estamos y hacia donde vamos*. Santiago de Chile: Centro de estudios publicos, 233–76.

Sabatini, F., Cáceres, G. et Cerda, J. (2001). Segregación residencial en las principales ciudades chilenas: tendencias de las tres últimas décadas y posibles cursos de acción. *EURE*, 27(82): 21–42.

Shirley, M.M., Xu, L.C. et Zuluaga, A.M. (2000). *Reforming the Urban Water System in Santiago, Chile*. Washington DC: The World Bank, 76.

Tiebout, C.M. (1956). A Pure Theory of Local Expenditures. *The Journal of Political Economy*, 64(5): 416–24.

Trom, D. (1999). De la réfutation de l'effet NIMBY considérée comme une pratique militante. Notes pour une approche pragmatique de l'activité revendicative *Revue française de science politique*, 49(1): 31–50.

Valenzuela, A. (1977). *Political brokers in Chile: Local Government in a Centralized Polity.* Durham: Duke University Press, 272.

Chapter 6

Governing Under Constraints: Strategy and Inherited Realities

Dominique Lorrain, Alain Dubresson and Sylvy Jaglin

If we had wished to begin this account of megacities and large cities with a film shot, we would have chosen a violent image that would convey the intensity of the urban phenomena we have been describing. Growth rates and the human masses involved, gaps in income and property, the challenge of integrating new inhabitants – all of these are bigger than in cities in industrial countries. The emerging cities we have studied radically switched directions in the late twentieth century, shaking up their urban societies and pulling them toward new political systems or accumulation regimes. History has not taken peaceful paths here. These large cities, gigantic energy accumulators and transformers, are intense, turbulent. This reality invites us to reflect on the factors of change that are leading some of them out of path dependence.

Santiago's evolution continues to be affected by the 1973 *coup d'Etat* involving abduction and death on a mass scale, the dismissal of local left-wing elected officials and a take-over of city government by the central state. It took many years to loosen that vice; several decades later its mark is still visible. In Cape Town and Mumbai, extreme poverty rubs shoulders with opulent wealth. These two cases operate at the extremes. Their elites have developed a discourse on competing with world-class cities while parts of the population still live without essential services. These cities do not seem to be able to handle the problem of housing. In Cape Town, nearly a third of the population – poor people, migrants, and blacks discriminated against by the former apartheid regime – live in slums. In Mumbai the phenomenon is quantitatively greater, and rents are so high that even the middle-class is affected. There is violence too in the fierce competition to acquire wealth, particularly in the form of housing and land. At the top we find the major operations, which generally proceed in accordance with 'good governance' rules and are characterised by alliances between public authorities and private actors that can be classified as 'growth coalitions'. However, when we look more closely at ordinary operations, we discover the negative side of accumulation. In Mumbai, real estate developers supported by local elected officials and in some cases criminal gangs are seizing entire neighborhoods. In Cape Town, the situation inherited from apartheid has not been improved everywhere, and certain economic activities in some Cape Flats townships are run or co-run by gangs. Shanghai has managed to escape most of these ills, though living conditions for the 'floating' population are very hard and not very well known. Overall, however, that city is an extremely powerful machine, massively accumulating, transforming goods and services, transforming itself. Old neighborhoods in central districts are being destroyed and replaced by modern towers and public facilities. In the 1990s, at the start of this transformation process, which called for building very fast, inhabitants were unceremoniously evicted and granted only minimum compensation. Gradually, rules were drawn up to regulate the process. The central government has been running some anti-corruption campaigns and has harshly sentenced some developers, to make it clear there is a line that must not be crossed.

The cities studied raise issues of governability related to their particularities as large and very large cities, but their development is also part and parcel of emergence contexts themselves characterised by both constraints and opportunities. Emergence implies a combination of high growth, confirmed integration into globalised markets, and consolidated institutional know-how; it also implies building rational, competent administrative apparatuses (Sgard, 2008). The changes observed in our cases are therefore both responses to urban management problems and part of broader processes specific to emergence trajectories such as the renewal of production modes and institutional structures. In large cities, which may be thought of as globalisation strongholds and anchorage points, local public authorities are having to learn to deal with the external forces of the market and exert effort internally to develop and supervise autonomous, efficient public policies likely to produce socially satisfactory results.

The question of whether urban institutions are converging, then, is raised in two ways. First, with regard to national economies' becoming globalised and competitive; here the institution construction process would seem constrained to comply with shared game rules. Second, with regard to the supposed convergence of metropolisation models themselves constrained by the diffusion of 'good' models as well as by technical solutions and funding mechanisms. Taking a critical view of the claim that national economies are being standardised for the purposes of international competition, other studies stress divergence and the weight of political and cultural institutions inherited from the national past and of public policies in explaining that divergence, thereby seeking to reassert the value of the autonomy left to national and local public authorities (Shatkin, 2007; Vietor, 2007). In fact, the point is not so much whether institutions affect the 'quality' of development trajectories as what a country and its regions' institutional infrastructure needs are and what processes and time spans are required for institutional rules to indeed rule (Rodrik, Subramanian and Trebbi, 2004). What makes ordinary economic principles compatible with a variety of institutions is having policy space that can be used to adapt institutions to those principles (Rodrik, 2008). As we have shown, not just states but also large cities use this maneuvering room to adapt their institutions to their economic ambitions. The results can only be assessed at the local level and over the long term of institutional change.

To understand institutional change, then, we have to return to the approach and questions we put forward in the introduction. Our two arguments are 1) institutions –

in contrast to other factors such as site and location, place in international flows, inherited situations – can still be changed by voluntarist actors; 2) institutional change is not a *sui generis* process but is constructed in response to specific challenges. To understand why and how actors transform their institutions, we first have to look at existing problems.

In what way is the construction of institutions an important vector for change? Are emerging cities governed, or do the forces of economic globalisation turn them into spaces entirely at the mercy of the market? How do large technical systems and utility industries contribute to city government? Do those networks help segregate the city or are they an anti-fragmentation device and a source for institutional learning at the municipal level?

Changes in Models of Urban Government

The four cities studied have one point in common: the problems their governments are confronted with all relate to development. These city governments cannot respond with hollow rhetoric; they have to act to find solutions, lest their cities implode politically.

Demography, both in terms of population growth rates and the size of the population masses involved, is clearly a central issue. To this must be added proportion of young people and low- or unskilled working adults under 30. The flexible accumulation regime that was established in the 1990s has changed labor markets, resulting in sharper polarisation and employment insecurity and putting an end to the practice of spending an entire career with one or a few companies. Moreover, many of the formal jobs created by current growth are not accessible to the poorest, who are also the least qualified, and particularly likely to be women. This change has had major consequences for all our cities, as shown by the cases of Mumbai and Cape Town, where exacerbated urban struggles to obtain wage-paid employment, as well as an increasing tendency to use nationalist, religious and ethnic terms to shape indentities (autochthones versus allochthones, nationals versus foreigners) are producing discourses on self-proclaimed 'priority' rights, and so on. That exacerbation is also patently at work in small-scale informal market activities, where tensions caused by struggles to gain control over a given occupation, network and/or specific intra-urban space are growing more intense.

Economic growth, and wealth accumulation and distribution, are required to cope with these problems, i.e., to absorb migrant flows, update often inadequate inherited facilities and infrastructure services, ensure social peace. If a city falls below a certain growth level, it moves into a high risk zone where the number of unemployed is simply too great. This is the case in Cape Town with the pro-growth policy, and in Shanghai. The housing situation and level of network service coverage also have to be improved; they are not yet up to the standards of cities in industrial countries. Here the term '*emerging* metropolis' acquires its full meaning and the question of economic development is central, whether it be for absorbing demographic excess or improving living conditions.

The issue of politics, the vision that forms the basis of the 'social contract', is at the heart of the development process. It is particularly complex given the heterogeneity of these large cities, due in turn to income gaps but also to diversity of population backgrounds and histories; that is, colonisation experiences embedded in long pre- and post-colonial histories, each with its accumulated institutions and rationales. To take up and try to meet these challenges, states as well as city governments have had to reform their initial direct-government model. Here the tie between action and acting institutions is obvious. The cities we have observed do present several cases of convergence around a movement to 'modernise' public administrations and operators.

The direct administration model, inherited for the most part from solutions initially put in place in the late nineteenth century in industrial countries, is based on public administrations and companies at the state, province or city level. With regard to network infrastructures, these are vertically integrated companies with a service provision monopoly. The whole is coordinated more through tax mechanisms and planning than market competition and contracts. In fact, this model has proven quite effective for it was what allowed the equipping of many of these large cities. The results are clear for Shanghai, Santiago and Cape Town; Mumbai's performance is not as strong. But when it becomes time to move into a higher gear, the flaws become apparent: this public, vertically integrated model is excessively sectorial and bureaucratic. Its primary funding mechanism is tax revenue, and given the levels of investment required, those revenues are running out. The figures speak for themselves: from 1991 to 2007, the city of Shanghai spent €390 billion on fixed assets; the 'Vision Mumbai' program estimates needs at €32 billion ($40 billion), and this is probably below the mark.

At a time when the initial public model is losing operating power, city governers are quite logically looking elsewhere for inspiration, particularly to the private sector. They have had strong incentive to do so. Policies to liberalise urban activities[1] have been undertaken since the 1980s, and powerful actors – the World Bank, the International Monetary Fund, international development institutions, consulting agencies, securities firms and investment funds – have been energetically promoting the move. The rise of the private sector paradigm constitutes a particularly striking change in the government of large emerging cities. These large cities are projecting themselves into the future, expressing growth ambitions; each wants to be a leader in some specific areas. Their elites have adopted the language of economic competition: rivalry and comparison, strategy, efficiency. The urban economy no longer seems organised as it was in the theory, i.e., around an export base that would fuel the economy and a domestic service base bolstered by a

---

1 The verb 'liberalise' refers to three operating modes: privatisation through sale of public enterprises, establishing public-private partnerships, applying market techniques to manage public enterprises.

public sector, both relatively protected (Davezies 2008; North 1966). According to the dominant vision, the competition principle seems to have been generalised and now informs all action. We should nonetheless observe the strong analogy between this and the analytic schemata used for large corporations, with their strategies, activity portfolios and core businesses.

In fact, the changes we are discussing correspond to deeper phenomena than the new combinatorics of actors suggested by the term 'urban governance'. They amount to changing the former models of urban government, and if we accept the idea of the model (Lorrain, 2005), we can say that the new models operate in several ways and at several levels, thus reconfiguring entire institutional architectures. At the highest level of the matrix the breadth of change is uneven (nature of property rights, competition structure, market operation, and so on.), and urban institutions are either more (Shanghai) or less (Mumbai) affected by recent developments. At the level we have been observing, that of second-rank institutions (Lorrain, 2008), those changes are affecting both actor systems – a greater role is being granted to private actors – and policy tools: new instruments are being used, instruments modeled on the world of private enterprise. All of this leads to convergence on new values. We can now examine the triptych institutions, instruments, and values.

With regard to *institutions* and actor systems, the change lies in the emergence of *growth coalitions* (Logan and Molotch, 1987). This term refers to an alliance between local rulers and private actors for the purpose of promoting urban development and working the given city up to world-class or reference status. Growth coalition effectiveness varies by city: the actors implicated in them may be more or less genuinely committed to the city, and this goes a long way to explaining the results. To account for this situation, we need to consider for a moment the cities' political elites and the nature of the companies participating in the urban fabric.

Mumbai has a development plan, but political parties and the business community are not yet used to working together; the two worlds were long separate. Moreover, there is no real urban corporation. Shanghai, on the other hand, has a growth supercoalition; the political and administrative elites are being merged and are supported by the central government. This model unquestionably produces results, but it operates without any real counter-power. Its internal mechanisms draw it up into a growth spiral – the city funding the city – that will be hard to get out of. Chili has been a laboratory for privatisation policy, and private interests largely dominate development of the city of Santiago. Local power is weak there and the growth coalition involves groups of big land-and-real estate developers who work with and around state-implemented public policies. Cape Town's government has set up a pro-growth policy to keep its pro-poor policy working, but the former is hard to implement. Overall, the private sector there is not really supportive of or mobilised around the municipal strategy. The strategies of major corporations in that metropolis (insurance, finance, business, and so on.) do not link them indefinitely to the city in which they began to develop. They are playing an 'accompaniment' role rather than fully committing themselves. Political behavior also weighs in. The instability that has characterised the political scene since the end of the apartheid regime has not facilitated exchanges between the political and corporate worlds, and relations with small and medium-sized businesses, which account for 90 per cent of productive units, are even more strained. This is compounded by municipal civil servants' distrust of the private sector, expressed notably with regard to the plan to delegate water supply management to the private sector. The private sector – particularly real estate developers – is involved in some projects (for example, 'city improvement districts'), but these are extremely circumscribed, localised partnerships in wealthy areas, where the private sector has been setting itself up as an intermediary between civil society and the city government.[2]

As our four cases make quite clear, it is not easy to find the right adjustment between the public and private poles and so to achieve equilibrium. What growth coalitions there are remain fragile. And in the two cases governed by such coalitions we have imbalance. In Shanghai, the principle of having two blocs of partners is losing ground in favor of a dominant public pole: the public pole as ultimate organiser, encompassing and fusing together administration, political class and private sector and behaving like a developer itself. In Santiago, private interests dominate when it comes to making urban planning decisions. In Mumbai as in Cape Town, the growth coalition is more an objective than a reality. Urban governments and private corporations do not seem ready to commit themselves to lasting partnerships for mutual benefits. This can only be due to the weight of history, the impact of deep forces that overdetermine actors' behavior despite the modernity discourse.

Table 6.1   Growth coalition factors

	Mumbai	Shanghai	Santiago	Cape Town
Local authorities	- -	+ +	- -	+
The state	+	+	+ +	+
Infrastructure companies	-	+ +	-	-
Developers	-	+	+ +	-
Other companies	+ +	-	-	+

---

2   Some authors are of the opinion that this imbalanced Shadow State-type situation could lead to privatising urban planning (Mitchell, 2000).

Instruments and visions. Ideas circulate from one continent to another and help define visions, models of government, city development strategies. City and/or state governments and the new local economic elites in the cities we studied thus share to a considerable degree the new representations of 'urban performance', representations heavily influenced by new public management models. These representations are impacting to various degrees on the modernisation of public utilities operators and are leading to accounting reforms (new procedures, computerisation), financial reforms (ring-fencing), changes in human resource and skills management (including aspects of the wage relationship), rate reform, and a redefinition of subsidy practices, lastly, a redefining of 'customer' relations and standards for providing services to users. We can also confirm the role of the finance and consulting industry and the power of information. On McKinsey's advice, Mumbai is now seeking to adopt a development model like Shanghai's; i.e. an infrastructure-based growth coalition. Mumbai is also applying a 'city manager' model imported from the United States. Ideas circulate at the ground level as well and are applied in the making of micro-decisions. It is worth mentioning a few of the instruments that get exported and are found in all the cities we studied.

The City Improvement District model, imported from the United States, is being applied in a modified version in Cape Town, and, in more general terms, our cities are all developing *project-based policies*. This technique, which involves autonomising every operation by creating an *ad-hoc* company with legal entity status, stockholders and financing, can be applied in every type of city subdivision – an activity area, a housing program, a megamall, an urban facility, a technical network. Individualising operations this way allows for 'hedging bets', varying partners and developing innovative funding mechanisms. However, it also carries a strong risk of fragmentation if projects scattered across the city are not really coordinated. Cities advised by financial sector actors have shown they are capable of creativity when it comes to funding their projects. Alongside classic techniques – public subsidies, borrowing, rates – they have learned to use the market, issue bonds, get some of their urban utilities companies listed on the stockmarket, and so on.

The city pays for the city is a principle applied in two ways. In Shanghai, the public development companies charged with funding infrastructure are using land-sale to pay for nearly 50 per cent of investment in fixed assets, so ground rent for city growth is becoming a more important mechanism than ordinary techniques like taxation and tariffs. However, it is important to understand that this technique is only possible because private property has to take account of state property. The situation is different in Santiago, where 'conditioned urban development' principles have been laid out since the 1970s in a regulatory plan; the idea is that building sale price has to include the cost of installing infrastructure.Though this solution seems simple and rational, it raises a great deal of implementation problems. First, it is not easy to reach agreement on the list of networks to be imputed to an urban development program, above and beyond those that have to be built in the area in question. If the rise in consumption brought about by the construction program saturates the long distance electricity grid or has a similar effect on a freeway or water treatment plant, can these costs be charged to the program? Definition difficulties have given rise to intense bargaining between the relevant ministry and major developers with good political connections. In reality, only secondary network infrastructure costs have been internalised and can thus enable the city to pay for the city; primary networks still have to be paid for by the public authorities.

Liberal economists' idea that *market competition* is the best means of improving utility services has had some impact. This principle explicitly guided land policy in Santiago in 1979, under the influence of economists trained at the University of Chicago. For competition to work in the housing market there can be no restrictions on supply, and this led to adopting an urban plan that increased the surface area officially available for urban development from 35,000 to 100,000 hectares. The same competition principle, imported from British reforms of 1986, may be found in Santiago and Shanghai bus transportation systems: private companies can easily obtain a license for running bus lines, and they can choose their ticket rates and running frequency. In this system, providers are competing at the level of the single bus line – a far cry from the historical model of public-transportation companies with a monopoly throughout the city.

Local Particularisms and Immutable Realities

Public policy and institution quality are not enough to explain the development path a city takes. Not everything is decided at the local level, nor does everything have to go through institutions. The weight of inherited situations also intervenes.

A city has *geographical attributes*: a site, a location on the given continent that positions it either more or less advantageously in relation to global economic flows and which can therefore give it a competitive edge or constrain it. Shanghai, at the mouth of the Yangzi, a port city in the vast country of China, is better situated than Santiago or Cape Town, both of which are located in the south of continents facing the ocean. The reforms in Shanghai have been facilitated by extraordinary economic accumulation; investment growth and the many projects made possible by it have enabled the city to attain several goals – a case of 'a rising tide lifts all boats'. Cape Town is not experiencing the same vigorous growth, and this is making it difficult for the city to reach its social goals or any political project its leaders might devise. In other words, though a city's economic performance depends on the quality of its institutions and its ability to invest in relevant sectors, it also depends on other factors, e.g. a possible turnaround in the markets. The notion of 'stranded costs' used in network industries to designate the risks for operators or a radical change in public policy[3] applies here to entire cities. Hard hit by the 2007–2008 financial and real estate crisis, Dubai offers a clear illustration of this notion.

---

3   E.g. the effect of a decision to put an end to nuclear power programs on operators that have invested in that technology.

A city is also a *built space* in which right-of-ways, technical networks and buildings of many shapes, heights and uses have been accumulating over a long period of time. This inheritance constitutes a massive constraint – unless wartime-type tabula rasa plans are implemented. Lastly, a city is characterised by an economic base and social classes. These two factors likewise imply great inertia and can amount to an extremely heavy inheritance, as in Cape Town, where the notion of social segregation is inscribed in the city's residential norms and the way identity groups are defined.

Cities are differentiated by *the way change is managed*, a factor that cannot be dissociated from inherited situations and contexts. In generalising the partnership approach (1999 to 2003) and formalising a particular kind of growth coalition, the city of Shanghai made use of knowledge it had begun to acquire in the mid-1980s, 15 years earlier. Its leaders concentrated on a few practical problems – they experimented. The method was gradual change. The central government set goals, while local actors had some freedom to act, to experiment, to adjust institutions to a format that suited them. This explains how it was later possible to speed up the pace of reforms and apply partnership methods throughout city government. The paths taken by our other cities were very different, often involving a more top-down, procedure-focused approach. In Santiago, it was the state that abolished autonomous city governments and imported liberal economic principles, and its method was authoritarian. The result 30 years later is that urban government is still profoundly state-dependent. In Cape Town, local actors had six years to get ready, i.e. the time between the formal end of apartheid in 1994 and implementation of the Unicity reform in 2000. But both the city reform program, discussed with the Urban Foundation, and the gradual adoption of new public management principles began much earlier, in the 1980s. The blockages that slowed consensus building and interfered with reaching a shared vision of change were therefore due less to insufficient time than to discrepancies between reform levels, between the various speeds at which institutions were changing and in the degree to which those institutions were rooted in social structures. The approach was comprehensive – a large number of programs targeting a wide range of social and political regulation dimensions – and the impetus, which then fueled a high number of gradual sectorial reforms, was political.

All these factors result from what new leaders inherit in the way of long-term collective actions. The three terms 'collective', 'long-term', and 'inheritance' are very important, and they stand in stark contrast to strategic actor discourse imported from sociology of organisations, management science and game theory, language we find in connection with discourse on growth coalitions, where mayors are said to be 'entrepreneurs'.[4] What may make sense in managing corporations works less well for cities. There the voluntarist actor is much more constrained.

---

4   France experienced the same enthusiasm for the 'strategic actor' in the 1980s, shortly after decentralisation. But this voluntarist discourse disappeared as if by magic when difficulties became more serious (Padioleau, 1991).

The idea of an activity portfolio and core businesses presupposes a leader in a position to choose between strengthening the entity in question in one activity and giving up others. City government does not work this way. First, the work of leading, guiding, is often divided up between different institutions. Second, except in societies that exclude a part of their population, mayors cannot simply abandon 'sections' of their cities. Urban management implies adding together, not separating. The city – its situation vis-a-vis the major flows, its economic base, its social groups, its morphology and its built environment – is first and foremost a set of inherited realities.

The differences between the large cities we studied are also to be found when we look beyond urban institutions. The idea that urban governments are strategists with autonomy to act needs to be seriously revised, first by taking into account the role of the *state*. State intervention goes a long way to explaining the results for our four cities. In Santiago, the state has been omnipresent since 1979; indeed, urban policy is steered directly by the president's office or the relevant technological ministries. Performances in Shanghai cannot be understood without taking into account the central government's decision around 1992 to make it the country's economic capital and the incarnation of a socialist market economy. This intention explains the decision to build the new city of Pudong, with its free zones, port, airport and financial district. Without all this, the story would have been different: part of the economic flows would certainly have been captured by Hong Kong and the special economic zones of Guangdong and Fujian. But the role of the state can also be measured by absence of state intervention. Cape Town depends on aid from the central government to financially balance its pro-poor policy, but the state does not give it any special priority over other cities. Mumbai is unquestionably the economic capital of India, but it has to share its area of competence with the state of Maharashtra, and the support it gets from the federal state is much lower than what it would receive in the framework of a unitary state.

Differences are also reflected in the political organisation of society. Shanghai is of course not part of a political democracy; sectorial interests cannot have their say through independent organisations like political parties and unions, though a few associations have begun to take shape. The absence of an independent political sphere means that public action gets reduced to its professional dimension: technical solutions and actions for the common good. This gives it genuine efficiency. Policy is made through delegation to the CCP (Chinese Communist Party). Post-apartheid Cape Town operates in quite the opposite way. After the long period of apartheid, a means of legally excluding the black community, freedom of expression and individual rights have been made into the highest precepts. But those principles were introduced quite suddenly into a historically segregated society, a society in which ordinary categories – insider/outsider, 'race' (White, Coloured, Indian and Asian, Black) – were defined in complex ways. The categorising also covered such behavior as 'fought/did not fight apartheid', 'was/was not a civil rights activist', 'was/was not a prison inmate'. In a society made up of infinite subdivisions, the new freedom has had the effect of intensifying the atomistic nature of the city population, forcing the municipality to negotiate constantly to reach balances that then get called into question, over and over again. During the 17 post-apartheid years, the prevalence of politics has led to a sort of hypertrophy of the political, exacerbating particular rights that collide and clash with each other so often that they end up blocking public action. 'Disruption of routine' and political alliance instability have disorganising effects.

The question of elites, their nature, and the nature of their involvement in local affairs is also a variable that differentiates the cities we studied. Whether or not a public-sector elite has developed, and if so, how it intervenes in urban affairs is a major factor for differentiating these cities. This idea makes clear once again how important it is for public action analysis to examine how state and city work (or do not work) together. Some countries are organised to train and select elites through meritocratic selection, and reforms have made it possible to retain those elites. In Shanghai, the transforming of public bureaus and companies into joint-stock companies, some officially listed on the stockmarket, has made it possible to create well-paid public manager positions and prevent qualified persons from leaving the public sector. Conversely, in India and in Mumbai, there has been 'elite flight' toward private companies and international development institutions. In the early twentieth century, India was distinguished by the quality of its (British-trained) public administration (Nield 2002): a small number of elite administrators were able to manage the entire immense country. Since then, the quality of the public system has declined; it is criticized as inefficient and occasionally corrupt, and India's elites aspire to work in the private sector.

In some of our cities, then, elites are drained into international activities and contribute little; in others they have an acute sense of their common interests and a plan for 'their' city. In Cape Town and Mumbai, private elites are not much interested in the city; they invest only in certain activities and are interested above all in promoting their own affairs. For them, the city is not a comprehensive focus of action but a means of displaying their own strength and power, perhaps a market on which to do their own business. Shanghai's growth coalition is quite the opposite. Why do some elites have a Prussian or Colbertist conception of action while others are simply not interested? Elite approaches to development also vary considerably. In Shanghai and Santiago we find a rational approach dominated by guidelines and plans of action, whereas in Mumbai we find bricolage and arrangements that serve the interests of the 'arranging' parties. Officials there even refuse to create a structure for advising decision-makers for fear that the information thus produced would fuel opposition to the powers-that-be. Many basic technical studies are done there, often by specialised consulting firms, some of them foreign. But there is no public synthesis. The leaders insist on arbitrating between proposals themselves.

In several cases we discover a *dual action structure* involving both *formal*, readily interpretable *institutions*, similar to what can be found in developed countries, and *informal practices*. The first reaction to this is to impute this to economic backwardness, assumed to give rise to dual organisation of the production sphere in that it keeps in place inherited realities that preexisted the market and survive at the edges of 'modern' capitalist enterprises. This dualism thesis, fashionable in the 1970s and still occasionally put forward by political elites, e.g. in South Africa, where the point is to integrate the 'second' economy into the first, is generally not considered acceptable today. A great number of later studies have shown that informal arrangements and relations, far from amounting to an anomic, marginal residue that is bound to disappear, are in fact part and parcel of the urbanisation process (Lautier, 1994; Portes et al., 1989). For authors with a neo-Marxist approach, informal economic arrangements constitute a vital dimension of the capitalism that developed on the edges of the US-EU-Japan Triad in the second half of the twentieth century (Castells et al., 1989; Sassen, 1991). Some neoliberals have even theorised 'the informal' as a possible foundation for pure, salutary capitalism, the vector of an alternative development path (De Soto, 1986; De Soto, 2000). However that may be, field studies uniformly show how complex and organic the ties are between formal and informal economies. Depending on the situation being examined, relations between industry, crafts and small urban businesses may amount to induction, functional fitting together, connection or dissociation. In emerging megacities, non-conventional activities are in fact required if the poorest city-dwellers' basic needs are to be met, which is why the public authorities tolerate some of them.

Reciprocity relations and the intertwining of formal and informal affect not just the economic sphere but also political practices. The frequent confusing of public and private leads to operation modes that often resemble patronage and nepotism. These modes make use of informal networks. The public administration is not an autonomous entity or guarantor of the notion of general interest everywhere. Whether these practices were inherited from a long history of resisting some authority – the emperor, the colonial authorities – or constitute a particular native mode of exercising power, it is clear that they continue to be reproduced.

Above and beyond relatively superficial model convergence, then, there is some room for maneouver, and this is what enables urban governments to develop original institutions. However, the efficiency of those institutions when it comes to steering change varies greatly across our four cities. It is not our aim here to analyse institutional arrangements and whether they do or do not fit the models, but rather to consider how the specific constraints of context and social practices are taken into account and inscribed within a dynamic of change. We need to beware of overly causalist approaches. Efforts to cope with unprecedented problems produce institutional structures that are themselves complex scaffoldings, arrangements that often slip the grip of their initial creators, giving rise to uncertainty once again (North, 2005). Furthermore, economic and institutional change itself brings about disorder: in modifying the income hierarchy and access gates to opportunities, it threatens the security of certain groups and individuals. In other words, institutions are never 'good' in any absolute way but good to the extent that they can be adapted to pre-existing problems and the disorders they themselves provoke: they are good to the extent that they are capable of continuous change. This is clear in the four cities we studied. In all of them, considerable efforts have been undertaken to change institutions, but not all city governments have the same degree of control over the effects thereby induced. It is primarily through the gradual process of adaptation, rather than during crucial, founding moments in which an urban society breaks with an old system (in fact, the cathartic virtue of such moments may have an anesthetising effect on dissent and conflicts, as it did in South Africa during the first post-apartheid decade) that institutions' legitimacy and efficiency in situations of change are tested, along with the solidity of relationships based on trust and credibility, and the appeal of the social contract.

The quality and effectiveness of the change process derives from the ability to create and rally coalitions, to surmount immediate disruptions while eliciting trust. All change provokes resistances. To overcome those resistances, power struggles between economic and political elites in possession of the main resources have to be neutralised by arrangements that enable their interests to converge (Meisel and Ould Aoudia, 2008). Conceived to apply at the national scale, this analytic framework can be adapted to large cities, where the nature of coalitions is essential to understanding types and directions of change. Indeed, as our four cities show, elites' interests may be aligned in quite different ways: top-down or bottom-up; authoritarian or more democratic; tightly framed by formal, non-personalised rules or not framed in this way. Elites also have to be able to mobilise a significant fraction of the city population around a shared project, either by creating convergence between the interests of what are often heterogeneous social groups or inducing their belief in such convergence; lastly, by convincing each actor to respect the new rules in a lasting way, or supporting them when they do so. What is at issue here is the ability of coalition actors to design and implement a shared political project.

Dimensions of Emerging Metropolis Governability

The four large cities also give us a better grasp of several of the recurrent problems involved in organising such vast, intensely populated urban areas. Does size always produce complexity? Does segregation originate in informal, non-regulated urbanisation, technical networks or housing production? These factors have not always been clearly distinguished in research studies; we shall now see how each should be weighted.

Having Institutions that Fit Together and Work Together is More Important Than City Size.

Our four cases differ by size. Cape Town with its 3.7 million inhabitants is less than one-fifth the size of Shanghai with its 23 million. Should we conclude that the second is less governable? There is no reason to think so. Our study does not justify the claim that framing arrangement complexity or efficiency is proportionate to city size. We find the same three-level system in each of the four cities studied (see table below). However, despite the relatively similar administrative architectures, governability varies greatly. Shanghai is more governable than Cape Town because the works are politically 'oiled' by the single party system. And regardless of size, the weight of the state as actor varies by whether the metropolis in question is or is not the capital.

Table 6.2   Three institutional levels

Shanghai	Municipal government	Urban districts (19)	Streets
Mumbai	Metropolitan government	Municipalities	Districts
Santiago	Metropolitan (*intendant*)	Provinces	Cities (37)
Cape Town	Metropolitan government, Unicity	Sub-councils (23)	Wards (105)

As we see it, differences in governability have less to do with size than with *three institutional variables*. First, is the territory covered by the urban government congruent with the built metropolitan area, as in Shanghai, or is it divided up between several institutions, as in Mumbai and Santiago? In the latter, five out of 32 cities of the metropolitan area belong to different provinces. Cape Town is quite interesting on this point: its explicit simplification strategy has led to merging 61 administrative units into a single entity, the City of Cape Town.

Second, is that local government strong or weak? Does the mayor have enough resources to give him or her significant weight in the political-institutional field (Goldsmith and Page, 1987; Page 1991)? Caught as he is between the central state on one hand, and city and regional councillors on the other, the *Intendant* in charge of governing the metropolis of Santiago has very little power. Even when the local public authority in place clearly means to exercise power over the entire metropolis, as in Cape Town with Unicity, this does not amount to real power if the local institution lacks sufficient financial resources and so finds itself dependent on the state for funding its major policies, which already have to comply with strategic provincial and national preferences. And what are we to say of Mumbai, where power is shared twice over? The government of greater Mumbai is two-headed, with a municipal superintendant (a state civil servant) and a city council that elects the mayor, but the metropolis is also co-governed by the state of Maharashtra. Indeed, several organisations crucial to managing the city – planning, highway construction, electricity management – are controlled by the state of Maharashtra. What is decisive, then, is multi-level government fluidity and whether or not the interests of central and local powers converge.

Third is the political variable. In this connection, our cities exhibit two opposed types of organisation. Shanghai is characterised by strongly implicated political officials; however, the single party system and the absence of elections neutralises the diversity factor. The metropolitan government process in this city is therefore largely explained by functional organisation. If we add the close connections between political and administrative elites, all these factors narrow the field of possibilities – we see how and why this gigantic metropolis can be governed with such (relative) efficiency. By contrast, Mumbai and Cape Town exhibit political hypertrophy. In those cases the administrative and political spheres are independent of one another; the spaces they define do not overlap: the 24 wards of Mumbai correspond to 227 electoral committees, and Cape Town's electoral wards were only grouped together into planning zones in 2011. Each sphere operates according to its own logic. The multiparty regime provokes fierce competition and regularly topples majorities. This way of running political life compounds the coordination problem induced by strictly administrative division of the territory, resulting in confrontations that may block projects. In Cape Town and Mumbai, political opposition groups have slowed down land reform, thereby threatening the social housing policy; they have also delayed modernisation of the electricity sector.

In other words, these large and very large cities are complex entities made up of heterogeneous forces with different not to say divergent interests, and a great number of institutions with diverse jurisdictions intervene in them. Governing them is no easy task. The existence of a higher-rank power is a crucial factor in making them governable, as it allows for defining common objectives, arbitrating, and assembling resources to implement projects. This condition is not really met in our cities due to the high number of institutions intervening in interlocking spaces. The fact that those institutions are also headed by elected officials – the most common way of satisfying people's aspiration to democracy – often leads to intra- and interinstitution competition, then aggravated by competition between individual politicians. In places where the political game should be framed by the principle of moderation – lest it results in a zero-sum game – we find instead fierce, unregulated competition. In truth, this situation is not specific to large emerging cities; it is to be found in all democratic, multiparty countries with a long institutional history. But in large cities the phenomenon is even more striking due to the number of institutions intervening in the same territory and the close connections between political institutions and projects-developing ones.

Table 6.3   Three factors of convergence

	Mumbai	Shanghai	Santiago	Cape Town
Congruence between institutions and built metropolis	-	+	-	+
Strength of local authorities	+/-	+	-	+/-
Political/administrative alignment	-	+	+	-

Lack of Control Over the Informal has a Greater Effect Than Depth of Divisions

The speed with which emerging large cities get populated and the accelerated occupation rate of new spaces in them overwhelm institutions. Though large cities are governed more intensely and better than small ones, there are still fringes inside the city and on its edges that escape formal institutional control. The phenomenon may be minor, as in Shanghai with its shady, illicit spaces at the edges of urban districts or between the city and neighboring towns. In these less regulated areas – between a canal, a freeway, and high-voltage electricity lines, for example – populations settle, barges moor along the waterway, various activities such as recycling city refuse get organised around market garden areas. Informality is often a fundamental feature of these urban fringes. What distinguishes our large cities from each other here is the intensity of competition for control of these spaces and their resources. The formal political system meanwhile, overwhelmed, is incapable of preventing private and in some cases criminal groups take over (gangs in the Cape Flats, mafiosi in Mumbai slums). It may also deliberately withdraw, leaving governance up to the private sector, as in large housing projects in Santiago, management of which has been delegated to the private sector. Those areas may turn into neighborhoods and end up becoming virtual mini-cities in their own right.

Entire neighborhoods and districts thus operate at the margins of the organised metropolis, beyond the control of formal government institutions. Contrary to our initial presupposition, these are not temporary accidents due to delay but enduring urbanised situations. Several data converge here. These built spaces are vast and contain large populations who settled there some time ago. The phenomenon is massive, and there is no good reason to believe it can be absorbed or dispelled merely by a few voluntarist policy programs. The persistence of these districts has been tolerated by institutions because it contributes structurally to the balance of the system as a whole. The areas generate land income – often invisible, yet essential to social regulation. They make it possible to receive migrant flows at low cost and they enable the public authorities to handle things on a day-by-day basis, freed from the burdens of drawing up a comprehensive plan and making major investments in fixed assets. The second-class inhabitants of these areas help regulate job markets: employers can maintain flexible organisation and thereby stay competitive; they are not constrained to develop a new organisational model.[5] Symmetrically, public institutions save time on constructing social and labor rights (Castel, 1995). The dark side of this kind of objective flexibility is that social issues become problems for families.

As the example of South Africa retrospectively shows, the problem for city government is not so much segregation – even in very large cities – as the proliferation of territories that escape regulation by the instituted political power

---

5   See studies by business historians linking company development with company organisation modes (Chandler and Hikino 1997).

(Jaglin, 2008). The persistence of these informal territories and activities calls into question our conception of urban government; i.e. our vision of a strata of public institutions that serve all inhabitants of a given territory, with political institutions granting the right to vote to all citizens while practical institutions organised around the concept of public service deliver those services to every inhabited area and every user of an officially governed territory.[6] This way of organising urban government, inherited from a political system and institutional choices that go back to the late nineteenth century (Lorrain, 2005; Rosanvallon, 2004), corresponds to the idea of a city's needs being 'covered' to near-perfection by its institutions. Problems may exist, e.g. some users' income may not be sufficient with regard to public service rates, but those problems are not seen to call into question the universal nature of political or technical solutions. This vision simply does not correspond to the reality of major emerging cities.

More than three decades after the first International Labor Organization report on the informal economy (1972) and the Habitat I conference held in Vancouver (1976), informal dynamics have been theorised and investors and governments are more careful to take them into account, though the disparity on the ground between real practices and the representations diffused by development institutions and international consultants remains great. Investors and governments are interested above all in big programs; they do not pay much attention to the informal economy and small operations. And yet those activities too produce the city, including 'global' cities. The existence and resistance of the informal economy is moving both researchers and decision-makers to revise their dominant notions, one of them being the thesis of urban convergence put forward by Michael Cohen (1996). For Cohen, cities of the North and South, despite their unequal degrees of development, all have to face the same set of problems of the same nature. For Gavin Shatkin (2007), on the other hand, divergence is the key: contrary to the situation in Northern cities, the megacities of the various Souths are being globalised by informal activities and flows, though this does not make them global cities as defined by Saskia Sassen and GaWC (Globalization and World Cities) researchers. The weight of local contingencies and the fact that informal activities have remained in place and may actually be 'taking off' cannot be ignored; both constitute strong city differentiation criteria.

Real Estate Development Increases Urban Fragmentation More Than Infrastructure Networks

While our studies confirm that informal processes are a major problem for city government, they also make it clear that in emerging cities, it is much harder to gain firm control over land and real estate production mechanisms than over large technical systems. Access to land and housing, then, rather than network services is what causes intra-urban social inequalities of the sort that stabilise and

---

6   See 'Aux marges des réseaux', special issue of *Flux* 76–7 (Apr.–Sep. 2009).

deepen segregation. As early as the mid-1980s, studies by radical sociologists and geographers analysing capitalism in global terms brought to light the spatial effects of the new international division of labor (NIDL) (Friedman, 1986; Harvey, 2000). Activity specialisation and transformation of the dominant (Fordist, to be brief) mode of work organisation was leading to greater spatial specialisation and sharper polarisation of social groups (Castells, 1985; Marcuse, 2000; Sassen, 1991). Other authors stressed dynamics deriving from urban actor behavior (Fainstein, 1994; Graham and Marvin, 2001) or owners' demands for security, which led to fenced-in spaces. These analyses converge on the point that the great global city is a segregated one. In this connection our surveys provide several new results.

In three of the cities studied, spatial heterogeneity is strong. Nearly 60 per cent of Mumbai inhabitants live in slums or unsafe, unhealthy housing – this is an extremely high figure. But not all these people are poor, and this attests to the extremely high real estate prices in residential neighborhoods and the lack of public housing. The situation in Cape Town 17 years after the political abolishing of apartheid remains strongly split. If we include slums and backyard shacks, we can estimate that almost a million inhabitants (approximately 30 per cent of the population) live in precarious housing. In Santiago, the issue of social housing has dominated the political scene for more than two decades. It was a fundamental demand of the social movements that brought Allende to power, and failure to resolve the problem quickly fueled criticism of Allende's government. After the *coup d'Etat*, the Pinochet government implemented a radical policy: more than 250 slums were razed and 150,000 inhabitants displaced and rehoused. But that action did nothing to reduce inequality, as populations who had been living in slums situated in wealthy neighborhoods were relocated to much poorer ones. This aggravated segregation situation may be understood as a combination of the economic mechanism of land prices, they have to be low enough to remain compatible with the cost of public housing construction – and the political position of wealthy groups, who want to keep to themselves – one writer has even spoken of 'secession" (Massey, 2005). Shanghai is the only city that shows no such tendencies. It has no slums, though some housing remains insalubrious. The city that was inherited from the communist period was socially quite uniform: people obtained housing via their employment in a state company, meaning the entire status hierarchy, from managers to rank-and-file workers, could be found in the same neighborhood. The fact that part of the population has become significantly wealthier since the late 1990s, and the existence of a private ownership housing regime, has been fueling separation tendencies. The cost of housing (or rent) in relation to income works as a social filter; controlled-access apartment complexes are being built in the new districts (Wu, 2002: 164). But these new developments have not yet upset the inherited housing situation, even if pressures for segregation are growing.

In sum, our studies show that the observed increase in urban segregation is due to real estate development and construction operations rather than urban infrastructure. In all our cities, making utility services universally available is a stated goal; those services are also strictly regulated by the public authorities. Even in Santiago, a prototype of free-market city management, the policy has been to ensure that city services are available to all. The slums replacement programs enacted under the dictatorship included providing access to housing, drinking water and electricity. When water supply delivery was privatised in 1999, the policy decision was to connect all housing to the sanitation system, and rates were revised accordingly. Interestingly, the politically and institutionally segregated city of apartheid-ruled Cape Town was an integrated city in terms of utility service provision.

Like the convergence thesis, then, the 'splintering urbanism' thesis (Graham and Marvin, 2001; Marcuse, 2000) is open to debate. According to this radical geography approach, globalisation and privatisation policies are producing urban segregation worldwide. As this critical view would have it, the culprit is urban network privatisation. Private, listed corporations that have to make a profit are said to be likely to give priority to areas whose populations are solvent ('cherry picking') while excluding others ('social dumping'). This argument fails to hold up either descriptively or logically. Let us recall the essential point here (Lorrain, 2001). First, urban system history shows that the intention has always been for utilities to provide universal service but before they could do so, they served particular sets of actors (solvent populations and businesses) in central spaces. So to understand utility service distribution today we have to take into account the time factor. It seems that some types of networks get universalised relatively quickly (cellular phones) while others are slower (running water, sanitation systems). This is a combined effect of economic factors (high fixed costs), anthropological factors concerning the desire to pay for modernity, and political factors concerning the nature and effectiveness of incentives and support measures decided by public authorities. Second, infrastructure systems cannot be governed by pure market logic. Operators everywhere are regulated, including in countries such as Chili that have taken the privatisation road. The obligation to connect housing units to the system is one of the tasks that public authorities delegate to private operators. Third, the radical geography argument grants little weight to corporation logic. As the history of industrial cities shows, a systems operator intervening in a given territory for a certain length of time is likely to serve a high proportion of residents in that area as a function of two considerations. From an economic perspective, the best way to decrease unit costs in an activity where fixed costs are by nature high is to increase the number of 'subscribers' to that service or utility. This behavior is reinforced by political logic: an operator that focuses entirely on solvent districts and ignores poor ones would be taking a serious political risk that might lead to outbursts of social unrest and being dismissed as a service provider.

But this may not be the most crucial point (Jaglin and Zérah, 2010). Even when utility companies seek to extend service coverage[7] or when those services

---

7   See various World Bank reports demonstrating that even in cases of broken contracts, private operators have invested heavily in connecting housing units (Gassner et al., 2009; Marin, 2009); see also more critical studies, e.g. of the particularly controversial area of

have not been privatised, as in Mumbai and Cape Town, there are poverty pockets and occupied spaces beyond reach of all city planning and programs, areas that resist service universalisation. In some cases they may amount to a significant proportion of the city. Here the causes must be sought elsewhere than in the public or private nature of the enterprise, which, if it performs well and is correctly regulated, will have shown its efficiency within the urban area it was originally called upon to serve – the planned city, where land is legally owned – to the benefit of customers instructed in 'normal' operation rules and in the framework of a business relationship considered legitimate overall. Once again, in emerging large cities this situation cohabits with other spaces, termed 'informal' or 'precarious', where the aforementioned service relation rules are not securely in place. This has nothing to do with the manager's public or private status. Lastly, business, including innovative business practices (Botton, 2007), cannot change the extreme poverty of many users, and social policies have not be able to manage this problem in many situations (Boccanfuso et al., 2005; Kayaga and Franceys, 2007). Universal service coverage is perhaps not the most difficult problem to solve, however. Service universalisation also depends on how land and real estate markets function, and the coexistence of formal and informal in those markets raises extremely difficult challenges for urban development planning. In some cases, the development of infrastructure networks follows on non-planned housing production by developers or private citizens. Second, infrastructure building is complicated by the imprecision of land ownership rules and the absence of planned roadways. When there are too many rules in emerging cities and when city government is too weak to enforce them, then land value appreciation strategies become too powerful for institutional frameworks to contain. Those strategies are applied at the edges or in the 'hollows' of the city, in poorly defined spaces where anticipations can be richly remunerated. Large operators in Santiago practice strategic anticipation, and similar informal practices are to be found in Cape Town and Mumbai. Real estate developers serve a preexisting dynamic for localising the 'rich' while price mechanisms distribute the poor.

In addition, if we consider the structuring factor of large real estate project location, it becomes clear that the role of utility networks in creating urban spatial coherence (our original thought) must be reassessed. Voluntarist public policies that include spatial planning and investment in infrastructure networks *before* buildings get built, as in Shanghai, do facilitate control over urban development. But this is not the most commonly encountered reality. Moreover, improving the situation presupposes a voluntarist government with action tools. And this works better when private land ownership is not one of the society's highest principles. When land and real estate markets are free, entirely unregulated, the capturing of land income by big landowners associated with real estate developers wins out over all other considerations. The potential value of urban land is so high that real

---

drinking water provision (Estache and Fay, 2009; Kirkpatrick et al., 2006; Prasad, 2006; Trémolet, 2006).

estate developers set out to acquire vast stretches of it and urbanise them, as in Santiago and Mumbai. The lack of infrastructure is not crippling because actors can acquire the land at farmland prices, then maximise the ground rent. The rest is a matter of sharing the work with other firms, the ones that build the networks. In such cases, the land appreciation dynamic is what triggers the entire urbanisation process, leaving political authorities struggling to catch up with private-sector initiatives. To this must be added informal urbanisation processes – once again, a city is not produced by major operations alone; it is also the product of thousands of decisions by small actors (smaller-scale property developers, private citizens). They too play a role in urban change.

Much of the difficulty of governing emerging large cities and aligning their urbanisation with policy projects and goals has to do with just this coexistence of formal and informal land ownership regimes, a situation over which public authorities have little control. Unsurprisingly, Chinese cities (here illustrated by Shanghai) figure prominently among emerging megacities that are successfully controlling their rapid growth; further examples are Hong Kong and Singapore. In those cases, the community is the ultimate landowner; private ownership rights exist and make commercialisation of built areas possible, but they are secondary rights, granted for limited periods. This gives the public power a formidable tool for organising the city and obtaining part of the land income itself, which can then be used to fund heavy infrastructure. The whole process depends on institution building, as is demonstrated by the opposite situation. In developing countries where the state has not yet been fully constructed as an institution,[8] individual ownership dominates. And land and real estate ownership are extremely important capital investments. This is a case of 'owners' capitalism' in the primary sense of the term;[9] that is, expressed by something other than assets management by insurance companies or investment funds. Here ownership is direct and strategies for increasing or decreasing the value of a property are quite explicit. This bolsters owner and developer vigilance with regard to public projects. They are well-informed, keep a close eye on institutions, and are capable of influencing those institutions.

Interactions between actors and existing interests thus work to intensify city segregation. Nobody living in a wealthy neighborhood wants social housing there, as demonstrated by the examples of slum resorption in Santiago and Mumbai. Inhabitants prefer to be with their own kind; that way they can keep up their property while maintaining facility and service quality and the atmosphere of their neighborhood. In slums – highly organised locales despite being situated on the fringes of the formally governed city – secondary rights develop that favor the status quo or slow change. 'Owners' without legal property rights rent the property in question or sell buildings on it; an economy of non-contractual services (refuse

---

8 For the historical case of France see Charle 1987 and Bezes 2009.

9 In current debates on the financialisation of the economy, the rise of shareholder power has led some to speak of 'owners' capitalism', with the understanding that it has reduced the power of managers (Djelic and Zarlowski, 2005; Agglietta and Rebérioux, 2004).

collection, water-carriers) gets set up to compensate for the lack of essential services. This world entertains a strong tacit understanding with local elected officials, and decentralisation reforms have strengthened the ties between them everywhere in the last decades. So what may seem astonishing from the outside persists, settles in, becomes path dependence.

While regulatory modes do change in informal districts, they do not immediately converge on or link up with the formal, instituted rules produced by official changes in city governance. Urban societies thus operate by accumulating different regulation modes rather than by substituting one for another, and some actors can play on several fields at once. Accelerated adoption of new institutions and governing rules does of course work to strengthen the efficiency and 'modernity' of vast metropolitan spaces, but in some cases it has no more than a limited impact on the life of ordinary city-dwellers, i.e. residents of ungoverned or unmanaged neighborhoods working in informal micro-undertakings. The reforms of the last decades have in many cases increased the complexity of urban economic, social and political regulation systems, leading to the coexistence of inherited institutions that are likely to be eroding and formalised institutions that are as yet only partially able to normalise social functioning. Here lies one of the primary challenges for governing emerging megacities.

****

Let us conclude the book where we began it. Are these megacities and large cities governed, and if so who steers them: the public authorities, the market, a spontaneous process? Or is the grim prophecy becoming reality? Our investigations show that size is not the most important variable. All institutional systems beyond a certain size are complex, and going from 4 to 23 million inhabitants does not proportionately multiply complexity. In fact, the most important point is whether or not there is a government endowed with legal authority and recognised legitimacy. That government may have been determined by an election system, but as the case of Shanghai shows, it may also involve other mechanisms. Furthermore, the examples of Mumbai and Cape Town make it clear that having such a government is not a sufficient condition. This result is puzzling. As we see it, it should be added to those of recent institutionalist studies probing the tie between political democracy, government quality, and economic performance (Holmberg and Rothstein, 2010; Rothstein and Teorell, 2008). Governability presupposes a legitimate governing power endowed with resources, able to make the important decisions and to rally and concentrate collective energies. Legitimacy depends more on the 'quality' of government – that is, having rules that are stable and impartial enough to enable actors to act – than on whether or not that government is elected. All of these observations suggest the relevance of studying institutions all the way down to the level at which they actually intervene in and exercise some degree of control on the action, and this in turn presupposes 'unbundling' them (Acemoglu et al., 2008) and being more attentive to second-order institutions (Lorrain, 2008).

Our studies also show that these large cities in many respects are indeed governed, and that steering by infrastructure networks greatly contributes to the quality of that government. Large technical systems and utility services constrain actors to reach decisions, to learn, and to make their way out of path dependency. A networked city is relatively well governed because the economy of each network is highly regulated. Whether or not the firms are private or public is fairly secondary at this level; being private does not necessarily mean the market in question is a free one. Public authority makes itself felt in Mumbai, Shanghai and Cape Town; it is also present in Santiago, despite the liberal economic model chosen there. But our studies also show that the 'organised' city can be overwhelmed by its fringes, and this time the explanatory factor concerns land ownership and poorly organised urbanisation processes. In a deliberate oversimplification of the case, we might say that there are two antagonistic forces at work: infrastructure organisation and housing production. Because large technical systems require public permits and substantial funding, they have to be 'governed' by precepts of order and planning. By contrast, the various forces involved in land and real estate development are doubly market forces, partaking both of a market organised by public rules *and* an unregulated market where the imperative needs of inhabitants and the promise of quick and easy gain mobilise actors and create situations that overwhelm government. This second component of megacity dynamics seems to us extremely important and not very well understood. Shanghai, which is well organised (like other cities in the region such as Hong Kong and Singapore), is an exception in many ways, with its combination of strong political institutions, planning tools and limited land ownership rights – a winning combination when it comes to controlling the urban fabric. Elsewhere the combination of individual land and real estate property rights and small or medium-sized actors free to make whatever decisions they please produces less stable cities.

The problem is whether the situation produced by these urbanising processes at the city's edges and fringes (Agier, 2009) is going to persist or whether with time these city fragments will be brought back into the dominant model of a governed, equipped city. Four questions remain. The first is political: At what pace will these districts and neighborhoods be integrated into the local political system, with rights of their own and the possibility of putting forward plans and projects for themselves? The second concerns global regulation of the economy in Michel Aglietta and Robert Boyer's sense of the term. Fringe areas may be thought of as a spatial representation of the flexibilisation process affecting production, but above all they are a spatial representation of the specific ways in which cities are becoming inscribed in the globalisation process. As long as this process remains weakly regulated, the vast pools of potential labor in developing countries will enable these flexible arrangements to persist. In his fine book on the emergence of the social issue in Europe, Robert Castel (1995) shows that in order to integrate migrants and a low-skilled labor force into political society, labor regulations and property rights had to be developed. People who had nothing were 'disaffiliated'. There is a connection between the way wealth is produced, how it is redistributed, and the impact this has on cities. The third question is a macro-economic one. Producing a city that meets standards for facilities and large technical networks requires accumulating considerable resources. To reach this goal, it is preferable (to put it lightly) to have a growth economy. In other words, the fight against urban poverty, like improvements in governability, require integrating those goals into wealth production mechanisms and they require willingness on the part of elites to invest part of produced value in fixed urban assets. The fourth question concerns technologies: Does the solution for emerging megacities necessarily require replicating the Western model of vertically integrated utilities with a monopoly? If decentralised technologies were to appear in the urban fabric tomorrow as happened with cellular phone, micro computer and web communications, this would have significant impact on existing forms of urban government.

References

Acemoglu, D. and S. Johnson. (2008). The Role of Institutions in Growth and Development. Working paper no. 10, The World Bank, Washington, D.C.

Agier, M. (2009). *Esquisse d'une anthropologie de la ville.* Louvain: Bruylant-Academia.

Aglietta, M. and A. Rebérioux. (2004). *Dérives du capitalisme financier.* Paris: Albin Michel.

Bezes, P. (2009). *Réinventer l'Etat: Les réformes de l'administration française (1962–2008).* Paris: Presses Universitaires de France.

Boccanfuso, D., A. Estache and L. Savard. (2005). A Poverty and Inequality Assessment of Liberalization of Water Utility in Senegal: A Macro-Micro Analysis. Cahier de Recherche/Working Paper no. 05–13, Groupe de Recherche en Economie et Développement International (GREDI), Université de Sherbrooke, Sherbrooke, Canada.

Botton, S. (2007). *La multinationale et le bidonville: Privatisations et pauvreté à Buenos Aires.* Paris: Karthala.

Castel, R. (1995). *Les métamorphoses de la question sociale.* Paris: Fayard.

Castells, M. (1985). *High Technology, Space, and Society.* Beverly Hills: Sage.

Castells, M. (1989). *The Informational City.* Oxford: Blackwell.

Castells, M. (1989). World Underneath: The Origins, Dynamics and Effects of the Informal Economy. In A. Portes, M. Castells, L. Benton (eds), *The Informal Economy.* Baltimore, Md.: Johns Hopkins University Press.

Chandler, A.D. and T. Hikino. (1997). The Large Enterprise and the Dynamics of Modern Economic Growth. In A.D. Chandler, F. Amatori, T. Hikino (eds), *Big Business and the Wealth of Nations.* Cambridge: Cambridge University Press.

Charle, C. (1987). *Les Elites de la République, 1880–1900.* Paris: Fayard.

Cohen, M. (1996). The Hypothesis of Urban Convergence: Are Cities in the North and South Becoming More Alike in an Age of Globalization? In M. Cohen, B. Ruble, J. Tulchin, A. Garland (eds), *Preparing for the Urban Future: Global Pressures and Local Forces*. Woodrow Wilson Center Special Studies. Baltimore: Johns Hopkins University Press.

Davezies, L. (2008). *La République et ses territoires: La circulation invisible des richesses*. Paris: Editions du Seuil.

De Soto, H. (2000). *The Mystery of Capital: Why Capitalism Triumphs in the West and Fails Everywhere Else*. New York: Basic Books.

De Soto, H., E. Ghersi and M. Ghibellini (1986*). El otro sendero: La Revolucion informal. Instituto Libertad y Democratia. Lima: El Barranco*. Published in French under the title *L'Autre sentier: La révolution informelle* (Paris: La Découverte, 1994) and in English under the title *The Other Path* (Harpercollins, 1989).

Djelic, M.L. and P. Zarlowski (2005). Entreprises et gouvernance en France: perspectives historiques et évolutions récentes. *Sociologie du Travail*, 47(4): 451–69.

Estache, A. and M. Fay (2007). *Current Debates on Infrastructure Policy*. Policy research working paper no. 4410, The World Bank, Washington D.C.

Fainstein, S. (1994). *The City Builders: Property, Politics and Planning in London and New York*. Oxford: Blackwell.

Gassner, K., A. Popov and N. Pushak (2008). *Does Private Sector Participation Improve Performance in Electricity and Water Distribution?* Washington, D.C.: World Bank Publications.

Goldsmith, M. and E.C. Page (1987). Britain. In E.C. Page and M. Goldsmith (eds), *Central and Local Government Relations: A Comparative Analysis of West European Unitary States*. London: Sage.

Graham, S. and S. Marvin (2001). *Splintering Networks: Networked Infrastructures, Technological Mobilities and the Urban Condition*. London: Routledge.

Holmberg, S. and B. Rothstein (2010). Quality of Government is Needed to Reduce Poverty and Economic Inequality. Working paper series 2010:3, University of Gothenburg, Göteborg.

Jaglin, S., coordinator (2008). Territorialisation des espaces urbanisés dans les grandes villes: une confrontation nord/sud. Rapport final. ACI Espaces et territoires, Latts, Paris.

Jaglin, S. (2001). Villes disloquées? Ségrégations et fragmentation urbaine en Afrique australe. *Annales de géographie*, 619 (May–June): 243–65.

Jaglin, S. and M.-H. Zérah (2010) Introduction: Eau des villes: repenser des services en mutation. *Revue Tiers Monde*, 203: 7–22.

Kayaga, S. and R. Franceys (2007). Costs of Urban Utility Water Connections: Excessive Burden to the Poor. *Utilities Policy*, 15(4): 270–77.

Kirkpatrick, C., D. Parker and Y.-F. Zhang (2006). An Empirical Analysis of State and Private-Sector Provision of Water Services in Africa. *The World Bank Economic Review*, 20(1): 143–63.

Lautier, B. (1996). *L'économie informelle dans le tiers monde*. Paris: La Découverte.

Logan, J.R. and H.H.L. Molotch (1987). *Urban Fortunes: The Political Economy of Places*. Berkeley, Ca.: University of California Press.

Lorrain, D. (2001). Gigacity: the Rise of Technological Networks in Daily Life, *Journal of Urban Technology*, 8(3): 1–20.

Lorrain, D. (2005). Urban Capitalisms: European Models in Competition. *International Journal of Urban and Regional Research*, 29(2): 231–67.

Lorrain, D. (2008). Les institutions de second rang. *Entreprises et Histoire*, 50 (Apr.): 6–13.

Marcuse, P. and R. van Kempen, (eds) (2000). *Globalizing Cities: A New Spatial Order?* Oxford: Blackwell.

Marin, P. (2009). *Public-Private Partnerships for Urban Water Utilities: A Review of Experiences in Developing Countries*. Trends and Policy Options no.8. Washington D.C.: The World Bank, Public-Private Infrastructure Advisory Facility.

Massey, D. (2005). *For Space*. London: Sage.

Meisel, N. and J. Ould Aoudia (2008). La 'bonne gouvernance' est-elle une bonne stratégie de développement? Working paper, Agence Française de Développement, Paris.

Mitchell, K. (2000). The Culture of Urban Space. *Urban Geography*, 21(5): 443–9.

Nield, R. (2002). *Public Corruption: The Dark Side of Social Evolution*. London: Anthem Press.

North, D.C. (1966). *The Economic Growth of the United States 1790–1860*. New York: The Norton Library.

North, D.C. (2005). *Understanding the Process of Economic Change*. Princeton: Princeton University Press. Published in French under the title *Le processus du développement économique* (Paris: Éditions d'Organisation, 2005).

Padioleau, J.G. (1991). L'action publique urbaine moderniste. *Politiques et Management Public*, 9(3): 133–46.

Page, E.C. (1991). *Localism and Centralism in Europe*. Oxford: Oxford University Press.

Portes, A., M. Castells and L. Benton, (eds) (1989). *The Informal Economy: Studies in Advanced and Less Developed Countries*. Baltimore, Md.: Johns Hopkins University Press.

Prasad, N. (2006). Privatisation Results: Private Sector Participation in Water Services After 15 Years. *Development Policy Review*, 24: 669–92.

Rodrik, D. (2008). *One Economics, Many Recipes: Globalization, Institutions, and Economic Growth*. Princeton and Oxford: Princeton University Press.

Rodrik, D., A. Subramanian and F. Trebbi (2004). Institutions Rule: The Primacy of Institutions over Geography and Integration in Economic Development. *Journal of Economic Growth*, 9 (June): 131–65.

Rosanvallon, P. (2004). *Le modèle politique français*. Paris: Editions du Seuil.

Rothstein, B. and J. Teorell. (2008). What is Quality of Government? A Theory of Impartial Government Institutions. *Governance: An International Journal of Policy, Administration and Institutions*, 21(2): 165–90.

Sassen, S. (1991). *The Global City: London, New York, Tokyo*. Princeton: Princeton University Press.

Sassen, S. (1994). *Cities in a World Economy*. Thousand Oaks, Ca.: Pine Forge Press.

Sgard, J. (2008). Qu'est-ce qu'un pays émergent, et est-ce un concept intéressant pour les sciences sociales ? Paper presented at the conference 'Emergences: des trajectoires aux concepts', Bordeaux, November 27–28. http://emergence.u-bordeaux4.fr/programme_038.htm.

Shatkin, G. (2007). Global Cities of the South: Emerging Perspectives on Growth and Inequality. *Cities*, 24(1): 1–15.

Tremolet, S. (2006). Un point sur les privatisations de l'eau en Afrique. *Responsabilité & Environnement*, 42: 59–68.

Veltz, P. (2000) (2nd ed.). *Mondialisation, Villes et Territoires: L'économie d'archipel*. Paris: Presses Universitaires de France.

Vietor, R. (2007). *How Countries Compete: Strategy, Structure and Government in the Global Economy*. Boston: Harvard Business School Press.

Wu, Fulong (2002). Real Estate Development and the Transformation of Urban Space in China's Transition Economy with Special Reference to Shanghai. In J. Logan (ed.), *The New Chinese City:Globalization and Market Reform*. Malden, Ma.: Wiley-Blackwell.

Index

Printed in the United States
by Baker & Taylor Publisher Services